New Pedagogical Approaches in Game Enhanced Learning:

Curriculum Integration

Sara de Freitas
University of Coventry, UK

Michela Ott
*Institute for Educational Technology of the Italian National Research
    Council, Italy*

Maria Magdalena Popescu
Carol I National Defence University, Romania

Ioana Stanescu
Advanced Distributed Learning, Romania

Managing Director:	Lindsay Johnston
Editorial Director:	Joel Gamon
Book Production Manager:	Jennifer Yoder
Publishing Systems Analyst:	Adrienne Freeland
Development Editor:	Austin DeMarco
Assistant Acquisitions Editor:	Kayla Wolfe
Typesetter:	Deanna Jo Zombro
Cover Design:	Jason Mull

Published in the United States of America by
Information Science Reference (an imprint of IGI Global)
701 E. Chocolate Avenue
Hershey PA 17033
Tel: 717-533-8845
Fax: 717-533-8661
E-mail: cust@igi-global.com
Web site: http://www.igi-global.com

Library of Congress Cataloging-in-Publication Data

New pedagogical approaches in game enhanced learning : curriculum integration / Sara de Freitas, Michela Ott, Maria Magdalena Popescu, and Ioana Stanescu, editors.
    pages cm
Includes bibliographical references and index.
Summary: "This book addresses the major challenges associated with adopting digital games into a standard curriculum, providing fresh perspectives from current practitioners in the education field"--Provided by publisher.
    ISBN 978-1-4666-3950-8 (hardcover) -- ISBN 978-1-4666-3951-5 (ebook) -- ISBN (invalid) 978-1-4666-3952-2 (print & perpetual access) 1. Educational games--Design and construction. 2. Simulation games in education. 3. Computer games--Design. I. Freitas, Sara de, editor of compilation.
  LB1029.G3N46 2013
  371.39'7--dc23
                                    2012048159

British Cataloguing in Publication Data
A Cataloguing in Publication record for this book is available from the British Library.

All work contributed to this book is new, previously-unpublished material. The views expressed in this book are those of the authors, but not necessarily of the publisher.

Table of Contents

Detailed Table of Contents

    Michela Ott, National Research Council (ITD-CNR), Italy
    Maria Magdalena Popescu, Carol I National Defence University, Romania
    Ioana Andreea Stănescu, Advanced Distributed Learning Association, Romania
    Sara de Freitas, University of Coventry, UK

This chapter tackles the issue of Serious Games (SGs) curriculum integration approached from different perspectives (different levels, subject areas, instructional contexts, pedagogies, views, and visions over what it is already in practice and what is yet to be implemented). In light of the title of this book, it refers to Game-Enhanced Learning and not simply to game-based learning, thus supporting the concept that games can really contribute to improving and enhancing both collaborative and individual learning processes. The chapter is meant to trigger reflections on the potential of Serious Games in the present learning/teaching panorama and to explore how SGs can be considered suitable tools for sustaining the development of some relevant skills required to live and be proactive actors in the Knowledge Society, namely the so-called 21st Century Skills. Further, key challenges in the field of game-enhanced learning, with particular regard to pedagogical aspects are also in-depth explored by emphasizing the important role of teachers as to the choice of the SGs, their deployment, and the overall conduction of learning experiences.

    Leona Achtenhagen, Jönköping International Business School, Sweden
    Bengt Johannisson, Linnaeus University, Sweden & Jönköping International Business
       School, Sweden

An increasing number of education institutions, including many universities and colleges, are offering entrepreneurship education. This development is driven by the hope that more entrepreneurs could be "created" through such efforts, and that these entrepreneurs through their newly founded ventures will contribute to economic growth and job creation. At higher education institutions, the majority of entrepreneurship courses rely on writing business plans as a main pedagogical tool for enhancing the students' entrepreneurial capabilities. In this chapter, the authors argue instead for the need for a pedagogy that focuses on supporting students in crafting an entrepreneurial mindset as the basis for venturing activities. They discuss the potential role of games in such entrepreneurship education and present the example of an entrepreneurship game from the Swedish context, which was developed by a group of young female entrepreneurs. The authors describe the game and discuss their experiences of playing it with a group of novice entrepreneurship and management students at the master's level, and they review the effectiveness of the game in terms of how it supports students in crafting an entrepreneurial mindset. The authors conclude the chapter by outlining how entrepreneurship games could be integrated into a university curriculum and suggest some directions for future research.

Chapter 3
Ronald Dyer, Grenoble Ecole de Management, France

In an age of technological tools ranging from social media to virtual environments, higher education institutions need to re-examine the context of their content delivery, creating an opportunity for more realistic learning methodologies across the education spectrum more closely aligned with expectations from the world of work. Today's learners consist of a cadre of individuals aptly described as "digital natives" (Prensky, 2001) whose proclivity for technology adoption is natural, as most grew up with access to computing technology and have directly experienced its evolutionary path. As such, higher education professionals are now challenged to specifically treat with a generation who perceive technology as a natural extension of their daily lives, recognizing that traditional approaches inclusive of e-learning are no longer sufficient to engage their student population.

Chapter 4
Dores Ferreira, University of Minho, Portugal
Pedro Palhares, University of Minho, Portugal
Jorge Nuno Silva, University of Lisbon, Portugal

In the last few years, the authors have been carrying out a study involving elementary school students from 3rd to 6th years of schooling. The main goal of this study is to identify the possible relationships between the ability to identify patterns and the ability to play games, in particular mathematical games. The research methodology is quantitative and most of the analysis is concerned with the verification of correlation between variables. The analysis takes into account seven factors (besides the ability of pattern recognition) identified through a factor analysis carried out on data. With these tools, the authors have been able to differentiate games according to the different measurements. In this chapter, they disclose the important steps of this research as well as the results and main conclusions reached so far.

Chapter 5
Thorkild Hanghøj, University of Aalborg, Denmark

This chapter outlines theoretical and empirical perspectives on how Game-Based Teaching can be integrated within the context of formal schooling. Initially, this is done by describing game scenarios as models for possible actions that need to be translated into curricular knowledge practices, pedagogical knowledge practices, and everyday knowledge practices. Secondly, the chapter emphasizes how teachers must be able to shift back and forth between various interactional roles in order to facilitate game scenarios. Finally, a discussion is presented on how teachers choose different pedagogical approaches to game-based teaching, which may or may not correspond with the pedagogical models of particular games.

Chapter 6

The amount of research done on educational game integration has lately witnessed a large development. Many scholars believe that games can motivate, engage, and stimulate students' higher order thinking skills, and studies have shown that the integration of commercial and popular games in the classroom provide positive impact on students' learning. On the other hand, there are other voices that reveal the multitude of factors hampering the integration of these games into the educational environment. Generally, these factors are derived from the lack of instructional games designed to cater for classroom teaching and learning processes. In this respect, there are efforts made by the educational researchers and game designers to minimize the hampering factors. One alternative some scholars offered to this was for teachers and students to act as game designers, developing games to be used for classroom integration. This chapter explores the possibilities for both trainers and trainees to design games tailored for classroom integration.

Chapter 7

The game-based learning approach has already shown its strengths from the learners' point of view. However, there are numerous unrevealed ways to support teachers' work within the game-based approach. Unfortunately, games that exclude the teacher from the game-based learning process dominate the markets, which is of great concern. Thus, the aim of this chapter is to study the use of novel game features that enable teachers to participate in game-based learning events. In this chapter, the teacher's role in the game-based learning process is considered through several different game examples that are designed to fulfill both learners' and teachers' needs. The examples show that there are both computational and non-computational methods that can be used to support learning and teachers' work in the game world. Based on previous results it can be argued that the diffusion of game-based learning can be facilitated only if both learners' and teachers' needs and goals are taken into account.

Chapter 8

This chapter presents a framework for understanding the elements of educational exergames that combine both cognitive and physical gameplay. The aim of the framework is to provide a foundation to develop engaging and effective educational exergames as well as to provide a blueprint to define reasonable research settings. By using the framework, designers can scrutinize their game designs, either in research or commercial settings, and reveal new ways to optimize learning effects, health effects, and user experience in educational exergames. The chapter describes a case study in which the framework was used to fine-tune an educational exergame called "Yammy Attack." The results showed that the framework was a useful tool to imagine and discover novel design solutions that would not necessarily otherwise emerge. Furthermore, the chapter discusses the usefulness of educational exergames and possibilities to incorporate them into the schools.

Mathematical literacy is a core literacy that functions as a critical gatekeeper for participation in many aspects of modern society. Research has shown that the way mathematics is taught at school is highly associated with students' achievement and interest levels. Declining interest in mathematics and the need to raise the educational standards of youth in this discipline set a critical agenda for the revision of pedagogical practices. Digital games hold a lot of promise as tools for improving mathematics instruction at the school level. This chapter reports the main insights gained from a study that implemented a game-enhanced learning environment for the training of pre-service elementary school teachers. Teachers experienced some of the ways in which online educational games could help students internalize key mathematical concepts across the school curriculum and build their problem-solving skills, while at the same time improving their attitudes towards the subject. The course also familiarized teachers with the design principles for constructivist gaming environments. Findings indicate a positive impact on teachers' competence in selecting, evaluating, and productively using online games as an instructional tool.

In this chapter, the authors explore an innovative educational classroom scenario where commercial video games are used as an educational tool. They analyse an experiment involving students between the ages of 12 and 13, during the second semester of 2010, in a "Language and Literature" class of a Spanish Secondary School. The main aim of this chapter is to develop new literacies through new educational strategies. These relate commercial video games with the curriculum in order to improve students' specific cultural competences and social skills. The authors show how the social simulation video game "The Sims 3" can be used as a learning resource for students to create narratives and descriptions using a variety of media.

Managers tend to recruit individuals of highest educational standards who deserve quality jobs and attractive remuneration. Equally, disabled persons should enjoy the same benefits. In our era of unprecedented technological development, education should be flexible in order to meet the contemporary demands and the needs of all persons. This chapter analyzes the use of aids, including educational games that can be helpful in supporting people with disabilities. Types of games and games for disabled persons are considered. A more active involvement of international managers in the use of games in educational/ training courses for disabled persons is also proposed. Their duties must be amended to include participation in curricula design for any level of vocational/technical education.

Medical knowledge has increased exponentially in the last decades. Healthcare professionals face a lifetime challenge in keeping abreast with current medical education. Continuing Medical Education (CME) is an ongoing challenge. Traditional adult education, largely used in medical training, shows little effectiveness. Problem-based-learning has been proposed as a student-centred pedagogy to overcome failure of traditional medical instruction. In this chapter, the authors review the status quo of medical education, certification, and recertification in Europe. A summary of the history of simulation in medical education is presented. In recent years, there has been a growing interest in using video games for educational purposes. This is also true for medical education. The use of serious games in medical education is reviewed, and its integration in medical curricula is discussed. The efforts to raise awareness of policy makers are described. Finally, a critical assessment of the strengths and weaknesses of these technologies as well as a proposal to overcome some of its limitations are made.

From primary and secondary educational levels to higher education and lifelong learning, the use of games for educational purposes has become a focus of increasing interest for instructional designers, teachers, and researchers. To ensure the achievement of learning objectives and competency in the use of games for educational purposes, the use of Game-Based Learning (GBL) in the curriculum should be considered in terms of its learner-centred characteristics, game dynamics, and interactional requirements. A dimension that involves all these characteristics is the time factor. Time is considered in this chapter from three different points of view: learner's psychological time; temporal gameplay; and the "interaction tempo" required for successfully including games in the curriculum. This chapter describes four typologies of the time factor: time-on-task; temporal perspectives of learners; temporal gameplay; and interaction tempo. Finally, the chapter proposes practical ideas for game designers and teachers when using GBL in face-to-face and online contexts.

Preface

Recently, considerable interest has been devoted to the pursuit of learning through, and with, digital games. Many studies have highlighted the potential of computer games to support immersive, situated, and learner-centered learning experiences. Proponents of the educational use of games see them as a means for active construction, rather than passive reception, of knowledge and as prime opportunities to practice the kind of soft skills considered crucial in the knowledge society, such as problem-solving, decision-making, inquiry, multitasking, collaboration, and creativity. Such abilities can be trained in different ways and can be acquired in different educational contexts.

A fundamental distinction with regard to the context of the educational use of digital games regards formal and informal educational settings.

To date, much of the attention has regarded the use of games in informal settings where learning results are not necessarily obtained through the guide of a teacher or an educator; thus, most cases are spontaneous and unintentional from the learner's perspective.

Nevertheless, the widespread pervasiveness of games has encouraged many teachers to look at their use in classes and, helped by the simultaneous bottom up push from students, games are more likely to become a part of the curriculum over the coming years. A growing body of experience is already being accrued in the deployment of digital games within formal education settings, and, in light of these experiences, it is also recognized that their adoption for learning purposes calls for a radical rethinking of pedagogical approaches so that their potential can be fully exploited and their effectiveness maximized.

In an effort to lay the foundations for more effective use of digital games in formal educational contexts, this book focuses on the major issues and challenges of Game-Enhanced Learning.

It pays particular attention to pedagogical aspects to support teachers and educators in the adoption of the new pedagogical approaches needed for successfully introducing games into the curriculum.

It is intended as a mean to provide fresh perspectives on how to guide and sustain a pedagogically effective use of games. In this light, it explores a broad spectrum of pedagogical issues in light of influential contextual factors such as target population, subject, roles, methods, curricula, place, time, objectives, skills, and the specific type of technology involved.

On the one hand, the book looks at how games are currently being employed in education by presenting relevant best practices in different educational areas. On the other, it examines key theoretical issues and proposes innovative ideas related to their adoption for learning purposes.

In most of the chapters the issue of curriculum integration is explored by paying particular attention to the new role that the teacher/educator assumes in games-based learning environments, namely that of "teacher as coach."

The book's intended target audience encompasses both researchers in the fields of Game-Based Learning and Technology-Enhanced Learning and educators, teachers, and educational practitioners interested in exploiting the potential of games for educational purposes; game designers and developers will also find matters of specific interest for them in this book.

Chapter 1
Game–Enhanced Learning:
Preliminary Thoughts on Curriculum Integration

Michela Ott
National Research Council (ITD-CNR), Italy

Ioana Andreea Stănescu
Advanced Distributed Learning Association, Romania

Maria Magdalena Popescu
Carol I National Defence University, Romania

Sara de Freitas
University of Coventry, UK

ABSTRACT

This chapter tackles the issue of Serious Games (SGs) curriculum integration approached from different perspectives (different levels, subject areas, instructional contexts, pedagogies, views, and visions over what it is already in practice and what is yet to be implemented). In light of the title of this book, it refers to Game-Enhanced Learning and not simply to game-based learning, thus supporting the concept that games can really contribute to improving and enhancing both collaborative and individual learning processes. The chapter is meant to trigger reflections on the potential of Serious Games in the present learning/teaching panorama and to explore how SGs can be considered suitable tools for sustaining the development of some relevant skills required to live and be proactive actors in the Knowledge Society, namely the so-called 21st Century Skills. Further, key challenges in the field of game-enhanced learning, with particular regard to pedagogical aspects are also in-depth explored by emphasizing the important role of teachers as to the choice of the SGs, their deployment, and the overall conduction of learning experiences.

INTRODUCTION: SERIOUS GAMES AND THE FUTURE OF LEARNING

When we speak about the Four Pillars in UNESCO's Task Force on education for the 21st Century, we are inherently speaking about learning to know, learning to do, learning to live together, and learning to be. Underpinning these pillars are the 21st Century skills that have been so hard to define and so hard to model in traditional learning conditions. However, once defined, the task of teaching all these skills to a vast array of students requires a major rethink of what education is and how it can be delivered to answer the 21st Century challenges. This is due to the fact that today's educational infrastructure,

DOI: 10.4018/978-1-4666-3950-8.ch001

models and approaches are not consistent with a more skill-centred, personalized and self-paced vision for future learning. The future of learning therefore needs a consideration of 21st century skills, the future classroom *and* the best methods for educational delivery.

This rethink in education follows the need to reshape and reconsider the requirement for new competences tailored for the "generation.com" (Garris, Ahlers & Driskell, 2002) or the "new millennials". In the past, education could have simply been considered as a way to deliver a framework for prescribed educational knowledge and curriculum, in line with the classical tradition of the trivium and quadrivium. Today, the requirements of knowledge management have prescribed new sets of data and new sets of skills needed to adapt to fast changing technological advances, globalization and the need to collaborate in order to achieve goals and post-industrialism, with an emphasis upon service culture and servitisation. In the light of these changes, e-learning methods have emerged, while a parallel change in society has driven interest in social communities, game play and use of web-based services into the forefront of our work, leisure time and education, as part of this transition of technology enhanced learning into the classroom.

As a result, many of us are used to using the internet to educate ourselves, to inform ourselves, work more effectively from home and communicate with individuals and groups all over the world. Related to this, research has shown that highly interactive virtual learning imprints a permanent transformation of the educational landscape, as it has the ability to produce better academic results (Hamza-Lup & Stănescu, 2009; Wei, Lee, Hinchley, Corriveau, Kapralos & Hogue, 2010; Kapp, 2012). Moreover, the emergence of game-based learning approaches has recently found favour with learners, tutors and policy makers because games can engage and motivate learners, including those learners who are disengaged from the traditional methods of *chalk and talk* and *age and stage*.

In support of all this, Aldrich (2009) presents three arguments in favour of highly interactive virtual environments adoption:

- **Games as a learning tool:** Games are a more natural way to learn than traditional classrooms. As they are the most ancient vehicle for education, they are able to create the optimal learning state and immerse the learners into specific contexts that build knowledge and skills.
- **Context and Emotional Involvement:** Knowledge becomes entirely useful only in context. Serious games can provide the context in which the educational content can be used and also bring the learner into an emotional stake that stimulates memory.
- **Participation:** Participation with content may be necessary for learning. The process of converting experiential expertise into linear materials such as books might strip out what is most valuable in the content.

Serious Games (SGs) make learning fun, blending game elements more usually associated with entertainment games and thereby showing evidence of better retention of students on courses and higher grades. Where 'learning by doing' has become such a commonly referred practice for the proponents of Computer-Based Training (CBT), Games-Based Learning (GBL) enables both teachers and students to get a new perspective on learning, as well as enhance knowledge transfer, simultaneously offering good hands-on practice and chances for rehearsing skills and making errors without a negative consequence.

While high fidelity simulations have been the primary educational tool for decades (especially in aviation and the military), computer-based and console-based games (e.g., Xbox, Playstation) have become the focus of recent research and training because they offer an easily accessible low-cost, yet effective alternative for learning (e.g., Belanich, Sibley, & Orvis, 2004; Driskell,

& Dwyer, 1984; Rieber, 1996). Schaffer, Squire, Halverson and Gee (2004) have shown that games can instantiate a new approach to learning by allowing players experience different worlds and learn by trying to solve issues/problems inside the game: learning by doing; Holland, Jenkins and Squire (2003) have argued that games also have, to some extent, the power to shift some attitudes. Nonetheless, research has also shown that not all subject-matters can be taught via SGs and, opponents to this issue argue that games only lead to superficial learning and thus do not satisfy students' educational needs. In this respect, Clark (2003, cited in Mitchell & Savill-Smith, 2004) points out that there are several risk factors that would have a negative impact on learning via games: he argues that the learning outcomes may not meet the game objectives, in which case the game can distract the student from learning due to a score and win target. Despite the lack of supporting evidence in this respect, the popularity of games for education and training has lately been constantly increasing (e.g., Arnseth & McFarlane, 2012; Fletcher & Tobias, 2006). This has brought with it a renewed interest and development in simulation and gaming organizations (e.g., North American Simulation and Gaming Association, International Simulation and Gaming Association), scientific journals (e.g., *Journal of Educational Multimedia and Hypermedia* Special Issue on Learning and Teaching with Electronic Games) and gaming initiatives.

SERIOUS GAMES AND THE 21ST CENTURY SKILLS

If the future of learning relies upon new skills, then we need to define these 21st Century skills and to consider how they can be delivered via innovative means such as serious games.

In order to understand whether SGs are appropriate tools to contribute to build the so called 21st Century skills we need to clarify in advance what

we exactly mean when we refer to these new skills. The question has attracted considerable attention in the literature, with different definitions and classifications proposed by researchers who have considered the matter from different perspectives. As highlighted by Kickmeier-Rust and Dietrich (2012) the major obstacle to reaching a shared definition arises from "the unclear, probably vague, and highly informal nature of these 21st Century skills." The concept is, then, an overarching term for many kinds of meta-abilities, soft skills, communication and collaboration skills, of attitudes, self-awareness, strengths in non-linear thinking, and innovative problem solving, as well as the ability to reflect about one's own thinking and being. Despite this over-generalized definition, there is, anyway, a general agreement that 21st Century skills "bring together skills considered necessary in the knowledge society" (Ananiadou & Claro, 2009).

That said, a number of serious attempts have been made both by individual researchers and by relevant institutions in the field not just to define 21st century skills but to provide a systematic 21st century skills framework or structured classification. Recently Voogt and Pareja Roblin performed a meta-analysis of six relevant frameworks (namely: P21, ENGAUGE, ATCS, ISTE, OECD, CASE). These authors, thus, also produced (2010) a thorough list of the skills mentioned in the considered frameworks. In Table 1, the list of the skills mentioned in all or at least in most of the considered frameworks according to Voogt and Pareja Roblin is reported.

Consistent with this, leaders from education, business and government aspire to improve their institutions' outcomes and values to society, and, therefore, they are interested in identifying ways in which technology can support skills development. As an example, The Games for Learning Institute (G4LI) is a multi-disciplinary, and multi-institutional gaming research alliance initiated by Microsoft that aims to provide the fundamental scientific evidence to support games as learning

Table 1. List of the 21ˢᵗ century skills mentioned in all/most of the six considered frameworks (from Voogt, et al., 2010)

Mentioned in *all* frameworks	Mentioned in *most* frameworks (i.e., P21, EnGauge, ATCS, and NETS/ISTE)
• Collaboration • Communication • ICT literacy • Social and/or cultural skills; citizenship	• Creativity • Critical thinking • Problem solving • Develop quality products/productivity (except in ATCS)

tools, since Microsoft is interested in enhancing computer science curriculum, and correspondingly the student attraction, comprehension and retention rates, with innovative use of computer gaming concepts and assets[1]. In discussions with Academia and partners in industry, Microsoft has come to the conclusion that one way to improve student's interest and participation in Computer Science is to provide curriculum embedded themes that resonate with today's students' profile.

Additionally, IBM has identified five directions in which technology can improve the quality and the way education is delivered[2] where serious games are a critical component of these signposts: Technology immersion; Personalized learning paths; Knowledge skills; Global integration, and Economic alignment.

Should we now look at Serious Games as means to develop the 21ˢᵗ Century skills, we argue that they can be highly valued. We, thus, do not mean that SGs always have the potential to develop such skills *per se*, but that:

- Educators can reasonably adopt these tools to address and improve the development of such skills
- SGs can be highly effective, provided they are properly used, according to suitable and effective pedagogies

As a matter of fact (Figure 1), as underlined by Bottino et al. (2007) a wide variety of SGs can be adopted to improve "critical thinking" and "problem solving" strategies while "creativity, productivity, and ICT literacy" can be profitably

addressed by means of game building environments (Kiili, Kiili, Ott, & Jönkkäri, 2012). Should we, then, think of collaborative games (among which the competitive multiplayer games reside) we realize that games can be an interesting tools to promote "collaboration" and cooperation, exchanges, "communication" and "social skills" at large.

Of course, skills can be addressed (and the related educational objectives can reasonably be set and pursued) by means of SGs but it should be highlighted that game-based activities need to be carefully planned and guided: the role of educators/teachers is a key one and suitable pedagogies should be adopted (Arnab, Berta, de Freitas, Earp, Popescu, Romero, Stanescu, & Usart, 2012).

What research still has to cover is a rethinking of all the elements in terms of educational effectiveness, given this landmark has got new dimensions with the 21ˢᵗ Century. Questions like "are SGs good for education or training?" have already been answered by inordinate numbers of research papers and case-studies. What we still do not know is to what extent SGs do teach, train and entertain and—most importantly—how we can boost their use and effects to better serve education, irrespective of age, place, time, subject, performing characters (i.e. the student and teacher/trainer), methods, curricula, objectives and skills, technology involved.

Should we speak about integrating 21ˢᵗ Century skills via games in K-12 and Higher Education curriculum, we must acknowledge that the integration of games in schools and their adoption within formal curricula has been widely discussed over

Figure 1. SGs and the 21st century skills

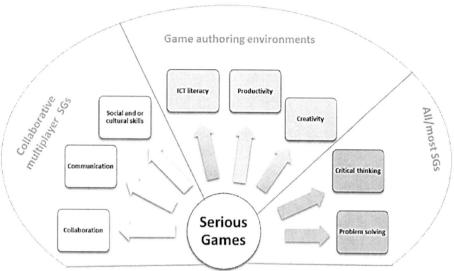

the last ten or so years (e.g. Mitchell & Savill-Smith, 2004; Squire, 2005; Michael & Chen, 2006). While most authors have underlined the benefits of using digital games for educational purposes (de Freitas & Oliver, 2006; Sandford, et al., 2006; Pivec, 2007; Hong, et al., 2009), some have also underlined the lack of enough proof of the educational outcomes/results (Hays, 2005). More recent reviews and investigations (Hainey, Connolly, Baxter, & Boyle, 2012) have highlighted that game-based learning has not been widely adopted in the educational systems both because educators still need the appropriate guidance on how to use games in their daily educational practice (Van Eck, 2006; Becker, 2007) and also because there are issues of the acceptability of games in formal educational contexts. As a matter of fact, it appears that still teachers and educational practitioners:

1. Are to be convinced of the potential of the medium as well as of its limitations (Whitton, 2012);
2. Need to become aware of the educational methodologies to be adopted (Bedwell & Salas, 2010), and

3. Need to know how the students' performance and actual learning can be assessed (de Freitas, 2006; Bottino, Ferlino, Ott, & Tavella, 2007).

Besides, we need not forget that countries in Europe are already experiencing these tools- if we have data on funds invested for the US into Serious Games uptake (1.5 billion $ in 2009 – Derryberry), about the UK we know that 35% of those involved in education have already used this tool while 65% of them are willing to do it; as far as Denmark is concerned, serious games are culturally accepted and mentioned in the curriculum, while in France there is a growing interest of SGs for individualized learning in curricular reform, and in Spain the phenomenon is at its dawn. Despite all the visible incremental uptake, experiments have never ceased to demonstrate the effectiveness of games for learning in general, as a cognitive process; yet there are questions that still remain pending when it comes to formal education, especially if our focus turns to higher education and adult learning.

FROM GAME-BASED LEARNING TO GAME-ENHANCED LEARNING

When we refer to the adoption of games in education we generally speak of Game-based-learning.

This expression refers to learning/teaching actions carried out in formal and/or informal educational settings by adopting games. It encompasses the use of both games designed expressly for fulfilling learning objectives (SGs/Educational games) and "mainstream games," those games that are developed "solely for fun" (Kirriemuir & McFarlane, 2004).

The term "game-based learning" has a very long tradition in theory and practice of pedagogy and psychology, although in its original meaning it was not expressly related to computer games (Martens, et al, 2008), nowadays it is broadly felt as a synonym of "Digital game- based learning", that is, it almost exclusively refers to the use of digital games for learning purposes (Pivec, 2007; Prensky, 2001b).

According to Squire (2005 b) a characterization of the term from the designer perspective is:

1. Having learning driven by personally meaningful scenarios;
2. Constructing problems to extend previous understandings and shape future ones;
3. Paying close attention to users' pre-existing beliefs;
4. Carefully designing for what the user experiences from moment to moment; and
5. Situating facts and knowledge in the context of doing.

Searching, alternatively, for a definition of the Game-based-learning process from the viewpoint of the user, one can outline this as:

- The process where creative teachers use certain tools that come as a complementary help and do not ask for teachers' demise (Pivec, Koubek, & Dondi, 2004).

- The teaching environment where a game is used and a scenario is created around this game to stimulate learning to occur.
- The teaching space which facilitates learning and not merely playing a game.

The emerging term Game-Enhanced Learning (which actually appears in the title of this book) on the one hand represents an attempt to underline the strong connection of this specific research field with the one of TEL (Technology Enhanced Learning), the well-established research field that "aims to design, develop, and test socio-technical innovations that will support and enhance learning practices of both individuals and organizations" (Manouselis, Drachsler, Vuorikari, Hummel, & Koper, 2011) and, on the other hand, it underlines the high potential of games not only to support but rather to improve and enhance individual and collaborative learning.

INTEGRATING SERIOUS GAMES IN LEARNING CONTEXTS

Speaking about implementing Serious Games into the educational continuum, there are elements to consider same way we do when adopting other types of learning/teaching tools the only specificity being that the tool used is a game or a part of a game. Therefore first, when selecting the game or a certain part of the game for educational purposes, the educator should bear in mind at least the following:

- What he wants his students to be able to do at the end of the instruction (educational objectives to be met)
- What students' level is
- What they already know
- What skills are stirred to reach the goals
- Which are the additional materials to be employed to best serve the set educational scopes

- How he intends to make use of the selected game: sequencing, timing, practice and class management
- How much he should insist on certain aspects in the steps of learning event- timing the events of instruction
- How to warm-up and wind-down the teaching/training event to give it all a sense of closure and fulfilment

Educators should recall and bear in mind that they can address all the educational objectives considered in the Bloom's revised taxonomy. If we look at Table 2 we easily understand that all these objectives, referring to both high order and low order thinking skills, can be profitably addressed by means of SGs. Examples can be found in literature for all of them, including creativity (Ott & Pozzi, 2011).

This view of the "reachable" educational objectives is important because it supports the idea that SGs can be compared to other more traditional educational resources, and, thus that they can be adopted as interchangeable tools with the aim of fulfilling the standard learning objectives or rather as privileged means to address further and more ambitious learning goals.

Skills and curriculum are basic ingredients one must consider when taking into consideration game-enhanced –learning. One of the key questions here is how we succeed in shaping the above mentioned skills? What is the added value for using educational alternative materials such as SGs? To what extent the materials we use in the educational process are good is a matter not only of the way we design them but also of when and how we use them.

The success of the game-based learning interventions is, thus, deputed to both game designers (IT, pedagogy and psychology specialists) as well as educators (irrespective of field and target audience) not to mention the ones who benefit from the successful outcome and actually who are the best metrics of the educational process, the students themselves.

While defining serious games, Michael Zyda considered they "have more than just story, art, and software, (…) they involve pedagogy: activities that educate or instruct, thereby imparting knowledge or skill" to our end-product, the students (Zyda, 2005, p. 26). Having mentioned the educational framework, the skills, and the curriculum, it is of paramount importance to recall that students are the main actors in the process of

Table 2. Learning objectives adapted from Churches (2008)

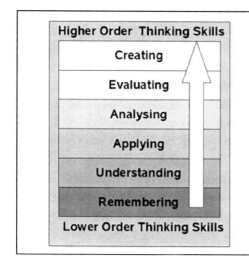

Higher Order Thinking Skills	Key verbs associated with skills
Creating	**Creating:** Designing, constructing, planning, producing, inventing, devising.
Evaluating	**Evaluating:** Checking, hypothesizing, criticizing, experimenting, judging, testing, detecting, monitoring.
Analysing	**Analysing:** Comparing, organising, deconstructing, attributing, outlining, finding, structuring, integrating.
Applying	**Applying:** Implementing, carrying out, using, executing.
Understanding	**Understanding:** Interpreting, summarising, inferring, classifying, comparing, explaining, exemplifying.
Remembering	**Remembering:** Recognising, listing, describing, identifying, retrieving, naming, locating, finding.
Lower Order Thinking Skills	

Game Based Learning (and Game-Based Teaching implicitly).

These key "elements" in our paradigm, the students, nowadays tend to prefer:

1. Receiving information quickly from multiple multimedia sources;
2. Parallel processing and multitasking;
3. Processing pictures, sounds, and video before text;
4. Random access to hyperlinked multimedia information;
5. Interacting/networking simultaneously with many others;
6. Learning "just-in-time";
7. Instant gratification and instant rewards; and
8. Learning that is relevant, instantly useful, and fun (Derryberry, 2007).

Educators as well as game developers must consider very carefully all these aspects in order to boost serious games effectiveness (Marlow, 2009). More thoughts should be, then, dedicated to explore the moment, possibility and effectiveness of game-integrated curricula as well as the best ways for implementation.

HOW TO IMPLEMENT SERIOUS GAMES IN THE CURRICULUM

First Steps

Should we tackle this generally, there are four ways educators approached the idea of integrating games into the learning process: students as game-designers; educators and/or developers as game designers, use of proprietary game-based learning content and the use of Commercial Off-The-Shelf (COTS) games. In the first approach, students learn the content and at the same time they also can develop problem-solving skills; if they do not adopt ad–hoc developed dedicated and facilitated environments (such as the MAGOS environment

see Kiili, Kiili, Ott, & Jönkkäri, 2012) they also learn programming languages.

What we consider an effective but also efficient method is integrating purpose designed game-based content and using them in educational environments. In this approach, the game is a support or means to deliver and/or assess learning. This approach is currently the most cost-effective in terms of money and time and can be used with any domain and any learner. This is an approach to be used on a short term-basis because of its practicality and efficacy and in the long term because of its potential to generate the living proof that we need to get game companies develop more serious games. An already existing proof that this is effective is the more and more frequent use of games to be in-house tailored with basic means or even the authoring tools more and more used by teachers to adjust the games that can be personalized- this is evidence of constant preoccupation in the practical field but also of the effectiveness and incremental uptake even among the IT-challenged educators, due to their practicality.

Even with some positive experiences (Bottino & Ott, 2006), there is little evidence that COTS are effective as a learning tool in classrooms. Even though integrating games into the curriculum seem to be a more and more positive and effective method, it has its drawbacks, especially if the game in focus is not designed for learning from the start. Commercial games are not designed to teach, so subject-matter may not all find their correspondent, while the content may be incomplete in relation to what we teach. This is the biggest obstacle to implementing COTS: it requires careful analysis and a matching of the content, gaps, and things to be speculated of the game to the content to be studied.

Needless to say that not all games we find interesting are suitable for learning, or if they cover the subject-matter they might not fit the age and student's profile, his interests and particular learning style. Adjustment is thus the key and teacher's creativity to find ways to get the most out of what a game offers.

Choosing a Suitable Game

A plethora of literature has been trying to categorize games from different perspectives; the most commonly referred ones are:

1. Serious games classification[3], a large database ordering games according to several criteria like gameplay, purpose, market, target audience,
2. The ENGAGE website[4] which provides an online catalogue with "ratings and case studies" (Kearney, 2011), and also
3. The classification made by Djaouti, Alvarez, and Jessel (2011) which at present is the latest in the field and offers significant cues for reflection.

Classifications of games based on learning outcomes are a good way to start in choosing a game, yet the catalogues are far from being complete as they lack other integration details that would otherwise shorten the time for a teacher to select, implement, and use the game for various subject-matters, ages, learning styles, backgrounds, environment. To exemplify, we can for example take a look at the categorization offered by *serious games classification*, by the ENGAGE program that render general characteristics of—mostly—games designed for entertainment. Despite the fact that these tools are well received, they are time consuming if taken by educators, due to the need for personal exploration and trial, which can be a hindrance in implementing the game, strengthened also by some of the educators' reluctance to the unknown. In order to facilitate games uptake into training, catalogues of games with specific, structured information for teachers' use strive for supremacy in terms of usefulness; large-scale accessibility to specific didactic information about games has to be provided, to help their embedding into curricula and also to serve the further scope of evaluating their learning impact.

At a first trial, the *serious games classification* gives information on gameplay, purpose—which is rather generally expressed: training; market-education/healthcare; audience, etc. Should we take, for example, games like *A walk in the park*[5], *1492*[6], *Emergency Evacuation Simulator*[7], or *Enchanted palace*[8] a trainer, educator, curriculum designer or student looking at this classification has minimum information on what games can do or on how they can/should be deployed; rarely educators get really helpful and self-sufficient information in relation to the targeted learning goals the game might cover.

Conversely, the ENGAGE learning site offers an improved classification, more suitable for parties interested in educational or training endeavours; thus, games are classified according to genre, game platform, age, learning objective or purpose, stating that they affirm or deny any cultural reference, player mode and time for different activities seen as sequential or global. This classification is more complex, yet more improvements would be required to increase its efficiency to support educational choices.

In the search for bringing up a tool focusing on what an educator would look up first when searching for educational materials, a table of such classification of games based on the learning outcomes (Table 3) has been projected. This is meant to be a start in mapping games with learning outcomes, a first-hand tool in designing a game-based curriculum.

Information thus drawn from various sources (Kebritchi et al. 2008; Vogel et al. 2006) has been as such organized.

Aligning the Game with the Curriculum

A game may be used as a preamble to teaching something, as a co-instructional element (to exemplify, consolidate, and practice learning in a domain), or as a post-teaching device (for as-

Table 3. Games classification based on learning objectives: prospective approach (Popescu, 2012)

Field/ skills	Skill based Learning Objective (L.O.)	Declarative knowledge LO	Procedural Knowledge LO	Strategic Knowledge LO	Affective LO
	Drill & practice	Reproduce/ recognize	Apply knowledge, rules, skills	Know when and why to apply	Foster attitudes, self-efficacy, confidence
Business & management		Gamenomics		Gamenomics	
Engineering& manufacturing		Daedalus' End Hephaestus	Daedalus' End Hephaestus		
Health & Fitness		Biohazard Fizziees	Biohazard Fizziees		
Security, safety & Crisis management		-Army Excellence in leadership (AXL) -Discover	-Full Spectrum warrior -SLIM-ESJ -Peacemaker		
Humanities & Heritage		Global Conflicts: Palestine			
Personal & social Learning &Ethics		Army Excellence in Leaderships (AXL)	Global Conflicts: Palestine	-simSchool -KM quest	
K-12	-Destination Math -La Jungla de Optica -Quest Atlantis -DimensionM -Genius Series -Jr Series				

sessment). This decision is partly determined by the curriculum and partly by the game. A balance between the needs of the curriculum and the structure of the game must be achieved to avoid either compromising the learning outcomes or forcing a game to work in a way for which it is not suited; this is why it may happen that both teachers and students can render the learning inefficient and the educational process time-consuming and futile.

Aligning the Game with the Content

Research and practitioners have concluded that games are effective educational tools and that they are worth being introduced in the curriculum.

However, this process has its limitations. Therefore, when we evaluate and select games to later use and assimilate them to the subject matters taught, we have to ask ourselves several questions. What is covered in the game? A game like *Civilization*[9] will cover a huge range of history across continents and cultures, whereas a game like *Call of Duty*[10] will focus on one snapshot of history. Obviously, this has implications on how the games align with the curriculum. Also, for instance, cultural awareness games lend themselves to more than one subject-matter; this kind of games can be used for history, language, cultures and civilizations, psychology and geography, anthropology as well.

Along with what can be used from the game we must consider also what is not covered but necessary in relation to the topic in the learning sequence, yet still missing in the game. A thoughtful educator will complement this with other didactical tools so that a continuous learning process can be unfolded.

Using the Game

Once we have chosen a game, we have become familiar with its content, and pinpointed what can be used for teaching, consolidation, guided practice, or assessment, we have to decide how to implement the content to flow nicely with the other topics in the curriculum. We can either analyse this on our own or throw it as such to students and by developing their creativity to let them apply and create, divert but stay within the topic and still head for the targeted learning outcomes silently, as whenever we can maximize students' responsibility, we should not miss any chance of doing it.

In this respect, we should not let any stone untouched on designing activities as logical continuations of the game activities, skills, and environment.

Pedagogies

Simultaneously, in the process of learning, activities entailed by Serious Games follow different pedagogical approaches and use different didactic concepts to accomplish the educational goal.

For ease of use, a taxonomy of SGs based on underlying pedagogies would better help game designers entail proper dimensions within the games so that these could correspond from the start to certain educational objectives. Conversely, once games would be associated to pedagogies and didactical methods, directories of TEL (Technology Enhanced Learning) tools would help better sustain and spread the adoption of games as teaching tools.

When they are used for supporting learning, games must be educationally sound so that the player could recall rules, elements of game mechanics previously used so that they could proceed with the next levels in a game and the educational process would not be hindered.

In this light, a taxonomy of games proposed by BinSubaih, Maddok and Romano (2009) considering underlying pedagogies would give a picture of how to better achieve certain learning goals by using a certain type/game.

1. Games based on *behaviourism* where learning occurs through conditioning with the game element typically being a reward for the correct response to the stimuli. These games are often called edutainment. An example as such is *Mathblaster*[11] where the player's reward is to shoot balloons if getting a sum correct – the sum itself is separated from the reward. Brain training games would fall into this category as well.

2. Games based on *cognitivism* where the learner becomes the centre of attention and acquires knowledge through a variety of different modalities (eg.: text, pictures, sounds). These enable the player to identify and analyse problems and apply past learning, where learning is the process of connecting symbols in a meaningful and memorable way (for example, exploring microworlds).

3. Games based on *constructivism*, that is, learning by making, where the player is immersed in a world that enables them to include feelings and emotions with the social while the player can interact with his fellow participants in the virtual environment as well as acquire and use knowledge gained (for example military simulations to develop knowledge of convoy driving with colleagues).

4. Games based on *constructionism* (former constructivism) where learning is reinforced by having to explain it. Examples in this re-

spect can be the games *VentureSim[12]*, *Global Conflict: Palestine[13]*.

5. *Situated learning* has been incorporated as information used in context, through a creation of a setting close to reality, which can easily be transferred to the real world. An example can be the socio-cultural theory which describes how games can be used as tools to mediate learning through discussion, reflection and analysis—while learning is facilitated by the culture and identity of the learner. The final model mentioned by Bin Subaihand et al. considers that a full-learning cycle is one that starts with an initial understanding, then knowledge is tested, and the feedback results in a refined model.

6. Games that blend the conditional (the rules, etiquette, software or learning goals) with the *experiential* (the sense of play, agency, learning, improvisation and feedback). In these games you know or can determine the goal but need to have the ability to identify and enact your preferences, exercise your own choice, and, possibly, make mistakes and correct them. Successful games, here, are a combination of potentially adaptive structures (such as rules), and the timely delivery of information, both of these being relevant to sustain learning (Ulicsak & Wright, 2010).

Other Elements inside the GAME

The ability of the adopted tools to be appealing for the users, to capture his/her attention, and keep his/her concentration high are of utmost importance to guarantee the reaching of the learning objectives. As far as serious games are concerned, once they are introduced in the educational flow, it is mandatory for the educational provider using the game to focus on:

- Elements in the game that match the expectations and requirements of the learner.

- Elements like time management (different with age and type of user) concentration span (which varies with age also) and sustained engagement (longer engagement with more varied activities and crossroads on the way, so that interaction could bring vividness to the process) must be measured and well catered for in the economy of the lesson plan, for sequencing the game-play to the objectives in focus. It would even be idealistic if the tutor identified sub-skills and sub-objectives to be exploited from sequences of the game, thus obtaining serious games—educational chunks to be incorporated in the learning context.

- The most important thing when we employ a game in the educational process and try to embed it in the curriculum is to make sure that the selected chunk teaches the player a new skill, and then immediately afterwards lets the player practice this skill until near mastery, creating cycles of expertise with information that is presented to them just-in-time instead of upfront (Gee, 2005), bearing in mind that games can be used to teach declarative, procedural and conceptual knowledge, train cognitive skills such as problem solving, enhance motor skills, change a person's attitude or intrinsic motivation and teach people to communicate and work together (Ratan & Ritterfeld, 2009; Wouters, Van der Spek & Van Oostendorp, 2009; Sitzmann, 2011).

In summary, we feel the need to say that games are considered effective training tools provided that learning occurs in a meaningful context (i.e. what you learn is directly related to the other subject matters inside the curriculum); plus, another condition is that the learning one gets via a game is not only relevant but applicable and practicable in that given context. Learning that occurs in meaningful and relevant contexts is then more effective than learning that occurs outside of those contexts, as is the case with most formal instruction. This leads us to highlighting the need for games embedded curriculum in an environment conducive to immediate learning and trans-disciplinary skills.

Assessment of the Educational Effectiveness

As mentioned above, when bringing up the issue of introducing game-based learning in the educational practice we face the issue of challenging current thinking about the effectiveness of Game Enhanced Learning (Whitton, 2012); in this line we also need to address the issue of how learning is assessed, taking into account that the evaluation process is key for educator's acceptance of any educational action and tool. Of course the issue should be regarded in the light of the already mentioned fact that teachers play a major role in supporting, guiding and monitoring the students' learning process (Arnab et al., 2012) and that therefore, in terms of learning results, much depends on "how" the games as instructional tools are used.

Considering a definition of games out of the inordinate ones existent, we should say that games can be considered complex software artifacts that receive continuous input from the user and return immediate feedback (Bloomfield & Livingstone, 2009). In particular when dealing with the educational use of games (and the consequent need for actual evaluation of the learning outcomes), this exchange can be observed and logged, gathering vast amounts of information about how the students interact with the game. This opens up new assessment models, potentially semi-automatic, in which the interaction can be analysed to learn about the entire gaming activity and to infer information about the learning process. Tracking and logging the activity of a student become central elements in game-based learning because this information can be used to calculate students' grades (automatically or with instructor's participation) (Moreno-Ger, Burgos, & Torrente, 2009).

Actually we see that, here, new frontiers can be opened by making use of Learning Analytics, namely those features embedded in the software to allow "the measurement, collection, analysis and reporting of data about learners and their contexts, for purposes of understanding and optimizing learning and the environments in which it occurs" (Siemens & Long, 2011).

As underlined by Serrano et al. (2012) "in educational games if in-game evaluation exists, it is usually based on a series of simple goals, whether these goals are achieved (i.e. assessment)," but "evaluation can be improved by taking advantage of in-game interaction, such as the user behaviour during the game and the type and number of interactions performed by the user while playing"; these authors then provide an example of how it is possible to collect data about user interaction and how relevant information can be extracted from these data and presented to the educators, so as to address their need for a thorough assessment of students' performance and, more at large, of games learning effectiveness.

FINAL REFLECTIONS ON SERIOUS GAMES AND CURRICULUM INTEGRATION

While games have been shown to be effective for supporting learning, its use as part of development and teaching 21st Century skills is in its infancy. The approach needs to be studied and researched further to indicate its validity as a teaching tool and as a method for assessing and tracking learners.

While the advantages of game-enhanced learning include: social interactive learning, collaboration, engagement, motivation and adding fun to learning, the introduction of games into the classroom requires well-defined plans and a step-by-step incorporation of game elements in the early stages of learning design. Even if there are many initiatives in this direction, trying to jump straight into game-based curricula does not guarantee success and performance; moreover, it is not an easy endeavour at all. This is why efforts are being made to support a game-based curriculum. For example, Curriculum Games is a directory of games that helps to teach the UK National Curriculum including a variety of games (online games, video games, board games and classroom games) for four key stages: age 5-7, age 7-11, age 11-14, and age 14-16. A Question Matrix for Teacher Reflection has been developed with the Game Enhanced Learning Project.[14] It targets the teachers interested in using games and it includes questions such as "What is my context in terms of curriculum?", "Why do I want to integrate games?", "What is the purpose of the use of the game?" (Ney, Emin & Earp, 2012).

In the light of game-enhanced-learning, deviations from the standard-based curriculum represent a paradigm shift for many teachers. Developing a curriculum based upon 21st Century skills begins by the identification of the skills and knowledge that students need to attain and then requires mapping against these skills a model or models for game and learning design (Lund & Tannehill, 2009). Teachers are responsible for choosing the content and the activities that will allow students to reach these standards but support from policy makers and the scientific community is necessary for validating that learning approach and for ensuring that quality and improving standards of education are reached. Curricular assessments are also necessary in standards-based curricula, to enable students to track their success and teachers to determine if the curriculum allows students to meet the standards.

In this context, the need to provide higher standards for all students has led to the development of both content and performance standards. Content standards are a key element of standard-based education. They indicate what students should know and be able to do, and they specify what schools should teach. They are designed to encourage every student's highest achievement. Content standards define the essential knowledge, understandings and skills, while performance standards establish specific expectations and examples of what it means to be proficient (McMillan, 2008).

Ultimately, while developing SG curricula, it is important to consider all the opportunities that standards can offer in order to develop future-proof integrated approaches in education. The future of learning looks very different from current and traditional practices, but that is because the content and skills that need to be taught are informed by globalization, cultural practices, and new approaches to learning that aim to close the gap between learning and doing. The work around game-based approaches fits well into the current structures because they allow users to dip in and out of game experiences, to map curriculum objectives against game elements such as missions and quests, but centrally because they engage and motivate young and older learners.

The potential of game-based approaches is just beginning to be quantified and this book brings together some of the ways that this is occurring in current leading edge practices. This work frames a new approach to learning, and one that means we need to reflect upon the fundamentals such as what is education, what are the 21st century skills, and how can we inform and enrich blended learning practices through game play.

REFERENCES

Aldrich, C. (2009). *Learning online with games, simulations, and virtual worlds: Strategies for online instruction.* San Francisco, CA: Jossey-Bass.

Ananiadou, K., & Claro, M. (2009). 21st century skills and competences for new millenniumm learners in OECD countries. EDU Working paper no. 41. *Organization for Economic Cooperation and Development.* Retrieved from http://www.oecd-ilibrary.org/education/21st-centuryskills-and-competences-for-new-millennium-learners-in-oecd-countries_218525261154

Arnab, S., Berta, R., de Freitas, S., Earp, J., Popescu, M., Romero, M., Usart, M. (2012). Framing the adoption of serious games in formal education. *Electronic Journal of e-Learning, 10*(2), 159-171.

Becker, K. (2007). Digital game-based learning once removed: Teaching teachers. *British Journal of Educational Technology, 38*(3), 478–488. doi:10.1111/j.1467-8535.2007.00711.x

Bedwell, W. L., & Salas, E. (2010). Computer-based training: Capitalizing on lessons learned. *International Journal of Training and Development, 14*(3), 239–249. doi:10.1111/j.1468-2419.2010.00355.x

Belanich, J., Sibley, D. E., & Orvis, K. L. (2004). *Instructional characteristics and motivational features of a PC based game*. Washington, DC: US Army Research Institute for the Behavioral & Social Sciences.

BinSubaih, A., Maddock, S., & Romano, D. (2006). A serious game for traffic accident investigators. *International Journal of Interactive Technology and Smart Education, 3*(4), 329–346. doi:10.1108/17415650680000071

Bloomfield, P. R., & Livingstone, D. (2009). Multi-modal learning and assessment in second life with quizHUD. In *Proceedings of the 2009 Conference in Games and Virtual Worlds for Serious Applications*, (pp. 217-218). IEEE.

Bottino, R. M., Ferlino, L., Ott, M., & Tavella, M. (2007). Developing strategic and reasoning abilities with computer games at primary school level. *Computers & Education, 49*(4), 1272–1286. doi:10.1016/j.compedu.2006.02.003

Bottino, R. M., & Ott, M. (2006). Mind games, reasoning skills, and the primary school curriculum. *Learning, Media and Technology, 31*(4), 359–375. doi:10.1080/17439880601022981

Churces, A. (2008). *Bloom's taxonomy*. Retrieved from http://edweb.sdsu.edu/courses/EDTEC470/sp09/5/bloomstaxanomy.html

de Freitas, S. (2012). *Learning in immersive worlds: A review of game-based learning JISC e-learning programme*. Retrieved from http://www.jisc.ac.uk/media/documents/programmes/elearninginnovation/gamingreport_v3.pdf

de Freitas, S., & Oliver, M. (2006). How can exploratory learning with games and simulations within the curriculum be most effectively evaluated? *Computers & Education, 46*, 249264. doi:10.1016/j.compedu.2005.11.007

Derryberry, A. (2007). *Serious games- Online games for learning*. Retrieved from http://www.adobe.com/products/director/pdfs/serious_games_wp_1107.pdf

Djaouti, D., Alvarez, J., & Jessel, J. P. (2011). *Classifying serious games: The G/P/S model*. Hershey, PA: IGI Global. doi:10.4018/978-1-60960-495-0.ch006

Driskell, J. E., & Dwyer, D. J. (1984). Microcomputer videogames based training. *Educational Technology Research and Development, 44*(2).

Egenfeldt-Nielsen, S. (2005). *Beyond edutainment, exploring the educational potential of computer games*. (Unpublished Dissertation). IT University of Copenhagen. Copenhagen, Denmark.

Fletcher, J. D., & Tobias, S. (2006). Using computer games and simulations for instruction: A research review. In *Proceedings of the Society for Advanced Learning Technology Meeting*. Orlando, FL: IEEE.

Garris, R., Ahler, R., & Driskell, J. (2002). Games motivation and learning: A research and practice model. *Simulations and Gaming, 33*.

Gee, J. (2004). *Learning by design: Games as learning machines*. Paper presented at the Game Developers Conference. San Jose, CA.

Hainey, T., Connolly, T., Baxter, G., Boyle, L., & Beeby, R. (2012). Assessment integration in games-based learning: A preliminary review of the literature. In *Proceedings of the 6th European Conference on Games-Based Learning*. IEEE.

Hamza-Lup, F., & Stănescu, I. A. (2010). The haptic paradigm in education: Challenges and case studies. *The Internet and Higher Education, 13*, 78–81. doi:10.1016/j.iheduc.2009.12.004

Hays, R. T. (2005). *The effectiveness of instructional games: A literature review and discussion*. Washington, DC: Naval Air Warfare Center.

Holland, Jenkins, & Squire. (2003). Theory by design. In *Video Game Theory*. New York, NY: Routledge.

Hong, J. C., Cheng, C. L., Hwang, M. Y., Lee, C. K., & Chang, H. Y. (2009). Assessing the educational values of digital games. *Journal of Computer Assisted Learning, 25*, 423437. doi:10.1111/j.1365-2729.2009.00319.x

Kapp, K. M. (2012). *The gamification of learning and instruction: Game-based methods and strategies for training and education*. San Francisco, CA: Pfeiffer.

Kebritchi, M., & Hirumi, A. (2008). *Examining the pedagogical foundations of modern educational computer games*. Paper presented at the International Technology, Educational, Research. Orlando, FL.

Kickmeier-Rust, M. D., & Dietrich, A. (2012). A domain model for smart 21st century skills training in game-based virtual worlds. In *Proceedings of ICALT 2012*. ICALT.

Kiili, K., Kiili, C., Ott, M., & Jönkkäri, T. (2012). Towards creative pedagogy: Empowering students to develop games. In *Proceedings ECGBL 2012*. ECGBL.

Kirriemuir, J., & McFarlane, A. (2004). *Literature review in games and learning report 8: Futurelab series*. Retrieved from http://archive.futurelab.org.uk/resources/documents/lit_reviews/Games_Review.pdf

Kolb, D. (1984). *Experiential learning: Experience as the source of learning and development*. Englewood Cliffs, NJ: Prentice Hall.

Lund, J., & Tannehill, D. (2009). *Standards-based physical education curriculum development*. Sudbury, MA: Bartlett Publishers.

Manouselis, N., Drachsler, H., Vuorikari, R., Hummel, H., & Koper, R. (2011). Recommender systems in technology enhanced learning. In Ricci, F., Rokach, L., Shapira, B., & Kantor, P. B. (Eds.), *Recommender Systems Handbook* (pp. 387–415). Berlin, Germany: Springer. doi:10.1007/978-0-387-85820-3_12

Marlow, C. M. (2009). *Games and learning in landscape architecture*. Paper presented at the Conference of Digital Landscape Architecture. New York, NY.

McMillan, J. H. (2008). *Assessment essentials for standards-based education*. London, UK: Corwin.

Michael, D., & Chen, S. (2006). *Serious games: Games that educate, train, and inform*. Boston, MA: Thomson.

Mitchell, A., & Savill-Smith, C. (2004). *The use of computer and videogames for learning: A review of the literature*. Retrieved from http://www.lsda.org.uk/files/PDF/1529.pdf

Moreno-Ger, P., Burgos, D., & Torrente, J. (2009). Digital games in e-learning environments: Current uses and emerging trends. *Simulation & Gaming, 40*(5), 669–687. doi:10.1177/1046878109340294

O'Neil, H. F., Wainess, R., & Baker, E. L. (2005). Classification of learning outcomes: Evidence from the computer games literature. *Curriculum Journal, 16*(4), 455–474. doi:10.1080/09585170500384529

Ott, M., & Pozzi, F. (2011). Digital games as creativity enablers for children. In *Behaviour and Information Technology*. New York, NY: Taylor & Francis.

Pivec, M. (2007). Play and learn: Potentials of game-based learning. *British Journal of Educational Technology, 38*, 387393. doi:10.1111/j.1467-8535.2007.00722.x

Pivec, M., Koubek, A., & Dondi, C. (Eds.). (2004). *Guidelines on game-based learning*. Berlin, Germany: Pabst Vrlg.

Pivec, P., & Pivec, M. (2009). Collaborative online roleplay for adult learners. In Ratan & Ritterfeld (Eds.), *SG: Mechanisms and Effects*. Hershey, PA: IGI Global.

Rieber, L. P. (1996). Seriously considering play-Designing interactive learning environments: Based on the blending of microworld, simulations and games. *Educational Technology Research and Development, 44*(2). doi:10.1007/BF02300540

Sandford, R., Ulicsak, M., Facer, K., & Rudd, T. (2006). Teaching with games. *Futurelab report*. Retrieved from http://archive.futurelab.org.uk/projects/teaching-with-games

Schaffer, S. Halverson, & Gee. (2004). *Video games and the future of learning*. Retrieved from http://www.wisconsin.gov/state/core/education.html

Serrano, A., Marchiori, E. J., del Blanco, A., Torrente, J., & Fernandez-Manjon, B. (2012). A framework to improve evaluation in educational games. In *Proceedings of the Global Engineering Education Conference (EDUCON)*. IEEE.

Shi, W., Lee, G., Hinchley, J., Corriveau, J.-P., Kapralos, B., & Hogue, A. (2010). Using a virtual learning environment with highly interactive elements in second life to engage millennial students. In *Proceedings of the International Conference on e-Education, e-Business, e-Management, and e-Learning, 2010*, (pp. 255-259). IC4E.

Siemens, G., & Long, P. (2011). Penetrating the fog: Analytics in learning and education. *EDUCAUSE Review, 46*(5).

Sitzman, T. (2011). Analytic examination of the instructional effectiveness of computer-based simulation games. *Personnel Psychology, 64*(2), 489–528. doi:10.1111/j.1744-6570.2011.01190.x

Sitzmann, T., Ely, K., Brown, K. G., & Bauer, K. N. (2010). Self-assessment of knowledge: A cognitive learning or affective measure? *Academy of Management Learning & Education, 9*(2), 169–191. doi:10.5465/AMLE.2010.51428542

Spires, H. (2008). *The 21st century skills and serious games – Preparing the N generation in serious educational games*. Rotterdam, The Netherlands: Sense Publishing.

Squire, K. (2003). Video games in education. *International Journal of Intelligent Simulations and Gaming, 2*(1).

Squire, K. (2005). Game-based learning: An X-learn perspective paper. *MASIE Center: e-Learning Consortium Report*. Retrieved from http://www.masieweb.com/research-and-articles/research/game-based-learning.html

Squire, K. (2005b). *Game-based learning: Present and future state of the field*. Retrieved from http://www.newmediaforlearning.com/research/Game-Based_Learning.pdf

Squire, K. D. (2006). From content to context: Videogames as designed experiences. *Educational Researcher, 35*(8). doi:10.3102/0013189X035008019

Tang, S., Hanneghan, M., & El Rhalibi, A. (2009). Introduction to games-based learning. In Connolly, T. M., Stansfield, M. H., & Boyle, E. (Eds.), *Games-Based Learning Advancement for Multisensory Human Computer Interfaces: Techniques and Effective Practices*. Hershey, PA: IGI Global. doi:10.4018/978-1-60566-360-9.ch001

Thatcher, D. (1990). *Promoting learning through games and simulations.* Thousand Oaks, CA: Sage Publications.

Ulicsak, M., & Wright, M. (2010). *Games in education: Serious games.* Futurelab.

Van Eck, R. (2006). Digital game-based learning: It's not just the digital natives who are restless. *EDUCAUSE Review, 41*(2).

Vogel, J. J., Vogel, D. S., Cannon-Bowers, J., Bowers, C. A., Muse, K., & Wright, M. (2006). Computer gaming and interactive simulations for learning: A meta-analysis. *Journal of Educational Computing Research, 34*(3), 229–243. doi:10.2190/FLHV-K4WA-WPVQ-H0YM

Voogt, J., & Pareja Roblin, N. (2010). *21st century skills – Discussion paper.* Enschede, The Netherlands: University of Twente. Retrieved 25 November 2012 from http://onderzoek.kennisnet.nl/onderzoeken-totaal/21stecentury

Wagner, T. (2008). *The global achievement gap.* New York, NY: Basic Books.

Whitton, N. (2012). The place of game-based learning in an age of austerity. *Electronic Journal of e-Learning, 10*(2), 249 – 256.

Wouters, P., van der Spek, E. D., & van Oostendorp, H. (2009). *Current practices in serious game research: A review from a learning outcomes perspective.* Retrieved from http://www.cs.uu.nl/docs/vakken/b3elg/literatuur_files/Wouters.pdf

Zemliansky, P. (Ed.). (2010). *Design and implementation of educational games: Theoretical and practical.* Hershey, PA: IGI Global. doi:10.4018/978-1-61520-781-7

Zyda, M. (2005). From visual simulation to virtual reality to games. *IEEE Computer, 38*(9), 25–32. doi:10.1109/MC.2005.297

KEY TERMS AND DEFINITIONS

Assessment (In the Serious Games Field): Serious Games assessment corresponds to the evaluation of the players' performance in terms of in-game achievements or learning outcomes that can be carried out within the game (where the game represents the evaluation tool) or outside of the game.

Curriculum: Curriculum represents a planned and guided program of learning, usually segregated by subject area, carried on in groups or individually, inside or outside the school, composed of four main categories: content, instruction, assessment, and context.

Game-Based Learning: Game-based learning refers to the innovative learning approach derived from the use of computer games that possess educational value or different kinds of software applications that use games for learning and education purposes such as learning support, teaching enhancement, assessment and evaluation of learners (Tang, Hanneghan, & El-Rhalibi, 2009).

Serious Games: Games that do not have entertainment, enjoyment, or fun as their primary purpose (Michael & Chen, 2006).

Standard-Based Curriculum and Assessment: A standard-based approach enables practitioners apply a common understanding of benchmarks, refine the curriculum as to be aligned with self-established exit outcomes, as well as with relevant standards, and implement specific strategies to make sound decisions about curriculum, instruction, and assessment.

ENDNOTES

[1] https://www.facultyresourcecenter.com/curriculum/DE/6646-Gaming-Resource-Toolkit-2006-.aspx?c1=de-de&c2=DE

[2]   http://www.redbooks.ibm.com/redpapers/pdfs/redp4564.pdf

[3]   http://serious.gameclassification.com

[4]   http://www.engagelearning.eu/teachers/?page_id=26)

[5]   http://serious.gameclassification.com/EN/games/16847-A-Walk-in-the-Park/index.html)

[6]   http://serious.gameclassification.com/EN/games/14557-1492/index.html

[7]   http://serious.gameclassification.com/EN/games/17985-Emergency-Evacuation-Simulator/index.html)

[8]   http://serious.gameclassification.com/EN/games/16732-Enchanted-Palace/index.html

[9]   http://armorgames.com/play/5151/civilizations-wars

[10]   http://www.callofduty.com/

[11]   http://www.mathblaster.com/free-game.aspx?pid=googpd&cid=online%20math%20games%20for%20kids

[12]   http://www.wiley.com/college/fin/smith322873/site/buyaccess/student.html

[13]   http://playthisthing.com/global-conflicts-palestine [14]http://www.gel.itd.cnr.it/

Chapter 2
Games in Entrepreneurship Education to Support the Crafting of an Entrepreneurial Mindset

Leona Achtenhagen
Jönköping International Business School, Sweden

Bengt Johannisson
Linnaeus University, Sweden & Jönköping International Business School, Sweden

ABSTRACT

An increasing number of education institutions, including many universities and colleges, are offering entrepreneurship education. This development is driven by the hope that more entrepreneurs could be "created" through such efforts, and that these entrepreneurs through their newly founded ventures will contribute to economic growth and job creation. At higher education institutions, the majority of entrepreneurship courses rely on writing business plans as a main pedagogical tool for enhancing the students' entrepreneurial capabilities. In this chapter, the authors argue instead for the need for a pedagogy that focuses on supporting students in crafting an entrepreneurial mindset as the basis for venturing activities. They discuss the potential role of games in such entrepreneurship education and present the example of an entrepreneurship game from the Swedish context, which was developed by a group of young female entrepreneurs. The authors describe the game and discuss their experiences of playing it with a group of novice entrepreneurship and management students at the master's level, and they review the effectiveness of the game in terms of how it supports students in crafting an entrepreneurial mindset. The authors conclude the chapter by outlining how entrepreneurship games could be integrated into a university curriculum and suggest some directions for future research.

DOI: 10.4018/978-1-4666-3950-8.ch002

INTRODUCTION

Since the 1990s, many universities worldwide have initiated entrepreneurship education, which mainly aims at increasing the number of potential entrepreneurs (Kuratko, 2005). This development follows the commonly shared understanding that new ventures play a crucial role in achieving economic growth and value creation, as well as that young growth firms create the majority of new jobs (e.g. Kirchhoff & Phillips, 1988). As pointed out by Katz (2003), homogeneity as to what is considered to be appropriate content for entrepreneurship education has increased over the past years, and today there exists a widely shared agreement that such education should:

1. Increase the understanding of what entrepreneurship is about (leading to a concern for economic wealth creation);
2. Focus on the entrepreneurship process, which entails learning to become entrepreneurial; and
3. Prepare individuals for careers as entrepreneurs.

Here, business plan assignments are typically used to imitate 'action learning'—although the 'action' is largely restricted to the linguistic exercise of developing a business plan document without much 'real' action related to it.

Our point of departure is the need for a pedagogical approach that centres on the crafting of an entrepreneurial mindset, and enforces this process through different types of pedagogical tools. Following the American Heritage Dictionary definition, we associate mindset with "[a] fixed mental attitude that determines one's responses to and interpretations of situations". An entrepreneurial mindset is not only relevant when taking on a narrow definition of entrepreneurship as a new venture creation, but is equally (if not more) important when recognizing the potential of entrepreneurial activities for all types of creative organizing in public as

well as in private life. Nevertheless, we argue that having an entrepreneurial mindset does not mean that the individual immerses into an entrepreneurial identity that directs all existential choices. Rather, students can craft their entrepreneurial mindsets without directly becoming entrepreneurially active in venture creation, i.e. without enacting their entrepreneurial identities at this point in time. We argue that such a mindset is the prerequisite for the later crafting of an entrepreneurial identity which takes place when immersing 'in' entrepreneuring (rather than learning 'about' or training 'for' entrepreneurship). For the context of formal educational settings, such as university, we think that influencing attitudes towards crafting an entrepreneurial mindset, supported by tools such as games, is a realistic ambition.

In many entrepreneurship courses, students are asked to write business plans for real, rudimentary or fictitious venture ideas, hoping that this exercise would simulate the real world of entrepreneurship as a practice. The predominance of this approach was confirmed by Honig (2004), who found that 78 out of the top 100 US universities offered courses that specifically referred to business plan education. The proposed experiential learning is assumed to inspire students to start their own (business) ventures after the program. There are, though, some fundamental flaws in the underlying assumptions of such a programme design when it comes to helping students to (re-)discover their talents as entrepreneurs.

First, it is taken for granted that all students are already interested in entrepreneurship as a career choice, since they are already equipped with an entrepreneurial mindset. However, this is typically not the case. Through socialization and formal education they have most probably 'unlearned' their entrepreneurial mindset and the playfulness that they once had as children (Johannisson, 2010). Thus, for this (usually large) group of students, entrepreneurship education needs to provide an arena which supports students in crafting (or rediscovering) their entrepreneurial mindsets.

Second, for the effectiveness of entrepreneurship education (in the sense of leading to a higher number of successful start-ups), it is probably fundamental whether students consider entrepreneurial activities to be simply a part of their educational journey, an element in their emerging careers or associated with those existential issues that subsequently build an entrepreneurial identity. For students who already know that they want to become entrepreneurs, business plan assignments can be a helpful learning tool for important aspects of entrepreneurial life. However, many students enrolled in entrepreneurship courses have in fact not yet had the chance to craft an entrepreneurial mindset and associated action orientation.

Third, business planning is a crucial component in a management logic that in many respects contrasts with that of entrepreneurship (e.g. Hjorth, Johannisson & Steyaert, 2003). Formal planning only makes sense when the future is foreseeable and thus can be controlled. From, for example, chaos theory we know that that is not the case (Stacey, 1996). A generic assumption in entrepreneurship is instead that the (future) environment can be enacted, meaning that it is possible to co-construct it together with other actors. This calls for experimenting and intense interaction, which are activities that are certainly different from business planning as an analytical exercise. Even in education programmes which include internships in entrepreneurial firms, such practical experiences are usually not enough to turn students into entrepreneurs. Rather, this experience might train students to become administrators who know how to help business leaders to remain entrepreneurs (Johannisson, 1991).

Fourth, an entrepreneurial mindset can be applied to a much broader context than that represented by the common, narrow view on entrepreneurship as a profit-oriented activity, which is typically in focus in business plan exercises. While an entrepreneurial mindset is applicable to most spheres of life, it is also important that entrepreneurship education embraces other highly relevant types of entrepreneurial endeavours, such as those taking place in the social, cultural or public sphere (e.g. Berglund, Johannisson, & Schwarz, 2013; Fayolle & Matley, 2010; Klamer, 2011).

Elsewhere we have presented our view on how the academic setting may be turned into a learning context for entrepreneurship (Achtenhagen & Johannisson, 2011, 2013b). This view includes, among other aspects, the need for a learning context that offers diversity and variety and recognizes that the boundaries between the university and society must be permeable, inviting dialogues with different stakeholders. In internationally diverse student groups (as is common in many study programmes today), such variety with respect to (cultural) outlook, family backgrounds and academic profile is provided by the student cohort itself, but can be amplified by different modes of organizing (for example, in group assignments conducted by mixed student groups). To make the university's boundaries more permeable, interaction with different external stakeholders can be nurtured. For example, students' experiential learning will increase if they conduct company projects addressing challenges identified either by the companies (or mediating organizations) or by the students. Such collaboration will help the students to gain an insight into how companies work and will make them realize how theory relates to practice. Participating organizations can not only get ideas for their own development, while connecting firms and students, but also access to a group of potential recruits.

The discussion so far has underlined that sets of experientially oriented pedagogical tools appear to be well suited to guiding students on their journey of crafting an entrepreneurial mindset. Games can be one useful pedagogical tool to facilitate this process.

To avoid misunderstanding, it is important to point out that an entrepreneurial mindset does not include the assumption that entrepreneurs have a tendency or like to act as 'gamblers.' Despite the fact that entrepreneurs certainly thrive on chaos, this does not mean that entrepreneurs typically tend to take risks that cannot be calculated, something that in economic theories, such as game theory, is associated with uncertainty. We rather ascribe to entrepreneurs the ability to cope with ambiguity. The difference between risk-taking, dealing with uncertainty and managing ambiguity was explained very well by Sarasvathy (2001). Describing the logic that experienced entrepreneurs tend to apply in their decision-making, she very pedagogically uses the example of an urn that cannot be looked into and that contains balls of different colours. If the colour of the balls and their proportions are known, risk refers to the probability of picking a ball with a certain colour out of that urn (i.e. the probability can be calculated). A situation characterized by uncertainty, such as that of gambling, means that the colours of the balls are known, but their proportions are not. This means that the probability of picking a ball of a specific colour cannot be calculated. An example of an uncertain situation is the commercialization of a radical innovation where what to do is known but not the outcome of the action. Sarasvathy (2001) argues that while human beings in general, including managers, prefer the 'risky or known distribution' over the 'uncertain or unknown distribution' urn, entrepreneurs might have a preference for a third situation, namely that of ambiguity. Then the colours of the balls in the urn are not at all known, but by keeping to add own balls of a certain colour, over time that colour will dominate that of the balls originally in the urn. Thereby the whole situation is changed in a mode that is partially controlled by the actor. Entrepreneurial activities often call for creativity and innovativeness, and no probabilities on their outcome can be calculated before embarking on them. Coping with ambiguity demands, among other things, experimenting and interacting in order to influence and 'enact' the context of the venturing activity. Playing games in entrepreneurship education can help students to experience such experimentation and interaction in a 'safe' setting.

This chapter is structured as follows. First, we present our view on entrepreneurship and the current state of the art of entrepreneurship education in the contemporary university-level business school setting (in Sweden) and review the mainstream pedagogical paradigm underlying much of that teaching, and we position the entrepreneurship game approach as one tool in an alternative approach to entrepreneurship education. Then we tell the story of a game developed by young Swedish entrepreneurs, arguing that despite formalized rules, a game can contribute to rediscovering the creativity typical of play. Following the presentation of the game, we reflect on the role that this game can play in entrepreneurship education. We evaluate the impact the game has had on our current student cohort in a master's-level class on entrepreneurship, by assessing the course evaluation as well as reflective blog entries (for elaborations on this pedagogical setting, see Achtenhagen & Johannisson, 2011), in which the students discuss their experience and learning from playing the game. We conclude with lessons learned and reflections targeted at entrepreneurship educators about in which contexts and related to which contents this entrepreneurship game might be beneficial to use.

ENTREPRENEURSHIP: AN INSTRUMENT OR AN APPROACH TO LIFE?

In the search for legitimacy as an academic field in its own right (rather than continuing to be viewed as a subsection of strategic management, small business management or similar areas), entrepreneurship scholars have created a rather high level of institutionalization of the field, for example with regard to the number of teaching programmes, professorships, conferences and scientific journals and that institutionalization has also contributed to a standardization of pedagogical approaches, as has been confirmed for the

United States by Katz (2003) and Honig (2004), and more generally by Kuratko (2005).

However, for example in Europe alternative images of entrepreneurship have emerged that, for example, widen the common perspective in the entrepreneurship field to focus on different learning approaches (e.g. Hjorth & Johannisson, 2007). Taking such a perspective decouples entrepreneurship from the stereotype of entrepreneurs as white, male heroes with superior personal attributes (Ogbor, 2000), and also liberates it from the focus on for-profit business ventures (Berglund & Johansson, 2013). Instead, such a perspective allows us to view entrepreneurship as generically associated with the creative organizing of people and resources according to opportunity, which stretches into the mundane settings of everyday life (e.g. Steyaert, 2004). Thus, we acknowledge that entrepreneurship is intimately associated with human activity, complementing the questions of who the entrepreneur is, what happens when entrepreneurship is carried out, and how entrepreneurship is enacted. As much as entrepreneurship brings commercial and social innovations to the market and society, it also expresses intrinsic human characteristics that are deeply embedded in our existence. Thereby, we complement the common instrumental dimension of entrepreneurship with an expressive one. This activity-centred perspective on entrepreneurship can more accurately be labelled 'entrepreneur*ing.*'

Elaborating upon the expressive dimension of entrepreneurship, we can recall what we as human beings all were before we were socialized into society (not least by institutions like the school system). We were born as entrepreneurs (Johannisson, 2010). As children we all practise entrepreneurship, or rather entrepreneuring (because it is an ongoing activity, see above), in our play. Typical dimensions of our play as children are being creative, imaginative, and courageous, and taking initiative and responsibility, while collaborating with others. The role of the context, in particular family members, but also (pre-)school

teachers, then, is to provide a feeling of security that allows us to immerse ourselves in the practice of entrepreneuring (Winnicott, 1971). As pointed out by the Swedish author and mathematician Helena Granström, children's play does not need any language but is genuinely embodied (Granström, 2010, p. 43). Just as the young child is literally illiterate, the grown-up is bodily illiterate (p. 49). This means that children are able to spontaneously practise entrepreneurship. While grown-ups associate play with relaxation, children seem to see it both as a voluntary and as an existential necessity. Yet, adults play for instrumental reasons—in order to have fun (or, in some cases, for money)—while children play for expressive reasons, for its own sake.

Huizinga (1938), with his seminal work *Homo Ludens*, puts the spotlight on play as a generic feature in human life. Although the brief title signals play as the core feature of human self-identity, adults' play is very much reduced to an activity that makes grown-ups temporarily break away from everyday life and behave foolishly on special occasions, such as carnivals, or in special places, such as clubs. But such limits in time and space represent a kind of regulation. Huizinga thus associates play with a 'game' that signals a planned (inter)activity. Rules are stated above the head of the players involved before the exercise starts and the designed activities are demarcated in time and space, play being explicitly a game of make-believe, usually representing established cultures. As with any other human activity, play and game are thus enforced and/or restricted by their institutional setting, which also defines what type of entrepreneurship is appropriate (Baumol, 1990). Institutions provide 'the rules of the game' (*sic!*) (North, 1990) which offer a basic order as a platform for the spontaneity and improvisation that characterize entrepreneuring. In contrast to this understanding of the 'playful' (adult) human being, for children, play is the core of their existential being. Play makes childhood unique. When children play, rules may be established, but usually by the children themselves and then only for occasional and local use. Besides, children's play often takes off spontaneously. Children play at any time in any place, and what is considered to be fact or fiction in children's play remains ambiguous in the potential spaces that the presence of a caring and trusted adult provides. While play is exciting to adults it is self-evident to and, as indicated above, embodied by children. In many societies, parents play parlour games with their children, which often have aims beyond having fun together—namely, during these games parents try to familiarize their children with institutionalized 'rules of the societal game' through restricting the parlour game by following its established rules.

The discourse above has at least three implications for what we will discuss in more detail below. First, the rules that accompany a game as a tool in entrepreneurship education should not control or streamline the activities concerned, but rather communicate a feeling of comfort that invites entrepreneuring. Second, in an academic setting, entrepreneuring could fruitfully be taught by focusing on helping students recognize and craft the entrepreneurial mindset they all once had as children. As indicated above, if such a foundation is not firmly built, activities such as writing business plans may rather put students off entrepreneurship—as they often at this stage have not yet crafted their entrepreneurial selves. Thus, we propose that for students with unclear entrepreneurial aspirations (as well as for students with clear entrepreneurial aspirations but a lack of confidence to put these into practice), focus might be put on guiding students in crafting an entrepreneurial mindset. Then it is important to experience entrepreneuring through a variety of exercises and tasks. An important aspect of entrepreneuring is reflexivity as a mode of building actionable knowledge (Jarzabkowski & Wilson, 2006). We argue that despite their rules, games can contribute to rediscovering the creativity typical of play (for elaborations on a pedagogical setting which fosters reflexivity, see Achtenhagen

& Johannisson, 2011), in which the students discuss their experience and learning from playing the game. This is a kind of self-reflection that we would like to associate with all education for and in entrepreneurship.

If successful, the game activity has to be contextualized into the social setting of the students. This has to be done both in a systematic way jointly by the course organizers and by the students themselves in the interface between their public and private life spheres. In Table 1, we position the game in relation to alternative approaches to enforcing entrepreneurial learning and the crafting of an entrepreneurial mindset. Five such pedagogical approaches are presented in order of declining control over the process by the programme management and, accordingly, increased student self-control (but also increased difficulties of evaluating learning outcomes in established ways).

The teaching of 'business planning' has, despite the criticism we present above regarding the over-reliance on this approach in settings that invite entrepreneurship, some strengths also in the context of venturing. One is that it helps develop analytical skills and holistic perspectives. Another advantage is that its causal logic makes it easy to communicate and points out the importance of not just the uniqueness of a venture concept but also the significance of building legitimacy among different stakeholders (Honig & Karlsson, 2004). The cognitive normative bias of business planning, however, means that practical skills, needed to move from decision to concrete action, are devalued. As pointed out by Sarasvathy (2001), entrepreneurial venturing is guided by a logic of effectuation that is by 'making do' whatever the means are.

'Games' can be appropriate for developing specific skills, which have been demonstrated to be important in feeding entrepreneurial processes, such as creativity, decisiveness and social skills. Entrepreneurial processes of 'becoming' often call for instant action, and time pressure can be integrated into games. However, entrepreneur-

Table 1. Positioning the game as a mode of enforcing entrepreneurial capabilities

Approach	Strengths	Weaknesses	Contributions to crafting of entrepreneurial mindset
Business plan	Systematic analysis including stakeholders	Cognitive/normative bias denies role of hands-on experience	Points out the importance of legitimacy
Game	Develops creativity, encourages teamwork, coping with time pressure	Decontextualized laboratory setting, little concern for timing	Reveals a hidden creativity potential, builds self-confidence
Internship	Combines action and reflection, bridges academia and community	Partner organization may not be role model; time- and resource-consuming	Develops responsibility and social skills
Enacting an own venture idea	Develops personal responsibility and social skills	Practicalities absorb most of the time, no space for reflection	Enforces social learning and commitment
Everyday practising of entrepreneuring	Ongoing identity building, networked reflexivity	Some parts of the private sphere remain closed	Integrates public and private life spheres

ing even calls for timing (*kairos*) (Johannisson, 2011), a capability that is difficult to encourage considering that games are arranged in a laboratory setting, which by definition is decontextualized from all the coincidences that invite alert action to turn coincidences into opportunities. Having said this, the ability of games to enforce hidden capabilities such as creativity and decisiveness feeds self-confidence, which is a basic requirement when crafting an entrepreneurial mindset and subsequently activating it in real situations.

'Internships,' where students spend part of their time in a partner firm, have been practised in Sweden in academic programmes in small business management and entrepreneurship since the 1970s (Johannisson, 1991). Internships, of course, invite experiential learning, where theoretical frameworks are challenged by industry and organizational practices. However, not all (small) organizations are entrepreneurial, and to contribute to entrepreneurial learning, the approach requires a guided reflection about practice (Cunliffe, 2004; Gray, 2007). Internships also trigger students' own networking, crucial for future venturing (e.g. Johannisson, 2000; Sarasvathy, 2001). However, internships are challenging to organize and administer, and they need to be combined with academic contents in order to qualify students to receive credit points.

Some programmes in entrepreneurship may invite students to 'enact an own venture,' that is to take control over their own creative organizing of resources according to an opportunity they have imagined. In order to be able to state the business or social value of that emerging venture, of course, students have to interact with actors outside the university and create practices beyond existing routines. Students have to take responsibility for the development of both the venture itself and the social skills that are needed to build a context that supports the emerging organization. However, while the business plan approach runs the risk of remaining an intellectual exercise, enacting an own venture may imply that practicalities absorb most of the available time at the expense of the reflexivity that is needed to build a sustainable venture. Nevertheless, the very attempt provides relevant lessons with regards to social learning and the importance of building commitment, both personally and among different stakeholders.

As indicated, entrepreneuring as a verb reflects an existential approach to life, 'an everyday practice,' where ongoing change is considered to be a natural state. This attitude is generic and should frame even the other approaches mentioned above, as long as it is not restricted to different roles, for example that of a student or a project leader, but concerns building an entrepreneurial mindset that guides the student when s/he crafts her/his identity. Learning and entrepreneuring then become interchangeable with each other. Although some part of what energizes the ongoing identity-crafting process may be subconscious, hidden also to the student her-/himself, this approach means that the boundaries between public and private lives dissolve. Of course, it is difficult to teach such existential challenges, even though this practice was once, when we were children, natural to all of us. Our experience tells us that the teacher her-/himself has to adopt such an approach to life in order to be trustworthy and accordingly listened to.

Keeping this positioning of the game approach in mind, we now turn to the presentation of a Swedish game that, properly managed, can serve as a facilitator to support students in crafting their entrepreneurial mindsets.

THE ENTREPRENEURSHIP GAME

Here, we present an entrepreneurship game, in Swedish 'Entreprenörsspelet 1.0,' and its integration in a master's programme at Jönköping International Business School, internationally recognized for its entrepreneurship research and education. This tool was developed by a group of young (female) entrepreneurs in Sweden, with their venture 'Go Enterprise!'. The game is played in seminar groups of around 25 people, divided into five teams. Based on a real company case, the teams have to complete a number of tasks to develop solutions for that case under high time pressure. The tasks trigger a number of key entrepreneurial competences, such as being analytical, reflective, creative, courageous, strategically realistic, communicative, and daring. After each task, the groups present their solutions (again within strict time limits) and then the groups and the facilitator jointly vote for the best solution. At the end of the game, the team with the best overall ranking wins. Below, we will first introduce the company and its business model, before describing the game in more detail.

In order to evaluate the feasibility of the academic teaching about/for/in entrepreneurship we think that it is important to be informed about the societal context in which the educational activities take place. In 2009, the Swedish Government gave the National Agency for Education, as the central administrative authority for the public school system, the publicly organized preschooling, school-age childcare and adult education, the task to develop means to stimulate the work with entrepreneurship in the school system. With the clearly expressed aim that schools should pay more attention to supporting pupils in crafting their entrepreneurial mindsets, the game developed by Go Enterprise! had a good starting position, offering a tool aimed at pupils and students at high school and in higher education. However, despite the lip service paid by the government and many schools to foster entrepreneurship through focusing on entrepreneurship in education, in practice rather little change has happened—not least because the teacher education programmes were, and still are, not adjusted to prepare future teachers to handle entrepreneurship or enterprising contents.

The Company: Go Enterprise!

The founders of the company Go Enterprise! tell the story of how they came up with the idea for the entrepreneurship game as follows on their home page:

Three entrepreneurs went on a combined travel trailer holiday and parlour game tour. With around 40 different games in our cupboards, we parked in front of our friends' houses and invited them to spend the evenings playing games with us. These evenings were a great success, and the competitions, laughter and companionship made the windows foggy and the time fly by. It was during one of those evenings that the idea was born—to produce our own parlour game. Partly, we enjoyed playing, and partly we were fascinated by parlour game as a tool and the emotional involvement it creates.

As dedicated entrepreneurs, for many years we have wanted to stimulate other people to make use of their entrepreneurial skills. In our business, we work with inspirational concepts and presentations. (…) With this background, identifying the opportunities of games became a business idea. Just imagine if we could develop a parlour game that inspired people to entrepreneurship. Now we have developed the idea further, and in summer 2009 we launched the Go Enterprise! entrepreneurship game (http://goenterprise.se/ historien-bakom-spelet; our translation).

The founding team successfully participated in the Swedish version of the TV programme *Dragons' Den* (in which entrepreneurs pitch their ideas to a group of risk capitalists for financing) and received venture capital. This success for the young, female entrepreneurs created much media attention, which facilitated the marketing process, and especially brand building. In order to refine the concept and gain further legitimacy, the female entrepreneurs invited a number of experts—including one of the authors of this chapter—to a process evaluation of a prototype of the game (implying participating in a game session).

The Business Model

The entrepreneurship game is based on a twofold revenue model. First, licences to play the game (including a game case with materials) are sold to schools and higher education institutions. However, this revenue model alone would be very difficult to scale up, as market saturation would be quickly reached. Also, cases to play need to be continuously updated and renewed. Therefore, Go Enterprise! offers companies and other types of public and private organizations the opportunity to have cases on their organizations. They pay a fee to Go Enterprise!—receiving in return not only higher visibility among Swedish pupils and students, but also solutions developed by teams playing the game, uploaded on the enterprise's

home page. In other words, entrepreneurship educators who purchase the licence for playing the game receive a code which can be used to enter an online community (at http://community. goenterprise.se/). Here, pupils and students have the opportunity to upload their solutions and receive feedback on them from the companies and other participants. However, the decreasing activity on this site demonstrates the challenge of maintaining such an interactive community site, which is highly time-consuming for the moderator and of limited interest to participants in the game. Based on the underlying concept of the entrepreneurship game, the company Go Enterprise! also offers consulting, training and coaching services around entrepreneurship and innovation to private and public organizations, as well as competence development sessions for schoolteachers.

The Rules of the Game

At the beginning of the game session, the game leader presents a case, which the teams of 'entrepreneurs' will work with and solve during the session by drawing on their creativity, communication skills and courage. During the game, eight 'activity cards' challenge the 'entrepreneurs' to make use of their skills to solve the case. Their achievements are evaluated by the group and the teacher who give points for the best presentation after each activity. These points are tracked by the teacher on an 'entrepreneur barometer' throughout the game, and the team with most points on the barometer wins. An Internet community is linked to the game, where the teams could upload their case solutions, receive comments on them and compete with other players (at community. goenterprise.se; however, this site shows very little traffic, see above). The number of players can vary between 7 and 30 in one session, which can take one to two hours of playing time.

The game proceeds as follows. The game leader is the person in charge of ensuring that the game is played according to the rules (usually the entrepreneurship teacher). Four to five teams of two to six 'entrepreneurs' (a more 'ideal' number is three to four players) are formed and spread out in the room. The game outline is fastened to a whiteboard in front of the class, displaying the 'start', phases 1, 2, 3, and 4, and the 'finish.' Each phase focuses on one area (i.e. research, idea, concept or action), and 'plays with' two different entrepreneurial skills associated with each phase respectively.

Phase 1: Research

At the beginning of this phase, the game leader instructs the 'entrepreneurs' to get familiar with the written case (which is about one page long). The participants are told that the two entrepreneurial skills 'played on' in this phase are being *analytical*, i.e. analysing the case in a mature, reflective manner and seeing it in its context, and being *reflective* of the environment, making smart use of available information. The first activity card asks the players to be analytical by summarizing the case in one sentence, focusing on what the case company wants to get help with. Each team gets four minutes to jointly write down the sentence, with the game leader strictly keeping time. When the time is up, each team gets to read its sentence to the entire session group, without providing any further explanations. Then each team, as well as the game leader, must vote for which presentation they liked best. The votes are written down and held up at the same time. One or a few teams are asked to explain the reasons behind their vote (and/ or the game leader provides her/his explanation). The second activity card asks the teams to be reflective by identifying which target group the case company wants to address. Again, the teams are given a short time (three minutes) to write down a sentence, which they read for the entire group without further explanations, followed by the voting procedure described above.

Phase 2: Idea

Moving on to the second phase of the game, the game leader announces to the participants that the focus will now be on developing several solutions to the case's challenge. The key skills to make use of in this phase are being *creative*, thinking outside of given frames and generating ideas, and *courageous*, daring to take charge of one's and others' ideas. The first activity card in this phase asks the players to be creative and develop three different solutions to the case's challenge. The teams are asked to write down one key word for each solution, which should be creative and presented after only two minutes of working with this task. Again, each team votes for the best solution. The second activity card in this phase asks teams to be courageous and develop a solution, assuming that no resource restrictions exist, within two minutes. With the support of a maximum of three words written down, each team then presents the solution. Again, the best solution is voted for.

Phase 3: Concept

In this phase, an idea is chosen to be further developed towards feasibility. The focus is on how the idea could be implemented. The two entrepreneurial skills to 'play with' in this phase are being *realistic*, i.e. developing ideas which are feasible, and *strategic*, i.e. planning implementation and preparing for different kinds of situations. The first activity card for this phase asks the teams to choose one of the ideas presented (by themselves or another team) in the previous phase and to further develop that to make it realistically feasible. They have four minutes to fulfil this task and present their solution, based on the three words written down. After the usual voting for the best solution, the second activity card asks the teams to develop, within two minutes, a five-step strategy for its implementation, again followed by presentations and the voting procedure.

Phase 4: Action

This phase is introduced by pointing out the focus on developing a storyline around the solution before the final pitch. Thus, in this phase teams work with justifying why their own solution is best. The two entrepreneurial skills to draw on in this phase are being *self-confident* and being *communicative* in a pedagogical and concrete manner. The first activity in this phase asks the teams of 'entrepreneurs' to write down, in two minutes, one selling sentence about why the team's solution is outstanding. When each team has read their sentence to the group, the best solution is once again voted for. The last task for each team in this phase is to draw an easily understandable picture representing their solution within two minutes, supported by three keywords.

After the voting, following the presentation and explanation of the pictures, all teams have three minutes to prepare their final pitch. This 45-second pitch will present each team's own solution to the challenge that the case company is facing. These pitches are evaluated through two rounds of voting, one for the best presentation and one for the best solution.

The game leader has updated the 'barometer', which keeps track of the points of each team, throughout the game, and can announce the winner. The case solutions can then be uploaded onto Go Enterprise!'s home page, where even the other case solutions can be read.

Experiences with Playing the Game

We have experimented with playing the entrepreneurship game in different entrepreneurship courses at Jönköping International Business School (JIBS) in Sweden. It is JIBS' strategy to focus on entrepreneurship and business renewal in its activities. The game is now included in the curriculum of an introductory course to the master's programmes on entrepreneurship and management. This course is called 'Introduction to Business Creation', and its main focus is on crafting an entrepreneurial mindset. (For more information about the pedagogical approaches to this course and the entrepreneurship master's programme, see Achtenhagen & Johannisson, 2013a, 2013b).

Here, we report students' experiences from playing the game. According to the course evaluations and meetings with students acting as course developers, the entrepreneurship game was highly appreciated. The following quotes from blogs which students wrote during the course illustrate their own reflections on the game:

I particularly liked the game where we had to practise creativity. It is amazing how quickly a group of people can come up with ideas, however it is also important to remember to further analyse and evaluate how feasible the idea really is (Swedish student, female).

After having the seminar where we played the entrepreneurial game and the one by Science Park, many new aspects came to my mind that got my brain working. Combining these inputs with the articles from de Bono (1995) and Ko and Butler (2007) widened my knowledge of how to act creatively. (…) To be creative you must practise being creative (Austrian student, male).

Being creative and innovative is probably the hardest and most challenging part (as experienced in the game) in a new business set-up. After the mentioned game and the guest lecture from the guys from the Science Park I realized how important it is to think out of the box and go unusual ways in order to create unexpected ideas, which in the end are the basis for entrepreneurial success. (…) In the end, my awareness towards creativity sharpened regarding its various facets and I think it will be helpful in any kind of solution finding in everyday life, not just business ideas (German student, female).

During the entrepreneurship game (…), I came to the conclusion that creativity can often be found (and tested) when you ask people, under time pressure, to think and come up with different ideas and ways to go about things. For some, thinking of something on the spot wasn't difficult, but for others, it proved to be a bit of a struggle (Dutch student, male).

The entrepreneurship game we played in class actually gives one the feel of being an entrepreneur, trying to provide solutions to business problems taking into consideration the challenging factors that restrict the process of achieving your business objectives. This kind of activity helps to develop one's creative ability (Ghanaian student, male).

I do understand your point, however what I meant by 'teaching and trying to encourage' people in order for them to be more entrepreneurial and more interested in entrepreneurship is that the method of teaching should be more like the one we used in yesterday's seminar—The Entrepreneurship Game. So, I would like teachers to use a more practical and fun way of encouraging people, instead of having boring theoretical lectures. Personally, I had lots of fun in yesterday's seminar and I actually got more interested in this subject and entrepreneurship overall than I was before (Turkish student, male).

However, during the Science Park lecture and the entrepreneurship game we certainly must have used creativity, since we all came up with some pretty good ideas. Perhaps in order to be creative we just need a hint, a different environment, or a game like in the seminar. I'm starting to believe that people possess more skills than they actually know about (Swedish student, male).

The entrepreneurship game really trained the brain in being creative and to think fast. [I believe …] that we are all born creative. But it is like a car or physical health, you need maintenance. You need

to keep the creativity going or it will slow down. And just like physical well-being I think you can get better at it (Swedish student, female)

Thus, when the students reflect on their own learning from the entrepreneurship game, they bring up a number of aspects which we consider to be important for, and fully in line with, crafting an entrepreneurial mindset. These include the positive experience of practising creativity, which leads to surprising solutions, reflecting on which skills one already feels comfortable with and which skills might deserve more practice, and developing trust in one's own skills. The experience of playing the game provides input into further reflection on entrepreneurship, creativity and the link between theory and practice. The increased understanding of the usefulness of an entrepreneurial mindset, even for everyday life, is also important.

A relevant aspect of how the game enhances the crafting of an entrepreneurial mindset is that playing the game is considered to be fun, while recognizing that it reflects the 'feel' of entrepreneurial activity to some degree. 'Experiencing' entrepreneurship in this way as a practical activity (rather than in theoretical exercises only) is viewed as valuable, triggering further interest in the topic of entrepreneurship.

CONCLUDING DISCUSSION AND FUTURE RESEARCH

The report from and evaluation of the game presented above confirm the usefulness of playing it as one activity (among others) to help students develop an interest in entrepreneurship and rediscover their entrepreneurial selves. More precisely, playing this game (or similar ones) has the potential to arouse interest in the topic of entrepreneurship for novices, thereby facilitating their learning journey towards becoming an established (social) entrepreneur or business person (Dreyfus & Dreyfus, 1986; Markowska,

2011). Thus, in a university setting, this game can be fruitfully used in introductory courses to entrepreneurship or corporate entrepreneurship (i.e. focusing on entrepreneurship in existing organizations). Due to the need of companies to strive for constant innovation of products and/or processes, it becomes increasingly important that employees have an entrepreneurial mindset. Therefore, this game can also be used as a pedagogical tool in management classes to support students in crafting such a mindset. While in entrepreneurship classes, the imitated entrepreneurial setting reflects the entrepreneurial process, from developing a venture idea to making it feasible to be enacted, in management classes the same process can be linked to mirroring improvement processes in existing organizations. In any case, the explicit rules of the game serve as a safety structure which lets students experience entrepreneurial skills in a setting with clearly stated goals. While playing the game in collaboration with fellow students, the students become aware of their unique capabilities, which in turn will increase their self-confidence—certainly an asset that will inspire and help with enacting an entrepreneurial career or acting on their entrepreneurial mindset to improve existing organizations.

Considering the very diverse backgrounds of the students, culturally, socially, as well as with respect to (lacking) prior education concerning entrepreneurship, we find such a controlled approach to help the students to craft their entrepreneurial mindsets appropriate. In many countries, academic teaching is still dominated by hierarchical models, far away from the bottom-up approach that entrepreneurial training calls for. In addition to facilitating self-reflection regarding the own set of entrepreneurial competences and identity, the game also invites the student on the laborious but necessary journey where learning by trial/experiencing and learning by reflection must be combined (see the seminal work by Schön, 1983). In an entrepreneurial context, creativity, so often alluded to by the students when commenting on

the learning experiences from the game, first has to be turned into 'creactivity,' that is integrated with different hands-on measures to become new 'actionable' knowledge, feasible for entrepreneurial projecting. Once instigated, such venturing must be reviewed, in the case of students reflecting with the help of appropriate course literature.

Reconsidering the lessons with respect to their implication for the curriculum, that is the content of educational programmes, and processes such as pedagogy and teacher-student relationships, the game implies a different kind of critical and reflective conduct that is usually argued for in the management and entrepreneurship literature (e.g. Reynolds, 1999). At least when it comes to the use of games for training in entrepreneurship, the student's ability to imagine new openings and enact new opportunities becomes more important than revealing hidden assumptions and dominant power relationships. Accordingly, 'process' is more important than 'content', which, for example, means that course literature should be used to reflect, individually or in a group, upon the 'gaming' and how it evolved rather than for preparation of the game activities. As regards the importance of socio-cultural considerations, we think that the fact that the game was constructed by young women, that its content is recreated in collaboration with real corporations, and that its playing takes place in a very heterogeneous setting with respect to students' cultural and educational backgrounds, continuously feeds reflection. We also think that the close relationship between students and committed teachers stimulates reflexivity that is not just intellectual but existential as well – although we, as indicated, do not elaborate further on this aspect here.

The role of the game approach in the successive crafting of an entrepreneurial mindset among the students as presented in Table 1 can be reconsidered in view of the lessons learned from our experiences at Jönköping International Business School. Most master's students have previously experienced, with different subject foci, education that has been dominated by a linear management logic (i.e. belief in decision-making rationality, systematic planning and quantitative analysis). When continuing with such logic, it seems feasible to introduce students to the field of entrepreneurship by giving them the opportunity to write plans for the enactment of a new venture, as done at many business schools. Being able to use the management tools that students are used to can construct a bridge between the contrasting logics of management and entrepreneurship. However, business plan writing then represents more of the same type of educational logic that these students have already been exposed to. And while such an exercise can provide legitimacy, which can indirectly add to self-confidence, crafting an entrepreneurial mindset provides a different approach to entrepreneurship as well as management education.

Introducing the game approach, even in a setting dominated by a more critical management logic (e.g. Alvesson & Willmott, 1996), will still cause a rupture as regards the understanding of how controllable the environment is. Since this learning experience, as outlined above, is embedded in different measures which communicate safety, reflexivity rather than anxiety will be enforced. This in turn helps the students to meet the real world of (social) enterprise, for example by getting involved in internships. Then they will encounter a reality where their conceptually dominated training will become challenged by the everyday life of organizing people and resources. What has been learned in the game setting, such as the need for alertness, immediacy and decisiveness, will then be expanded into insights as regards the need for coping with ambiguity and practising timing. The students will also get the opportunity to train their entrepreneurial skills, which are indispensable when they move on to take responsibility for their own venture. This, however, does not have to be the beginning of

an irreversible career as a business or social entrepreneur. Rather, testing one's capabilities and potential by launching a venture may 'just' be the final step in the creation of an entrepreneurial mindset—namely building an identity that makes the individual approach (even everyday) life as an adventure, with the responsibility and the opportunity to make a difference.

The game as designed and played in the course above can easily be elaborated with respect to both content and process. As regards the former, the inclusion of cases that cover social and cultural entrepreneurship will not only broaden the scope of the game as a means for professional training, it will also give students more opportunities to integrate private interests in their academic education and invite students outside the business school context to practise and reflect upon entrepreneurship. Obviously, the game as a pedagogical tool is able to mobilize not only cognitive but also other human powers, such as passion, and then takes the learning experience beyond that of training certain attitudes. With respect to goals other than that of enhancing skills, the game as practised in our education also gives the students an opportunity to take responsibility for their own evaluation. This in turn challenges the norm in both formal and informal learning settings—that the more experienced (teacher) should take the lead (e.g. Dreyfus & Dreyfus, 1986). Here, the students are invited to bring in their own criteria related to assessing the specific task solutions in relation to the practised 'skill' when making collective choices about the vote.

Future research could attempt to operationalize and measure the learning outcome of playing such games at different educational levels from high school to university, with the aim of statistically validating our claim that it contributes to enhancing pupils' and students' entrepreneurial mindset.

REFERENCES

Achtenhagen, L., & Johannisson, B. (2011). *Blogs as learning journals in entrepreneurship education – Enhancing reflexivity in digital times.* Paper presented at the Scandinavian Academy of Management Conference (NFF). Stockholm, Sweden.

Achtenhagen, L., & Johannisson, B. (2013a). Context and ideology of teaching entrepreneurship in practice. In Weber, S., Oser, F., & Achtenhagen, F. (Eds.), *Entrepreneurship Education: Becoming an Entrepreneur.* Rotterdam, The Netherlands: SensePublishers.

Achtenhagen, L., & Johannisson, B. (2013b). The making of an intercultural learning context for entrepreneuring. *International Journal of Entrepreneurial Venturing.*

Alvesson, M., & Willmott, H. (1996). *Making sense of management: A critical introduction.* London, UK: Sage.

Baumol, W. J. (1990). Entrepreneurship: Productive, unproductive, and destructive. *The Journal of Political Economy*, 98(5), 893–921. doi:10.1086/261712

Berglund, K., Johannisson, B., & Schwarz, B. (Eds.). (2013). *Societal entrepreneurship – Positioning, penetrating, promoting.* Cheltenham, UK: Edward Elgar.

Berglund, K., & Johansson, A. W. (2013). Dark and bright effects of a polarized entrepreneurship discourse … and the prospects of transformation. In Berglund, K., Johannisson, B., & Schwarz, B. (Eds.), *Societal Entrepreneurship – Positioning, Penetrating, Promoting.* Cheltenham, UK: Edward Elgar.

Cunliffe, A. L. (2004). On becoming a critically reflective practitioner. *Journal of Management Education*, 28(4), 407–426. doi:10.1177/1052562904264440

Dreyfus, H. L., & Dreyfus, S. E. (1986). *Mind over machine: The power of human intuition and expertise in the era of the computer.* New York, NY: The Free Press.

Fayolle, A., & Matley, H. (Eds.). (2010). *Handbook of research on social entrepreneurship.* Cheltenham, UK: Edward Elgar.

Granström, H. (2010). *Det barnsliga manifestet.* Stockholm, Sweden: Ink bokförlag.

Gray, D. E. (2007). Facilitating management learning: Developing critical reflection through reflective tools. *Management Learning*, 38(5), 495–517. doi:10.1177/1350507607083204

Hjorth, D., & Johannisson, B. (2007). Learning as an entrepreneurial process. In Fayolle, A. (Ed.), *Handbook of Research in Entrepreneurship Education: A General Perspective* (pp. 46–66). Cheltenham, UK: Edward Elgar.

Hjorth, D., Johannisson, B., & Steyaert, C. (2003). Entrepreneurship as discourse and life style. In Czarniawska, G., & Sevon, G. (Eds.), *Northern Light – Organization Theory in Scandinavia* (pp. 91–110). Malmö, Sweden: Liber.

Honig, B. (2004). Entrepreneurship education: Toward a model of contingency-based business planning. *Academy of Management Learning & Education*, 3(3), 258–273. doi:10.5465/AMLE.2004.14242112

Honig, B., & Karlsson, T. (2004). Institutional forces and the written business plan. *Journal of Management*, 30(1), 29–48. doi:10.1016/j.jm.2002.11.002

Huizinga, J. (1938). *Homo ludens: A study of the play element in culture.* Boston, MA: Beacon Press.

Jarzabkowski, P., & Wilson, D. C. (2006). Actionable strategy knowledge: A practice perspective. *European Management Journal*, 24(5), 348–367. doi:10.1016/j.emj.2006.05.009

Johannisson, B. (1991). University training for entrepreneurship: Swedish approaches. *Entrepreneurship and Regional Development, 3*(1), 67–82. doi:10.1080/08985629100000005

Johannisson, B. (2000). Networking and entrepreneurial growth. In Sexton, D., & Landström, H. (Eds.), *Handbook of Entrepreneurship* (pp. 368–386). London, UK: Blackwell.

Johannisson, B. (2010). In the beginning was entrepreneuring. In Bill, F., Bjerke, B., & Johansson, A. W. (Eds.), *De)mobilizing the Entrepreneurship Discourse: Exploring Entrepreneurial Thinking and Action* (pp. 201–221). Cheltenham, UK: Edward Elgar.

Johannisson, B. (2011). Towards a practice theory of entrepreneuring. *Small Business Economics, 36*(2), 135–150. doi:10.1007/s11187-009-9212-8

Katz, J. A. (2003). The chronology and intellectual trajectory of American entrepreneurship education. *Journal of Business Venturing, 18,* 283–300. doi:10.1016/S0883-9026(02)00098-8

Kirchhoff, B. A., & Phillips, B. D. (1988). The effect of firm formation and growth on job creation in the United States. *Journal of Business Venturing, 3*(4), 261–272. doi:10.1016/0883-9026(88)90008-0

Klamer, A. (2011). Cultural entrepreneurship. *The Review of Austrian Economics, 24,* 141–156. doi:10.1007/s11138-011-0144-6

Kuratko, D. F. (2005). The emergence of entrepreneurship education: Development, trends and challenges. *Entrepreneurship Theory & Practice, 29*(5), 577–598. doi:10.1111/j.1540-6520.2005.00099.x

Markowska, M. (2011). *Entrepreneurial competence development: Triggers, processes & competences.* (Dissertation). Jönköping International Business School. Jönköping, Sweden.

North, D. C. (1990). *Institutions, institutional change and economic performance.* Cambridge, MA: Cambridge University Press. doi:10.1017/CBO9780511808678

Ogbor, J. O. (2000). Mythicizing and reification in entrepreneurial discourse: Ideology critique of entrepreneurial studies. *Journal of Management Studies, 37*(5), 605–635. doi:10.1111/1467-6486.00196

Reynolds, M. (1999). Critical reflection and management education: Rehabilitating less hierarchical approaches. *Journal of Management Education, 23,* 537–553. doi:10.1177/105256299902300506

Sarasvathy, S. D. (2001). Causation and effectuation: Toward a theoretical shift from economic inevitability to entrepreneurial contingency. *Academy of Management Review, 26*(2), 243–263.

Schön, D. (1983). *The reflective practitioner: How professionals think in action.* New York, NY: Basic Books.

Stacey, R. D. (1996). *Complexity and creativity in organizations.* San Francisco, CA: Berret-Koehler.

Steyaert, C. (2004). The prosaics of entrepreneurship. In Hjorth, D., & Steyaert, C. (Eds.), *Narrative and Discursive Approaches in Entrepreneurship* (pp. 8–21). Cheltenham, UK: Edward Elgar.

Winnicott, D. W. (1971). *Playing and reality.* Harmondsworth, UK: Penguin Books.

ADDITIONAL READING

Anderson, A., & Jack, S. L. (2008). Role typologies for enterprising education: The professional artisan? *Journal of Small Business and Enterprise Development, 15*(2), 259–273. doi:10.1108/14626000810871664

Begley, T. M., & Tan, W.-L. (2001). The socio-cultural environment for entrepreneurship: A comparison between East Asia and Anglo-Saxon countries. *Journal of International Business Studies, 32*(3), 537–553. doi:10.1057/palgrave.jibs.8490983

Berglund, K., & Johansson, A. W. (2007). Entrepreneurship, discourses and conscientization in processes of regional development. *Entrepreneurship & Regional Development, 19*(6), 499–525. doi:10.1080/08985620701671833

Cabral-Cardoso, C. (2004). Ethical misconduct in the business school: A case of plagiarism that turned bitter. *Journal of Business Ethics, 49*, 75–89. doi:10.1023/B:BUSI.0000013864.76547.d5

Cerulo, K. A. (1997). Identity construction: New issues, new directions. *Annual Review of Sociology, 23*, 385–409. doi:10.1146/annurev.soc.23.1.385

Chell, E., Karata-Özkan, M., & Nicolopoulou, K. (2007). Social entrepreneurship education: Policy, core themes and developmental competencies. *International Journal of Entrepreneurship Education, 5*, 143–162.

Copeland, W. D., Birmingham, C., de la Cruz, E., & Lewin, B. (1993). The reflective practitioner in teaching: Towards a research agenda. *Teaching and Teacher Education, 9*(4), 347–359. doi:10.1016/0742-051X(93)90002-X

Fayolle, A., Gailly, B., & Lassas-Clerc, N. (2006). Assessing the impact of entrepreneurship education programmes: A new methodology. *Journal of European Industrial Training, 30*(9), 701–720. doi:10.1108/03090590610715022

Fiet, J. (2000). The pedagogical side of entrepreneurship theory. *Journal of Business Venturing, 16*, 101–117. doi:10.1016/S0883-9026(99)00042-7

Fletcher, D. (2003). Framing organizational emergence: Discourse, identity and relationship. In Steyaert, C., & Hjorth, D. (Eds.), *New Movements in Entrepreneurship* (pp. 125–142). Cheltenham, UK: Edward Elgar.

Freire, P. (1970). *Pedagogy of the oppressed.* New York, NY: Herder and Herder.

Gartner, W. B., Bird, B. J., & Starr, J. A. (1992, Spring). Acting 'as if': Differentiating entrepreneurial from organizational behavior. *Entrepreneurship Theory and Practice,* 13-31.

Gibb, A. (2002). In pursuit of a new 'enterprise' and 'entrepreneurship' paradigm for learning: Creative destruction, new values, new ways of doing things and new combinations of knowledge. *International Journal of Management Reviews, 4*(3), 13–29. doi:10.1111/1468-2370.00086

Gibb, A. (2007). Entrepreneurship: Unique solutions for unique environments: Is it possible to achieve this with the existing paradigm? *International Journal of Entrepreneurship Education, 5*, 93–142.

Gore, J. M., & Zeichner, K. M. (1991). Action research and reflective teaching in preservice teacher education: A case study from the United States. *Teaching and Teacher Education, 7*(2), 119–136. doi:10.1016/0742-051X(91)90022-H

Harding, R. (2004). Social enterprise: The new economic engine? *Business Strategy Review, 15*(4), 39–43. doi:10.1111/j.0955-6419.2004.00338.x

Henry, C., Hill, F., & Leitch, C. (2005). Entrepreneurship education and training: Can entrepreneurship be taught? Part 1. *Education + Training, 47*(2), 98-111.

Johannisson, B. (2004). Entrepreneurship in Scandinavia: Bridging individualism and collectivism. In Corbetta, G., Huse, M., & Ravasi, D. (Eds.), *Crossroads of Entrepreneurship* (pp. 225–241). Boston, MA: Kluwer Academic. doi:10.1007/0-306-48742-X_13

Johansson, A. W. (2010). Innovation, creativity and imitation. In Bill, F., Bjerke, B., & Johansson, A. W. (Eds.), *De)mobilizing the Entrepreneurship Discourse: Exploring Entrepreneurial Thinking and Action* (pp. 123–139). Cheltenham, UK: Edward Elgar.

Karakas, F. (2011). Positive management education: Creating creative minds, passionate hearts, and kindred spirits. *Journal of Management Education, 35*(2), 198–226. doi:10.1177/1052562910372806

Kirby, D. (2004). Entrepreneurship education: Can business schools meet the challenge?. *Education + Training, 46*(8/9), 510-519.

McBeath, J. (2010). Leadership for learning. In Peterson, P., Baker, E., & McGaw, B. (Eds.), *International Encyclopedia of Education* (3rd ed., pp. 817–823). Amsterdam, The Netherlands: Elsevier. doi:10.1016/B978-0-08-044894-7.00454-1

Moon, J. A. (2004). *A handbook of reflective and experiential learning: Theory and practice.* London, UK: RoutledgeFalmer.

Schofer, E., & Meyer, J. W. (2005). The worldwide expansion of higher education in the twentieth century. *American Sociological Review, 70*(6), 898–920. doi:10.1177/000312240507000602

Schön, D. A. (1987). *Education the reflective practitioner.* San Francisco, CA: Jossey-Bass.

Shane, S. (2003). *A general theory of entrepreneurship- The individual-opportunity nexus.* Cheltenham, UK: Edward Elgar.

Shane, S. (2009). Why encouraging more people to become entrepreneurs is bad public policy. *Small Business Economics, 33*(2), 141–149. doi:10.1007/s11187-009-9215-5

Spinosa, C., Flores, F., & Dreyfus, H. (1997). *Disclosing new worlds – Entrepreneurship, democratic action and cultivation of solidarity.* Cambridge, MA: The MIT Press.

Steyaert, C. (2007). Entrepreneuring as a conceptual attractor? A review of process theories in 20 years of entrepreneurship studies. *Entrepreneurship & Regional Development, 19*(6), 453–477. doi:10.1080/08985620701671759

KEY TERMS AND DEFINITIONS

Entrepreneurial Mindset: An individual's attitude to identify and act on opportunities for entrepreneuring in everyday situations.

Entrepreneuring: Activity-centered perspective on entrepreneurship, which acknowledges the existential dimension of everyday entrepreneurial practices as ongoing processes.

Entrepreneurship: The creative organizing of people and resources according to opportunity, not only related to the founding of for-profit start-ups, but also in all different types of existing organizations and societal settings as well as the personal life-sphere.

Mindset: A fixed mental attitude that determines one's responses to and interpretations of situations.

Chapter 3
Games in Higher Education:
Opportunities, Expectations, and Challenges of Curriculum Integration

Ronald Dyer
Grenoble Ecole de Management, France

ABSTRACT

In an age of technological tools ranging from social media to virtual environments, higher education institutions need to re-examine the context of their content delivery, creating an opportunity for more realistic learning methodologies across the education spectrum more closely aligned with expectations from the world of work. Today's learners consist of a cadre of individuals aptly described as "digital natives" (Prensky, 2001) whose proclivity for technology adoption is natural, as most grew up with access to computing technology and have directly experienced its evolutionary path. As such, higher education professionals are now challenged to specifically treat with a generation who perceive technology as a natural extension of their daily lives, recognizing that traditional approaches inclusive of e-learning are no longer sufficient to engage their student population.

INTRODUCTION

The opportunity for Game-Enhanced Learning (GEL) within higher education lies in its ability to mitigate the degree of abstraction between theory and application of content. Students today represent a new generation, Generation C. This generation as defined in a seminal article by Booz Allen Hamilton in Strategy and Business (2011) is described as follows:

They are realists, they are materialists. They are culturally liberal, if not politically progressive. They are upwardly mobile, yet they live with their parents longer than others ever did. Many of their social interactions take place on the Internet, where they feel free to express their opinions and attitudes. They've grown up under the influence of Harry Potter, Barack Obama, and iEverything—iPods, iTunes, iPhones. Technology is so intimately woven into their lives that the concept of early adopter is essentially meaningless.

DOI: 10.4018/978-1-4666-3950-8.ch003

Higher education is faced with the challenge of a large influx of Generation C students given their demographic (18-34 years). This catchment now pervades all aspect of the systems from freshman to graduate students and those taking continuing education units to remain current in their workplace. What is consistent across the higher education spectrum is that these students are not traditional brick and mortar students of two decades ago. Their interest and attention span cannot be captured simply through dissemination of content in a traditional classroom. As such higher education needs a new pedagogical approach to engage this present cadre of students. The approach should allow for richer learning experiences that are contextual, theoretically grounded and present a degree of realism while providing students with a more acceptable "*ah ha*" i.e. (similar to the famous statement by Archimedes eureka "I found it") moment post content dissemination. The linkage between theory and experience within higher education for these students must be closely aligned so as to allow for an easier translation of the content into workable schemas, across multiple digital domains which they can apply in the workplace post graduation.

Similarly, professors and academic administrators alike need to first recognize that the present mode of curriculum design and by extension its integration does not fit with prevailing audiences. They further need to be convinced of adoption and adaptation of the curriculum underpinned by its ability to measure the impact of games enhanced learning on student performance much in a similar manner as traditional test are administered presently. It is only through valid and visible measurable impact of new media technologies such as games will they take their place on the curriculum design table becoming relevant and sustainable within an academic context. To ensure such an ambitious effort higher education institutions need to re-think the way they presently teach and dis-seminate content. As most institutions are already aware even the perception of universities in their current brick and mortar institutional format are rapidly being challenged with the advent of so many virtual university models.

In examining games-enhanced learning in higher education its opportunities, expectations, challenges, and curriculum integration one has to be wary of the very traditional and somewhat inflexible landscape that needs to be changed. Even the slightest modification to existing curricula within higher education institutions can possibly be met with extreme resistance.

The major questions therefore are: How do institutions effectively integrate gaming approaches into the curriculum? What is the best way to gain buy-in and adoption and how do they measure the effectiveness of these games post curriculum integration?

The best way to commence this discussion is to introduce this topic with some definitions of the term game-enhanced learning, also referred to as game-based learning or serious games.

Serious Games Definitions:

- According to Corti (2006) game-based learning or serious games as it is mostly referred "is all about leveraging the power of computer games to captivate and engage end-users for a specific purpose, such as to develop new knowledge and skills" (p. 1)
- Zyda (2005) defined serious games as "a mental contest, played with a computer in accordance with specific rules, that use entertainment to further government or management education, education, health, public policy and strategic communication objectives" (p. 26)
- Michael and Chen (2006) define a serious game as "a game in which education (in its various forms) is the primary goal, rather than entertainment" (p. 21)

Game-Based Learning Definition:

- **Game-Enhanced Learning (GEL): A** branch of serious games that deals with applications that have defined learning outcomes. Generally they are designed in order to balance the subject matter with the game-play and the ability of the player to retain and apply said subject matter to the real world
- **Digital Game-Based Learning (DGBL):** An instructional method that incorporates educational content or learning principles into video games with the goal of engaging learners. Applications of digital game-based learning draw upon the constructivist theory of education. Drawing from the constructivist theory of education, Digital Game-Based Learning (DGBL) connects educational content with computer or video games and can be used in almost all subjects and skill levels (Coffey, 2009).

These definitions provide a robust starting point articulating not only what sectors these games represent as learning tools but also the expected outcomes of these games. Technology is forcing the academic landscape to change rapidly and with it the modes of content delivery. Academic environments are continuously struggling to keep up with these technological advancements. For decades higher education curricula has been delivered in the tried and tested manner of *design, teach, and test.* Institutionally, this curriculum approach has been predominantly centered on professors and academic administrators with the student simply a passive recipient. Students in the past have had little or no contribution or flexibility as it relates to content delivery, its mode of gestation or the best strategies for possible retention.

This chapter's contribution seeks to examine the integration of game-enhanced learning into higher education's curriculum. It further seeks to define a framework to support buy-in and adoption

by higher education professionals by building a convincing argument for both cost wary fiscal gate keepers responsible for academic budgets coupled with academic traditionalist who still question some of today's technology advances in learning perceiving them as mere distractions.

As higher education professionals grapple with the challenges of integrating myriad technologies into the existing curricula, investigation of the potential of games enhanced learning as a key component for successful engagement of students is critical. Identification of its ability to support the curriculum design process, its relevant both from an academic perspective and in the eyes of the ultimate beneficiaries, i.e. students and employers necessitates institutional survival. Furthermore, while games represent an innovative curriculum integration step in the evolution of higher education's pedagogical approach designers must bear in mind the important factor of ensuring measurement. The promotion of the successes of games in higher education can only be heralded with defined, measurable outcomes which identify and are linked to specific learning objectives as set out in the institution's curriculum vision. Institutions must be mindful that it is not fancy technologies that will convince communities of academics but robust learning outcomes that attest to assessment and learner retention.

The objectives of this chapter will therefore be to:

1. Provide an introduction to the attributes of games enhanced learning and their relevance in higher education curriculum integration.
2. Identify applicable measurement models to assist higher education professionals with measuring the impact of game-enhanced learning integration.
3. Provide recommendations for higher education professionals with an implementation framework to assist with the adoption of game-enhanced learning within their respective institutions.

BACKGROUND

For centuries, games have been a source of entertainment specifically as a recreational form. More importantly the computer gaming industry which gained much relevance in the 1980 represents billions of dollars in revenue and has been responsible for the implementation of some of the most advanced technologies in computing available today. While more commonly referred to as serious games, game-enhanced learning have over the last few decades become a "hot topic" on the lips of academics and corporate trainers. The US Military's utilization has been evident for decades but it was the advent of their game America's Army 2002 (www.americasarmy.com; Gudmundsen 2006) that serious games began to receive real attention. Further legitimacy for game-enhanced learning came with the creation by the Woodrow Wilson International Centre for Scholars (http://www.wilsoncenter.org) in Washington DC of the Serious Games Institute (www.seriousgames.org/index2.html) and hence the term's adoption. Michael and Chen (2006) cited by Susi, Johannesson and Backlund (2005) indicated that serious games are becoming ever more important in the global education and training market which was estimated to be approximately $2 trillion as at (2003). They further predicted that 40% of US companies would have adopted serious games in their corporate training efforts by 2008. According to TJ Keitt (2009) "serious games adoption will remain highly vertical in 2010 and beyond—it is expected firms in the defense industry will make the strongest moves to acquire serious gaming and virtual world companies to serve their military and healthcare clients.

Serious games are the accepted term for games with an educational intent, they are required to be engaging, immersive, not necessarily fun, with the learning being predominantly implicit or explicit. Mary Ulicsak (2010) a senior researcher at Futurelab did a comparison of the use of serious games (including simulations and virtual worlds) in multiple domains to determine if the practice could be transferred to the formal educational domain. She found that training simulations, integral to military and health care given their provision of a safe cost-effective mechanism for training tasks in generally hazardous circumstances have become prevalent amongst users of game-enhanced learning technologies citing (Stone 2008). However, while military and health embrace the advent of serious games higher education institutions have been much slower to adopt. Unlike the arenas of the military or health care one of the major challenges to adoption continues to be measurement. Measurement of students represents the overarching goal of the institution's curriculum whose aim is to improve the performance of students post-graduation.

Deriving appropriate methods to measure the impact of learning technologies is essential for both buy-in and adoption by institutions of higher learning especially given their acquisition cost.

Game-enhanced learning or serious games as it is often termed for educational intent requires an engaging and immersive approach with the learning being predominantly implicit or explicit. Bruce Dixon (2011) in his blog asked a very pertinent question; "When will educators get serious about gaming?"

He begs the question as to why such a long period for educators to adopt despite all the conferences, papers and other roundtable discussions on the topic. Furthermore, he laments the fact that if the reason behind the lag in higher education buy-in is driven by subversive pedagogy then the much anticipated wide spread adoption will never come as fundamental shifts in higher education are a challenge to academia's status quo and as such will remain at best a boutique curriculum integration project within more progressive institutions.

Exploration of the progress of game-enhanced learning to date coupled with some examples of its application within the higher education environment reveals an upwardly trending evolutionary path. However, this evolutionary path has not necessarily been driven by higher education institutions but what can be classified as education entrepreneurs. In a much broader sense as it relates to innovations in curriculum delivery and integration we are currently seeing a rise in what can be classified as education start-ups. These startups such as Udacity, Udemy, Coursera, and the Khan Academy have already pushed the envelope as it relates to what integrated curriculum could possibly look like in the future. More specifically they represent a model for university education specifically targeted to Generation C participants. It is only a matter of time before these emerging institutions adopt game-enhanced learning approaches as part of their pedagogical undertaking and with it launch a frontal attack on the academic status quo. According to Nick DeSantis (2012) in his article A Boom Time for Education Start-Ups, he stated that investment in education technology companies has tripled over the last decade shooting up to $426m in 2011 up from $146m in 2002. The aim of these companies being to revolutionize the online education market. What does the advent of education start-up companies and the increased investment have to do with higher education? More specifically what is the relevance to this chapter's game-enhanced learning focus? There are two underlying observation that need to be noted.

The first is the shift to a truly digital modality which now is markedly identified by these increases in funding. Higher education needs to wake up and take notice as these companies are catering or at least plan to cater to students with content engineered more in line with their digital expectations. Secondly, the development of the online imperative is only happening as a result of the huge advances in computing especially within higher education establishments to meet the dictates of its students. As such there is increased thrust by higher education institutions to ensure the most ubiquitous technology experiences (wireless connectivity, social networks, cloud computing, etc.) What role do games play given this increased

technological thrust? First, we need to understand something critical to the curriculum integration process of game-enhanced learning within higher education institutions. Academics will only integrate what they have experienced whether it be academic or experiential subject matter. Despite all the technologies available on campuses games are not resident in the toolboxes of curriculum designer/integrators as opposed to its prevalence on the digital devices of the recipients of the curriculum, i.e. students. The decision to introduce game-enhanced learning into the curriculum needs to start firstly with encouraging the integrators to become familiar through play. Younis and Loh (2010) citing Baek (2008) identified some fundamental factors that debilitate games adoption in education environments. Baek (2008) cited by Younis and Loh (2010) states some relevant factors that need to be recognized in the game-enhanced learning transition decisions within higher education:

1. Experienced and older teachers often worry about students becoming addicted
2. Lack of supporting material to support integrating serious games into the classroom
3. Rigid curriculum and fixed class schedules are major obstacles to adoption of serious games by teachers and
4. More experienced (older) teachers are more resistant to the use of serious games in the classroom than their less experienced (younger) colleagues.

The above statements attest to a problem which has less to do with the degree of investment required by higher education institutions to adopt the "best" technologies but with internal organizational culture. The current demographic of academic staff within the higher education hierarchy debilitates wider exploration of games and as this book seeks to examine the issues and challenges of curriculum integration. Let us now examine some of the issues, challenges and controversies as preliminarily identified by Younis and Loh (2010) citing Baek (2008) in the main focus of the chapter.

GAME-ENHANCED LEARNING: THE CHALLENGES OF ADOPTION AND CURRICULUM INTEGRATION

The focus of this book revolved around the major issues and challenges of game-enhanced learning, with particular attention to pedagogical aspects providing a fresh perspective on how to guide and sustain pedagogically effective use of games and lay the foundations for more effective use in a formal educational context. In order for the book and more so this chapter to achieve these objectives the issues, controversies and problems associated with integrating games into the curriculum must be addressed. Let us first establish some perspective within the context of the objectives outlined.

Attributes of Game-Enhanced Learning

What are the attributes of game-based learning and why should higher education even care about integration into the existing curricula? Games provide a different pedagogical perspective within a higher education context. They are not a natural fit to the pedagogical landscape but they do represent two critical factors which need to be considered:

1. They are impactful and
2. They are emerging as a potential source of disruption in current teaching models

Given these two factors, some attributes of games are as follows:

1. They are task specific
2. Ability to concentrate on the task (deep immersion)
3. Task have clear goals
4. They provide immediate feedback
5. They provide a high degree of autonomy.

These attributes are directly correlated to curricula and when aligned to curriculum design as they leverage the impact of course delivery. The impact-correlation factor between game-based learning and higher education curriculum integration lies in the increased engagement, learner retention, reduction in cognitive load and increased student participation and attendance. These represent key factors for consideration not just for game-based learning integration but the validity of curricula in general.

Arnab et al (2012) in their article on framing game adoption in formal education make a valid point when they cite the need for a problem-type taxonomy (Gee 2007; Kiili 2007; Van Eck & Hung 2010). Treating with the deconstruction of game-based problems events into atomic units can greatly assist academic designers and developers better indicate what types of game-play will appropriately fit the learning goals and objectives. This represents a key attribute of game-enhanced learning approaches as curricula gets chunked into bite size pieces that can better be digested by students. A value added effect is the reduction in the load on working memory.

This brings us to the attributes of measurement, the second objective identified. To successfully integrate games into the pedagogical architecture of higher education current measurement approaches cannot be effectively utilized. The measurement approach needs to be significantly modified to include such factors as; degrees of engagement, collaboration, knowledge creation, problem solving and a significant shift in the role of the teacher to that of facilitator. The use of such measurement approaches as cognitive load and flow as mechanisms for identification of learner retention become valuable resources in the integration process.

Game-enhanced learning while novel, perceived as pedagogically innovative, effective and perhaps even revolutionary by some academics is not without its controversies and pitfalls. Let us examine some of these factors.

Issues

In a general sense one of the greatest bug bears to game-enhanced learning could possibly be the generational disconnect within academic institutions. Prensky (2001) used the term digital natives to describe today's technology savvy user population. However, there exists another group as defined by Prensky (2001) which needs to be considered in any deliberations over game-enhanced learning, i.e. digital immigrants. Digital immigrants are defined as follows:

Digital Immigrants learn—like all immigrants, some better than others—to adapt to their environment, they always retain, to some degree, their "accent," that is, their foot in the past. The "digital immigrant accent" can be seen in such things as turning to the Internet for information second rather than first, or in reading the manual for a program rather than assuming that the program itself will teach us to use it (Prensky, 2001, p. 46).

This is a key issue relevant to the introduction of game-enhanced learning within higher education as most of the prevailing academic staff to a greater extent are digital immigrants teaching digital natives. As such their proclivity to adopt games as a teaching tool much less integrate into the existing curriculum framework can be problematic. It is not to say there is not interest but cultural differences based on generational factors, which act as a natural barrier in the adoption process. This is further perpetuated by the type of education that would be adopters of game-enhanced learning have acquired. The more traditional the education the less likely are these "immigrants" to see the correlation between content integration

in the classroom and the development of games to impart delivery. Arnad et al (2012) speaks to the traditionalist role of teachers as providers of information and students as recipients. These two roles are perceived as strictly separate with analogy of teachers as squares and students as circles, cited again by Arnab et al (2012). Complicating the dilemma further those educated in less traditional subjects such as informational technology, computer science are more inclined to attempt to adapt games in their curriculum vs. those from humanities and arts.

The second issue with the use of game-enhanced learning in higher education curriculum integration is design. Curriculum design and its integration are already challenging. Professors and academic administrators are faced with insurmountable levels of information to distill and ensure that this information is informative, instructional, relevant, digestible, and engaging. This all has to be done in an environment where available knowledge changes at the speed of thought with the advantage of students they engage having much faster access to the same information on their various digital devices than their designers. To facilitate such approaches places much duress on educators who are now forced to ramp their competencies to include both subject matter and technological expertise.

Digital immigrants (professors/administrators) speak a different language from digital natives (students) and as such would naturally struggle with development of curricula that meets the needs of this demographic. The traditional curriculum integration can treat with students from various view points. While higher education curriculum integration process can best be described as interdisciplinary vs. that of the elementary school system which are truly more integrated, games require a much higher degree of interdisciplinary collaboration amongst faculty. This is primarily based on the fact that at the college or higher education levels curricula is more likely to be based around problem solving. The rationale makes sense as a key goal of higher education institutions is to create a cadre of individuals who can think and by extension solve problems in the work place. Furthermore, the interdisciplinary approach presupposes given blocks of time, with traditional groups of subjects e.g. Science, Business, and Humanities, which are assigned to a defined set of teachers, allocated a specific number of students per class. Introducing a game-enhanced learning environment would be at best chaotic as much logistics needs to take place to simply allow the relevant content modification and teaching time. The time constraint i.e. the time set for delivery is fixed thirty minutes, an hour, or three at most and as such not enough time to truly get the level of traction required to deliver a game in the classroom. Secondly, at the higher education level it is very rare that the relevant faculty areas will work with each other in a collaborative format. Game-enhanced learning requires a collaborative space as games represent a realistic experience that does not possess just one dimension of the curricula.

Finally, there is the issue of standards. Each curriculum area has its own which are not easily integrated across faculty and by extension students. The rigueur of current curriculum integration across areas is rare with professors and designers working mostly in a silo. Based on these issues alone from a curriculum perspective game-enhanced learning is already out the starting gate with some very severe obstacles to overcome.

Controversies

Perhaps the most controversial issue which faces higher education in its pursuit of game-enhanced learning is its perceived frivolity. Caroline Pelletier (2009) in her journal article cites Sutter-Smith (1977) who examined the ideological values that underpin theories of play.

Sutter-Smith (1977) identified between a number of rhetoric's of play theories, including the rhetoric of "play as progress," in which play is seen as a source of moral, social, and cognitive development and the rhetoric of "play as frivolity," which is applied to describe the activities of the idle or the foolish who rebut the classical work ethic; and the rhetoric of the self in which play is about individual desires and feelings such as fun and relaxation rather than about any external consequences. This theory though old in relation to some of the more recent findings about games as an academic learning tool strikes an appropriate chord albeit thirty-five years later. As in many academic circles, the value of adopting game-enhanced learning remains to some a frivolous undertaking. In fact what makes the argument stronger for those who perceive games as nothing more than a distraction is the demographic associated with game play mostly composed of the *net generation*. Furthermore, there is also the inherent controversy surrounding the appreciation of the skills inherently associated with game play and by extension game-enhanced learning as it represents endless hours of perceived mindless "shoot em up," zombie fighting and alien invasion styled play activities that still stigmatize the game industry. Academics in higher education whose approach to teaching has always been methodical: one concept at a time, one individual with total control of the classroom and lastly serious in their delivery are now being asked to undo decades or perhaps maybe centuries of structured learning simply to appease digital natives who find their approach at best boring. Adding salt to the controversial wound around game-enhanced learning is that there is the general rule that "the learners are the same as they have always been" (Prensky, 2001). Therefore, the same method which worked for them as students way back then will work within the present environment.

Moreover, given the rigid unionization of some academic environments there is also the issue of legacy academics whose belief is to stand and teach in a traditional manner based on a job description designed many years prior to fundamental shifts in teaching with technology. While it would be fair to admit that the controversies mentioned are slowly eroding and these gaps are narrowing as it relates to the adoption of advanced learning technologies within the walls of higher education much still needs to be accomplished.

The concept of loss of operational autonomy, i.e. the right of being self-governing is a concept very much shared within higher education and by extension professor and lecturers. Game-enhanced learning creates a new and emerging controversy through the loss of operational autonomy. Where as in the traditional classroom the teacher is in control, game-enhanced learning first strips some portion of control at the curriculum level. A second stripping occurs in the classroom, as the teacher becomes facilitator of learning and not necessarily sole driver of the learning process. Shazia Mumtaz (2006) provides ample support citing Robertson et al (1996) who indicated that resistance to outside interventions was one of the factors that prevented teachers from using technology. Given the high degree of operational autonomy associated with both classroom teaching and curriculum integration inclusion of game activities requires much higher degrees of collaboration, dependence and shift the teaching paradigm. Teachers need to be more facilitative possessing an inter-disciplinary approach with other teachers and perhaps external providers of input to reduce integration challenge.

Another controversy looming over higher education is the external perception of curriculum relevancy. Many outsiders including employers have challenged the relevancy of what is being thought in the classroom at university level and demand reforms. One of the key challenges of curriculum integrators is making the classroom experience more applicable to the real world. Caroline Pelletier (2009) articulates this point in her article stating:

One of the ideological premises of much research on digital games and learning is the belief that education institutions are failing—failing to adequately prepare students for the demands of the digital age, failing to engage students in the curriculum, and failing to make best use of the digital technologies now available. The ideological consequences of framing the education system as "failing" have been explored elsewhere (Rancière, 1991; see also Pelletier, 2012), and can be understood in part in terms of ascribing to the education system an originating purpose from which it has been diverted, and under-emphasizing its institutional role in certifying the distribution of social functions (Pelletier, 2009, p. 84).

What Pelletier (2009) indicates is the failure of higher education to graduate students who can integrate effectively into the workplace. Many lay the blame on a curriculum process that has not kept up with the times. As stated earlier the traditional curriculum integration process focuses on one class, teacher and subject. Students are somewhat siloed with limited integration so that credits do not connect during but at the end of the degree process. The traditionalist curriculum needs to be replaced with one that is increasingly problem-solving based and as such shift the "teach to text" philosophy to teach for practice. To this extent games enhanced learning represents the opportunity for a new paradigm i.e. a curriculum that is designed around a problem-based model allowing for easier integration of appropriate technologies. This approach provides for the integration of many more disciplines in the curriculum integration process and lends support to finding a solution that is more akin to real world approaches, which in themselves are not unitary in dimension.

The advantage of this model of integration is that it offers potential for the identification of relevant, highly motivating problems which make for a learning experience that is more aligned to specific learning outcomes. These outcomes should go beyond gauging conceptual understanding of theoretical principles. Furthermore, they should allow the student to "appreciate" the inquiry process involved in finding the solution as opposed to struggling with the course curricula to pass an exam. A disadvantage of this model is the difficulty of assuring that the curriculum framework and standards are fully addressed within the game-enhanced learning model. The challenge is always the balancing act between an appropriate use of technology that addresses the needs of digital natives and ensuring that the desired learning outcomes are achieved.

Problem of Measurement

This chapter's focus has so far examined the broader issues of game-enhanced learning and the components which can affect its successful integration. While cultural, generational and even technological knowledge can provide great challenges as it relates to the pedagogical integration of games into higher education the greatest challenge remains measurement. There is an old adage "what gets measured gets done," often associated with the likes of Drucker, Deming and Lord Kelvin. True, as we can only measure results that are tangible. Therein lays the greatest challenge for the introduction of game-enhanced learning. Like its technological predecessor e-learning the only way to ensure that the approach is effective is in the ability to measure its success.

The issue of measurement is a continuous phenomenon. In the realm of higher education, measurement becomes ever more important as its success is determined by performance of students both in the classroom and the workplace. Measurement becomes a linking pin as it determines such important factors as student quality, university ranking and by extension the companies which choose to recruit on campuses based on the quality of former graduates.

Game-enhanced learning requires a radical shift in the prevailing testing mechanisms as what is now required is a combination of traditional testing and innovative observation of competencies acquired during play. The assessment of game-enhanced learning and measurement of its impact to ascertain curriculum Return On Invest-

ment (ROI) as it relates to successful integration is an important concern not only for higher education professionals but within the wider societal context. According to Fang and Neufeld (2007) while numerous studies have compared learning outcomes between traditional and online courses the findings are still mixed with limited conclusive evidence on which type's leads to better learning outcomes. They support the view based on supporting research cited from Arbaugh and Duray (2002); Marks et al. (2005) that perceived flexibility of technology used for content delivery has been positively associated with perceived learning and satisfaction. Additionally they also cite research by Benbunan-Fich and Hiltz (2003) which indicated that perceived convenience of access leads to better perceptions of learning effectiveness. As such, it can be assumed that measuring learning is perhaps as much an assessment of technology as it is content. Fang and Neufeld (2007) concluded that technology plays an important role in learning environments and more so student learning outcome effectiveness indicating a two-dimensional impact between the people who are involved and the design of the courses influencing participant psychological processes and actual learning activities.

This makes for an interesting curriculum integration challenge in that not only do we need to design the curriculum well but just maybe we need to involve students in the process at the beginning to ensure positive engagement. A radical shift indeed from the present processes utilized to instill learning.

The main aim of measuring game-enhanced learning should be firstly, assess its effectiveness, and secondly, ascertain its impact on various areas of improvement in delivery. Several models for evaluation of curriculum effectiveness have been developed over the years. When we examine the present curriculum integration process, the objectives for assessing student learning are pretty straightforward:

1. Assessment that guides and encourages effective approaches to learning.
2. Assessment that validly and reliably measures expected learning outcomes, in particular the higher-order learning that characterises higher education; and
3. Assessment and grading that defines and protects academic standards.

These objectives work well within traditional curriculum integration efforts for identification of the effectiveness of learning outcomes in the present university setting. They are straightforward in their measurability of traditional programmatic delivery but are these best suited for the integration of game-enhanced learning. The challenge with game-enhanced learning and curriculum integration is the subtle balancing act of technology and good design practices coupled with achieving the higher-order learning characteristics of the assessment process. This first problem that game-enhanced learning faces is translation of the theoretical concepts associated with the subject matter learning into a useable format. Secondly, game-enhanced learning faces another challenge of measurability when it comes to curriculum integration i.e. the degree of flexibility assigned to current curriculum approaches, their standards, and the degree to which the game can allow students to independently explore concepts, draw conclusions, and explore the role of the technologies that are so commonplace in their lives. Measurement of game-enhanced learning cannot be designed into the existing higher education framework without a decided shift from traditional to more problem based and thematic curriculum methodologies. Theme based learning as an additional component to the game integration process offers the ability to higher education personnel to identify with specific disciplines, allow students to make relevant connections with learning objectives and still meet the required standards.

An extremely valid point is made by Pellegrino and Quellmalz (2010) in discussing the need for a distinction being made between assessments of the outcomes of learning, typically used for grading and accountability purposes (summative assessment), and assessments for learning, used to diagnose and modify the conditions of learning and instruction (formative assessment) citing (Stiggins, 2005). In fact research repeatedly shows the use of formative assessment to significantly benefit student achievement (Black & Wiliam, 1998; Wiliam, 2007) cited by Pellegrino and Quellmalz. They also note that technology is well suited to support many of the data-collection, complex analysis, and individualized feedback and scaffolding features needed for the formative use of assessment (Brown, Hinze, & Pellegrino, 2008).

In order for higher education to adopt game-enhanced learning they must examine formative assessment methodologies which integrate and lend to the quality of feedback provided to participants, inclusive of self-reflection and action as a part of their integration strategy. The immersiveness of games as a learning technology requires adjustments to the curriculum integration process not because students are not learning under the present pedagogical processes but because the inclusion of games will require measurements that involve evaluation for more "realistic" assessment of learning outcomes given that the approach will now be more interdisciplinary. Interestingly, Pellegrino and Quellmalz articulate that assessment of student knowledge and skills in highly structured problems can also support the design of complex, interactive tasks that extend the range of knowledge, skills, and cognitive processes that can be assessed citing (Quellmalz & Haertel, 2004). A role for which game-enhanced learning can provide great value. They use the example of simulations, which can assess and promote understanding of complex systems by superimposing multiple representations and permitting manipulation of structures and patterns that otherwise might not be visible or even conceivable. For game-enhanced learning to be successful, it must be perceived as assessment tools for complex problem solving and learning activities. The measurement of the learning will be based firstly on the curriculum's design to include multi-dimensional approaches to problem perception and secondly, inclusion of variables that allow for solutions that are akin to those in real world situations. Furthermore, the measurement of games must probe basic foundational knowledge and more importantly, measure the student's knowledge of how components of the courses act in cohort and impact the solutions they seek in line with the content provide through the theory, i.e. integration. A unique point given that games can take this approach a step further by not only allowing for the probing of foundational knowledge but integrating a realistic approach to identification and analysis of changing variables through multiple scenarios, which can represents a challenge in traditional curriculum design. Higher education institutions thinking about game-enhanced learning need well designed and implemented measurement frameworks, which provide foundational assessment during content delivery to monitor and improve student progress and measure the instructional delivery period so as to establish the evolution of the higher order learning as it progresses. A good example of this approach would be where the curriculum integration is treated like level design. This approach would allow for documenting learning and identify remaining needs in an almost real time manner as each stage of the course is completed, thus making measurement and corrective action much more effective. This would make games a credible component of a multilevel assessment system. It also adds validity to the concept of cognitive load as the doing and learning are happening in a seamlessly simultaneous environment thus improving working memory.

The architecture of game-enhanced learning integrated into the curriculum provides the landscape for formative assessments during instruction providing an immediate opportunity for contingent feedback and adaptive coaching especially with problematic knowledge and skills subject matter.

Higher education professionals need appropriate measurement data to inform the correct impact of the curricula within their respective departments and across the institution. Game-enhanced learning can only successfully integrate if it collects performance data in a timely manner a role it can easily play as a learning technology. Furthermore, given its immersion component and the ability to integrate most of the learning task into a play environment which focuses on realism it can allow for a seamless flow of performance data in a real time manner.

Relevance of Game-Enhanced Learning in Higher Education

We have discussed the basis attributes of games and the issues and challenges associated with curriculum integration. How then are games relevant to higher education?

There exists first target audience relevance. We are in the age of the net generation or as aptly classified in an article by Friedrich et al (2011) as Generation C (Connected). They are consummate consumers of content, digital devices and gaming. Their perception of technology is rooted not in adoption but in a natural orientation. Most importantly they are today and definitely tomorrow's student. The need to connect with them on their own terms in the classroom is not only an issue of relevance for higher education but survival as they will easily find substitutes amongst the emerging players.

Secondly, they are very responsive to storytelling as they create learner-centred, learner-guided environments Dziorny (2005) citing Klaila (2011). Higher education can take advantage of this element of games as they allow the students freedom to freely explore, experiment and adapt learning within their own environmental context.

Thirdly, and as final food for thought they allow educators to gain a more concrete understanding of leaner dynamics through the lenses of educators as:

1. Instructor
2. Guide
3. Explorer and
4. Playmaker

A concept articulated by Arnab et al (2012) citing Hanghoi and Brund (2012). In this context the teacher's context becomes complementary and positions the knowledge not as a forced procedure associated with the overall learning process but as reinforcement of the existing theoretical knowledge.

Solutions and Recommendations

The challenge for game-enhanced learning is adoption and sustainability. Despite the myriad number of factors that may debilitate and detract its benefits, games will become a main stay in not just higher but across all spectrums of education over the next few years. While naysayers may perceive games in higher education as frivolous they cannot deny the value of utilizing tools in the classroom that both appeases the presentation of content to users as well as provides a richer learning experience though digital media. The key to the challenge of game enhanced learning in higher education is neither the availability of technology nor access to content but the monumental task of paradigm shifts within the administration to give this approach a robust push forward.

So what is the course of action that must be taken for the successful integration of games?

The first step is to deal with the issues associated with curriculum integration and its adaptation to a game-enhanced learning framework. To achieve this requires a change in higher education's learning behavior. This can be achieved through three fundamental steps (see Figure 1).

Step 1: Plot a Course Based on Components of Present Curriculum that Can Benefit from Game-Enhanced Approaches

This approach involves the dissection of the curriculum into components, e.g. If we took an introductory statistics course and dissect into:

1. Statistical theory
2. Worked examples and
3. Final component that applies worked example to a real world problem

The game-enhanced learning integration can either occur at the second or third stage. Hence,

Figure 1. Game-enhanced learning integration

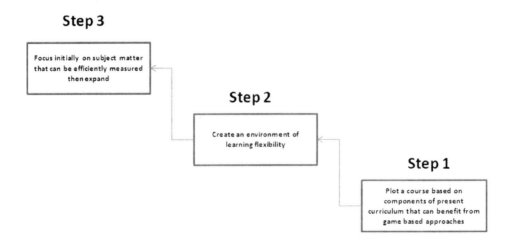

it does not challenge curriculum integrators to re-design existing theory into a game but simply how the theory is put into practice. Furthermore, it allows for a direct benefit of game integration at the best point of leaner interaction in that the learner is not a passive player in the process. It further lends to reinforcement of the theoretical underpinnings of the subject matter as the learner now has a tool that provides a causal approach to the content and its outcomes.

Step 2: Create an Environment of Learning Flexibility

Theoretically learning requires a movement through various stages. One of the flaws of present curriculum integration is that it is perhaps not as fluid as it should be in its movement. To increase the fluidity of the curriculum for game-enhanced learning integration there needs to be a motivational factor for students to expend the required effort. In this instance that factor is "play." The play imperative allows the student to perceive the learning not as work but as a natural extension of everything else they already do and with which they are familiar. Learning flexibility removes in-built perceptions, attitudes and belief structures akin with traditional curriculum. So as learners shift and sift through content learning moves from those who need to be tested to learners whose desire is to understand through the causality associated with games play.

Step 3: Focus Initially on Subject Matter that Can Be Efficiently Measured then Expand

In step three, the focus on subject matter which can be efficiently measured then expanded for

game-enhanced learning into the curricula is critical. What this means is to apply a systematic approach for game integration by:

1. **Removing learning barrier:** The virtual wall between learners and academics needs to be sufficiently removed to allow the student to perceive their teachers more as coaches than academic stalwarts. The challenge being to develop a layered approach to the learning so that the curriculum becomes a facilitated activity very much like in games where the mission is provided at the beginning as a brief to the task at hand prior to game play.

2. **Enable the subject matter:** For games to be successfully integrated into the curriculum academics need to try something new. As such game enhanced curriculum should include some "easter egg" i.e. hidden messages or clues which support and encourage students to take a new direction or re-think an existing theoretical principle given new information. This approach further allows the subject matter to be developed much in the same fashion as level design in games which leverages the content of the curriculum in the game as a stage and assist in removing learning barrier as stated earlier.

3. **Direct subject matter flow:** This component in step three provides a good way to measure initial subject matter through strategically mapping subject content to specific elements of the game enhanced curriculum. The mapping processes assist in the individualization of student learning experiences so that each student determines their own flow and by extension achieves a pace suitable to retention of the content over the requisite period of time.

Additionally, as part of the solution academic institutions truly interested in game-enhanced learning need to take a progressive step towards learning resource management. This concept requires higher education curriculum personnel to develop learning resource material, which can be accessed according to need. This will assist greatly in creating a framework for game-enhanced learning as content can now be pulled into the game by individuals or teams on a just in time basis, similar to traditional games where the player has access to these resources as they play through the various levels. This approach can also assist in reducing the degree of cognitive load experienced by students, as they are no longer faced with large amounts of content all at once but can "nugget" content as required.

Another solution to put on the table to successfully integrate games into the curriculum is to establish appropriate measurement frameworks. While many may differ on the method of measurement in support of curriculum integration no one can argue the actual need to measure the impact of game-enhanced learning on student performance. Given the marked difference between game-enhanced learning and traditional curricula, the question becomes what approaches represent a good starting point to ascertain game effectiveness. While there are many possible ways to measure effectiveness three come to mind that represent an excellent starting point (see Figure 2).

Leveraging Cognitive Load

Cognitive Load Theory (CLT) (Sweller, 1988, 1989) is concerned with the manner in which cognitive resources are focused and used during learning and problem solving. Many learning and problem solving procedures encouraged by instructional formats results in activities by participants far removed from the task at hand or lost soon thereafter post learning. This theory's relevance to the topic, its integration, and impact on higher education rest in its ability to be utilized as a measurement tool given its focus on

instructional design. Cognitive load represents an excellent starting point for measurement of games within higher education environments from an evaluation perspective as the approach has the ability to:

1. Create problem-solving methods, which avoid means-ends approaches that impose a heavy working memory load, by using goal-free problems or worked examples. Thus, integrating game-enhanced learning allows academics to measure the degree of cognitive processing naturally built in as a result of re-focusing on instructional design.
2. Allows for measurement by eliminating the working memory load associated with having to mentally integrate several sources of information by physically integrating those sources of information.
3. Allows for increase working memory capacity by using auditory as well as visual information under conditions where both sources of information are essential. I.e. game play along with its visual elements not only allows for visual integration of all the curriculum elements but through play itself allows for easy recall due to the flow experience.

Figure 2. Measures of effectiveness in GBL

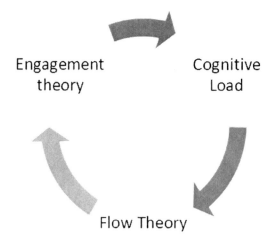

The value of integrating cognitive load as a measurement tool in support of game-enhanced learning lies in its ability to focus on measurement of task related outcomes via working memory vs. the tradition testing approaches that are defined through traditional pedagogy. Measuring games impact on cognitive load can go a long way in presenting robust evidence to academic naysayers. The basic premise of (CLT) being to reduce the load for difficult task so that it becomes easier to remember within a working memory context has no better home than being put to use to measure games which are in themselves load specific in their challenges.

Flow Theory

Flow theory represents another measurement tool to assist with game-enhanced learning adoption. Flow can best be defined as the mental state of operation in which a person in an activity is fully immersed in a feeling of energized focus, full involvement, and success in the process of the activity. The concept was first defined by Mihály Csíkszentmihályi, the positive psychologist who developed the theory back in the 1960s. The value of flow as a measurement tool rest in its defined components which if appropriately contextualized within the curriculum integration effort can lead to not only the integration of game-enhanced learning in higher education, but to a more engaging curriculum experience for its Generation C audience. The initial components as defined by Csíkszentmihályi initially in 1975 are as follows:

1. Control;
2. Attention;
3. Curiosity;
4. Intrinsic Interest

Csíkszentmihályi (1993) later refined these components going into further details through the development of eight dimensions of the flow experience.

1. Clear goals and immediate feedback
2. Equilibrium between the level of challenge and personal skill
3. Merging of action and awareness
4. Focused concentration
5. Sense of potential control
6. Loss of self-consciousness
7. Time distortion
8. Autotelic or self-rewarding experience

The relevance of these dimension to game-enhanced learning, curriculum integration and measurement are inextricably linked. Within each of these experiences lies existing dimensions from traditional game play. When translated into re-engineering of the curriculum within higher education the overarching philosophies of games are inherent in the flow experience. Game-enhanced learning's integration can easily follow the dimensions as previously mentioned through a simple translation of these dimensions into making them applicable to the curriculum integration efforts (see Table 1).

Engagement Theory

However, for any of the above to be adopted their must exist firstly the shifting paradigm of the human element. Academic institutions are slow to change and the struggle to influence the status quo has met with much resistance. Game-enhanced learning for all its novelty does have the potential to provide a high degree of engagement and as such would attract greater student interest simply because it appears to be more fun that traditional brick and mortar teaching approaches. As such, engagement forms a crucial element in the integration of games into the present curriculum offerings. The underlying philosophy behind engagement theory is that students must be meaningfully engaged through mutual interaction with others and an assignment of task that provide worthwhile/valuable experiences. It is essentially a conceptual framework for teaching and learning with technol-

Table 1. Flow experience and curriculum integration

8 Dimensions of Flow Experience	Curriculum Integration for GBL
Clear goals and immediate feedback	Integrating of mission style objectives into the curriculum design process,
Equilibrium between the level of challenge and personal skill	Implementation of hierarchically examples which allow for multiple starting points based on student knowledge
Merging of action and awareness	Integration of consequence based outcome assessment which provides both feedback and richer investigation of concepts
Focused concentration	Build learning momentum through (1) topic (1) task approaches
Sense of potential control	Student driven learning, with ability to determine starting points and evaluation
Loss of self-consciousness	Integration of flow and engagement. Learning is perceived as effortless, limited or no cognitive load barriers
Time distortion	Extend learning boundaries outside traditional mechanisms such as e-learning too m-learning and social networks
Autotelic or self-rewarding experience	Curriculum provides the ability for self-reflection

ogy. Given the philosophy of engagement, can we seriously say that the present curriculum design process offers best level of engagement based on its current design approaches which are focused on testing, learner retention and standards? This is not to say these elements are not important. When we look at the engagement track record in the classroom it is a known fact we all appreciated the professors who were able to spice up their classes with anecdotes, interactivity and other modes of delivery that made the class lively and fun. These activities created a high degree of student engagement. Similarly, game-enhanced learning through its interactivity, multi-dimensionality, and design creates an environment for greater engagement to the development of curriculum by creating stronger linkages via the following:

1. Collaboration
2. A problem based orientation and
3. Leveraging external focus, i.e. creating an opportunity for interactions external to the classroom which build on the theoretical perspectives of the curricula

Engagement hence forms the underpinnings of both good curriculum and game design as such no discussion or commencement of game-enhanced learning in higher education should begin without a re-evaluation of the present curriculum's engagement's perspective. To allow for such an evaluation it is integral that those considering game-enhanced learning within higher education consider Kearsley and Schneiderman (1999) engagement theory, which provided some simple markers for engagement as follows:

- **Relate:** Emphasizing teamwork, social skills, communication and management
- **Create:** Emphasize creativity and a sense of purpose, make students feel defined content context within a problematic domain
- **Donate:** Emphasize the importance of outcomes, helping student to understand the impat of their thinking, solutions on an external customer.

FUTURE RESEARCH DIRECTIONS

While games have been around for centuries and more specifically digital games have pervaded the lives of everyone since the advent of the Atari with such games as Packman, the future of games has never been brighter. In commercial circles, we see games pushing the envelope as it relates to such technologies as Microsoft's Xbox Kinetic, Nintendo's Wii and Sony's PS3. These games have pushed the envelope in terms of game play, digital storytelling, and graphics. The question remain where does the future of game-enhanced learning, serious games or whatever sobriquet we choose to use lie? While the industry for game-enhanced learning is still young, in fact from a lifecycle perspective we have now entered the growth stage there remains much to be done from a research perspective. The future of game research in this writer's opinion rest in three critical research domain areas:

1.   The first direction is continued development of robust research into the measurement and benefits of gaming. While much has been written on games as a learning tool not enough has been done to continue to demonstrate and promote its benefits within the academic administration and curriculum design suite. Strategic focus on the impact of games both psychological and from a learning perspective as well as the integration of games to assist in workforce development are critical to its future. Moreover, there needs to be more research into "best fit" adoption methodologies for higher education institutions, specifically best practices, and white papers, which illustrate practical use of games in institutions and act as a signpost for institutions wishing to adopt.

2.   The second area of future research can potentially be an examination of the experience curve of students focused on their experience with games. A translation of these experiences into useful insights for integration into the curriculum within higher education and a gauging of the overall impact of the experience as a value added component of the teaching and learning with technology process. The research approach can perhaps borrow from the world of marketing and innovation utilizing a framework based on

Rogers Adoption Curve (see Figure 3). Aptly applied this approach can research which academic departments adopt technology as a teaching tool fastest and as such utilize these departments as pilot programs for devolution to others. This research would be extremely valuable to academics as it would provide some greater insight into the key components required for content design, technology infrastructure and ensure that the resources are prioritized for game-enhanced learning. All departments would benefit from this approach and not simply perceive games as a cure all for curriculum design ills.

3.   The third are of research is a value added component. Researchers should more closely examine the role that game-enhanced learning can play in the developing learning analytics. Learning analytics much like other analytics such as business intelligence and informatics focuses on collection and analysis of data specifically related to students. Researchers can use the game play experience associated with GEL to capture valuable data on student learning through the integration of content into game play. Data can be gathered based on the complexity of content tackled, the duration spent on specific content as well as actions/solutions taken based on the content within the game-enhanced learning environment. This research can promote deeper insights into measurement, teaching and, content dissemination. It can re-engineer the present academic curricula to more closely align with the thinking and requirements of today's Generation C target audience.

CONCLUSION

Whether academic institutions choose to adopt game-enhanced learning or not its evolution is inevitable. The present cadre of students demands

Figure 3. Applying Rogers adoption curve to GBL

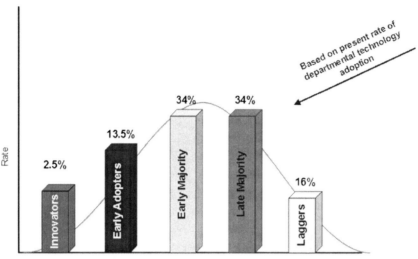

it and the ready availability of commercially available software supports its efforts coupled with eager education technology start-ups. Higher education institutions will for the most part remain pragmatic and even more so cautious in their adoption of games. However, the rapid pace of development of the new education start-ups as mentioned earlier in this chapter will push the curve for technology-based learning at a rate much faster than traditional institutions can manage. There are many consequences for established academia to not embrace game-enhanced learning within the curricula. Bearing in mind the sexiness of game-enhanced learning and its appeal students will simply gravitate to institutions whose curricula and mode of delivery are better suited to their style of learning. As such, academic institutions who fail to adopt the next wave of learning are doomed to lose their appeal to students who are already clamoring for customized content delivery, asynchronous in nature and relevant to their interest.

Academic institutions have a responsibility to at least attempt game-enhanced learning within their curriculum integration efforts. At worst they will have practical, evidenced based justification as to why they will not pursue adoption. At best

they will engage their students in an environment that despite their best efforts they are already familiar with and win their praises for recognizing the cries of the net generation.

At the beginning of our discussions I asked some pertinent questions such as:

1. How do institutions effectively integrate gaming approaches into the curriculum?
2. What is the best way to gain buy-in and adoption?

The integration of games into the curriculum needs to be an enterprise wide philosophy. By this I mean there must first be an organizational ethos which underpins the decision such as competitive advantage to the organization, a value proposition to its customers, i.e. students or an opportunity for closer alignment with industry players in offering practical experiences. Whichever the organization chooses as its ethos it cannot be underscored that game-based learning cannot be a siloed philosophy that only traverses a few people or departments. There must be a clear message sent throughout the organization that this is an enterprise change effort and we are going to try even if it fails. For in failing we learn that it was not only the wrong strategy for our institution but more about the processes associated with choosing an effect strategy for improved curriculum integration.

Additionally, this philosophical approach must have buy-in. Often we are faced with a do or die reality in academia because it is what the administration wishes. Buy-in towards adoption of game-enhanced learning must be aligned to a clear adoption strategy that is underpinned by:

1. A demonstrative approach, i.e. academic integrators must be able to try before they buy-in
2. Sufficient investment in the infrastructural components requisite for delivery in the classroom
3. Training prior to and for a sufficient period to support curriculum integration at the class as well as departmental level
4. Support staff, so that the burden is not on the professors to "do it all" and
5. A forum to vent perceived frustrations with the process so that those who choose to be either innovators or laggers in the process do not feel a sense of isolation.

Game-enhanced learning is a big change for any organization to undertake but changing an organization culture is an even bigger challenge. While we push the technological envelope let us not forget the human element in higher education institutions that are ultimately responsible for their success.

REFERENCES

Arnab, S., Berta, R., Earp, J., de Freitas, S., Popescu, M., & Romero, M. (2012). Framing the adoption of serious games in formal education. *Electronic Journal of E-Learning, 10*(2), 159–171.

Corti, K. (2006). *Game-based business and management skill development.* Retrieved from http://www.pixelearning.com/docs/games_basedlearning_pixelearning.pdf

DeSantis, N. (2012). *A boom time for education start-ups.* Retrieved from http://chronicle.com/article/A-Boom-Time-for-Education/131229/

Dixon, B. (2011). *When will educators get serious about gaming?* Retrieved from http://blogs.hbr.org/innovations-in-education/2011/03/when-will-educators-get-seriou.html

Dzinory, M. (2005). *Ids digital game-based learning (DGL) situated learning?* Austin, TX: University of Texas.

Fang, D., & Nuefeld, Y. (2007). The role of information technology in technology-mediated learning: A review of the past for the future. *Journal of Information Systems Education, 18*(2), 183–192.

Friedrich, R., Peterson, M., & Koster, A. (2011). *The rise of generation C.* Retrieved from http://www.strategy-business.com/article/11110

Gudmunsen, J. (2006). *Movement aims to get serious about games.* Retrieved from http://www.usatoday.com/tech/gaming/2006-05-19-serious-games_x.htm

Keitt, T. J., Daley, E., & Iqbal, R. (2009). *Predictions 2010: What's in store for serious games and B2B virtual worlds?* Boston, MA: Forrester Research.

Mapp, K. M. (2012). *The gamification of learning and instruction: Game-based methods and strategies for training and education.* New York, NY: Pfeiffer.

Mumtaz, S. (2006). Factors affecting teachers' use of information and communications technology: A review of the literature. *Journal of Information Technology, 9*(3), 312–342.

Pellegrino, J., & Quellmalz, E. S. (2010). Perspectives on the integration of technology and assessment. *Journal of Teacher Education, 43*(2), 119–134.

Pelletier, C. (2009). Games and learning: What's the connection? *International Journal of Learning and Media, 1*(1), 83–101. doi:10.1162/ijlm.2009.0006

Prensky, M. (2001). Digital natives, digital immigrants on the horizon. *MCB University Press, 9*(5).

Prensky, M. (2007). *Digital game based learning.* New York, NY: Paragon House.

Susi, T., Johannesson, M., & Backlund, P. (2007). *Serious games - An overview.* Skövde, Sweden: University of Skövde.

Ulicsak, M. (2010). *Games in education: Serious games 2.* Futurelab.

Younis, B. L. (2010). Integrating serious games in higher education programs. In *Proceedings of the Academic Colloquium 2010: Building Partnerships in Teaching Excellence.* Ramallah, Palestine: Virtual Environment Lab (V-LAB).

ADDITIONAL READING

Bolman, L., & Gallos, J. (2011). *Reframing academic leadership.* Indianapolis, IN: Jossey Bass Publishing.

Christensen, C., Johnson, C., & Horn, M. (2010). *Disrupting class, expanded edition: How disruptive innovation will change the way the world learns.* New York, NY: McGraw-Hill.

Corti, K. (2006). *Game-based business and management skill development.* Retrieved from http://www.pixelearning.com/docs/games_basedlearning_pixelearning.pdf

Davidson, C., Golberg, D., & Jones, Z. M. (2009). *the future of learning institutions in a digital age.* Cambridge, MA: The MIT Press.

De Freitas, S., & Maharg, P. (2011). *Digital games & learning.* London, UK: Continuum International Publishing Group.

Keen, J. M. (2011). *Making technology investments profitable: ROI road map for business case to value realization.* Hoboken, NY: John Wiley & Sons.

Mapp, K. (2012). *The gamification of learning and instruction: Game-based methods and strategies for training and education.* San Francisco, CA: Pfeiffer Publishing.

Milton, M. (2009). *Head first data analysis: A learner's guide to big numbers, statistics, and good decisions.* Sebastopol, CA: O'Reilly Media.

Rosenberg, M. (2005). *Beyond e-learning: Approaches and technologies to enhance organizational knowledge, learning & performance.* San Francisco, CA: Pfeiffer Publishing.

Squire, K. (2011). *Video games and learning: Teaching and Participatory culture in the digital age (technology, education, connections: TEC).* New York, NY: Teachers College Press.

Susi, T., Johannesson, M., & Backlund, P. (2007). *Serious games - An overview.* Skövde, Sweden: University of Skövde.

Zyda, M. (2005). From visual simulation to virtual reality to games. *Computer, 38*(9), 25–32. doi:10.1109/MC.2005.297

KEY TERMS AND DEFINITIONS

Cognitive Load: The tolerance of working memory to retain pertinent information over a period of time.

Digital Natives: Individuals belonging to the *net* generation, whose daily lives are fully integrated with technology.

Engagement: The degree to which participation, interest and continuity are maintained as it relates to an activity or project.

Flow: A degree of task immersion where the individual becomes totally engrossed in the activity oblivious to external situations.

Game-Enhanced Learning/Serious Games: An advanced learning technology designed with play in mind to achieve learning outcomes.

Generation C: A group of individuals who have grown up connected via social networks and mobile devices.

Learner Analytics: A data driven measurement method which can be utilized to track student performance end optimize curriculum impact.

Technology Adoption: The rate at which technology is embraced within various environments.

Chapter 4
A Perspective on Games and Patterns

Dores Ferreira
University of Minho, Portugal

Pedro Palhares
University of Minho, Portugal

Jorge Nuno Silva
University of Lisbon, Portugal

ABSTRACT

In the last few years, the authors have been carrying out a study involving elementary school students from 3rd to 6th years of schooling. The main goal of this study is to identify the possible relationships between the ability to identify patterns and the ability to play games, in particular mathematical games. The research methodology is quantitative and most of the analysis is concerned with the verification of correlation between variables. The analysis takes into account seven factors (besides the ability of pattern recognition) identified through a factor analysis carried out on data. With these tools, the authors have been able to differentiate games according to the different measurements. In this chapter, they disclose the important steps of this research as well as the results and main conclusions reached so far.

INTRODUCTION

Playing games is part of human culture and, according to Huizinga (2003), play is even older than culture. Actually, over the centuries, children and adults of different civilizations have occupied some part of their leisure time playing games, as we can see in a wide variety of archaeological artifacts, such as board games marked on stone

DOI: 10.4018/978-1-4666-3950-8.ch004

floors of Roman remains, some paintings, and on the beautiful book of games by Alfonso X. Nevertheless, so far it is impossible to establish where and when games started to be used, since some games require no specific material to be played. Fortunately, some of these games, namely board games, are played with pieces made in stone or wood that resisted over the years and now are preserved in museums. These artifacts prove that board games have been played for more than 4 000 years (Murray, 1952) (see Figure 1).

Figure 1. The royal game of Ur, from Ur, Southern Iraq, about 2600-2400 BC (British Museum)

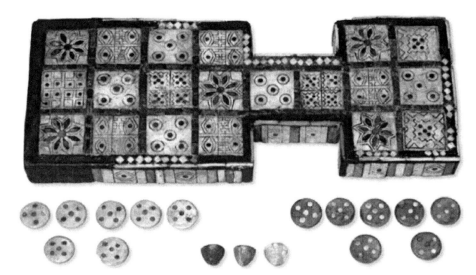

Nowadays, the interest in games remains. However, beyond the recreational aspect of games, the educational community has also become interested in possible pedagogical uses for them. The benefits of ludic environments, namely its motivating characteristics, may be used to promote the development of math skills, as is pointed by some guidelines of the Portuguese curriculum until 2011.

The word 'game' is used to describe different kinds of activities, such as children games, sport games, video games, guessing games, board games, among others. Consequently, it is essential to clarify the type of game that we are talking about. Although our interest rests on games in general, presently we are more focused on strategy games, known as mathematical games or abstract games (Neto & Silva, 2004). These particular games do not involve chance or hidden information. There is a large diversity of mathematical games, some well known, as chess, go and draughts. This kind of board games has been used in educational research and chess was perhaps the game that raised more studies in order to verify whether its practice improved math skills in their practitioners (Filguth, 2007).

In addition to games, another aspect that interests us in mathematics education is pattern identification. In fact, the ability to identify patterns is related to diverse areas of mathematics and some authors consider mathematics as the science of patterns (Devlin, 1997; Steen, 1990). This new concept of mathematics is very important and, the Portuguese curriculum of mathematic for elementary education, points to the development of the ability to identify and explore patterns in mathematical and non-mathematical contexts (DGIDC, 2007). Nowadays, mathematics educators should provide students the opportunity to visualize mathematical patterns to develop their mathematical power. In elementary mathematics education, teachers must be even more concerned about the improvement of the ability to find patterns in their students. According to Steen, "to grow mathematically, children must be exposed to a rich variety of patterns appropriate to their own lives through which they can see variety, regularity, and interconnections" (Steen, 1990, p. 8).

In this chapter we are going to focus on Chess, Wari, Traffic Lights, Dots and Boxes, Cats and Dogs, Dominoes, and Syzygies (a word game invented by Lewis Carroll), among other games.

We will present the major steps and principal results of a study which main goal is to identify the relationships between the ability to play each one of these games and the ability to identify patterns in elementary school students.

GAMES AND PATTERNS IN THE CURRICULUM OF MATHEMATICS EDUCATION

Usually, playing games is an activity related with leisure time and pleasure. However, this is not always true for everyone and depends on the situations. It is well known that sometimes a game is one of the different activities that people have to develop throughout the working week and not always bring happiness. Players suffer when they lose the game or when they are about to lose. Nevertheless, players like to play precisely because they do not know for sure whether they will win or not. The uncertainty about the outcome is the very essence of the pleasure of playing. This motivating characteristic of games makes them seen as a potential tool in education. As Caillois (1990) claims, "each game reinforces and stimulates any physical or intellectual activity" and this is an important issue in education. In fact, game has never been indifferent to the different civilizations and, over time, man has shown interest in different dimensions of games (Caillois, 1990; Huizinga, 2003).

The use of games in mathematics education is not new. In the 11th century an educational game named Rithmomachia was invented, played by students of arithmetic, astronomy and astrology (Silva, 2007). However, for many years games have been removed from the educational process, probably due to their strong connection to play environments and a different educational philosophy. More recently, researchers call renewed attention on the potential of games. Krulik and Rudnick (1993), claim that the competences acquired by or with pleasure are more durable, which makes

games a good ally of education. Games started to be seen as a facilitator of the process of teaching and learning, manly for their motivating characteristics and because they promote the development of mathematical skills (Lopes et al., 1990, Moreira & Oliveira, 2004).

The use of games with educational propose can be very positive for students who develop skills and acquire knowledge in a pleasant way. But such use must be clearly defined purposes and have underlying the curriculum. Silva and Santos (2011) point out that the games do not replace mathematics, not even to transmit particular curriculum. However, they also claim that games should be used as a complementary activity. Aware of the potential for certain games, these authors selected some of which they consider useful to mathematics education, stating some relations between these games and mathematics. Some recent research seems to justify these claims. Bottino, Ferlino, Ott and Tavella (2007) have conducted a study on the introduction of some mathematical games in a digital environment in two 4th grade classes in Italy. They could observe that children deviated from random work to a strategies search and application kind of work. They could also perceive positive impact on children's reasoning abilities by playing these games.

The important role of motivation in the teaching and learning process and the potential of games as a motivating source of learning are present in some curriculum guidelines. For instance, the recreational aspects of mathematics are mentioned in the *Principle and Standards for School Mathematics* of the American National Council of Teachers of Mathematics (NCTM) as being part of a cultural heritage that students have to appreciate and understand (NCTM, 2007). Another example are the *Standards for Excellence in Teaching Mathematics in Australian Schools,* adopted by the Australian Association of Mathematics Teachers (AAMT), which highlight the aims of excellent teachers, seeing that these teachers are aware of a range of effective strategies and techniques for promoting enjoyment of learning and positive attitudes to mathematics (Bragg, 2006). The Portuguese curriculum also point to the use of some games in mathematics education as one of the different activities that students should be involved (DGIDC, 2007).

Another aspect that is highlighted in the Portuguese curriculum and also in the NCTM standards is the study of patterns. These documents emphasize the importance of developing the ability to identify patterns in students, stating that visualizing and exploring numerically and geometrically is essential to build early algebra skills in elementary school students. In fact patterns are very connected with mathematics both in terms of numerical and geometrical issues, as functions or symmetry. According to (Steen, 1990), seeing and revealing hidden patterns is what mathematicians do best and, consequently, learning to visualize mathematical patterns enlists the gift of sight as an invaluable ally in mathematical education. As Devlin (1997) states, mathematics is the science of patterns. Furthermore, identify patterns is one of the most powerful strategies for problem solving (Posamentier & Krulik, 1998) and helps children appreciate the beauty of mathematics (NCTM, 1989). Appreciate the beauty of mathematics is very important in mathematics educations, among other things, because it is well known that we learn best what we like.

THE RELATIONSHIP BETWEEN GAMES AND PATTERNS

Games Involved in the Study

In this study, we decided to use two distinct categories of games. The first one consists of board games without chance involved or hidden information. Wari, Traffic Lights, Dots and Boxes, and Cats and Dogs were the games selected for this category. The second one consists of others games that do not belong in the first category.

In this case we selected a Dominoes game, and Syzygies, a word game.

The first game in the list above is Wari[1] also known as Oware, Awari, Awale and Ouri. It is an ancient game and a variant on African mancala games that have been played all over the world for centuries as it can be proved by archeological artifacts. According to de Voogt (1999, p. 104) "mancala boards games show an extensive range of distribution from West Africa to the Caribbean and parts of South America, from Northern to Southern Africa, from South East Asia, to South Asia and the Middle East" (see Figure 2).

The game is played by to players on a wooden board with six holes in each side. Usually the board game is a simple one, but there are also beautifully decorated boards that are preserved in museums. Sometimes the six holes are just made in the ground. The pieces, originally seeds or beans, are 48. The game starts with four pieces in each hole and players take turns in taking all the pieces from any one hole in his side of the board and spreading them anti-clockwise one by one in successive holes. If the last piece is dropped into an opponent's hole that gets, after the move is made, with two or three pieces the player captures these pieces. Captures are simultaneously made in all opponent consecutive holes counting back from the final hole, which also contains two or three pieces. The main goal of the game is to capture more pieces than the opponent (Botermans, 2008). These are the general rules, but there are also other specific rules and some particular exceptions.

Traffic Lights[2] is a board game invented by Alan Parr in 1998 (Neto & Silva, 2004). The game is played by two players on a 3x4 squares board and uses green, yellow, and red pieces. Only the green pieces can be placed in an empty place; the yellow pieces are used to replace the green ones; the red pieces are used to replace the yellow ones. Each player, on his turn, must do only one movement. The goal is to make three-in-a-row with pieces of the same color (see Figure 3).

Figure 2. Wari board and seeds from Camaroon

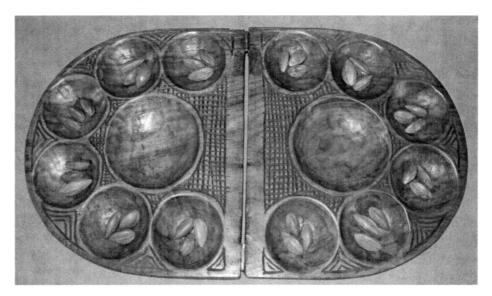

Dots and Boxes[3] is a pencil and paper game for two players. The board is an empty grid of dots and may be of any size. Each player, in turn, must draw a horizontal or vertical line connecting two adjacent points. The player that completes

Figure 3. Students play traffic lights in the Portuguese championship of mathematical games

one or more squares must make one more move before passing the turn to the opponent. The goal is to get more squares than the opponent. Despite being a simple game, Berlekamp (2000) reveals in his book how sophisticated it can be (see Figure 4).

Cats & Dogs[4], also known as Snort, is a board game invented by Norton Simon, probably in the 1970s (Neto, 2012). The game is played on an 8x8 board with pieces of two different colors, one

Figure 4. D&B game in progress

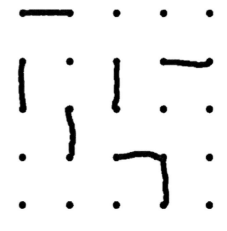

for cats and the other for dogs. On each turn, each player places one of his pieces on an empty square. A piece may not be placed in a square that shares an edge with some opponent pieces. The goal is to make the last move.

The word dominoes[5] is used to refer a system of games played with a set of particular pieces named also dominoes. Although is not yet know for certain the origin of dominoes, there are historians who assume that this is a game originating in China and has been introduced in Europe by merchants (Sanz, 2000). What we know for sure is that in Europe the game first appeared in the eighteenth century in Italy (Kelley, 1999; Sanz, 2000). The game of dominoes selected for the study is known in Portugal as Dominó Belga (Belgian). This game is extremely similar to Muggins and All Fives or the French version Cinq Partout (Clidière, 1968). This game is played by 2, 3, or 4 players with a double-six dominoes set. The main goal is to obtain as many points as possible, making the open ends of the layout add up a multiple of five. Usually, the first player to reach a score of 500 wins the match.

The word game Syzygies was invented by Lewis Carroll in 1879 (Wakeling, 1995). This game is an elaboration of the game Doublets also invented by the same author. The main goal of this game is to link two words following a set of definitions and rules. These starting words are given in a Syzygy-problem with the characteristic sense of humor of Lewis Carroll. Syzygy is the name given to the letter or group of consecutive letters that belong to two consecutive words. There are also some rules for scoring as well as a formula.

Aims of the Study

Our interest in games and its connection with elementary mathematics education was one of the major points that led us to carry out a research involving elementary school students.

The main purpose of this study was to identify the possible relationships between the ability to play games and the ability to identify patterns. Nevertheless, given the existence of a large variety of games, the interest was focused on board games without chance involved or hidden information, known as mathematical games or abstract games. Other games, such as dominoes and word games, were also used to disclose the existence or not of differences between the ability to play these different types of games concerning the ability to identify patterns. Another aim of the study was to ascertain the existence of significant differences between each one of the games involved in the analysis that could be used as a framework to differentiate these games.

Concerning the game of Chess, the literature point to the existence of relevant differences between Grand Masters and lower level players (Simon, 1992) or experienced and less experienced players (Charness, Reingold, Pomplun & Stampe, 2001). The conclusions point out by these authors led us to be focused also in the existence of possible differences between best and worst players. Consequently, finding differences between best and worst players of each one of the games involved in the study has emerged as an additional goal of the study.

The study comprised different phases of which this article will address only the part related with the correlational analysis. It takes also into account some previous analysis, namely a Factor analysis that revealed the existence of seven factors behind the ability to find patterns. Considering these results became relevant the identification of possible relationships between the ability to play games and the identifications of each one of the seven patterns, taking also into account the group of best and worst players.

Finally, as in Portugal elementary school students are every year assessed in mathematics by standardized tests, with this study we intend also to find the existence or not of relationships between the ability to play games and the results obtained in the national assessment in mathematics, regarding the group of 4th grade students.

Methodology

The methodology of the study is quantitative with a correlational design. The option by a correlational study is due to the fact that our interest is concerned with understanding the relationships between the ability to play games and the ability to identify patterns. Correlational studies are appropriate in educational investigations when there is a need to discover or clarify relationships and little or no previous research has been undertaken (Cohen & Manion, 1989). In fact, in Portugal there is little research about games in the framework of mathematics education. Therefore, as Cohen and Manion state, the investigation and its outcomes may subsequently be used as a foundation for other researches or as a source of additional hypotheses.

The population of the study consists of elementary school students from 3rd to 6th year of schooling (eight to twelve years old) from Portuguese schools. The process of data collecting was done in different ways: among the finalist of a national championship of mathematical games; organizing championships at schools with one or more classes involved. The sample was constituted by around 400 students, most belonging to 6 different schools. Only a small data was collected from a sample constituted by students participating in the Portuguese National Championship of Mathematical Games at the beginning of the research. The time duration of each tournament ranged between 1 and 4 months, depending of the number of participants. The specific tournaments where players have played with each other were the de ones that have spend more time. Remains to add the time spent on explaining and teaching the game (two or more sessions, depending on the number and complexity of rules) and collecting data (one session). Each session had the duration of around 45 minutes. The word game Syzygies do not required the Swiss system because it is an individual game and was implemented over 16 weeks.

In the study, we intend to investigate the existence of relationships between two variables: the ability to play games and the ability to identify patterns. The ability to play games was measured by the ranking of the respective championship. The software Swiss Perfect was used to organize the respective tournaments of these championships. The Swiss Perfect (available at http://www.swissperfect.com) is a computer program usually used in chess tournaments or other tournaments that pair opponents by Swiss or round-robin pairing rules, such as Go, bridge or Scrabble. In this study, the tournaments were mainly used the Swiss system and the Swiss Perfect software provided a valuable support. The option to this system is due to the fact that it is pointed as useful when a large number of players are competing and we have lack of time to carry out the tournament (Snyder, 2007). In a Swiss tournament, players are sorted according to their cumulative scores, which it means that each player plays against another player who has done the same or similar score to that point. In the first round of our tournaments players were paired according the alphabetic order or the numeric order that students have in their classes. Apart from being very useful the Swiss system does not eliminate anyone, which became an advantage when we are interested in having everyone participating in the game. Another advantage is that the final ranking gives us some indication of relative strength for all participants. On the other hand, players never play each other twice.

To measure the ability to identify patterns we have constructed and validated a test consisting of 24 questions involving numeric and geometric patterns. The structure of this test was based on the structure of similar questions used by other authors, such as Krutetskii (1976) and it was also based on the conclusions of Krutetskii's research. This author states the existence of three types of mathematical ability: analytical, geometric and harmonic (combining the other two). The questions of the test have the following structure:

identification of the following element of a pattern; identification of the element that does not fit in the pattern; producing patterns.

In this methodology, it is very important following some essential steps, such as the validation of the test, a pilot application, the analysis of its reliability, the elaboration of the test correction criteria and the normality of data. The steps concerning the test have been taken in a previous study carried out by Ferreira and Palhares among chess players and non-chess players (2008). In this study the strength of play was measured through the ELO rating of the players, as published by the chess federation, at the time when the test was implemented. The ELO rating is a statistical system, adopted by many different chess organizations, for calculating the relative skill levels of players in some games as chess and Go. The several tests used for statistical analysis have been applied using the software SPSS for Windows. The first step was the validation of the test made by a panel constituted by two university professors, one teacher of mathematics of the 2nd cycle (teaches students from ten to eleven years old) and a elementary school teacher (teaches students from six to nine years old) specialized in mathematics education. From this panel 26 questions have been selected. The correction criteria of the test were based on the principles reported by Charles, Lester, and O'Daffer (1992). The reliability of the test was measured by the statistical analysis of Cronbach's Alpha, which measures the internal consistency of items. Cronbach's Alpha must be greater than 0.70 (Fraenkel & Wallen, 1990), being accepted values slightly below 0.70 (Santos, 1999). After the implementation of a pilot application to 105 students, the analyses of the 26th questions revealed a Cronbach's Alpha coefficient of 0.756, which is an acceptable value. Nevertheless, to improve the reliability level we decided to remove two questions and the Cronbach's Alpha established was 0.763. With the reliability value appropriate to start the study remained to test the normality, which was made using the Kolmogorov-Smirnov

test. The statistical analysis revealed that the data was not different from a normal distribution, its means that we could use parametric tests as the Pearson coefficient.

All these steps were important to subsequently be able to draw reliably conclusions.

In the analysis of the relationship between variables we mainly used the Pearson (r) coefficient using the square of this coefficient (R^2) for interpretation because it can be interpreted as a ratio (Chen & Popovich, 2002). Kendall's Tau (τ) coefficient was used for the variables that contain a considerable amount of ties. However, in the analysis involving chess we have also used the point-biserial correlation coefficient (*rpb*), which is appropriated when one of the variables is dichotomic, as in gender (Field, 2000).

The interpretation of the correlation coefficients was undertaken according to the criteria mentioned in literature. Therefore, it was considered that coefficients between 0.2 and 0.35 reveal a small relationship between variables and may have some significance in exploratory research; coefficients between 0.35 and 0.65 reveal a moderate relationship between variables that allows group prediction, requiring at least a value of 0.5 for individual prediction; coefficients between 0.65 and 0.85 reveal a strong relationship between variables; coefficients above 0.85 indicate a very strong relationship between variables (Cohen & Manion, 1989; Fraenkel & Wallen, 1990; Christmann & Badgett, 2009). It analysis was also taken into account the level of significance, accepting only coefficients with a level of significance lower than 0.05 ($p < 0.05$ or $p < 0.01$). For instance, if the *p*-value (level of significance) is 0.05, that means that there is a 5% chance of observing a difference as large as we observed even if the two population means are identical. Therefore, we only report results that are consistent with these levels.

Concerning pattern recognition as a general ability that possibly will enclose other more specific abilities, Ferreira and Palhares (2009) carried out factor analysis existent on data, from more than six hundred elementary school students, and identified the existence of seven factors behind the ability of pattern recognition. The interpretation of the seven factors was done taking into account the category of patterns grouped in each factor. As a result of the analysis these seven factors emerged: numeric progressions (Factor 1); three terms repetition – ABC ABC (Factor 2); both geometric and numeric progressions (Factor 3); counting (Factor 4); odd and even numbers (Factor 5); rotation (Factor 6); more than one rule (Factor 7). After these results, the following analysis began to take into account also the seven factors.

Finally, in Portugal students from of 4th year of schooling are assessed in mathematics trough standardized tests. These tests are constituted by four sub-categories or areas: Number and Calculations; Geometry and Measurement; Algebra and Functions; Probability and Statistics. Data collected from five classes of 4th year students allowed us to verify the relationships between some games and this national assessment in mathematics both in the global results and the partial results of each area.

The process of data collecting required some recurring actions, namely teaching the rules of the game, clarify doubts, organize championships and pass the test.

Results of the Analysis Concerning Each Game

In the statistical analysis, when variables have the same direction we expect to find positive coefficients, it means that if a variable increase the other also increase. The negatives coefficients of correlation presented in the results are explained by an opposite direction between variables (e.g. in the ranking of players, the highest the number, the worse the player).

Concerning the previous analysis with chess, the sample was constituted by 65 chess players from the 3rd to the 6th year of schooling participants in the national championships. The statisti-

cal analysis revealed the existence of a positive relationship between the strength of play and the ability to find patterns, with a coefficient of correlation of $r = 0.458$ and a significance of $p < 0.01$. The analysis of a point-biserial correlation (*rpb*) and the R^2 interpretation showed that the variable School grade (year of schooling) affects the relationship between strength of play and the ability to find patterns. However, when we exclude its effects, the relationship is still above 0.38.

Results Concerning the Game Wari

The game Wari implicated the organization of championships in primary schools. The first championship involved 41 students from 3rd and 4th year of schooling. The statistical analysis revealed the existence of a negative relationship between the strength of play and the ability to identify patterns ($r = -0.398, p < 0.01$). The negative coefficient is explained by the different direction of variables, since in the ranking of players the highest the number, the worse the player, what did not occur with the score of the test. Another championship involving 148 students revealed a negative relationship between the best players and factor 7, that represent patterns involving more than one rule ($\tau = -0.542, p < 0.01$). Concerning the standardized national tests the analysis revealed e negative relationship between the strength of play and the domain of Geometry and Measurement ($r = -0.366, p < 0.05$).

With these results we conclude that for these students the game Wari has a moderate relationship significant at the 1% level (more accurate than the 5% level) with patterns recognition and with the mathematical domain of Geometry and measurement in the national standardized tests. In the group of best players the moderate relationship identified at the 1% level of significance allows us to conclude that the best you are; the more successful you are at identify patterns where more than one rule is intrinsic (see Figure 5).

Figure 5. Relationships concerning the game Wari

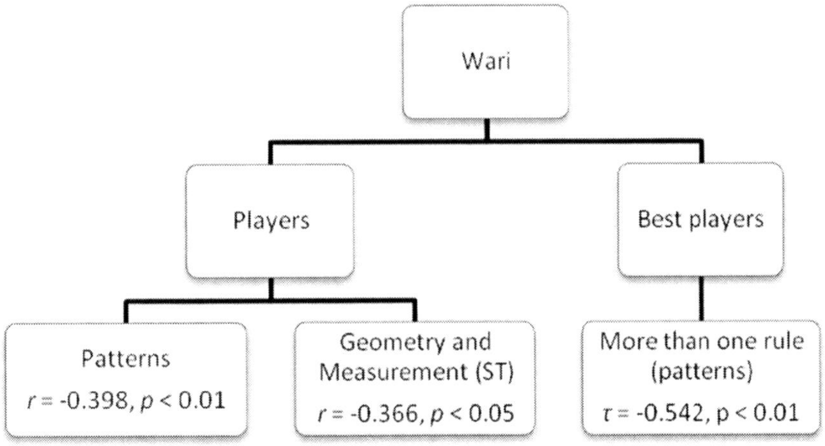

Results Concerning the Game Traffic Lights

In 2004, the organization of the first edition of a Championship of Mathematical Games (CNJM – Campeonato Nacional de Jogos Matemáticos) was a landmark in dissemination of mathematical games in Portuguese schools. The game Traffic Lights was introduced in the 2nd edition of this championship and has remained in the following championships. The final of this championship brings together students from different schools all over the country, which provided a good opportunity to collect data. Data collected in one of these finals from students of 3rd and 4th year of schooling, players of Traffic Lights, revealed a negative relationship between the strength of play and the ability to identify patterns ($r = -0.757$, $p < 0,05$). Subsequently, a championship organized in a primary school with 40 students from 3rd and 4th year revealed a negative relationship between the strength of play and the ability to identify patterns ($r = -0.316$, $p < 0.05$). The analysis of the best players of the championship reveled that this relationship was stronger ($r = -0.808$, $p < 0.05$) and close to the values obtained from the participants in the final of the national championship (CNJM). In a different situation,

as part of a quasi-experimental research, we have the opportunity to organize a championship with 24 students from 4th year where all students competed with each other, instead of using the Swiss Perfect tournament management software. The statistical analysis revealed a negative relationship between the strength of play and the ability to identify patterns ($r = -0.486$, $p < 0.05$). Concerning the seven factors, a championship involving three primary schools and 148 students showed the existence of a negative relationship between strength of play and the identifying patterns that involve three terms repetition for the best players ($\tau = -0,549$, $p < 0,05$). The analysis of the group of worst players of this championship showed a positive relationship between the strength of play of these players and the ability to find patterns involving odd and even numbers ($\tau = 0.324$, $p < 0.05$). This relationship was positive because the variables have the same direction. Concerning the standardized national tests (ST) the analysis revealed e negative relationship between the strength of play and the global results in these tests ($\tau = -0.486$, $p < 0.01$). Taking into account the four areas of these tests it was found negatives relationships between the strength of play and the following areas: Numbers and Calculations ($\tau = -0.448$, $p < 0.01$); Geometry and Measurement (τ

= -0.428, $p < 0.05$); Algebra and Functions ($\tau =$ -0.431, $p < 0.05$). The results concerning the area of Statistic and Probability were not significant at least at the 5% level so they are not reported (see Figure 6).

Results Concerning the Game Dots and Boxes

In this study, the Dots and Boxes players from 3rd and 4th year were organized in two distinct championships: the first one with 41 students;

the second with 148 students. The results of the analysis disclosed a negative relationship between the group of the best players and the ability to identify patterns ($r = -0.788$, $p < 0.05$), for the first championship. In the second one and concerning the seven factors identified behind the ability to identify patterns, there was also discovered a negative relationship between the strength of play of the best players and the ability to identify patterns involving numeric progressions ($\tau = -0.451$; $p < 0.05$) and counting ($\tau = -0.447$; $p < 0.05$). Concerning the group of worst players a positive

Figure 6. Relationships concerning the game traffic lights

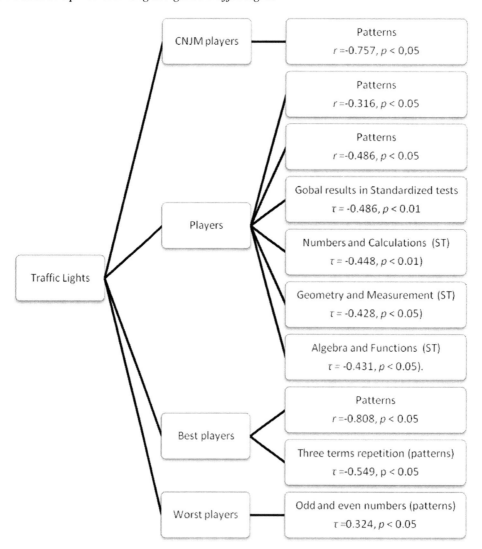

relationship was found between the strength of play and the ability to identify patterns involving odd and even numbers ($\tau = 0.287$; $p < 0.05$). In this game, we do not collect data from the standardized tests.

Concerning the results presented, we can say that for the best Dots and Boxes players the best you are, the more successful you are at identifying patterns involving numeric progressions or counting. However, for the group of worst players it seems to be important the relationship with a different factor although small (see Figure 7).

Results Concerning the Game Cats and Dogs

To collect data from Cats and Dogs players we have organized a championship with 31 of 4th year students. In this game the only significant result obtained in the statistical analysis was a relationship identified between the strength of play of the worst players and the ability to identify patterns involving more than one rule ($\tau = 0.626$; $p < 0.05$). The remaining results analysis were not significant, including the analysis concerning the national standardized tests.

Results Concerning the Game Dominó Belga

Dominó Belga was implemented on 41 students from two classes: one constituted by 23 of 3rd year students and other by 18 of 4th year students. Although it is a popular game, most of the students do not know how to play it, finding it hard to spot the connections between two dominoes. Therefore, the first sessions were devoted to teaching the rules of the game and clarify doubts. It was notoriously the most difficulty of the 3rd grade students in playing according to the rules. The championship for this game was also organized using the Swiss Perfect software, but the ranking was obtained from the total points of the cumulative score over the championship. Therefore, the variables have the same direction. In this game the significant relationships were found only concerning the seven factors. The analysis of the coefficients of correlation pointed out the existence of a positive relationship between the strength of play on these players and the ability to identify patterns involving both numeric and geometric progressions ($r = 0353$, $p < 0.05$). Concerning the best players, a negative relationship between the strength of play and the ability to find patterns

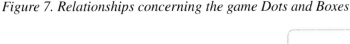

Figure 7. Relationships concerning the game Dots and Boxes

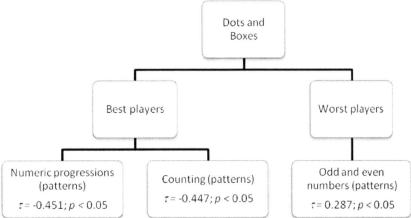

involving odd and even numbers have been found ($\tau = -0.632$; $p < 0.05$).

Regarding the results of the game Dominó Belga we are able to conclude that for these players this game has a moderate relationship with the ability to identify patterns involving both numeric and geometric patterns. The relationship concerning the group of best players close to be considered stronger and allows us to say that for this group of students the best you are at playing Dominó Belga, the more successful you become at identify odd and even numbers (see Figure 8).

Results Concerning the Game Syzygies

The last game in analysis is the word game Syzygies. To implement this game some syzygy-problem have been invented based on the implemented by Lewis Carroll. The next step was teaching the basic rules of the games as well the rules of scoring to the students involved in the study of this game. Then, over twelve and thirteen weeks, respectively, 18 students of 4th year and 26 of 5th year have to solve a syzygy-problem once a week. Every session, before knowing the syzygy-problem of the week, the students received their own result of the previous game with corrections and comments. Then, the best solution was written on the blackboard with the respective score. The students also knew the ranking of the week. The ranking of these championships is the cumulative score of each player, as well as in the Dominó Belga championship. The statistical analysis of data collected from these players has revealed some interesting results. For instance, in the group of 4th year students, the statistical analysis revealed a positive relationship between the strength of play Syzygies and the ability to identify patterns involving odd and even numbers ($r = 0.617$, $p < 0.01$). The analysis from students of this 4th year of schooling do not revealed significant relationship concerning national standardized tests. Regarding the group of best players of the 5th year students we found a negative relationship between the strength of play and two factors: one related with the ability to find numeric progressions ($r = -0.906$, $p < 0.05$); the other with the ability to find patterns involving counting ($r = -0.949$, $p < 0.05$). The group of worst players also revealed a relationship with the factor interpreted as numeric progressions but positive because in this game the variable worst play and strength of play have the same direction ($r = 0.878$, $p < 0.05$). In fact, this

Figure 8. Relationships concerning the game of dominoes

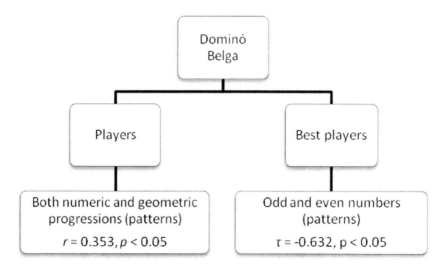

group also pointed out a relationship with patterns involving counting with significance close to the 5% level ($r = 0.791$, $p = 0.061$).

The results presented above allow us to say that in the 4th grade Syzygies players the ability to play is related with the ability to find patterns where odd and even numbers are intrinsic.

Another conclusion to be drawn is that in the 5th grade Syzygies best players the best you are, the more successful you are at identifying patterns involving numeric progressions or counting. Moreover, these results are consistent with those of the worst players for which we can say that the worst players they are, the worst at identifying patterns involving numeric progressions or counting they become. We think we can take into account the results of the factor represented by counting because the significant level is not too far from the default values. It is important to point out also that the relationships identified concerning the best and worst players, besides being taken with a small group of students they are very strong (see Figure 9).

Results Concerning the Relationship between Games and the Seven Factors

At this point, we have just displayed the results that are relevant and statistically significant at least of the 5% level ($p < 0.05$). However, the results presented until now were focused in each one of the different games. A different approach can provide us some interesting interconnections between the results for some games. For instance, an approach focused on the seven factors as following shows us more clearly which games are related to the same factor (see Figure 10).

As we can see in the Figure 10, four of the seven factors are related to two or three games. Consequently, the remaining factors, namely Factor 2 (three terms repetition – ABC), 3 (both geometric and numeric progressions), and 6 (rotation) are only related to one game or are not related to any games. In fact, Factor 6, interpreted as rotation, has no significant relationship to any game, in the analysis carried out in this

Figure 9. Relationships concerning the game syzygies from 5th year students

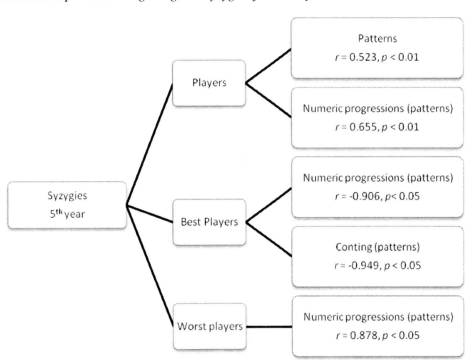

Figure 10. The seven factors that are related to more than one game

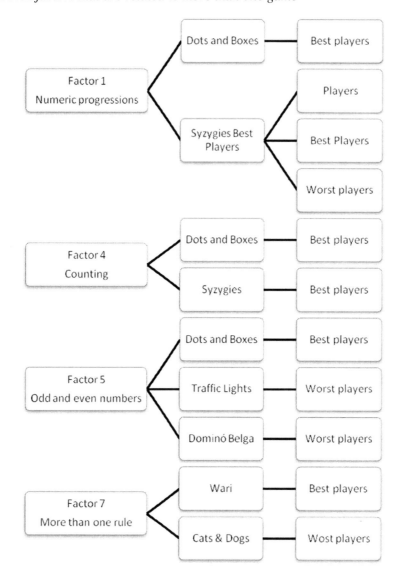

study. Factor 2 interpreted as three terms repetition is related only with the game Traffic Lights and Factor 3 with the dominoes game.

CONCLUSION

This study attempted to identify relationships between games and patterns with the objective that the results achieved could help the educational community as well as being a contribution to games studies.

The several relationships identified reveal the link between these games and the patterns present in the test. However, the different relationships also reveal that different games are related to patterns in a different way and some of them are more related than others.

It seems that for all games used in this study, Traffic Lights is the one that is more consistent in the analysis. This game has the largest number of relationships with different kind of patterns and also with the national standardized tests in mathematics as well as almost all the areas of these tests. In fact, of the games used in the research only for Dots and Boxes data was not collected that could enable the analysis concerning the national standardized tests. And only Traffic Lights and Wari have revealed being related with these tests. In the game Traffic Lights, besides some of the results were obtained with a small sample, as in the best and worst player's analysis, the several outcomes show us a certain consistency. Nevertheless, more research in this field is recommended to help make the result more robust. As a conclusion, we can state that playing Traffic Lights, and more precisely playing it well, could develop abilities in practitioners that are useful in pattern recognition. Traffic Lights is a good game to promote-among students for different reasons: it has simple rules; it is quick; it is easy to make; it is related with pattern recognition.

The game on the opposite side of Traffic Lights is the game Cats and Dogs. This game did not reveal almost any significant relationship with patterns, having just one result concerning the worst players. However, we believe that more research must be done with more students since we have analyzed only a group of thirty students. Other reason for the lack of significant relationships may be due to the fact that in our analysis the students are only from 4th grade and perhaps the game is not the most suitable for students of this level. Therefore, we recommend also more research concerning other grades.

Besides being a word game, Syzygies seems to be a good game to helps students develop their ability to identify patterns, mainly patterns involving numeric progressions and counting. The results analysis concerning this game point at the significant relationships identified on students of 5th grade, being more consistent than the results from 4th grade. The rules and definitions of this game are not so easy to learn as those of Traffic Lights, for instance. However, the relationship identified from the 4th grade students was very close to be considered strong and is significant at the 1% level. So we conclude that playing Syzygies could help 4th grade students identify patterns involving odd and even numbers. The different patterns related to Syzygies depending on the grade could be explained by differences in the strategies used by each one of the grade students in scoring well. Moreover, the different strategies used by players are probably the reason for the different links between patterns and games, as well as the particular characteristics of each game. Another aspect important to analyze in the game Syzygies is it possible connections with native language, such as vocabulary, grammatical mistakes and the national standardized tests. This game can also be used to establish connections between two different areas as is pointed by the curriculum guidelines (DGIDC, 2007): mathematics and Portuguese language (or other native language) or foreign languages.

The analysis focused on factors has shown distinction among games. It is clear that these games are not related with patterns where rotation is implicit. However, it is also clear that Traffic Lights is the only game related with repetition patterns, being the game of dominoes the only related to patterns involving both numeric and geometric patterns. Other important aspect is that some factors are shared by two or three games. For instance, Dots and Boxes and Syzygies are the only ones to share the link between patterns involving counting or numeric progressions. These interconnections possibly reflect that these two different games, a paper and pencil game and a word game, have in fact something in common, which makes them important to develop the ability to find a specific kind of pattern.

As a final point, this research highlights some aspect of the link between mathematical games and other games and patterns. We hope that the outcomes of this research will be useful for educators in general and enthusiasts of games and mathematics, as well as a contribution for future researches.

IMPLICATIONS ON THE CURRICULUM

For many years, mathematics educators had to deal with the lack of success of a large number of students. Many students consider mathematics as a nightmare because they have difficulties in this field and some of these students have also lack of motivation to learn mathematics. This lack of success could have diverse reasons and interpretations that we will not discuss in this chapter. Nevertheless, it is well known that students learn better what they like, being the motivation a central point in education.

Almost all the students like to play games, enjoying this activity even when they are not always successful. The reason for this motivation is probably intrinsic to games and to the pleasure acquired in playing. Curriculum guidelines on elementary mathematics are not indifferent to the inherent characteristic of games stating its uses as one of the different activities that students must be involved in. However, in the last few years, changes to the curricular documents have decreased the focus of the role of games in mathematics education. As Pacheco (2000) states, the curriculum policy is not always rational or based on research. Curiously, in the kindergarten, the focus on games was highlighted by supporting textbooks for early childhood educators pointing the use of games, including dominoes, for developing the number sense in students (Castro & Rodrigues, 2008). For some educational guidelines, it seems there is a huge difference having 5th or 6th years old, since for the 6th years old students, games are only a brief reference on the more recent documents. The reason is probably due to the fact that curriculum of mathematical education starts in the 1st grade with 6th years old students, starting also more formal education where playing is no longer well accepted. The results found in our research reveal that playing some particular games it is an important activity to implement in elementary schools students. These games are related with the ability to find mathematical patterns in a distinct way. As we stated above, there are games related to the ability to find a specific pattern whereas others games are related with the ability to find another pattern. These different patterns have inherent different kind of mathematical concepts. Educators can use the results of this research to choose at any given time, one or another game to help students developed the ability to identify patterns related to a particular aspect of mathematics. For instance, if a teacher needs to develop skills related to numerical progressions in their students or in a particular student can suggest or use the game Dots and Boxes to help them develop these skills. This possibility seems to be an advantage in the curriculum.

The link between some games and mathematics is not new. Several mathematicians have been enthusiastic about the analysis and practice of games. This interest has also promoted the emergence of another branch of mathematics, namely the theory of games (Neumann, 1972). Muniz (2010) classifies mathematical games as games of recreational mathematics, pointing out the link between this category of games and mathematics. In fact, both games and mathematics involve abstract thinking and reasoning, especially some kind of games, as mathematical games. In some games, players use the same strategies and steps that students use in solving problems (Krulik & Rudnick, 1993), namely the step states by Polya, which is an important field in mathematics education. As Palhares (2004) states, problem solving activities provided by strategic games contribute to the development of the ability to solve problems.

As we have mentioned before, the results of the study reported, as well as its conclusions, both are relevant for elementary school students. Knowing that a specific mathematical skill is related to the ability to play some games could be helpful for elementary school teachers, for parents and others educators. Moreover, they have a reference to help them choose the most appropriate game for the goals they want to achieve, when these goals are linked to the kind of pattern identification envolved in this study. If students like to play games and playing these games helps them to better identify patterns, then it is only necessary to provide the best moment and space for the students play. As students remain many hours at school, the school environment is probably one of the best places to implement the practice of some games. In fact, this practice can be found in some school clubs. Nevertheless, the coordination of these clubs represents an extra workload for teachers and many of them become unmotivated. Perhaps the results of this study may be used as a source of motivation. Another source of motivation is the National Championship of Mathematical Games[6], which has been a major contribution in promoting mathematical games stimulating its practice as evidenced by the large number of students present in the finals.

The extracurricular activities are also an excellent opportunity to implement the practice of good games as mathematical games or other games related to mathematics.

Finally, although games do not replace mathematics, some games can be used in an educational context as a tool for learning mathematics. However, it must be clear that the focus is not the playful activity itself, but the concepts or skills that we want to reinforce with a particular game. If we want that students play some specific games that can help them develop mathematical skills, as pattern recognition, first it is very important to motivate them and provide the opportunity to play them. Actually, really important is the activity itself, not the place where it takes place. Games provide the opportunity to socialize and learn to respect your opponents; learn the value of rules; know how to deal with defeat; learn from mistakes; develop new strategies of thinking; challenge own abilities, look for improvement; develop the abstract thinking and reasoning, as well as develop problem solving skills.

REFERENCES

Berlekamp, E. (2000). *The dots-and-boxes game: Sophisticated child's play*. Boston, MA: A. K. Peters.

Botermans, J. (2008). *The book of games: Strategy, tactics & history*. New York, NY: Sterling Publishing Co., Inc.

Bottino, R. M., Ferlino, L., Ott, M., & Tavella, M. (2007). Developing strategic and reasoning abilities with computer games at primary school level. *Computers & Education*, *49*(4), 1272–1286. doi:10.1016/j.compedu.2006.02.003

Bragg, L. A. (2006). *The impact of mathematical games on learning, attitudes, and behaviours*. (Doctoral Thesis). La Trobe University. Melbourne, Australia.

Caillois, R. (1990). *Os jogos e os homens*. Lisboa, Portugal: Cotovia.

Castro, J. P., & Rodrigues, M. (2008). *Sentido de número e organização de dados: Textos de apoio para Educadores de Infância*. Lisboa, Portugal: DGIDC, ME.

Catarino, I. (2007). O metromachia, um jogo geométrico. *Boletim da Sociedade Portuguesa de Matemática*, 105-122.

Charness, N., Reingold, E. M., Pomplun, M., & Stampe, D. M. (2001). The perceptual aspect of skilled performance in chess: Evidence from eye movements. *Memory & Cognition*, *29*(8), 1146–1152. doi:10.3758/BF03206384

Chen, P. Y., & Popovich, P. M. (2002). *Correlation: Parametric and nonparametric measures*. Thousand Oaks, CA: Sage.

Christmann, E. P., & Badgett, J. L. (2009). *Interpreting assessment data: Statistical techniques you can use*. Washington, DC: NSTA Press.

Clidière, M. (1968). *Le guide marabout des jeux de société*. Verviers, Belgium: Editions Gérard & C°.

Cohen, L., & Manion, L. (1989). *Research methods in education* (3rd ed.). London, UK: Routledge.

Devlin, K. (1997). *Mathematics: The science of patterns*. New York, NY: Scientific American Library.

DGIDC. (2007). *Programa de matemática do ensino básico*. Retrieved January 4, 2008 from http://sitio.dgidc.min-edu.pt/PressReleases/Paginas/ProgramadeMatematicadoEnsinoBasico.aspx

Ferreira, D., & Palhares, P. (2008). Chess and problem solving involving patterns. *The Montana Math Enthusiast, 5*(2-3), 249–256.

Ferreira, D., & Palhares, P. (2009). The ability to identify patterns. In *Proceedings of the Elementary Mathematics Education,* (pp. 209-216). Braga, Portugal: AEME.

Filguth, R. (2007). *A importância do xadrez*. Porto Alegre, Brazil: Artmed.

Huizinga, J. (2003). *Homo ludens*. Lisboa, Portugal: Edições 70.

Kelley, J. A. (1999). *Great book of dominoes games*. New York, NY: Sterling Publishing Co., Inc.

Krulik, S., & Rudnick, J. A. (1993). *Reasoning and problem solving: A handbook for elementary school teachers*. Boston, MA: Allyn and Bacon.

Krutetskii, V. A. (1976). *The psychology of mathematical abilities in schoolchildren*. Chicago, IL: Chicago University Press.

Lopes, A. V., Bernardes, A., Loureiro, C., Varandas, J. M., Oliveira, M. J. C., & Delgado, M. J. (1990). *Actividades matemáticas na sala de aula*. Lisboa, Portugal: Texto Editores.

Moreira, D., & Oliveira, I. (2004). *O jogo e a matemática*. Lisboa, Portugal: Universidade Aberta.

Murray, H. J. R. (1952). *A history of board-games other than chess*. Oxford, UK: Clarendon Press.

NCTM. (1991). *Normas para o currículo e a avaliação em matemática escolar*. Lisboa, Portugal: A.P.M e I.I.E.

NCTM. (2007). *Princípios e normas para a matemática escolar*. Lisboa, Portugal: A.P.M e I.I.E.

Neto, J. P. (2012). *Snort*. Retrieved April 2, 2012 from http://homepages.di.fc.ul.pt/~jpn/gv/catdogs.htm

Neto, J. P., & Silva, J. N. (2004). *Jogos matemáticos, jogos abstractos*. Lisboa, Portugal: Gradiva.

Neumann, J. (1972). *Theory of games and economic behaviour*. Princeton, NJ: Princeton University Press.

Pacheco, J. (2000). *A flexibilização das políticas curriculares: Actas do seminário O papel dos diversos actores educativos na construção de uma escola democrática*. Guimarães, Portugal: Centro de Formação Francisco de Holanda.

Palhares, P. (2004). O jogo e o ensino/aprendizagem da matemática. *Revista da ESEVC, 5,* 129–146.

Posamentier, A. S., & Krulik, S. (1998). *Problem-solving strategies for efficient and elegant solutions: A resource for the mathematics teacher*. Thousand Oaks, CA: Corwin Press, Inc.

Silva, J. N., & Santos, C. P. (2011). Jogos e matemática. In Palhares, P., Gomes, A., & Amaral, E. (Eds.), *Complementos de Matemática para Professores do Ensino Básico* (pp. 303–334). Lisboa, Portugal: Lidel.

Simon, H. A. (1992). The game of chess. In Aumann, R. J., & Hart, S. (Eds.), *Handbook of Game Theory with Economic Applications* (*Vol. 1*, pp. 1–17). Amsterdam, The Netherlands: Elsevier Science Publishers B.V. doi:10.1016/S1574-0005(05)80004-9

Snyder, R. M. (2007). *Winning chess tournaments: Methods and materials training guide.* Lincoln, NE: iUniverse.

Steen, L. A. (1990). *On the shoulders of giants: New approaches to numeracy.* Washington, DC: National Academy Press.

Voogt, A. J. (1999). Distribution of mancala board games: A methodological inquiry. *Board Games Studies*, *2*, 104–114.

ADDITIONAL READING

Bell, R., & Cornelius, M. (1991). *Board games round the world: A resource book for mathematical investigations.* Cambridge, UK: Cambridge University Press.

Chen, P. Y., & Popovich, P. M. (2002). *Correlation: Parametric and nonparametric measures.* Thousand Oaks, CA: Sage.

Delahaye, J. (2000). *Jeux mathématiques et mathématiques des jeux.* Baume-les-Dames. France: Belin.

Ferreira, D., Palhares, P., & Silva, J. N. (2010). Mathematical skills and mathematical games. In J. N. Silva (Ed.), *Proceeding of the Recreational Mathematics Colloquium,* (pp. 89-94). Lisboa, Portugal: Ludus.

Ferrero, L. (1991). *El juego y la matemática.* Madrid, Spain: Editorial La Muralla, S. A.

Gobet, F., Voogt, A., & Retschitzki, J. (2004). *Moves in mind: The psychology of board games.* New York, NY: Hove Psychology Press.

Linaza, J., & Maldonado, A. (1987). *Los juegos y el deporte en el desarrollo psicológico del niño.* Barcelona, Spain: Editorial Anthropos.

Ma, L. (2009). *Saber e ensinar matemática elementar.* Lisboa, Portugal: Gradiva.

Moreira, D., & Oliveira, I. (2004). *O jogo e a matemática.* Lisboa, Portugal: Universidade Aberta.

Murray, H. J. R. (1952). *A history of board-games other than chess.* Oxford, UK: Clarendon Press.

Neto, J. P., & Silva, J. N. (2006). *Jogos histórias de família.* Lisboa, Portugal: Gradiva.

Neto, J. P., & Silva, J. N. (2010). *Jogos velhos, regras novas.* Lisboa, Portugal: Clássica Editora.

Orton, A. (1999). *Pattern in the teaching and learning of mathematics.* London, UK: Cassell.

Parlett, D. (1999). *The Oxford history of board games.* Oxford, UK: Oxford University Press.

Ponte, J. P., & Serrazina, M. L. (2000). *Didáctica da matemática do 1.º ciclo.* Lisboa, Portugal: Universidade Aberta.

Sá, A. J. C. (1995). *A aprendizagem da matemática e o jogo.* Lisboa, Portugal: APM.

Schädler, U. (2007). *Jeux de l'humanité.* Genéve, Switzerland: Éditions Slatkine.

Smole, K. S., Diniz, M. I., & Cândido, P. (2007). *Jogos de matemática de 1.º ao 5.º ano.* Porto Alegre, Brazil: Artmed.

Vale, I., Barbosa, A., Borralho, A., Cabrita, I., Fonseca, L., & Pimentel, T. (2009). *Padrões no ensino e aprendizagem da matemática – Propostas curriculares para o ensino básico.* Viana do Castelo. Portugal: ESSE do IP de Viana do Castelo.

Whitehill, B. (2009). Toward a classification of non-electronic table games. In J. N. Silva (Ed.), *Proceeding of Board Games Studies Colloquium XI,* (pp. 53-66). Lisboa, Portugal: Associação Ludus.

KEY TERMS AND DEFINITIONS

Elementary School Students: Students from 3rd to 9th grade.

Mathematical Games: Games with no chance involved and no hidden information.

Pattern: Sequence of numbers or geometric figures according to a rule.

Seven Factors: Factors arising from factor analysis taken on the pattern test.

Significant: The *p*-value is at least equal or lower than 0.05.

Standardized Tests: Tests constructed by the educational department and implemented on all 4th grade students.

Strength of Play: The ability to play a game that can be measured.

ENDNOTES

[1] http://en.wikipedia.org/wiki/Oware

[2] http://www.boardgamegeek.com/board-game/1893/traffic-lights

[3] http://math.berkeley.edu/~berlek/cgt/dots.html

[4] http://en.wikipedia.org/wiki/Map-coloring_games#Col_and_Snort

[5] http://en.wikipedia.org/wiki/Dominoes

[6] http://ludicum.org/cnjm

Chapter 5
Game–Based Teaching:
Practices, Roles, and Pedagogies

Thorkild Hanghøj
University of Aalborg, Denmark

ABSTRACT

This chapter outlines theoretical and empirical perspectives on how Game-Based Teaching can be integrated within the context of formal schooling. Initially, this is done by describing game scenarios as models for possible actions that need to be translated into curricular knowledge practices, pedagogical knowledge practices, and everyday knowledge practices. Secondly, the chapter emphasizes how teachers must be able to shift back and forth between various interactional roles in order to facilitate game scenarios. Finally, a discussion is presented on how teachers choose different pedagogical approaches to game-based teaching, which may or may not correspond with the pedagogical models of particular games.

INTRODUCTION

This chapter addresses three recurring and inter-related challenges with Game-Based Teaching (GBT), which concern

1. How games are perceived and adopted within a formal school context,
2. How teachers facilitate games through different roles, and
3. The relationship between teachers' pedagogical approaches and the pedagogical models of particular games.

DOI: 10.4018/978-1-4666-3950-8.ch005

These three challenges are all addressed by conceptualizing games as scenario-based models for possible actions. This means that games are not viewed as self-explanatory aims or efficient "techniques," but as more or less open-ended scenarios that may or may not be integrated with the pedagogical and curricular knowledge practices of a school context. In this way, game scenarios involve both opportunities and challenges for teaching and for fulfilling particular learning objectives.

The chapter primarily adopts a teacher perspective on games and learning, a relatively overlooked aspect within the research field. A number of general pedagogical frameworks exist that describe how games can be integrated into educational contexts (Van Eck, 2009; Simpson & Stansberry, 2010; Arnab et al., submitted). However, only few empirical studies have been conducted on how teachers actually enact games within classroom settings (Squire, 2004; Sandford et al., 2006; Hanghøj & Brund, 2012). In order to generate knowledge that can be useful for practitioners in the field, it is crucial to conduct more empirical studies on the actual *practices* of teachers using games. Following this aim, the theoretical models and examples presented in this chapter are all based on empirical studies of educational gaming conducted by the author. These studies, each of which focuses on teacher use of a particular game, can be divided into three groups: the educational computer game *Global Conflicts* (Hanghøj & Magnussen, 2010; Hanghøj, 2011b; Hanghøj & Brund, 2012); the commercial off-the-shelf (COTS) game *Penumbra* (Bourgonjon & Hanghøj, 2011); and an ICT-supported debate game called *The Power Game* (Hanghøj, 2011a). Combined, these studies involve observations of game sessions conducted by approximately twenty-five teachers at the secondary and upper secondary level. In addition to classroom observations, the studies also include pre- and post-game interviews with the participating teachers.

The chapter is divided into five parts, the first of which defines game scenarios and why the scenario aspects of games are particularly relevant for educational purposes. Next, the three challenges mentioned above are introduced and then subsequently discussed in another section. Finally, the chapter concludes with a series of recommendations for GBT based on the opportunities and challenges discussed throughout the chapter. Based on a desire to put more emphasis on the crucial role of teachers as professional gatekeepers or "change agents" (Bruner, 1996, p. 84) when it comes to designing, facilitating and evaluating the outcomes of game-based learning environments, the term Game-Based Teaching instead of Game-Based Learning is used throughout

the chapter. In this way, the theoretical perspectives and empirical findings presented here can hopefully be used to qualify the choices teachers, designers and researchers make when using game scenarios for educational purposes.

GAME SCENARIOS

It is common knowledge among both children and philosophers that the term game is, to say the least, quite ambiguous (Wittgenstein, 1958). This uncertainty means that researchers, game designers, journalists, policy makers, parents, schoolteachers, and students rarely have an identical point of reference when they talk about games. Some of this confusion can be explained by the fact that the term game refers to a myriad of different game formats (e.g. video games, location-based games, board games), game genres (e.g. strategy games, edutainment games, massively multiplayer online role-playing games), and a diverse array of game dynamics (competition, exploration, resource management, etc.). In order to reduce this complexity, the *scenario* aspect of games will be stressed when describing how games can be used and understood in relation to educational contexts.

The main reason for describing games as scenarios, a term derived from Italian meaning "that which is pinned to the scenery," is that scenarios directly refer to the dynamic, future-oriented models for possible actions that are embedded in game designs. This points to a core dynamic of games, which is to make meaningful choices and to explore how these choices have consequences within a game world (Salen & Zimmerman, 2003). Following a pragmatist perspective, I assume that games are inquiry-based laboratories in which participants are able to imagine, engage with, and reflect upon their experiences (Dewey, 1916). Moreover, Dewey's theory of inquiry may also be understood as a theory of scenario-based inquiry (Hanghøj, 2011a), an interpretation of Dewey's pragmatism best illustrated by his term "dramatic rehearsal", which describes how individuals make moral and ethical decisions by going over "various competing possible lines of action" in their minds (Dewey 1922, p. 190). Dewey's compelling use of the drama metaphor implies that decisions cannot be reduced to utilitarian, rational, or mechanical exercises, but that they are resolved through the imaginative projection of outcomes that also have emotional, creative, and personal qualities. Based on this pragmatist perspective, game scenarios can be defined as *contingency models* that explicitly allow game participants to imagine, enact, and reflect upon the relationship between particular actions and their actual or possible consequences. In this way, game scenarios can be used to explore and experiment with the construction, deconstruction, and reconstruction of knowledge.

My second assumption, which follows from the first, is that games are well-suited for developing students' *scenario competence*, which can be defined as the ability to imagine, enact, and reflect upon game-specific choices and their consequences (Hanghøj, 2011). Thus, scenario competence represents a form of meta-competence, which involves three different aspects:

1.   Problem scenarios,
2.   Social scenarios, and
3.   Identity scenarios.

These three aspects correspond with the three major functions of education: qualification, socialization, and subjectification (Biesta, 2010).

The notion of problem scenarios, which refers to Dewey's theory of inquiry, concerns the ability of students to build and explore hypotheses in relation to the challenges that they encounter in a specific game world (Dewey, 1916). For example, a social studies course that uses the *Global Conflicts* game series may develop students' scenario competence by teaching them to understand the ideological conflicts as represented in the game. The key issue here is qualifications: What is to be learned through the game?

The second aspect, which concerns social scenarios, is based upon the assumption that the social interaction surrounding game encounters requires the ability to enact particular rules, roles, and frameworks within a given social context (Goffman, 1974). In this way, the same course with *Global Conflicts* games can be used to teach students how to work together in pairs to write journalistic articles based on their game experiences. The key issue here is socialization: How is the social interaction of the game session organized?

The third aspect of scenario competence, identity scenarios, refers to the player/student experience of projecting identities, and how this can be related to the individual's own beliefs and personal narratives (Bruner, 1990). When students take on the role of journalist in *Global Conflicts*, they may relate this experience to a number of other perspectives—e.g. what does it mean to see the world through the eyes of a journalist? What attitudes and ideological beliefs toward the conflicts are made available (and unavailable) in the game? The key issue here is subjectification: Who can I become when playing this game?

The final reason for conceptualizing games as scenarios is methodological. As Gee has argued, it is highly important that educational game researchers pay closer attention to the ways in which different games are related to larger learning systems, which can be termed Games, with a capital "G", as opposed to the current tendency to focus on games (with a small "g") as just isolated designs within educational contexts (Gee, 2011). Arguing along similar lines, the educational use of game scenarios can be seen as the creation of layered realities that involve both the scenarios embedded in the game and the scenarios of the educational context. In order to better understand this relationship, Game-Based Teaching can be described as an interplay and translation of knowledge practices, which involve different criteria for validating knowledge.

1ST CHALLENGE: GAMING VS. SCHOOLING

The challenges involved in Game-Based Teaching are often described in terms of "practical" problems or barriers, which need to be fixed or solved in order to further advance the educational use of games (Egenfeldt-Nielsen, 2004). Thus, several studies mention how the use of games is constrained by narrowly defined curricula, limited time schedules, technical problems, and insufficient resources for buying games (Sandford et al., 2006; Simpson & Stansberry, 2008; Van Eck, 2009; Williamson, 2009).

Seen from a pragmatist perspective, the challenges concerning the educational use of games cannot simply be reduced to a matter of practical problems to be solved. Instead, I wish to argue that the main challenge of Game-Based Teaching is a matter of integrating different *knowledge practices* with different criteria for what counts as valid knowledge—inside and outside school contexts (Barth, 2002; Hanghøj, forthcoming). In order to briefly illustrate this hypothesis, it can be helpful to take a closer look at the perceived dichotomy between "schooling" and "gaming" (i.e. school/serious versus leisure/fun), which is commonly reinforced among researchers, teachers, students, parents, politicians, and educational game designers. This perceived dichotomy is quite problematic given the fact that game practices and school practices in several respects have a common historical origin that can be traced back to Antiquity. In the words of the famous historian and play theorist Huizinga, "Meaning originally 'leisure,' [school] has now acquired precisely the opposite sense of systematic work and training, as civilization restricted the free disposal of the young man's time more and more" (1955, p. 148). Similarly, the Latin term for a teacher or schoolmaster, *magister ludi,* can literally be translated as "master of game activities" (Buttori & Loh, 2009). Today, these original meanings of the terms game and school are almost forgotten, mainly as a result of the last two-three hundred years of modernization taking place in Western societies, which has led to an increasing differentiation of play, work, and school activities. Thus, these two activities, gaming and schooling, have developed into two distinct "knowledge traditions" (Barth, 2002) that often rely on opposing validity criteria for determining what counts and what does not count as relevant knowledge.

Game-Based Teaching as an Interplay of Knowledge Practices

In order to provide a more context-sensitive framework for understanding how game scenarios can (and cannot) be taught within educational contexts, we argue that Game-Based Teaching represents a complex interplay of different knowledge practices. Inspired by Barth's anthropological theory of knowledge, a knowledge practice can be defined analytically in relation to a substantive corpus of assertions, a range of media and representations, and a social organization (Barth, 2002).

If we take games as an example of a knowledge practice, they embed a number of ideas and assertions in the organization of the game world, they embed different forms of game media and representation (including game boards, digital media, etc.), and they are distributed, communicated, employed, and transmitted within particular social institutions such as school settings (cf. Klabbers, 2009, p. 10). The three aspects of knowledge (assertions, representations, social organization) are interconnected and determine each other mutually (Barth 2002, p. 3). Moreover, any knowledge practice, whether it is game or school-related, generates tradition-specific criteria for validating knowledge that influences the ways in which certain knowledge practices are seen as being valid or invalid. This dynamic resembles Gee's notion of semiotic domains defined by distinct forms of "content", literacies, and social practices that can be designed to engage and manipulate people in certain ways (Gee 2003, p. 43ff). However, Gee has rightfully been criticized for a tendency to over-emphasize how particular game designs may determine particular forms of learning (Sefton-Green, 2006; Pelletier, 2008). In that sense, the term semiotic domain often reduces games to textual machines embedded with strong claims about how learning will or should take place. Consequently, I prefer to speak of knowledge practices and focus more on how the messy realities of teaching with games are actually carried out within a classroom context.

In order to provide a more detailed understanding of the complex translations involved in using games for educational purposes, I will conceptualize Game-Based Teaching as a dynamic interplay of four knowledge practices:

1. Specialized or curricular knowledge practices,
2. Pedagogical or "school only" knowledge practices,
3. Every day or non-specialized knowledge practices, and
4. Scenario-specific knowledge practices (Hanghøj, 2011b).

To give an example, a game-based course may involve the exploration of a particular game scenario in the *Global Conflicts* series, such as illegal border crossing between Mexico and the U.S. (scenario-specific knowledge practice), the specialized discipline of social studies (curricular knowledge practice), project-based group work (pedagogical knowledge practice), and leisure game experiences as well as commonsensical knowledge about politics and human rights (everyday knowledge practices). Figure 1 shows the interplay between the four knowledge practices.

As the model illustrates, the educational use of game scenarios always requires dynamic translations across the four knowledge practices. The term translation is used to describe the interpretations and choices that teachers have to make to "read" and re-design game scenarios for curricular practices and pedagogical practices while also paying attention to students' prior game experiences. Moreover, translations also refer to the fact that games are often seen both by teachers and students as somewhat unfamiliar learning resources and teaching methods in relation to the existing materials and pedagogical approaches

Figure 1. Game-based teaching as an interplay of knowledge practices

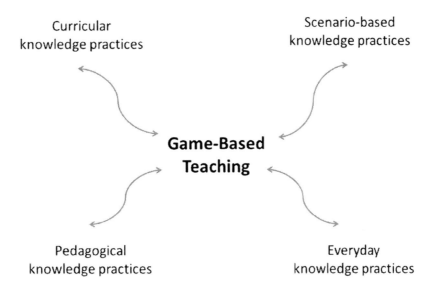

within a formal school context. Seen from a pragmatist perspective, the process of translating game scenarios into educational practices creates challenges that may—or may not—support valuable learning processes. Some of these challenges can be illustrated by briefly comparing two earlier empirical studies on Game-Based Teaching (Hanghøj, 2011b; Bourgonjon & Hanghøj, 2011).

Playing a "School Game"

In the first study, which is based on interviews with nineteen secondary teachers and classroom observations of their game sessions with the educational computer game *Global Conflicts*, the student experience of the game scenario often clashed with their everyday expectations of playing computer games (Hanghøj, 2011b). More specifically, the game scenario involved reading large amounts of text and was unable to provide sufficient forms of interaction for several students, who consequently termed *Global Conflicts* a "school game." Moreover, the teachers, who were using the game for the first time, often found it difficult to figure out how to link between the game scenario, curricular aims, pedagogical activities, and the students' everyday expectations toward games. As a result of clashing expectations, several students, especially boys, were disappointed by how much reading they had to do and by the lack of 3D interaction. One of the boys was eventually asked to leave the class for not playing the game as intended by the teacher. Some students, on the other hand, experienced the game far more positively, e.g. one girl, who did normally not receive high grades, was praised by her teacher for a feature article written based on in-game events.

Exploring "Horror Quality"

The aim of the second empirical study was to describe how secondary teachers try to design meaningful frameworks to promote students engagement with subject-related content when playing COTS games, e.g. by using the horror-adventure game *Penumbra* for teaching linguistic awareness and genre aspects in the context of mother tongue education (Bourgonjon & Hanghøj, 2011). In order to create an immersive atmosphere for the horror game scenario, one teacher in the study decided not to use the computer room and asked all the students to play the game on laptops using headphones in the darkness of the school's basement. Afterwards, the students would return to class and work in groups to write scenes that recreated their game experiences before ending with a plenary discussion on the "horror quality" of a selected sentence from each group. The teacher consequently managed to create a course that made meaningful translations across the four knowledge practices of the game scenario, the curriculum, the pedagogy, and the students' everyday game experience.

Teachers' Game Literacy

Comparing the two empirical studies clearly shows how teacher attempts to bring games into school contexts must meet a range of different validity criteria (Barth, 2002). First of all, both teachers and students must accept the games to be played as valid learning resources in relation to the existing ecology of learning materials within a formal school context. Secondly, GBT also requires close integration with the curricular aims of the teachers and their pedagogical organization of game sessions. However, in order to create meaningful translations across the different knowledge practices, it is crucial that teachers have developed *game literacy* based upon their experience with and understanding of different game designs. Similarly, it has been argued how teachers not only have curricular assumptions but also cultural assumptions on the use of games, i.e. teachers often assume that most students are quite motivated by games and that most students are competent gamers, which are both somewhat questionable assumptions when compared to empirical findings on how particular games are played by students in classroom contexts (Kirkland & Williamson, 2010).

The point here is that Game-Based Teaching requires an *alignment of expectations* between the intended possibility space of the game design, the teachers' understanding of how the game scenario can be used for educational purposes, and the students' experience of actually playing the game. As the first study shows, a serious game such as *Global Conflicts* may be able to provide both meaningful learning experiences as well as disappointment and frustration, all depending on how teachers facilitate the game and whether students accept the game. Similarly, the second study shows how a teacher was able to make meaningful translations across the four knowledge practices when re-designing a horror-adventure game for educational purposes. This involved a relevant setting (a dark basement) for playing the game that came close to the students' everyday experience of playing horror games, a pedagogical approach that required the students to collaborate and re-write scenes from the game, and a clear match with the curricular aims of Danish as a school subject.

The model shown in Figure 1 is descriptive and assumes no a priori hierarchy between the knowledge practices involved when teaching with games. Not surprisingly, most of the teachers and students who I have interviewed tend to value disciplinary and pedagogical knowledge practices as being the most valid or serious. However, as the two studies indicate, it is crucial that teachers are sufficiently game literate in order to make relevant translations from the knowledge practices of particular game scenarios into curricular, pedagogical, and everyday knowledge practices. This involves an understanding of the assertions of particular game scenarios (e.g. how the game worlds of *Global Conflicts* and *Penumbra* are constituted by specific rules, values, and ideas), an understanding of particular game media and

their genre aspects (e.g. what it means to play an adventure game), and how game scenarios may be meaningfully enacted within a school context (e.g. by organizing student collaboration). In this way, the development of teachers' game literacy is the primary prerequisite for overcoming the assumed dichotomy between "gaming" and "schooling."

2ND CHALLENGE: GAME-BASED TEACHER ROLES

Even though research on games and learning has been conducted for more than four decades, the actual practice of teaching with games has only come into focus in recent years. Consequently, the research literature only provides limited descriptions of the pedagogical choices and considerations that teachers make when they facilitate games. This lack of empirical knowledge about how and why teachers use games is quite striking, given the fact that teachers are crucial *gatekeepers* when it comes to actually selecting, enacting, and assessing educational games as a part of their teaching. This brings us to the second challenge of Game-Based Teaching: What roles should teachers assume when they facilitate educational games?

Game-Based Teaching should not be understood as a fixed practice as it involves a repertoire of shifting teacher roles. The term teacher role is commonly used among educational researchers and practitioners to describe how teachers respond to various demands and situations. Inspired by the work of Mead and Goffman, we will conceptualize teacher roles from an interactionist perspective (Atkinson & Housley, 2003). A role can be defined as, "the normative expectation of situationally specific meaningful behaviour" (Joas, 1993, p. 226). Following this definition, teacher roles are continually configured and re-configured in relation to the situated enactment of mutual norms and expectations. Thus, we conceive of teacher roles as a *relational property* of social interaction within a classroom context. This means that teacher roles should not be seen as fixed scripts or functions, but rather understood as more or less stable patterns of interaction and expectations based on processes of continual negotiation, i.e. between a teacher, a game scenario, and his or her students.

Four Teacher Roles

Based upon earlier empirical studies (Hanghøj & Magnussen, 2010; Hanghøj & Brund, 2012), we argue that teachers shift back and forth between four different roles when facilitating games for educational purposes, namely by performing as *instructor*, *playmaker*, *guide*, and *evaluator.*[1] The role as instructor concerns teacher planning and communication of the overall goals of a game scenario in relation to particular learning objectives. This role is an integrated part of most teachers' everyday practices, e.g. when giving overt instructions in relation to a curricular topic. The role as playmaker refers to the ability of teachers to communicate the tasks, roles, goals, and dynamics of a particular game scenario as seen from a player perspective. This term is borrowed from the domain of team sports, where it describes the ability to "read the game," i.e. by making passes that enable the offense to score. The reason for applying this metaphor to a classroom context is that educational games pose somewhat different challenges than required by the teachers' more familiar role as instructor. Thus, in order to understand how a given game can be played, teachers have to imagine how the different phases of the game scenario will unfold when preparing for the game session and how they plan to respond to the students' game interaction when facilitating the game. As a result, GBT requires that teachers make game scenarios "come alive" for the students. The role of the guide encapsulates how teachers support or scaffold students in their attempts to meet particular learning objectives when they play a game. Finally, games also require teachers to perform as evaluators in order to re-play relevant

game events and to provide a qualified response to student game experiences. These four teacher roles should not be understood as ideal types or as normative goals for teaching with games. Rather, they can be seen as heuristic categories based on empirical analysis of the game-based practices of teachers. Accordingly, the roles and their relationship are open to discussion and further analysis.

The similarities and differences between the four roles can be understood as a relationship between two dimensions of meaning making. The first dimension concerns the on-going *negotiation of meaning between the game practices and the curricular aims*, which may be converging or diverging depending on how the "game encounter" (Goffman, 1961) unfolds between teacher, students, and game scenario. Thus, in some cases, the game dynamics may be such a determining factor in the framing of student activities that making translations to the curricular aims may be difficult for teachers. In other cases, the game practices may not be meaningful or accepted by the students, which will often make teachers and students frame the game session as being a schoolish exercise. The second dimension of meaning making concerns the *shift of teacher perspectives* between viewing the game participants mainly as *students*—e.g. when linking the aims or outcomes of the game session to the curriculum—and viewing the game participants mainly as *players*—e.g. when addressing the students as actors within a game world. Figure 2 illustrates the relationship between the four roles.

Examples of Teacher Roles

In order to illustrate how these teacher roles can be performed, we will use examples from the empirical studies mentioned earlier. Following a pragmatist perspective, we will try to show both the challenges and the possibilities of performing the different roles.

Figure 2. The shifting roles of game-based teaching

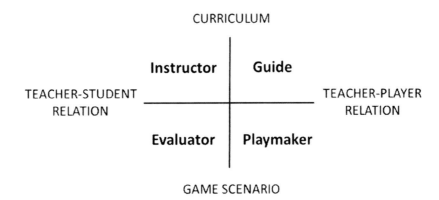

The Teacher as Instructor

One of the main challenges for the teachers in assuming the role as instructor was to explain the educational purposes for playing the game and to make clear links to the curriculum. One group of teachers provided lengthy, detailed introductions on the curricular objectives of using particular games, whereas other teachers perceived the games as experiments and left it more up to the students to set their own goals in relation to the game. Based upon the findings, identifying a proper way of introducing a game is difficult as doing so depends wholly upon the relationship between the game design, the curricular objectives, and the pedagogical approach chosen by the teacher, i.e. was the game primarily intended to be entertaining, as a drilling exercise, as an open-ended inquiry, or as a realistic simulation? However, no matter how and why the teachers decided to introduce a game scenario, the studies show that it was highly important for the student learning experience that the teachers were able to communicate a clear idea of how the game practices were linked to educational aims.

The Teacher as Playmaker

In contrast to the teacher role as instructor, which is strongly defined in all my studies of Game-Based Teaching, there were significant differences in the ways teachers performed as playmakers. In some cases, the teachers were thoroughly familiar with the game dynamics and enacted a strong presence as playmaker, e.g. by interrupting the game session in response to student game practices or by providing detailed information on different strategies for keeping within the time limit when interviewing non-player characters in the *Global Conflicts* games. Interrupting the game in this manner to present relevant information on the game scenario can also be described as "just-in-time" lessons (Squire, 2004). In other cases, teachers assumed a far weaker role as playmaker by communicating quite limited information on how to play *Global Conflicts*, which often had to do with the fact that the teachers were first-time users of the game. Other teachers deliberately chose not to provide too much information on how to play the game, as they believed the students were able to explore the games on their own. This final pedagogical choice is somewhat problematic as teacher expectations are often too high when it comes to how competent children are at playing games compared to how fast students actually grasp the key dynamics of a given game (Kirkland & Williamson, 2010).

The Teacher as Guide

Similar to the teachers' role as playmaker, there was also significant variation among the teachers regarding how they worked as guides for the students. One group of teachers would actively monitor how students progressed in the games and whether the students played individually or in pairs (e.g. *Global Conflicts*) or in larger groups (e.g. *The Power Game*). These teachers would regularly support students that were stuck in the game, promote on-going reflection in relation to the students' game practices or try to influence the game practices of those students that trailed too far off from the learning objectives, e.g. if students got bored with the *Global Conflicts* game and turned it into a click-a-thon with questionable educational value. Another group of teachers, in contrast, chose to stand back and observe the students more from a distance, by—to quote one of the teachers—"looking over their shoulders." Again, this choice may partly be explained by the teachers' lack of familiarity with the game scenario. However, for some teachers, it was a conscious pedagogical choice to assume the passive role of an observant guide who only responded when directly addressed by the students. This choice was based upon the assumption that it would be wrong to interrupt the students' experience of being immersed in the game. This finding points to an important discussion on how teachers should balance their guidance between assuming an active/interventionist role and a passive/observing role (Dorn, 1989; Belloti et al., 2010; Henriksen, 2010).

The Teacher as Evaluator

The fourth teacher role concerns the teachers' ability to evaluate the game outcomes and students' learning experiences. Again, there was significant variation among the teachers' roles as evaluators. One group of teachers' mostly referred to the student game experiences with *Global Conflicts* or *The Power Game* as curricular "content" at an overall level that more or less matched the curricular aims. These teachers would mainly assess the students' learning outcome through *summative assessment* by focusing on the game outcomes and on how well the students had solved a pre-defined task (e.g. by writing a feature article on the basis of their game experience). Another group of teachers was more interested in *formative assessment* and tried to explore the students' game-based learning processes when "re-playing" core game experiences and critical game events in the end-of-game discussions by relating the game actions of the students with their multiple consequences—both in relation to the game scenario and in relation to real-world events. In this way, these teachers mainly tried to evaluate student learning outcomes by projecting and expanding curricular themes that had emerged during the game scenario.

Teacher Roles vs. Game Design

When identifying game-based teacher roles, it is important to note that the specific modalities, activities, and affordances of particular game designs tend to be quite influential on how a given game can or should be facilitated (Hanghøj & Brund, 2012). Such differences become quite obvious when comparing studies of game sessions based on the 3D computer game *Global Conflicts* with game sessions based on the ICT-supported debate game *The Power Game*. The teachers in both studies were all first-time users, which meant that they had never previously taught with the games before. In spite of their lack of experience, two out of five of the teachers who taught with *The Power Game* decided to re-design important aspects of the game for their own purposes, e.g. by adding a procedure for forming a new government based on the parliamentary election of the game scenario. In contrast, only one out of nineteen teachers who taught with the *Global Conflict* games tried to experiment with different ways of teaching with the game and actively interrupted the students to provide relevant information or to guide students who engaged in disruptive gameplay. To some degree, this relationship between strongly and weakly defined teacher roles can be reduced to a matter of game literacy among the teachers, i.e. how familiar the teacher were with the games they taught. However, based on the significant differences across the two game examples, it is reasonable to assume that the design features and affordances of different game scenarios have quite an influence on the ability of teachers to fulfill *active* versus *passive* roles. In this way, it may be argued that the *Global Conflicts* series represent a relatively "closed" game design with few options for teachers to re-design different ways of playing the game, whereas *The Power Game* represents a more "open" game design, which can easily be re-designed for various educational purposes.

On the other hand, the third example, mentioned earlier with the teacher who used the COTS game *Penumbra* for his course on genres and linguistic awareness, indicates that game-based teacher roles are not simplistically determined by game designs. This particular horror-adventure game, based on a relatively linear game design, may arguably be seen as a more "closed" game space than the *Global Conflicts* games. Players may easily get stuck when solving riddles in *Penumbra*, which is rarely the case with *Global Conflicts*. COTS games such as *Penumbra* are often far more demanding to teach with than educational games, which are mostly designed to be taught, played and completed within the scope of a few hours (Squire, 2004; Sandford et al., 2006; Van Eck, 2009). However, the higher complexity of COTS games does not necessarily result in teachers who are more passive. On the contrary, teachers who are interested in using COTS games apparently also accept that they have to assume a more active role as teacher through higher levels of commitment as these games inevitably require more translation work, curricular re-design, and engagement in order to make sense in a classroom situation. The main point is that the facilitation of GBT is ultimately a question of teacher ownership of the games they teach, which is influenced not only by teacher game literacy and the affordances of particular game designs, but also by teacher game preferences and their pedagogical approaches.

3RD CHALLENGE: INTEGRATING PEDAGOGICAL APPROACHES

Having discussed the challenges of integrating game practices with school practices and the challenges of assuming game-based teacher roles, we will now turn to the third and final challenge, which concerns the relationship between the *pedagogical approaches* of the teachers and the embedded pedagogies of the games to be used for teaching. Here, the term pedagogy refers not only to the act of teaching, but also to the values, discourses, and theories of learning that support it (Alexander, 2008). In this way, teachers must not only be familiar with the games they teach and what roles to assume when teaching with them, but they must also be aware of their assumptions about how learning takes place and how they relate with the pedagogical models of particular games. Given the vast diversity of game formats, genres and dynamics, it is highly important that teachers are able to "read" the learning dynamics of particular games and understand how they may—or may not—relate with the teachers' pedagogical approaches and curricular aims. This challenge is further strengthened by the fact that game scenarios represent contingency models with relatively open-ended outcomes that are often difficult to predict.

Based on the empirical studies mentioned earlier, I have explored how GBT reflects individual teachers' different pedagogical approaches, which involve their own theories of learning, their attitudes towards GBT, and their views on how students can or should construct knowledge when playing games. Inspired by Bruner, the pedagogical approaches of teachers may be seen as "folk pedagogies," as teachers often have strong beliefs or assumptions about how and why they teach that they are not necessarily aware of (Bruner, 1996). This means that their pedagogical approaches toward games also represent different ways of *positioning* themselves in relation to the games they teach (Herrlitz et al., 2007).

Four Pedagogical Approaches

A summarization of my empirical studies of GBT makes it possible to identify four different pedagogical approaches among teachers who use games in their classrooms. These approaches include:

1. Explorative approaches,
2. Scripted approaches,
3. Pragmatic approaches, and
4. Playful approaches.

Table 1 shows that each of these approaches involves different perspectives on game scenarios and they forms of learning they can facilitate, i.e. games as inquiry, training/revision, tools, or self-expression. Finally, each of the four approaches also involves different knowledge criteria (Barth, 2002) for validating what kinds of knowledge that can—and cannot—be learned through games.

Care must be taken not to place teachers into one specific approach as individual teachers often—knowingly or unknowingly—mix several different pedagogical approaches when they teach

Table 1. Pedagogical approaches to GBT

Pedagogical Approach	Game As	Knowledge Criteria
Explorative	Inquiry	Produce new knowledge
Drill and skill	Training/revision	Reproduction of knowledge
Pragmatic	Simulation	Realistic knowledge
Playful	Self-expression	Fun and play

with games. Moreover, the aim of presenting the four approaches is not to advocate any of them in favor of other approaches to GBT. Seen from a pragmatist perspective, it is not possible to determine a priori which pedagogies and games will create the most educational value as this issue always depends on the complex interplay between contextual aims, means, and situations for learning (Biesta & Burbules, 2003). The point is simply that teachers should be *aware* of their own pedagogical approaches in order to create relevant links with the pedagogical models embedded in the games they wish to teach.

Similar to the game-based teacher roles described in the previous section, the relationship between the four pedagogical approaches can also be illustrated as a relationship between two dimensions of meaning making. The first dimension concerns the negotiation of aims—i.e. *curricular aims versus the aims of the game scenario*—which reflects a fundamental challenge when teachers position themselves in relation to their pedagogical approaches. The second dimension concerns *teachers' beliefs and assumptions on how students' game-based knowledge is or should be constructed*, which covers a broad continuum between realism and constructivism. These categories are chosen to describe the range of different validity criteria (Barth, 2002) teachers use when positioning themselves toward the intended and realized learning outcomes of game sessions. For example, one teacher may be quite focused on the use of games for learning basic skills and standardized forms of knowledge, which means that he or she mainly positions the use of games from a realist perspective. Another teacher may be more focused on how games can be used to play or to experiment, which means they primarily position their use of games from a constructivist perspective. Figure 3 shows the relationship between the four pedagogical approaches.

Figure 3. The pedagogical approaches of game-based teaching

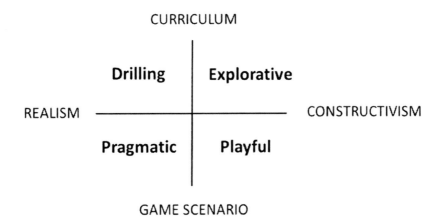

Examples of Pedagogical Approaches

In order to illustrate the challenge of integrating teacher pedagogies and game pedagogies, we will draw attention to two games, *The Power Game* and *Global Conflicts*, which we have studied being enacted by different teachers. The first game is an ICT-supported debate game, which divides players into four to six political parties. Players must then assume roles as politicians, journalists, and spin doctors in an attempt to win a national parliamentary election. The second game is a single-player adventure computer game, where players must explore 3D environments that represent different global conflicts by interviewing non-player characters and then finally confront "bad guys" with controversial information in order to write a journalistic article. In this way, the two games represent quite different game formats and genres with different game dynamics, which also implies different pedagogical models for creating learning environments. More specifically, *The Power Game* provides a multi-player open-ended model for embodied performances through political discourse within the dialogical space of a parliamentary election, whereas the *Global Conflicts* games offer a single-player cognitive model for finding information on particular

ideological conflicts through more or less linear narratives. The two game examples will now be used to illustrate the relationship between the teachers' pedagogical models and the "embedded pedagogies" of the games.

Explorative and Pragmatic Approaches

After observing and interviewing nineteen teachers who have taught using *Global Conflicts*, we identified recurring differences between the teachers who criticized and the ones who accepted the pedagogical model of the game (cf. Hanghøj & Brund, 2012). This variation can be seen as representing a difference between the teachers' *explorative* and *pragmatic* pedagogical approaches to the game. An ICT teacher at an English secondary school who preferred to conduct inquiry-based teaching is one example of a teacher who took an explorative approach to the game. This teacher taught with the game in three different classes and decided to experiment with various ways of playing the game, for example by comparing student findings in the game with Google searches on similar topics. However, in the post-game interview, he expressed some disappointment in the fact that the inquiry model of the game provided a narrow framework for exploration that was too difficult to combine with his open-ended approach to inquiry-based teaching. In contrast, another teacher, who taught secondary social studies at a Danish school, chose a more pragmatic approach by using the game to teach about the social conditions of people in Third World countries. For him, there were also obvious drawbacks with the game, especially the large amounts of text to be consumed by students with poor reading abilities. Still, his overall evaluation of the game was quite positive as he described the game as a tool that could be used to serve specific educational purposes by providing, for example, students with images of human conflicts in Third World countries.

Playful and Drilling Approaches

As mentioned, *The Power Game* is based on a rather open-ended pedagogical model that allows players a large degree of freedom when preparing and performing their roles as politicians, spin-doctors, and journalists. In this way, the game also offers greater flexibility for teachers to "re-design" than *Global Conflicts* does. An illustration of this flexibility is the two different pedagogical approaches to the game, i.e. a *playful* approach and a *drilling* approach, used by five upper secondary social studies teachers who we have observed and interviewed (Hanghøj, 2011a). One of the teachers who exemplifies the playful approach encouraged his students to deliver convincing, entertaining performances. Moreover, he finished the game session by telling his students that the game had shown how politics—just like oral student exams—were full of spin and lies. As a result, this teacher mainly focused on the playful aspects of the game and promoted no critical discussion of how the outcome of the election game was similar or different to the aims of the social studies curriculum or to real-world politics. As an example of a drilling approach to the same game, another teacher decided that *The Power Game* could be used as a revision of last year's introduction to political ideologies. Consequently,

she only touched briefly on the outcomes of the election game and concluded the game session by testing the students' existing knowledge of politics. During the post-game interview, this teacher stressed how she clearly preferred more traditional forms of instruction to games and that she initially felt like a "puppet" being controlled by the game.

Integrating the Pedagogies of Teachers and Games

As the examples suggest, GBT often involves discrepancies between the pedagogical approaches of individual teachers and the pedagogical models of the games they teach. This was illustrated by the teacher who felt challenged by the *Global Conflicts* game design when he attempted to re-design the game for more open-ended forms of inquiry-based teaching. Similarly, the two examples with *The Power Game* show how the pedagogical use of a relatively flexible game design may result in game sessions that either emphasize playfulness or end up testing student knowledge with only a limited relation to their game experience. Finally, the example with the teacher who used *Global Conflicts* shows how teaching with games may benefit from a pragmatic approach, where the teacher follows the intended pedagogies of a given game design to enact a realistic game world.

These findings should not be taken as a complete description of how GBT integrates teacher pedagogies and game pedagogies because several other curricular aims for teaching with games exist that extend the idea of using games as *teaching methods* to learn about particular topics. Examples of other aims for GBT include learning game design and game production (Kafai, 2006), media literacy (Klimt, 2009), and the use of game elements for facilitating innovation processes (Magnussen, 2011). These examples all differ from using educational games as a teaching method, for instance, by focusing on how games can be understood in terms of multimodal texts,

Table 2. Didactical aims for GBT

Didactical Aim	Game As
Teaching *about* games	Text/cultural phenomenon
Teaching *with* games	Teaching method
Teaching *through* game design	Design process and product

cultural phenomena, and design processes. Thus, distinguishing between three *didactical aims* for GBT, shown in Table 2, is helpful (Hanghøj, forthcoming).

As a result, the different pedagogical approaches teachers have toward games cannot be understood without relating them to their didactical aims.

THE FUTURE OF GAME-BASED TEACHING

The aim of this chapter was to present some of the main opportunities and challenges GBT faces. In the following, a number of recommendations will be provided that summarize the discussions and findings presented here as well inform future research and the use of games within educational contexts.

First of all, my description of GBT as an interplay of knowledge practices attempts to show how teachers need to be sufficiently game literate to "translate" game scenarios into the distinct knowledge practices of formal education, which involves curricular knowledge practices, pedagogical knowledge practices and students' everyday knowledge practices. This finding corresponds with other empirically based studies of GBT, which also stress the importance of teacher familiarity with the games they teach in order to create meaningful learning environments (Squire, 2004; Sandford et al., 2006). One answer to developing the game literacy of teachers is that games—along with other forms of digital media—should form a more important part of

teacher education, which rarely offers game-related courses (Sardone & Devlin-Scherer, 2010). However, the analytical framework presented here also points to the need for a more extensive analysis of the interplaying knowledge practices of GBT in order to empirically trace and overcome the perceived dichotomies between "schooling" and "gaming." As mentioned earlier, these categories are historical and cultural constructs, which can be contested and reconstructed—cf. the important on-going work with integrating game elements into the curriculum at the Quest 2 Learn school in New York. There is a strong need for more research on how the categories of work, school, and play/game can become reconfigured, as they all represent culturally defined forms of inquiry along a continuum of meaning-making practices (Dewey, 1916; Huizinga, 1955). By generating new research on the complex relationships between game scenarios, school cultures, curricular issues, and learners' everyday lives, it may be possible to challenge the dichotomies of gaming and schooling and support informed educational change.

Secondly, we have argued how the facilitation of GBT requires teachers to shift between different roles as instructors, playmakers, guides, and evaluators. As the examples show, there is significant variation in the ways that teachers are able to assume these different roles, especially for teachers who are first-time users of a particular game. In summary, the facilitation of games requires that teachers are willing to be *risk takers*, both in relation to the tension between game practices and curricular aims, and when shifting between perspectives on the participants as players and students. In order to gain further understanding of how games can be facilitated, we need more field studies at the micro level that describe game-related dialogue and the interaction between teachers and students (Silseth, 2012). The findings discussed earlier show how the design features of particular games may force teachers to assume more or less passive roles. Seen from a future perspective, it is crucial that educational game designers are able to develop "teacher sensitive" games (Arnab et al., submitted), which focus not only on creating immersive game experiences for players/students, but also on providing active roles for teachers to bring them closer to the game-based learning experiences of students. At the same time, teacher facilitation of games can also be supported in a variety of ways, e.g. by creating databases for sharing lesson plans and course designs (Van Eck, 2009), by creating more efficient communication on how particular game scenarios should be enacted, such as distributing online videos of actual game sessions, or by creating online learning communities around particular game scenarios such as the *Quest Atlantis* game world. Further research into such initiatives may help teachers avoid being positioned as passive observers and invite them to take more ownership of the games that they teach.

Thirdly, we have discussed how GBT may benefit from teachers being aware of their own pedagogical approaches and how they position themselves in relation to the pedagogies embedded in particular games. Teachers always embody pedagogical values and assumptions on learning that may or may not be successfully integrated with particular game designs. As the examples show, the pedagogical approaches of teachers to games can roughly be categorized as explorative, pragmatic, playful, and drilling, which mirrors the teachers' conceptions of games as learning resources and their knowledge criteria for validating what counts and what does not count as relevant game-based knowledge. Given the crucial significance of the teacher as a professional practitioner in choosing, facilitating, and legitimizing games for educational purposes, it is problematic to over-emphasize the importance of game design as an isolated aspect of educational gaming. Following this line of thinking, future research on GBT needs fewer de-contextualized studies of the inherent learning potential of "good game designs" (Gee, 2003; Becker, 2008) and more messy details on how teacher pedagogies

and game pedagogies can—or cannot—become integrated within classroom settings.

Finally, we wish to point to the methodological challenge of studying GBT, which is perhaps the largest challenge that researchers face when trying to understand and promote the use of games in formal education. With the growing number of empirical studies on GBT, the important role of the teacher is slowly receiving more recognition within the research field of games and learning, which has been dominated by relatively determinist approaches. Still, additional *contextualized* research on how games are used to teach is necessary. This is not an easy task. Seen from a methodological perspective, the study of the everyday use of games in schools is constrained by the fact that particular games or game environments are often only used a few times within quite limited time frames that must cover pre-defined curricular aims (Hanghøj & Meyer, 2010). As a result, providing context-sensitive descriptions of educational game sessions is difficult as they are mostly enacted and regarded as rather ephemeral phenomena within school settings. In response to this challenge, some researchers have studied games in more "game friendly" environments such as extracurricular activities designed for after school settings or summer schools (Squire, 2004; Shaffer, 2006). Even though these studies provide important knowledge on game-based learning, it remains questionable whether their findings can be adapted or retrofitted by teachers working within the curricula of mainstream compulsory education. Researchers interested in exploring GBT are consequently often faced with a difficult dilemma of whether to focus on the ideal contexts and convenience samples of designed experiments of games that generate findings that may be difficult to generalize, or to focus on everyday teaching practices with games that may often be difficult to locate even though surveys indicate that a significant percentage of teachers are indeed teaching with games on a regular basis (Williamson, 2009).

CONCLUSION

This chapter has presented analytical frameworks and concepts, which may be used to describe and understand the complex relationship between teachers, students, and game scenarios. The chapter aims to inform future studies of GBT that focus on teachers' translation of game-based knowledge practices, their assumptions and expectations toward games, their shifting roles, and on how their pedagogical approaches relate to the pedagogical models embedded in particular games. As mentioned at the outset, game scenarios represent contingency models for exploring somewhat unpredictable outcomes that mirror not only common conditions for being a citizen in a modern society, but also that offer valuable opportunities for learning scenario competencies. However, games do not facilitate learning on their own. By following the different perspectives on GBT presented here, it becomes possible to describe not only how teachers make pedagogical choices in relation to games but also how these choices reflect both the teachers' own positioning and the way that they become positioned by the games and the educational contexts in which they play and work.

Seen from a curricular perspective, the frameworks presented here can be used to conduct future studies of how games can be integrated into existing school curricula, for example, by analyzing how teachers translate game scenarios into particular curricular knowledge practices (i.e. subject-specific aims, themes, problems). Similarly, the frameworks could also be used for planning activities and aims within a game-based curriculum. The most demanding, but also the most important, part of this translation work involves matchmaking between particular game dynamics and curricular themes. In this way, future research can provide information on how teachers change their perspectives between being *designers of learning scenarios*, which address specific curricular aims, *facilitators of game scenarios*, which provide students with game activities that allow them to make complex and challenging choices, and being *reflective practioners* (Schön, 1983) who theorize and adjust their pedagogical assumptions. Thus, GBT continually requires teachers to design, facilitate, and theorize the educational value of game scenarios within their professional practice.

Due to the complexity and contingency of the game scenarios, the knowledge practices, roles, and pedagogies of Game-Based Teaching imply that game scenarios should not be reduced to "content" and the efficient delivery of pre-defined curricular packages. In this way, GBT fits poorly with the image of the teacher as a transmitter or implementer of existing curricula. Rather, the views on Game-Based Teaching presented here are inextricably bound to the notion of teachers as "curriculum makers" because they are an "integral part of the curriculum constructed and enacted in the classroom" (Clandinin & Connelly, 1992, p. 336; Shawer, 2010). What follows, then, is that the successful integration of games into the curriculum is ultimately a question of providing teachers with sufficient curricular autonomy, game literacy, and knowledge about how to design and facilitate meaningful learning experiences.

ACKNOWLEDGMENT

I wish to acknowledge the participation of all the teachers who have taken part in the empirical studies described here. Moreover, I wish to acknowledge my colleague, Max Møller, who has provided invaluable feedback on many of the ideas presented in this chapter.

REFERENCES

Alexander, R. (2008). *Essays on pedagogy*. London, UK: Routledge.

Arnab, S., Berta, R., Earp, J., de Freitas, S., Popescu, M., Romero, M., … Usart, M. (2012). Framing the adoption of serious games in formal education. *Electronic Journal of e-Learning*.

Atkinson, P., & Housley, W. (2003). *Interactionism: An essay in sociological amnesia*. London, UK: SAGE.

Barth, F. (2002). An anthropology of knowledge. *Current Anthropology*, *43*(1), 1–18. doi:10.1086/324131

Becker, K. (2008). Video game pedagogy: Good games = good pedagogy. In Thomas Miller, C. (Ed.), *Games: Purpose and Potential in Education* (pp. 73–125). New York, NY: Springer.

Bellotti, F., Berta, R., & De Gloria, A. (2010). Designing effective serious games: Opportunities and challenges for research. *International Journal of Emerging Technologies in Learning*, *5*, 22–35.

Biddle, B. J. (1997). Recent research on the role of the teacher. In Biddle, B. J., Good, T. L., & Goodson, I. (Eds.), *International Handbook of Teachers and Teaching* (pp. 499–520). New York, NY: Springer.

Biesta, G. (2010). *What is education for? Good education in an age of measurement: Ethics, politics, democracy*. Boulder, CO: Paradigm Publishers.

Biesta, G., & Burbules, N. (2003). *Pragmatism and educational research*. Lanham, MD: Rowman & Littlefield.

Bourgonjon, J., & Hanghøj, T. (2011). What does it mean to be a game literate teacher? Interviews with teachers who translate games into educational practice. In *Proceedings for the 5th European Conference on Games Based Learning*, (pp. 67-74). Reading, MA: Academic Publishing Limited.

Bruner, J. (1990). *Acts of meaning*. Cambridge, MA: Harvard University Press.

Bruner, J. (1996). *The culture of education*. Cambridge, MA: Harvard University Press.

Buttori, L., & Loh, C. S. (2009). Once upon a game: Rediscovering the roots of games in education. In Miller, C. T. (Ed.), *Games: Purpose and Potential in Education* (pp. 1–22). New York, NY: Springer. doi:10.1007/978-0-387-09775-6_1

Clandinin, D. J., & Connelly, F. M. (1992). Teacher as curriculum maker. In Jackson, P. (Ed.), *Handbook of Curriculum Research* (pp. 363–401). New York, NY: MacMillan.

Dewey, J. (1916). *Democracy and education: An introduction to the philosophy of education*. New York, NY: The Free Press.

Dewey, J. (1922). *Human nature and conduct: An introduction to social psychology*. New York, NY: Cosimo Classics.

Dorn, J. (1989). Simulation games: One more tool on the pedagogical shelf. *Teaching Sociology*, *17*(1), 1–18. doi:10.2307/1317920

Egenfeldt-Nielsen, S. (2004). Practical barriers in using educational computer games. *Horizon*, *12*(1), 18–21. doi:10.1108/10748120410540454

Gee, J. P. (2003). *What video games have to teach us about learning and literacy*. New York, NY: Palgrave Macmillan. doi:10.1145/950566.950595

Gee, J. P. (2011). Reflections on empirical evidence on games and learning. In Tobias, S., & Fletcher, J. D. (Eds.), *Computer Games and Instruction* (pp. 223–232). Albany, NY: State University of New York.

Goffman, E. (1961). Fun in games. In *Encounters*. Indianapolis, IN: Bobbs-Merrill Company.

Goffman, E. (1974). *Frame analysis: An essay on the organization of experience*. New York, NY: Harper & Row.

Hanghøj, T. (2011a). *Playful knowledge: An explorative study of educational gaming.* Saarbrücken, Germany: Lambert Academic Publishing.

Hanghøj, T. (2011b). Emerging and clashing genres: The interplay of knowledge forms in educational gaming. *Designs for Learning, 4*(1), 22–33.

Hanghøj, T. (Ed.). (2013). *Spil i undervisningen.* Aarhus, Denmark: Aarhus University Press.

Hanghøj, T., & Brund, C. E. (2011). Teachers and serious games: Teacher roles and positionings in relation to educational games. In Meyer, B., Sørensen, B. H., & Egenfeldt-Nielsen, S. (Eds.), *Serious Games in Education* (pp. 125–136). Aarhus, Denmark: Aarhus University Press.

Hanghøj, T., & Magnussen, R. (2010). *The role of the teacher in facilitating educational games: Outline of a game pedagogy.* Paper presented at the 2nd Designs for Learning Conference. Stockholm, Sweden.

Hanghøj, T., & Meyer, B. (2010). How to study something that does not exist: Making design interventions with educational games. In *Proceedings of the 4th European Conference on Games Based Learning,* (pp. 123-130). Reading, MA: Academic Publishing Limited.

Henriksen, D. T. (2010). *A little more conversation, a little less action, please: Rethinking learning games for organisational development and adult education.* Saarbrücken, Germany: Lambert Academic Publishing.

Herlitz, W., Ongstad, S., & van de Ven, P.-H. (Eds.). (2007). *Research on mother tongue education in a comparative international perspective: Theoretical and methodological issues.* Utrecht, The Netherlands: Rodopi.

Huizinga, J. (1955). *Homo ludens: A study of the play element in culture.* Boston, MA: Beacon Press.

Joas, H. (1993). *Pragmatism and social theory.* Chicago, IL: University of Chicago Press.

Kafai, Y. B. (2006). Playing and making games for learning: Instructionist and constructionist perspectives for game studies. *Games and Culture, 1*(1), 36–40. doi:10.1177/1555412005281767

Kirkland, K., & Williamson, B. (2010). Playschool: Linking culture and curriculum through games-based learning in schools. In *Proceedings for the 4th European Conference on Games Based Learning,* (pp. 168-176). Reading, MA: Academic Publishing Limited.

Klabbers, J. H. G. (2009). *The magic circle: Principles of gaming and simulation* (3rd ed.). Rotterdam, The Netherlands: Sense Publishers.

Klimmt, C. (2009). Key dimensions of contemporary video game literacy: Towards a normative model of the competent digital gamer. *Eludamos: Journal for Computer Game Culture, 3*(1), 23–31.

Magnussen, R. (2011). Game-like technology innovation education. *International Journal of Virtual and Personal Learning Environments, 2*(2), 30–39. doi:10.4018/jvple.2011040103

Pelletier, C. (2009). Games and learning: What's the connection? *International Journal of Learning and Media, 1*(1), 83–101. doi:10.1162/ijlm.2009.0006

Salen, K., & Zimmerman, E. (2003). *Rules of play: Game design fundamentals.* Cambridge, MA: The MIT Press.

Sandford, R., Ulicsak, M., Facer, K., & Rud, T. (2006). *Teaching with games: Using commercial off-the-shelf computer games in formal education. Research Report.* Bristol, UK: NESTA FutureLab.

Sardone, N. B., & Devlin-Scherer, R. (2010). Teacher candidate responses to digital games: 21st-century skills development. *Journal of Research on Technology in Education, 42*(4), 409–425.

Schön, D. (1983). *The reflective practitioner: How professionals think in action*. New York, NY: Basic Books.

Sefton-Green, J. (2006). Youth, technology and media cultures. *Review of Research in Education, 30*, 279–306. doi:10.3102/0091732X030001279

Shaffer, D. W. (2006). *How computer games help children learn*. New York, NY: Palgrave Macmillan. doi:10.1057/9780230601994

Shawer, S. F. (2010). Classroom-level curriculum development: EFL teachers as curriculum-developers, curriculum-makers and curriculum-transmitters. *Teaching and Teacher Education, 26*(2), 173–184. doi:10.1016/j.tate.2009.03.015

Silseth, K. (2012). The multivoicedness of game play: Exploring the unfolding of a student's learning trajectory in a gaming context at school. *International Journal of Computer-Supported Collaborative Learning, 7*(1), 63–84. doi:10.1007/s11412-011-9132-x

Simpson, E., & Stansberry, S. (2008). Video games and teacher development: Bridging the gap in the classroom. In Miller, C. T. (Ed.), *Games: Purpose and Potential in Education* (pp. 163–184). New York, NY: Springer.

Squire, K. (2004). *Replaying history: Learning world history through playing civilization III*. (PhD Dissertation). Bloomington, IN: Indiana University.

Van Eck, R. (2009). A guide to integrating COTS games into your classroom. In Ferdig, R. (Ed.), *Handbook of Research on Effective Electronic Gaming in Education* (pp. 179–199). New York, NY: Information Science Reference.

Williamson, B. (2009). *Computer games, schools, and young people: A report for educators on using games for learning*. Bristol, UK: NESTA FutureLab.

Wittgenstein, L. (1958). *Philosophical investigations* (Anscombe, G. E. M., Trans.). Oxford, UK: Basil Blackwell.

KEY TERMS AND DEFINITIONS

Game-Based Teaching (GBT): Refers to the teacher practices involved in selecting, facilitating, and validating the use of games for educational purposes. The term is also used in contrast to the commonly used term Game-Based Learning, which tends to neglect teacher perspectives on educational gaming by focusing more on issues such as student motivation, game design features, and the assessment of learning outcomes.

Game Scenario: Used to focus on the most important aspect of games as seen from an educational perspective. Basically, game scenarios refers to games as contingency models that explicitly allow us to imagine, enact, and reflect upon the relationship between particular actions and their actual or possible consequences.

Knowledge Practice: Refers to a "body" or "tradition" of knowledge that involves a substantive corpus of assertions, a range of media and representations, and a social organization (Barth, 2002). Moreover, any knowledge practice always involves specific criteria for validating knowledge. In this way, GBT may be understood as an interplay of different knowledge practices. For example, a game-based course may involve the exploration of a particular game scenario in the *Global Conflicts* series (scenario-specific knowledge practice), the specialized discipline of social studies (curricular knowledge practice), project-based group work (pedagogical knowledge practice), and leisure game experiences (everyday knowledge practices).

Pedagogical Approach: Refers not only to the act of teaching, but also the values, discourses and theories of learning that support it (Alexander, 2008). In this way, GBT always reflects individual teachers' different pedagogical approaches, which includes their own theories of learning, their attitudes towards GBT, and their views on how students can or should construct knowledge when playing games. The pedagogical approaches of teachers may also be seen as "folk pedagogies," as teachers often have strong beliefs or assumptions about how and why they teach that they are not necessarily aware of (Bruner, 1996). This means that the pedagogical approaches of teachers toward games also represent their different ways of positioning themselves in relation to the games they teach (Herrlitz, et al., 2007).

Scenario Competence: A meta-competence defined by the ability to imagine, enact, and reflect upon the relationship between particular actions and their actual or possible consequences in relation to specific knowledge practices. Analytically, scenario competence can be studied in relation to three interrelated aspects: problem scenarios, social scenarios, and identity scenarios. These three aspects may be seen as corresponding terms with the three major functions of education: qualification, socialization, and subjectification (Biesta, 2010).

Teacher Role: The notion of "role" is simultaneously one of the most widespread and most poorly defined terms within the social sciences, and this also goes for teacher roles (Biddle, 1997). Thus, the concept of a teacher role could refer to anything from a teachers' social position to actual classroom behavior to expectations toward his or her own role. In this chapter, teacher role is conceptualized from an interactionist perspective and defined as, "the normative expectation of situationally specific meaningful behavior" (Joas, 1993, p. 226). Following this definition, teacher roles are continually configured and re-configured in relation to the situated enactment of mutual norms and expectations. In this way, teacher roles represent a relational property of social interaction within a classroom context. This means that teacher roles should not be seen as fixed scripts or functions, but rather understood as emerging patterns of interaction and expectations based on processes of continual negotiation between e.g. the teacher, the game scenario, and the students.

ENDNOTES

[1] In an earlier study (Hanghøj & Magnussen, 2010), I have defined a fourth teacher role, which I call *explorer*. On-going feedback from researchers and practioners in the field, however, indicates that this term is too vague to grasp the important task teachers have in providing a formative and summative response to game outcomes and student learning experiences, e.g. by re-playing crucial game events or engaging in critical dialogue. Consequently, the term explorer has been replaced with the term *evaluator*.

Chapter 6
Teachers and Students as Game Designers:
Designing Games for Classroom Integration

Kamisah Osman
National University of Malaysia, Malaysia

Nurul Aini Bakar
Sultan Idris Education University, Malaysia

ABSTRACT

The amount of research done on educational game integration has lately witnessed a large development. Many scholars believe that games can motivate, engage, and stimulate students' higher order thinking skills, and studies have shown that the integration of commercial and popular games in the classroom provide positive impact on students' learning. On the other hand, there are other voices that reveal the multitude of factors hampering the integration of these games into the educational environment. Generally, these factors are derived from the lack of instructional games designed to cater for classroom teaching and learning processes. In this respect, there are efforts made by the educational researchers and game designers to minimize the hampering factors. One alternative some scholars offered to this was for teachers and students to act as game designers, developing games to be used for classroom integration. This chapter explores the possibilities for both trainers and trainees to design games tailored for classroom integration.

INTRODUCTION

Game is a phenomenon that influences most teenagers' lifestyle around the world. Nowadays, the integration of games within classroom teaching and learning processes has gradually become a

DOI: 10.4018/978-1-4666-3950-8.ch006

widespread phenomenon, congruent with their popular reputation among students. Hence, studies have reported on the promising outcomes for games to be integrated into the classroom- to motivate, engage and stimulate students' higher order thinking skills (Barab, et al., 2012; Papastergiou, 2009), while most of the research on this topic investigated the use of the existent commercial and popular games for the teaching and learning process (Amory et al., 1999; Charsky & Ressler, 2011; Sandford et al., 2006; Squire & Jenkins, 2003; Suh, Kim, & Kim, 2010), highlighting their successful integration into classroom activities (Charsky & Ressler, 2011; Facer, 2003; Prensky, 2001a; Squire & Jenkins, 2003; Suh, et al., 2010), even though some found these games to be unsuitable for teaching use (Ertzberger, 2008; McLester, 2005; Okan, 2003; Rice, 2007; Williamson, 2009).

Conversely, the inability of games especially commercial and popular games to be used as learning tools for students has been discussed in relation to various factors. One of the elements that hindered the integration of games in the classroom is the negative perception among teachers and parents to the idea of games used as educational components (Rice, 2007). The already mentioned groups stigmatized games as being merely entertainment devices. The negative perceptions also come from educators who debated on the danger of equating learning with fun, where students might build on a perception that there is no learning without fun. This possible change in the students' learning attitude is feared to have them take learning and studying lightly especially since higher educational level (post-secondary and tertiary) is not usually just fun and entertaining (Okan, 2003).

However, despite their negative perceptions, games are still being introduced in the teaching environment. While a majority of teachers would consider using games in the classroom (Ertzberger, 2008; Futurelab, 2009), there are more factors that prevent them from using these methods as instructional tools, to mention just a few of them: lack of cognitive value in the games due to the emphasized 'play' element (Hogle, 1996); lack of teachers' knowledge about the game/platform/software (Ertzberger, 2008; Williamson, 2009); expensive licensing and costs of games (Ertzberger, 2008; Williamson, 2009); lack of infrastructure capability in schools to effectively integrate the sophisticated and complex games

(Ertzberger, 2008; Williamson, 2009) as well as inflexible school hours to integrate the complex, challenging and time consuming games (Ertzberger, 2008; Williamson, 2009). In addition to the factors stated above, Kamisah and Nurul (2011) suggested that the most problematic nature of the commercial computer games to be used in teaching and learning process is their lack of relevance to the national educational curriculum. Essentially, any computer game needs to be relevant within the curriculum in order to be successfully implemented and integrated into the classroom teaching and learning process. Therefore, any pedagogically innovative game sequence or game on the whole must comply with the particular designated curriculum to a larger or lesser extent.

While there are efforts done by the educational researchers and designers to develop games that compromise the above stated factors, one alternative that has been raised by some scholars is for teachers and students to be game designers and develop suitable and effective games for the classroom integration (Ertzberger, 2010; Kafai, et al., 1998; Prensky, 2008). Hence, since both trainers and trainees are the people directly involved in the teaching and learning process equally, it is reasonable for them to design their own games by themselves. This way teachers and students will have no difficulty in embedding the content of a specific curriculum into the gaming sequence. This approach of designing an educational game will give those involved the opportunity to explore the potential these tools have for classroom integration and share their experiences with parents and educators. Hopefully, the effort would disseminate positive acceptance amongst teachers, parents and educators on the idea of integrating games into the classroom

This chapter will thus further explore the possibilities for both trainers and trainees to be game designers. The discussion will cover topics on

1. Development of educational games,
2. Educational game design,

3. Teachers as game designers, and
4. Students as game designers.

The discussion will focus on two types of learning conditions:

1. Students learning by playing the teacher's designed games, and
2. Students learning by designing and constructing games themselves.

DEVELOPMENT OF EDUCATIONAL GAMES

For years, the production of educational games/software has been dominated by educational software companies since the expansion of market needed electronic educational outputs in the 1990s (Buckingham & Scanlon, 2005). As for the current trend, the rapid pace of technological change makes it possible for the game companies to develop new, more sophisticated, complex and challenging games that can motivate, engage and stimulate students' higher-order thinking skills (Facer, 2003; Prensky, 2001a). There is a lack of coordination between the educational software and games companies and practitioners in the educational field in terms of training, education and instructional design input (Hirumi et al., 2010a). Although it has been proved that excellent commercial and popular games have benefitted from embedded educational value favourable to its players (Hirumi et al., 2010a; Facer, 2003; Prensky, 2001a; Squire & Jenkins, 2003), there are still inordinate factors that hinder classroom integration, as previously stated. In this respect, it is important for game (professional game designers) and education experts (subject-matter experts) to work together in designing and developing educational games (Roslina & Azizah, 2009; Tan, Neill, & Johsnston-Wilder, 2012), towards an effective classroom integration. Along these lines, the issue of scalability (Barbour et al., 2009) is equally important.

The collaboration between game and education experts perhaps is the best solution to produce effective educational games for classroom integration. However, is this approach scalable? We must consider that this asks for special resources and allows for the educational game development, especially since the production of a good quality educational game is extremely costly and requires lots of man's work and time. The educational game developed through this approach will then be expensive and impractical for most teachers wanting to use games in the classroom (Barbour, et al., 2009). Perhaps the approach could be applied by the game companies, but still, in terms of profitability issues, the design of the game would thus focus on broader consumer target and market, and not exclusively on classroom integration and specific curriculum content.

These are just some of the reasons why we propose such an approach to game design which requires both parties involved with the trainer and trainee to act as games designers for effective and practical alternatives to classroom integrated activities. Some might argue that teachers and students do not have the expertise to design and create games similar or to successful COTS (Commercial-Off-The-Shelf). On the one hand, this statement is true-the games designed and created by trainers and trainees might not be at par with sophisticated commercial games, nevertheless with a good game design principle and appropriate creating tools, the game will be able to provide an interesting and interactive teaching and learning environment for both teachers and students.

EDUCATIONAL GAME DESIGN

Mclester (2005) emphasized that design is the key to successfully integrate games into the classroom. A well designed game will be beneficial for students' learning while poorly designed game can actually harm (McLester, 2005). Research studies have revealed educational game design and development in various contexts: educational game design models (Amory, 2007; Garris, Ahlers, & Driskell, 2002; Paras & Bizzocchi, 2005; Roslina & Azizah, 2009), educational game design with specific instructional strategies (Huizenga et al., 2009; Kickmeier-Rust & Albert, 2010; Moreno-Ger et al., 2008; Roslina & Azizah, 2008) specific educational game design approach (Prensky, 2001a, 2008; Sandford, et al., 2006; Shelton & Scoresby, 2011). Based on the various educational game design approaches, there are two compulsory components which should not miss- the 'educational' component and the 'game' component (Roslina & Azizah, 2009). The balance between these two prerequisites in game design actually influence the effectiveness of educational games to provide a motivating and engaging learning environment.

Both students and younger children enjoy playing games due to the fun element. However, there is a contradicting view among students on this issue as well, thinking that fun factor will be lost (the 'game' component) when content knowledge is being infused into the game play (Charsky & Ressler, 2011). Moreover, this is backed-up by the idea that entertaining educational games are poor in cognitive values and 'educational' components as such (Hogle, 1996). Both contrasting views might be true to the extent to which interactions between the *educational* and *game* components are asymmetrical. Games that tend to be too academic overload the students and make the playing experience seem dull, with students that learn but are not motivated to play. On the other hand, games that tend to be too entertaining will lead to self-satisfaction as students will feel distracted from apprehending the knowledge embedded. In this situation, students perhaps will be motivated to play but barely learn. Therefore, to achieve the balance between the two components, both educational and game components need to be in harmony with each other. In addition, the balance between game design and instructional design is

something extremely difficult to acquire, making it thus very important for game designers to have the knowledge on both game design and instructional design as well.

Since teachers today are being trained to answer three knowledge perspectives- technological, pedagogical, and content (Technological Pedagogical Content Knowledge – TPCK) (Mishra & Koehler, 2006) this situation enables them to design the ideal educational games. TPCK depicted teachers' needs to attain technological, pedagogical, and content knowledge and explained how this knowledge domains interact with each other (Mishra & Koehler, 2006). The professional game designers, in general, are equipped with technological knowledge in developing games, while they lack the pedagogical and content knowledge, while teachers—on the other hand—are believed to have sufficient technological and pedagogical content knowledge for designing effective educational games for classroom integration (Barbour, et al., 2009).

Furthermore, students as the digital native generation (Prensky, 2001b) have the natural ability to explore the necessary technological skills required to design a game (Prensky, 2008) and since they are familiar with games, they have the experience and knowledge for motivating and engaging games. In this light, the creative process of game design and development with teachers' facilitation and supervision will be the platform for learning and constructing knowledge on the subject matter and improve generic skills. The educational games that students make could then be used by teachers for classroom integration.

TEACHERS AS GAME DESIGNERS

A creative classroom has long been promoted as one of the best condition for students' teaching and learning process (Morgan & Forster, 1999; Wallace, 1986). Thus, to build a creative classroom, teachers need to "become aware and interested"

(Morgan & Forster, 1999, p. 29) in instructional strategies that can encourage creativity. Integration of games into the classroom is an excellent way to promote students' creative thinking. However, it can only be successful when teachers are passionate to make the integration work. Quoting an educator regarding teachers' role in game-based classroom activitiess, one would state that "I would hate to see a room full of students playing a computer game, with a teacher sitting in the back, browsing a Web page" (McLester, 2005, p. 24). Conversely, teachers need to play an active role as a helper and facilitator to students' game play, so that students understand the subject matter embedded in the game, and not just have fun playing and feeling confused on what they should be learning. Therefore, instructional strategies and planning are crucial for teachers to ensure that the instructional objectives and learning outcomes are met during the game play, so these should be included in teachers' instructional design process.

In addition, one important aspect of teachers' instructional design is to cater for diverse learners' needs in today's constantly changing classroom (Gregory & Chapman, 2007). Since teachers are those who understand and recognize students' different standards then teachers' role as game designers would be the key to a successful classroom game integration. By designing the game themselves, teachers have the authority in determining how the instructional strategies will be embedded into the game to cater for students' standards and needs.

One example of how teachers can develop games is by using templates and editables that can be customized to create games, which are suitable for students' specific learning and curriculum needs (Barbour, et al., 2009; Ertzberger, 2010). These template games are created using standard software such as Microsoft Office and since most teachers are familiar with Microsoft Office, they do not need to spend lots of time learning how to employ the tools. PowerPoint and Word-based templates are among the popular ones available online for free, via educational websites such as:

- http://people.uncw.edu/ertzbergerj/ppt_games.html,
- http://jc-schools.net/tutorials/ppt-games/,
- http://it.coe.uga.edu/wwild/pptgames/, and
- http://facstaff.uww.edu/jonesd/games/

Templates provide teachers with pre-designed background story of the game, which just needs the learning materials added into the templates, so the games can be used immediately. That is why, teachers might find the templates and editable games to be very welcoming and effective tools (Ertzberger, 2010), yet some drawbacks of their use might also be mentioned.

While students today are familiar with COTS' sophisticated and complex design, they might find the simplistic template based games lack in challenges and complexity. Moreover, the use of templates also restrains teachers' instructional design and limits the gaming approach that could be integrated into the classroom. This is because most of the pre-designed templates are based on the drill and practise games approach—teachers insert questions related to a specific curriculum into the templates and then apply the games in the classroom. However, template based games can still motivate, engage and stimulate students' higher order thinking skills when they are used as classroom activities support, not as a main tool for classroom teaching and learning process. This type of games was labelled as 'trivial' (Prensky, 2005), containing narrow and shallow content without asking for multiple skills employment. Thus, in order to seriously integrate games into the classroom, it is important for teachers to design and develop specific games that incorporated multiple skills and knowledge.

According to Hong et al. (2009) "different games had different learning effects" (p. 424). Teachers as game designers can integrate different game genres, approaches and instructional strategies into the game design to create different creative and innovative learning environment. Teachers can choose from the various categories of game genres such as: action games, adventure games, role-playing games, as well as game approaches such as: drill and practise games, stable contest games, contextual games et. al. (Hong, et al., 2009), as individual or joint, to create the "game environments in which students' content, skills and attitudes play an important role during the game" (Hong, et al., 2009, p. 425). This approach of game design enables a certain degree of complexity and challenges which asks for the "learning of multiple skills, as well as for the ability to research and communicate outside the game" (Prensky, 2005).

Similar to the template based games, teachers can also create the specific games using standard software such as the PowerPoint. However, the use of this kind of software requires a detailed planning to design and makes the game work effectively. Ertzberger (2010) suggested that there are various types of game creation software that allow game development without programming knowledge needed. Some of the game creation softwares need to be bought and some are even free. Teachers are encouraged to explore this game creation software to ease their job as game designers. What it is also interesting to mention is that teachers can also use these types of software in the classroom as tools for students to construct and design their own games. Needless to mention that there are pros and cons on different softwares, issues which will not be detailed here. Below are some examples of game creation softwares including their website address:

- **GameMaker:** http://yoyogames.com
- **RPG Maker:** http://tkool.jp/products/rpgxp/eng/
- **Jump Craft:** http://jumpcraft.com

Research investigating teachers and students' effectiveness as games designers shows that teachers too, like students, can actually benefit from the act (Kafai, et al., 1998). Like any other

skill, it has been proven that designing games for classroom integration is also a skill that requires time retention to be mastered. In the case of Kafai, et al. (1998) teachers shifted from being extrinsic designers that viewed the content and game ideas separately, into intrinsic designers that integrated the content and game ideas, all the way throughout the process of designing games. However, it was a surprising outcome of the longitudinal research on how quickly teachers, like students, developed this idea and discovered the magnitude of the changes that occurred (Kafai, et al., 1998). The shift of roles shows that "both teachers and students move from either no productive representations or only symbolic representations to the use of pictorial representations, and in some cases multiple representations where the players could choose their representation from some given alternatives" (Kafai, et al., 1998, p. 175). According to Kafai et al. (1998) there are differences between teachers and students representations of game design. Students drew on their experiences through playing games, whereas teachers from their knowledge of the development of children thinking. Games designed by teachers take into account the important elements of students learning process such as the various degrees of students' ability and needs, although not all of the teachers were successful at reaching certain levels of sophistication during the research. (Kafai, et al., 1998). Yet, more experiences teachers will be able, in time, to design a good quality games for classroom integration, a thing proven based on Kafai et al. (1998) findings that teachers do have the ability to design and develop effective educational games for classroom integration.

STUDENTS AS GAMES DESIGNERS

Looked at from the students' perspective, latest research in the field has revealed that students learn better in the process of designing rather than playing a game during classroom integration (Vos, Meijden, & Denessen, 2011). According to Robertson and Howells (2008), the process of designing and developing games has the "potential to be powerful learning environment... that offers opportunities for children to exercise a wide spectrum of skills" (p. 559). Also, Gershenfeld (2011) summarized the potential skills improved by students through game design and development as follows:

Designing a digital game requires one to think analytically and holistically about games as systems, to experiment and test out theories, to solve problems, to think critically and to effectively create and collaborate with peers and mentors. These are all the skills that will be needed in a twenty-first century where virtually every job will involve navigating a complex, ever-changing, digital networked global landscape and where many of the future jobs have yet to be invented (p. 55).

In addition, when designing a game students are required to "have a deep understanding of the subject matter being explored in the game" (Gershenfeld, 2011, p. 56). Thus the designing process, besides being the platform for students' improvement of their twenty-first century skills, it is also a platform for students to construct deeper understanding of the content knowledge. Students as game designers will thus manifest a promising learning approach that could greatly benefit them. However, the implementation of this learning approach needs more "consideration of the educational principles behind this style of learning and strategies for teaching effectively within this framework" (Robertson & Howells, 2008, p. 575). Therefore, the support of teachers who are passionate and capable of handling the teaching and learning process through the game design approach is very important. They, as educators, need to facilitate, assist and aid students in their game design exploratory learning, so that the learning outcomes are successfully achieved.

According to Robertson and Howells (2008), the process of designing and developing a game is an exploratory learning process which gives students freedom to explore and work both independently and collaboratively with the game creating software. Needless to mention though that there are concerns regarding the justification of what students learn and what they achieve during the designing and developing process. That is why teachers need to ensure that there is a balance between the exploratory learning and instruction so that the knowledge gained while designing activities is aligned with the curriculum and learning objectives (Robertson & Howells, 2008). Consequently, teachers' roles are very important in

1. Facilitating the knowledge exchange between learners,
2. Facilitating cross-curricular learning and transferable skills, and
3. Evaluating successful learning (Robertson & Howells, 2008).

Along these lines, there were authors (Prensky, 2008; Robertson & Howells, 2008) who suggested ways to assist teachers in implementing this approach and to ensure that students gained the desired learning outcomes. Some of the suggestions in this respect could be: production of check lists consisting of success criteria for students' game design process (Robertson & Howells, 2008), production of summative questionnaires for students to assist their progress during the game design process (Robertson & Howells, 2008), as well as implementation of mini-game-based curriculum approaches where students are required to design and develop a game based on limited and specific curricular units or learning goals (Prensky, 2008). Examples of students' successful game implementation via student-designer approach can be seen in the works of Kafai et al. (1998), Robertson and Howells (2008), Vos, Meijden, and Denessen (2011) and Gershenfeld

(2011). The findings show that the approach will be effectively and successfully implemented in the classroom teaching and learning process by means of teachers' facilitation and supervision.

CONCLUSION

Teachers and students as game designers are considered as new approaches to integrate game in the classroom. Although there are obvious gaps within the literature review focusing on these topics, there is still a growing interest on the topic; consequently, more educational games will be produced via these approaches in the near future, as a result of the on-going research.

To conclude, this chapter has explored the possibilities for teachers and students to play the role of game designers. However, the discussions are still limited to the questions of why teachers should design games for classroom integration and why the classroom teaching and learning process should be done through game design approach. Thus, discussions on how these approaches should work and be implemented will need further exploration.

What is important is that *teachers as game designers* -approach challenges the concept of *teacher* per se, with the opportunity to develop specific games for their own teaching needs. Also, when teachers become game designers, there will be little concerns on the factors such as lack of cognitive value and relevance of the game to a specific curriculum. Moreover, teachers do not have to worry about the expensive licensing or the cost to implement games in the classroom. This is because they own the games and they themselves are the masters of the game. What is more, the problem regarding teachers who have little knowledge about the game and software will not occur under these circumstances. Additionally, through game design, teachers will be able to cope with the inflexible school hours and schools' infrastructure capability.

On the other hand, *students as game designers* approach offers students valuable learning experiences with wide spectrum of skills and knowledge. By designing and developing games, students will have the opportunity to be creative and experience fun learning through exploring and inventing something new. Also, game building by both teachers and students open the platform for effective students-teachers communication. Via teachers' facilitation and supervision, both students and teachers will be able to share and exchange opinions on how and what makes a game better in terms of both its educational and game component.

Moreover, teachers and students as game designers approach to classroom teaching and learning should be further extended as a compulsory school program or project so that teachers and students can both enjoy the substantial benefits offered by these approaches. Meanwhile government and education stakeholders should consider these approaches as an effective strategy to integrate games into the classroom. Perhaps the issue of budgeting and costing might hinder the national implementation of the program/project. However, taking into consideration the changing market demand which controls the production of consumer products, it is believed that once these approaches are being instigated in schools at national levels they will draw attention from the big budget game companies for funding. Nevertheless, it has to be clear that the intention of this program/project is to produce educational games that are relevant to the national curriculum. Educational games produced through these schools programs/projects then should be compiled in a database so that the games can be integrated into the classroom for free, by both teachers and students around the nation.

REFERENCES

Amory, A. (2007). Game object model version II: A theoretical framework for educational game development. *Educational Technology Research and Development, 55*, 51–77. doi:10.1007/s11423-006-9001-x

Amory, A., Naicker, K., Vincent, J., & Adams, C. (1999). The use of computer games as an educational tool: Identification of appropriate game types and game elements. *British Journal of Educational Technology, 30*(4), 311–321. doi:10.1111/1467-8535.00121

Barab, S., Pettyjohn, P., Gresalfi, M., Volk, C., & Solomou, M. (2012). Game-based curriculum and transformational play: Designing to meaningfully positioning person, content, and context. *Computers & Education, 58*(1), 518–533. doi:10.1016/j.compedu.2011.08.001

Barbour, M., Rieber, L. P., Thomas, G., & Rauscher, D. (2009). Homemade powerpoint games: A constructivist alternative to webquests. *TechTrends, 53*(5), 54–59. doi:10.1007/s11528-009-0326-2

Buckingham, D., & Scanlon, M. (2005). Selling learning: towards a political economy of edutainmnet media. *Media Culture & Society, 27*(1), 41–58. doi:10.1177/0163443705049057

Charsky, D., & Ressler, W. (2011). Games are made for fun: Lessons on the effects of concept maps in the classroom use of computer games. *Computers & Education, 56*, 604–615. doi:10.1016/j.compedu.2010.10.001

Ertzberger, J. (2008). *An exploration of factors affecting teachers' use of video games as instructional tools.* (Unpublished Doctoral Dissertation). Pepperdine University. Malibu, CA.

Ertzberger, J. (2010). *Everybody wins: A teacher's guide to customizing games for any curriculum.* Retrieved October 13, 2011, from http://www.uncw.edu

Facer, K. (2003). *Computer games and learning: Why do we think it's worth talking about computer games and learning in the same breath?* London, UK: Futurelab.

Futurelab. (2009). *NFER teacher voice omnibus February 2009 survey: Using computer games in the classroom.* London, UK: Futurelab.

Garris, R., Ahlers, R., & Driskell, J. E. (2002). Games, motivation and learning: A research and practice model. *Simulation & Gaming, 33*, 441–467. doi:10.1177/1046878102238607

Gershenfeld, A. (2011). From player to designer. *Educational Gaming, 40*(1), 55–59.

Gregory, G., & Chapman, C. (2007). *Differentiated instructional strategies: One size doesn't fit all* (2nd ed.). San Francisco, CA: Corwin Press.

Hirumi, A., Appelman, B., Rieber, L., & Eck, R. V. (2010a). Preparing instructional designers for game-based learning: Part I. *TechTrends, 54*(3), 27–37. doi:10.1007/s11528-010-0400-9

Hogle, J. G. (1996). *Considering games as cognitive tools: In search of effective "edutainment".* Retrieved October 13, 2011, from http://twinpine-farm.com/pdfs/games.pdf

Hong, J. C., Cheng, C. L., Hwang, M. Y., Lee, C. K., & Chang, H. Y. (2009). Assessing the educational values of digital games. *Journal of Computer Assisted Learning, 25*, 423–437. doi:10.1111/j.1365-2729.2009.00319.x

Huizenga, J., Admiral, W., Ackerman, S., & Dam, G. T. (2009). Mobile game-based learning in secondary education: Engagement, motivation and learning in a mobile city game. *Journal of Computer Assisted Learning, 25*, 332–344. doi:10.1111/j.1365-2729.2009.00316.x

Kafai, Y. B., Franke, M. L., Ching, C. C., & Shih, J. C. (1998). Game design as an interactive learning environment for fostering students' and teachers' mathematical inquiry. *International Journal of Computers for Mathematical Learning*, *3*(2), 149–184. doi:10.1023/A:1009777905226

Kamisah, O., & Nurul, A. B. (2011). *Implementation of educational computer games in Malaysian chemistry classroom: Challenges for game designers*. Paper presented at the 10th WSEAS International Conference on Education and Educational Technology (EDU 2011). Penang, Malaysia.

Kickmeier-Rust, & Albert, D. (2010). Microadaptivity: Protecting immersion in didactically adaptive digital educational games. *Journal of Computer Assisted Learning*, *26*, 95–105. doi:10.1111/j.1365-2729.2009.00332.x

McLester, S. (2005). Game plan. *Tech & Learning*, *26*, 18.

Mishra, P., & Koehler, M. J. (2006). Technological, pedagogical, content knowledge: A framework for teacher knowledge. *Teachers College Record*, *108*(6), 1017–1054. doi:10.1111/j.1467-9620.2006.00684.x

Morgan, S., & Forster, J. (1999). Creativity in the classroom. *Gifted Education International*, *14*(1), 29–43. doi:10.1177/026142949901400105

Okan, Z. (2003). Edutainment: Is learning at risk? *British Journal of Educational Technology*, *34*(3), 255–264. doi:10.1111/1467-8535.00325

Papastergiou, M. (2009). Digital game-based learning in high school computer science education: Impact on educational effectiveness and student motivation. *Computers & Education*, *52*(1), 1–12. doi:10.1016/j.compedu.2008.06.004

Paras, B., & Bizzocchi, J. (2005). *Game, motivation and effective learning: An integrated model for educational game design*. Paper presented at the DiGRA 2005 Conference: Changing Views - World in Play. New York, NY.

Prensky, M. (2001a). *Digital-game based learning*. New York, NY: McGraw-Hill.

Prensky, M. (2001b). Digital natives, digital immigrants. *On the Horizon*. *9*(5), 1-6. Retrieved October 13, 2011, from http://www.webcitation.org/5eBDYI5Uw

Prensky, M. (2005). In digital games for education, complexity matters. *Educational Technology*, *45*(4), 22–28.

Prensky, M. (2008). Students as designers and creators of educational computer games: Who else? *British Journal of Educational Technology*, *39*(6), 1004–1019. doi:10.1111/j.1467-8535.2008.00823_2.x

Rice, J. W. (2007). New media resistance: Barriers to implementation of computer video games in the classroom. *Journal of Educational Multimedia and Hypermedia*, *16*(3), 249–261.

Robertson, J., & Howells, C. (2008). Computer game design: Opportunities for successful learning. *Computers & Education*, *50*, 559–578. doi:10.1016/j.compedu.2007.09.020

Roslina, I., & Azizah, J. (2008). *Web based computer games as an educational tools: Mapping the Malaysian surrounding issues*. Retrieved October 13, 2011 from http://eprints.utm.my/24577/2/RoslinaIbrahim2009.pdf

Roslina, I., & Azizah, J. (2009). *Educational games (EG) design framework: Combination of game design, pedagogy and content modeling*. Paper presented at the International Conference on Electrical Engineering and Informatics. Selangor, Malaysia.

Sandford, R., Ulicsack, M., Facer, K., & Rudd, T. (2006). *Teaching with games: Using commercial off-the-shelf computer games in formal education*. London, UK: Futurelab.

Shelton, B. E., & Scoresby, J. (2011). Aligning game activity with educational goals: Following constrained design approach to instructional computer games. *Educational Technology Research and Development, 59*, 113–138. doi:10.1007/s11423-010-9175-0

Squire, K. (2006). From content to context: Videogames as designed experience. *Educational Researcher, 35*(8), 19–29. doi:10.3102/0013189X035008019

Squire, K., & Jenkins, H. (2003). Harnessing the power of games in education. *In Sight, 3*, 5-33.

Suh, S., Kim, S. W., & Kim, N. J. (2010). Effectiveness of MMORPG-based instruction in elementary English education in Korea. *Journal of Computer Assisted Learning, 26*, 370–378. doi:10.1111/j.1365-2729.2010.00353.x

Tan, W. H., Neill, S., & Johsnston-Wilder, S. (2012). How do professionals' attitude differ between what game-based learning could ideally achieve and what is usually achieved. *International Journal of Game-Based Learning, 2*(1), 1–15. doi:10.4018/ijgbl.2012010101

Vos, N., Meijden, H. V. D., & Denessen, E. (2011). Effects of constructing versus playing an educational game on student motivation and deep learning strategy use. *Computers & Education, 56*, 127–137. doi:10.1016/j.compedu.2010.08.013

Wallace, B. (1986). Creativity: Some definitions: The creative personality; the creative process; the creative classroom. *Gifted Education International, 4*(2), 68–73. doi:10.1177/026142948600400202

Williamson, B. (2009). *Computer games, schools and young people: A report for educators on using games for learning.* London, UK: Futurelab.

ADDITIONAL READING

Amory, A. (2010). Learning to play games or playing games to learn? A health education case study with Soweto teenagers. *Australiasian Journal of Educational Technology, 26*(6), 8100–8829.

Carro, R., Breda, A., Castillo, G., & Bajuelos, A. (2006). A methodology for developing adaptive educational-game environments. In De Bra, P., Brusilovsky, P., & Conejo, R. (Eds.), *Adaptive Hypermedia and Adaptive Web-Based Systems* (Vol. 2347, pp. 90–99). Berlin, Germany: Springer. doi:10.1007/3-540-47952-X_11

Hirumi, A., Appelman, B., Rieber, L., & Eck, R. V. (2010b). Preparing instructional designers for game-based learning: Part II. *TechTrends, 54*(4), 19–27. doi:10.1007/s11528-010-0416-1

Hirumi, A., Appelman, B., Rieber, L., & Eck, R. V. (2010c). Preparing instructional designers for game-based learning: Part III. *TechTrends, 54*(5), 38–45. doi:10.1007/s11528-010-0435-y

Ketelhut, D. J., & Schifter, C. C. (2011). Teachers and game-based learning: Improving understanding of how to increase efficacy of adoption. *Computers & Education, 56*(2), 539–546. doi:10.1016/j.compedu.2010.10.002

Kirriemuir, J., & McFarlane, A. (2003). *Use of computer and video games in the classroom.* Paper presented at the Level up Digital Games Research Conference. Dordrecht, The Netherlands.

Lee, J., Luchini, K., Michael, B., Norris, C., & Soloway, E. (2004). *More than just fun and games: Assessing the value of educational video games in the classroom.* Paper presented at the Conference on Human Factor in Computing System. Vienna, Austria.

Lewandowski, F. D. S., & Pereira, A. (2009). The development of educational games supported by a pedagogical tutor agent. In Tatnall, A., & Jones, A. (Eds.), *Education and Technology for a Better World* (*Vol. 302*, pp. 169–177). Boston, MA: Springer. doi:10.1007/978-3-642-03115-1_18

Moreno-Ger, P., Burgos, D., Ortiz, I. M., Sierra, J. L., & Fernandez-Manjon, B. (2008). Educational game design for online education. *Computers in Human Behavior*, *24*(6), 2530–2540. doi:10.1016/j.chb.2008.03.012

Overmars, M. (2004). *Game design in education.* Retrieved March 22, 2012, from http://archive.cs.uu.nl/pub/RUU/CS/techreps/CS-2004/2004-056.pdf

Tan, W. H., Johnston-Wilder, S., & Neil, S. (2011). Game-based learning with a dialogic teaching approach: A case of deep-learning and the use of Spore™ in a-level biology lessons. In Felicia, P. (Ed.), *Handbook of Research on Improving Learning and Motivation through Educational Games: Multidisciplinary Approaches* (*Vol. 1*). Hershey, PA: IGI Golobal. doi:10.4018/978-1-60960-495-0.ch039

KEY TERMS AND DEFINITIONS

Game Building: The act of designing and developing a game.

Game-Based Learning: A learning approach that employs electronic games as teaching and learning tools.

Instructional Game Design: Game design that caters for the need of instructional process which comprises of the technological, pedagogical and content knowledge components.

Instructional Games: Games that have been developed specifically for instructional purposes.

Integration of Game in Classroom: Integrating games in classroom teaching and learning processes, either as teaching or learning tools.

Student as Game Designer: A teaching and learning approach where students will build a game with teachers' facilitation. Through this game building activity students will have the knowledge transferred.

Teacher as Game Designer: Teacher designing and developing instructional games to be used as classroom teaching aid in the learning process.

Chapter 7
Integrating Games into the Classroom:
Towards New Teachership

Harri Ketamo
Eedu Ltd., Finland

Sylvester Arnab
Coventry University, UK

Kristian Kiili
Tampere University of Technology, Finland

Ian Dunwell
Coventry University, UK

ABSTRACT

The game-based learning approach has already shown its strengths from the learners' point of view. However, there are numerous unrevealed ways to support teachers' work within the game-based approach. Unfortunately, games that exclude the teacher from the game-based learning process dominate the markets, which is of great concern. Thus, the aim of this chapter is to study the use of novel game features that enable teachers to participate in game-based learning events. In this chapter, the teacher's role in the game-based learning process is considered through several different game examples that are designed to fulfill both learners' and teachers' needs. The examples show that there are both computational and non-computational methods that can be used to support learning and teachers' work in the game world. Based on previous results it can be argued that the diffusion of game-based learning can be facilitated only if both learners' and teachers' needs and goals are taken into account.

INTRODUCTION

If a teacher from 1910s would come to classroom at 2010, he or she would notice that something has changed, but not remarkably. However, the same reaction would not be possible either for doctors or process workers in factories. Why teaching

DOI: 10.4018/978-1-4666-3950-8.ch007

remains the same? If we take a deeper look into teachers work, we notice that classroom has not changed, but the skills required from a teacher have been dramatically changed. Nowadays teacher is seen more like a coach for learning. Furthermore, the real point for discussion is how the educational technology research has forgotten the practical dimension of the teachership, especially in game based learning solutions. It has become evident that teachers would need more effective tools for coaching, management, and assessment.

In recent years, Game Studies has rapidly developed into an important interdisciplinary research field as well as a nascent academic discipline. The rapid growth of the game industry has aroused wide interest, particularly among educational technology researchers as well as digital learning material producers and publishers. It is known that the possibilities to use digital games in education have been considered since the 70s. Nevertheless, the concrete and scientific ambitions to produce high quality educational games have been quite minor. Actually, the quality of produced games has not met the expectations of the educators and the use of games has not become as general as expected. Probably, the most significant factors that have lowered the quality of educational games have been the lack of a theoretical game design foundation as well as game developers' low yield expectations. In fact, the overall level of educational games indicates that the usefulness and the real power of game-based learning have still not been fully realized.

Apparently, the rapid growth of the entertainment game market has reawakened the interest of educational researchers and producers. It seems that games will get another chance to prove their usefulness in computer-assisted learning. At least the starting point for this revival is better than before. First of all, researchers have understood the meaning of pedagogical foundation in educational game design (e.g. Dunwell, de Freitas & Jarvis, 2011; Ketamo & Suominen, 2010; Kiili, 2007, Kiili & Ketamo, 2007; Amory & Seagram, 2003; Garris, Ahlers & Driskell, 2002). Secondly, the infrastructure of schools has developed a lot during the last decade. Thirdly, it has been argued that we are moving towards a new generation of educational use of games (e.g. Egenfeldt-Nielsen, 2007). According to Egenfeldt-Nielsen (2007) such third generation educational games rely on a socio-cultural approach, where the learning process is seen as being mediated in a social and

situated context. Furthermore, third generation educational games focus on the students' engagement with games (Gee, 2003) and emphasize the meaning of the teacher as a facilitator that expands the scope of computer games from just playing to learning (Egenfeldt-Nielsen, 2007). However, research dealing with third generation educational games has been mainly conceptual and is lacking of the empirical grounding of the approach.

In general, game based learning approach has shown its strengths and opportunities from the learners' point of view (e.g. Ketamo & Kiili, 2010a; Ketamo & Kiili, 2010b; Virvou et al., 2005; Ketamo, 2003; Sinko & Lehtinen, 1999). However, there are numerous unrevealed opportunities to support teachers' work with game based approaches. Support is not limited only to on-line game statistics, but game based approaches can extend teachers' role in very meaningful ways.

In this chapter, teacher's role in game based learning process is considered through several game examples that can be classified to third generation educational games. We consider teacher's role in game-based learning with the help of AnimalClass game, Eedu Elements game, Media Detective game, ALICE Fire Evacuation game, and Magos game-authoring environment. We argue that these game based solutions are rare, because the development of these games has focused on fulfilling both learners' and teachers' needs.

CASE STUDIES

This research is a meta study about authors' research between 2005 and 2012 in the area of educational games. The games have been studied in terms of educational sciences, usability, user experience and technology. Such exhaustive research results make it possible to create summaries about pedagogical use of educational games from classroom integration and a teacher point of view. The detailed list about used background research materials is presented in the Additional Readings section. The overall aim of this paper is to uncover the opportunities that third generation educational games can provide for schools and raise discussion about teachers' role in game based learning. Five case studies presented in this chapter consider educational use of games from several perspectives and that way provide quite exhaustive view on the theme. In general, the discussed approaches are meant to strengthen and speed up teachers' work in game based learning environments.

Integrating Games into Classroom: AnimalClass Case

The AnimalClass game series is developed according to Finnish curriculum. The background of the games is in Learning by Doing (Dewey, 1938/1997), Learning by Teaching and Learning by Programming (Papert, 1980). The idea of AnimalClass is to put a learner (player) into the role of a teacher. In AnimalClass the player has complete freedom to teach his virtual pet however he wants, even wrongly. The pet learns the things that are taught. The results described in this section are based on authors' previous studies and general feedback that teachers have provided after using the games in teaching.

Case Specific Background

In AnimalClass case, learning is discussed and analyzed in terms of conceptual change. Traditionally, most learning theories rely on the assumption that concepts change through an enrichment of prior knowledge (Vosniadou, 2007). Conceptual change differs from these learning theories, because it cannot be achieved through additive mechanisms involving only the enrichment of pre-existing knowledge. In fact, the conceptual change approach emerged from an effort to explain the radical reorganization of conceptual knowledge and acquiring an understanding of difficult concepts (Vosniadou, 2007).

Merenluoto's and Lehtinen's (2004) model of processes of conceptual change describes a learning situation in which the learner experiences tasks dealing with phenomenon calling for a new conceptual understanding. A learner's cognitive, metacognitive, and motivational sensitivity to the task influences how the learner perceives the task. With sensitivity Merenluoto and Lehtinen (2004) mean the extent to which the learner is aware of and interested in the novel cognitive aspects of the phenomenon. The model distinguishes three possible learning paths: the experience of conflict, the illusion of understanding, and having no relevant perception. These paths that form the theoretical basis of this research are briefly presented next (for a more detailed description, see Merenluoto & Lehtinen, 2004).

The first path, the experience of conflict may lead to radical conceptual change. The optimal level of prior knowledge of the phenomenon, sensitivity to novel features of the situation, and the process of tolerating the ambiguity resulting from experienced conflict are critical processes in conceptual change. The experience of cognitive conflict reduces a learner's certainty about the phenomenon. Thus, the learner does not rely only on his/her prior knowledge, but is ready to change his/her knowledge beliefs. Toleration of ambiguity is crucial. "Coping with a complex conceptual system is possible only if a learner has sufficient metacognitive skills to grasp the conflicting notions" (Merenluoto & Lehtinen, 2004, p. 525). Also motivational aspects affect how a learner deals with ambiguity. If tolerance of ambiguity is high, a learner feels that the experienced conflict is solvable. In contrast, low tolerance of ambiguity may decrease sensitivity or lead to a loss of trust, resulting in low certainty and avoidance behaviour.

In the illusion of understanding path, conflict is passed by unnoticed because of overconfidence. Self-efficacy and high motivation may increase a learner's tendency to take the illusion of understanding path. On this path, a learner recognizes some familiar elements in the new phenomenon, but his/her prior knowledge is not adequate for paying attention to the novel aspects of the phenomenon that go beyond his/her current conceptions. Familiar elements of the phenomenon arouse an illusion of understanding, which leads to an enrichment of naïve models or the construction of synthetic models. However, high motivation may lead to perception of the conflict and result in more radical conceptual change later on. In fact, Merenluoto and Lehtinen (2004) argue that cognitive change requires time. Thus, in mathematics learning games it is important to engage learners in playing for as long as possible in order to maximize the probability of conceptual change taking place.

In the no relevant perception path, the learner misses the conflict because of his or her broad cognitive distance to the phenomenon to be learned. The possible cognitive overload (Sweller, van Merrienboer, & Paas, 1998) confuses the learner and may lead to avoidance behaviour or routine activity unrelated to the cognitive demands of the task. Because any attempts to create cognitive conflicts are doomed in this path, game elements facilitating conceptual change cannot be designed for these learners. The only way to support these learners is to provide them with the information that is needed to understand the phenomenon and so be able to perceive the cognitive conflicts.

Description and Learning Activities of the Game

At the beginning of the game, a player gets his own virtual pet, a teachable agent, which wants to learn mathematics, natural sciences, languages or music depending on the game title. The task of the player is to teach his pet the content related to the subject of the game. In the beginning, the virtual pet does not know anything; its mind is an empty set of concepts and relations. The player has complete freedom to teach the pet what he wants. Teaching is performed in the classroom (see Figure 1). In AnimalClass games the teaching

Figure 1. Question construction (top-left); evaluating the question (top-right); calling a friend (bottom-left); competition (bottom-right)

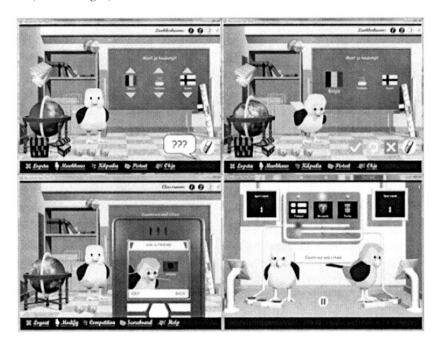

is always based on statements constructed by the player. The pet answers according to its previous knowledge. If there is no previous knowledge, it will guess. The player then tells the agent if pet's answer was correct or not, and based on this, the pet forms relations between concepts and pet's conceptual structure is updated.

The pet learns inductively: Each teaching phase increases and strengthens the network of concepts. During the game play the conceptual structure in the pet's AI evolves. When the virtual pet has achieved a conceptual network of a certain size, it starts to conclude. For example, if the virtual pet knows that concepts A and B belong in the same group and concepts A and C belong in the same group, it can conclude that also B and C belong to the same group. On the other hand, if the virtual pet knows that concepts A and B belong in the same group and concepts A and C belong to different groups, the virtual pet can conclude that B and C belong to different groups. Thus, player does not have to teach everything to their pet and the player can optimize his teaching.

A brain icon above the pet (see Figure 1) is used to describe the quality of learning. If the quality increases, the brains get bigger, and if the quality of learning decreases, the size of the brains get smaller. If the overall concept network is wrong, the brains is replaced by a cactus to show the player that he is doing something completely wrong. This kind of wrong teaching can be corrected by teaching the correct structure enough times. The game AI uses all the taught information behind its decisions and therefore it takes time to override the wrong learning.

The AnimalClass was designed to support reflective thinking. Usability issues were taken into account when there were no risks of decreasing reflective thinking. The major challenge was to design the user interface easy to use, but still leave the thinking and decision-making to the player. For example, the user interface does not inform of the wrong kind of construction of a question. The user can cancel the question and

construct it again if the user figures it out from the pets' answer or answering behavior. In Figure 1, top-left, the player has constructed a question that consists of two concepts that are related and one concept that is odd. When the question is ready, the player asks the question from the pet by clicking the 'ask' –button (balloon with three question marks). The pet answers according to its previous knowledge. The virtual pet answers anyway, even if it does not know the answer or, if the question is impossible, in these cases it will guess the answer. Gestures of the pet indicate whether it guesses or not.

In Figure 1, top-right, the virtual pet has given its answer by pointing out the concept, which it thinks that does not belong in the group. The player should judge the answer: if the answer is correct, the player should click the green 'correct'-button. If the answer is false, the player should click the red 'wrong'-button. If the player notices that he has done an impossible question, the question can be cancelled by clicking the yellow 'cancel'-button.

The classroom supports learning in two ways: In the beginning, constructing a task requires knowledge about the subject. If there is not enough knowledge, player is encouraged to discuss the problem with their friends. During this process, the player has to apply his knowledge and/or increase his knowledge. This process can also be seen as non-formal learning, where a player's interest (achieved by playing) directs the learning rather than formal instructions. Secondly, judging the answers requires specific knowledge about the question. Basically, a player can construct a question with less knowledge than answering requires. Now when the player should also judge the answer, the game also requires detailed knowledge about the subject combined with applied knowledge.

The player can send his/her pet to a competition (Figure 1, bottom right). In the competition, the pet competes in a quiz against someone else's pet that has been taught by a real person (possibly a friend or classmate). The game server constructs the questions and judges pets' answers that are determined based on players' previous teaching. The role of the player is to observe the successes and failures of his/her pet in order to grasp the pet's current skills and misconceptions. Of course, many players tend to encourage their pets in the competition by whispering comments to their pets, like "Hey, it's the one in the middle." Also this kind of encouragement supports learning: when a player tries to advise the virtual pet he has to solve the question at the same time. A competition challenge is automatically accepted; a player cannot refuse to compete. Because the competition is based on the conceptual structures of pets (previous teaching), the challenged player can be offline. Furthermore, in order to support social interaction a call-a-friend application was implemented into the game (see Figure 1, bottom left). Call-a-friend enables to ask questions (answers to created questions) from friends' pets.

Teacher's Role in the AnimalClass Games

The results of our previous studies support the possibility to mine (in terms of Data Mining) detailed information about learning and playing processes and provide such information for teachers (e.g. Ketamo & Kiili, 2010b). The teacher tool was designed to be easy and fast to use in classrooms. It was meant to improve teacher's capabilities to instruct pupil in real time. Because the semantic networks are slow to search or analyze manually, the most relevant information is mined, compressed and presented at four main areas of the teacher tool.

In the beginning, all the available concepts are on the 'not taught'-area. After teaching the virtual pet the concepts form a network with multiple relations and this structure is mined and compared to correct structure. According to this analysis, the concepts are presented either as 'correctly taught' or as 'wrongly taught' concepts. If the conceptual network is correct and strong around a concept, the concept will be upgraded into the well-taught area.

In just a few seconds a teacher can see what is wrong in some pupil's game play and after that teacher can help the pupil by providing some relevant correction suggestions. The idea is that a teacher can encourage pupil to think reflectively and point out problems in pupil's previous teaching. Teacher should not correct pupils' game play, but pupils should do it himself. With this tool, a teacher can manage game play even in large groups such as 20-30 pupils.

The game play can be used to support teacher's work also in terms of social networks: Because competing against classmates tells something about class's real world social networks, it could be useful to provide this information to a teacher. The formation of social networks is done with similar Data Mining methods than teacher tool's diagnostics. According to previous studies (e.g. Ketamo & Suominen, 2008) we can point out 1) two main types of social networks and 2) two clearly definable minor types of social networks.

First major type of social network is formed by the persons at the top of the ranking list of the game and their challengers. The cluster itself was not a surprise, but the clarity of the cluster from a modeling point of view is a bit of a surprise. Nevertheless, there was no hypothesis set in advance; the clusters were expected to be more 'noisy' and not as clear as structures. The second main group of the social networks was formed between, for example, classmates or other friend based groups (Figure 2). In these groups, the dominant feature was tightness of the group: There were many considerably strong two-way relations, but only a few one-way relations in these groups.

Two clearly defined, but not so frequent, types of social networks (less than 5% of the population) appeared, for example, in groups based around a central person and refer to a situation in which a center person has either two-way or one-way relations to other members, but other members do not even have one-way relations to one another themselves (Figure 3).

Figure 2. The social network structure of a 'classmates' type of group. The usernames are partially hidden in order to minimize the possibility of recognizing players.

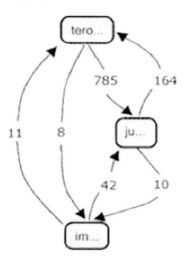

In Figure 3, left network, a central person is challenged by several classmates or friends. This can be explained either as a mobbing or as a leadership. In a case of mobbing, the classmates pick up an opponent that they know is e.g. low skilled in the game domain. However, if a person is likely to be mobbed, he/she can remain anony-

mous by not telling his/her username. Classmates cannot figure out a username in the game, but they certainly can force a mobbed pupil to tell his username. In a case of leadership, the classmates pick an opponent that is a central person of the class's real social network. Furthermore, if a person is a social leader of the class, he/she probably challenges his/her friends as in Figure 3 right network. To conclude, the visualization of players' social structures may facilitate the teacher to maintain better control of his/her class also in the virtual game world.

Findings and Discussion

In AnimalClass games the teaching of own virtual pet was found very motivating. The development of a virtual pet's conceptual structures makes possible to uncover the frequencies, dependencies, and patterns behind conceptual change. An interesting finding was that learners could use different playing strategies to achieve good results.

From teacher's point of view, AnimalClass enables almost any didactic approach: from teacher centered classroom management to social learning with peers and from Behavior-

Figure 3. Left network: possibly a case of mobbing? Right network: social leadership? The usernames are partially hidden in order to minimize the possibility of recognizing players.

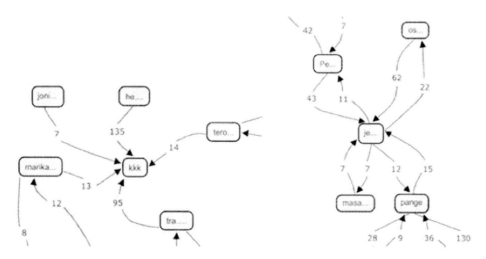

istic stimulus-response tracking to open ended learning-by-doing. Furthermore, the teacher tools in AnimalClass supports teacher in several way. In classroom level, teacher can check the progress in general at class or he/she can search themes that are difficult for most of the pupils. In individual level teacher can find in seconds what to discuss with individual pupil.

The biggest challenge in AnimalClass is the learning curve of the game itself. The gameplay and the aim of the game is difficult to realize for pupils. Furthermore, the teacher tools are like research tools, a teacher have to use time to start to use the tools.

Integrating Games into Classroom: eedu Elements Case

From educational outcome point of view, AnimalClass was a success. Furthermore, the game mechanics and AI was awarded in several educational and games industry contests. However, the game never made a worldwide breakthrough in everyday classroom use. One reason was that the gameplay was not easy to start. In other words, it takes more than 15 minutes to clearly understand the idea of the game. Finally, AnimalClass was only a collection of different themes, not a complete solution like a textbook and thus it was not appealing enough for teachers.

The following eedu Elements game solves these two major challenges: its gameplay can be learned in 15 seconds, it is extremely easy to take in use in schools and at home. Methodologically Eedu Elements applies similar solutions as AnimalClass (see: Ketamo 2009; Ketamo 2011). Finally, it is not just a game, it is a Finnish school (currently mathematics) delivered in a game format. In this way all children can access Finnish curriculum and learning-by-doing style of teaching. Basically the goal Eedu Elements is to produce equal education for all.

Game Description and Learning Activities

In the game mice can get cheese only by getting through mathematics labyrinths faster than cats can. Players' task is to teach necessary skills for their pets (mice). When their pets do have enough skills player can send it to labyrinth to survive on its own - catch the cheese before the cat.

Understanding the story is a critical point for player in order to get good gaming experience. In our first tests too many pupils didn't get the idea from external instructions, so the story and all instructions were embedded into the game as comic strips. Similar type instructions appear every time when a player moves into a new task or into a new kind of gameplay. The instructions can be skipped, but e.g. pre-school and first grade pupils like to watch the instructions time after time. In other words, they really perceive the ideas how to play the game and also like the comic strips as stories.

To give the pupils a feeling that characters are really their pets, there are several mice and cats to choose. If player chooses a mouse, it is expected that the mouse is taught correctly. In case player wants to help mice, he/she can start teaching cats wrongly. The idea in teaching wrongly is simple: many pupils are afraid of showing his/her weak skills. When the aim is to fail, it does not matter if you sometimes teach correctly. Eventually, before you can teach wrongly, you have to know correct answers, and so the process is same as when teaching correctly.

When starting teaching, the pet goes to classroom (Figure 4). In the classroom a teacher (owl) asks questions from mice and cats. Player can help his/her pet by pointing the pet's thoughts. The pet learns exactly according to the teaching. If the player teaches correctly, the pet learns correctly and vice versa. After the player has taught enough conceptual relations for his/her pet, a challenge

Figure 4. An example of the classroom (left); an example of the labyrinth (right)

icon appears on the screen. By clicking the icon, player sends his/her pet into the labyrinth to compete against the cat. In labyrinth (Figure 4) the pet is on its own and player's task is to observe how it manages in the competition.

In the labyrinth both characters pick the doors according to their taught knowledge. During the labyrinth player can observe what to teach more. If mouse wins, the level is completed and next level becomes playable. The achievements are auto-saved and all the completed levels remains playable—of course, the player may want to achieve the maximum numbers of stars into his/ her badge.

When all features are implemented in fall 2012, the game characters can compete against any other taught character any time, no matter if the human player is online, because all the taught behavior and skills in pets' AIs (brains) are always available in online. According to our previous studies, the social connections in the game and in the real world during the game play are important elements for the motivation (Ketamo & Suominen, 2008; Kiili, Ketamo & Lainema, 2011).

Each grade consists of 45 or more levels, containing hundreds of different exercises per level. The game as well as the content will evolve all the time, so players are not expected to get bored after played the game once. Furthermore, the production technology has been designed in a

way that enables very cost effective production. All assets are reusable and easily updated. Adding new exercises or new levels can be done in hours. Designing a whole new grade takes only few weeks if there is no need for new graphics. Graphics design, as design, we cannot speed up.

Teacher's Role in the eedu Elements

Eedu Elements game's skills -tool is meant for parents and teachers to quickly observe what the learner has taught for his/her pet. The visualization shows correctly taught concepts in the upper part of the skills-area and wrongly taught concepts in the lower part of the area. In a case pupil is teaching cats, it is expected that the most concepts are in the lower part of the area. The quantity of the teaching is visualized in a way that concepts that are taught a lot appears in the right side of the area and little taught concepts on the left side of the area. Quantity of teaching also means that what more relations a concept does have, that more right it is located. Concepts that have not been taught do not appear in the skills -area at all.

When focusing on dependencies between the taught conceptual structure of pets and pupils achievements measured with traditional paper tests, we can show that the taught conceptual structure is strongly related to the post-test score ($0.4 < r < 0.7$) with all tested content on mathematics and natural sciences. This is an important result in terms of reliability of the game as assessment/evaluation instrument. In the game one level represents approximately one school week in Finnish curriculum. In the game, the player can get one to three stars when completing the labyrinth. If the player completes the level with one star that represents satisfactory skills while three stars represent good skills. However, the results of the gameplay are always a bit fuzzy: a player can have just good luck and receive three stars with two stars performance. Furthermore, once and a while a nearly perfect mouse can lose in a labyrinth if there is just that one difficult question for it. So the evaluation/assessment with Eedu Elements in a single level is only indicative, but completing a whole grade requires skills that would be required to pass the same grade in a Finnish school.

Furthermore, when summarizing the game achievements, the schools and the national level policy makers can receive analysis about competences and skills in general level in order to develop their teaching or formal curriculum. The analytics are that detailed that we can point out general bottlenecks of education: e.g. in Finland there is an interesting bottleneck related to fraction numbers with odd nominator (Figure 5) that we have revealed from playing behavior. These numbers mediate or connect nearly all difficulties related to converting numbers between decimal numbers, fraction numbers and percent numbers. In other words, in Finland we should pay attention on how to teach odd nominated numbers for pupils.

When going deeper in details, wrong answers or misconceptions are not the only relevant factor explaining learning outcome. According to data received from gameplay, avoiding number (or concept) indicates directly poor performance in such concept. In Figure 6 some of the numbers and frequencies avoiding the numbers during the gameplay are presented. In fact we can see that once again the most avoided numbers are the odd nominated fraction numbers.

Findings and Discussion

From teacher's point of view, the easy start of the pedagogical activity in the classroom is one of the most important features. The second big feature is the gain. This does not mean only educational outcome, but also how a teacher can apply the tool in his/her classroom management. Thus, educational game should be designed in a way that it is 1) fast and easy to start, 2) requires only little or none technical support, 3) provides something useful for a teacher, and 4) does not restrict teacher's classroom management.

In the classroom use, eedu Elements is really easy to start: Teacher just gives tablets to pupils and playing can be start. Pupils, today, learns very fast how to use tablets and they are not afraid to

Figure 5. Misunderstood numbers and the strongest dependencies between misconceptions

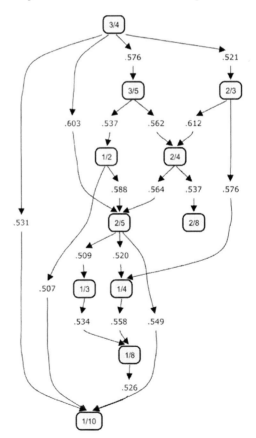

Figure 6. Frequencies of correct answers, wrong answers and avoided numbers. Unclear means that in some cases an individual player has understood such number correctly while in other cases he/she has not.

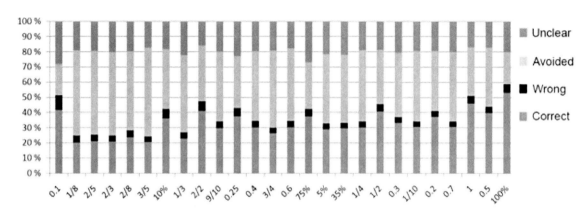

ask help from classmates when having troubles. Furthermore, the game play can be learned really fast, in seconds, so the teacher does not have to explain what to do. However, some teachers still feel themselves outliers when pupils are playing the game. They do not participate as much as they will participate when filling exercise book. However, important is, that even though some teachers do not participate in gameplay activities, all thought the game is very useful for kids.

Integrating Games into Classroom: Media Detective Case

Media Detective is a learning game designed for media education. Media education should not be confused to merely teaching through or with media. Instead, it should aim to develop children's media literacy so that they have the ability to access, analyze, evaluate, and create media in a variety of forms. This task is very challenging, because the required knowledge and skills are very broad and hard to teach. This was also the driving force behind the development of Media Detective game that aims to develop students' media literacy and ability to produce, evaluate, and interpret media messages critically. Furthermore, game includes elements that teach copyright issues, safe use of Internet services, and other data security themes.

The learning content is embedded into a realistic story that integrates the challenges and learning tasks into a coherent and harmonious entity. The aim of this case is to present how teacher can actively participate in game events and can guide players directly in the game world.

Game Description and Learning Activities

In this section a superficial description of the story and the game activities are presented. In Media Detective a player takes on the role of an undercover agent working as a journalist who tries to clear up a theft and a related copyright offense. The master disk of the forthcoming movie has been stolen and pirate copies are sold in Internet and streets of Mediaville. The police have reduced the suspects to six persons that are all actors of media industry and they have somehow participated in the production of the stolen movie. In the game the agent (player for now on) interviews suspects, becomes familiarized with their work and does feature stories about them while trying to solve the crime (Figure 7). The player has a partner, an experienced agent, who helps and guides him during the game. The partner called Silva comments the decisions of the player and tries to activate player to think the content more deeply.

Figure 7. Interviewing a suspect (left); writing a feature story (right)

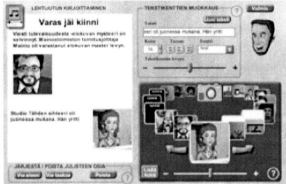

The interviews form the core of the game. They include both theoretical content about producing media messages (related to interviewee's work) as well as content needed to solve the crime. When the player has conducted an interview he is allowed to familiarize with suspect's work more deeply by performing a production task. Production tasks allow player to apply the theories that he has learned during interviews in practice. For example, in advertising agency, the player is obliged to produce an advertisement for a soft drink company and in LudusPoint game company player is obliged to design a level and related storyline for a platform game (Figure 8). The use of production tasks is justifiable because several studies have shown that challenging learn-

ers as producers of materials increase the learners' understanding of the subject matter (e.g. Kiili, 2005; Stern, Aprea, & Ebner, 2003; Hall, Bailey & Tillman, 1997). Furthermore, the creation of media messages supports also the formation of player's interpreting strategies of media messages. In fact, during the game player faces numerous media messages that he has to interpret and analyze in order to solve the game.

Teacher's Role in Media Detective Game

Players demand some intelligence from educational games due to their prior playing experiences with entertainment games. However, the develop-

Figure 8. Advertisement creation tool (left); game level editor (right)

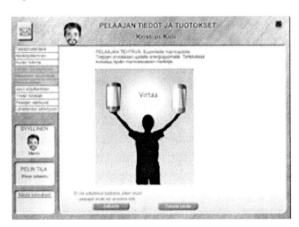

ment of AI-based game elements is expensive and challenging—especially in an educational context where the characters should provide constructive feedback for players. Furthermore, it is extremely challenging to form AI-based game elements that trigger reflection, which is a key process in learning. Therefore, Media Detective uses an alternative method of forming intelligence into the game, in which a teacher has a significant role. This method is called illusion of intelligence (Kiili, Ketamo & Lainema, 2011).

The idea of illusion of intelligence approach is that a teacher can communicate with players through non-player game characters included in the game world. It can be said that a teacher has many faces and identities. In Media Detective a teacher has two ways to communicate with players. Firstly, the teacher can take the role of player's partner, agent Silva. In other words, the teacher can create speech lines for the partner and aim them at a certain player. This kind of tutoring system allows the teacher to give constructive feedback to players and makes differentiation of teaching easier in a game context. Secondly, the teacher can communicate with players with game's internal e-mail system. The teacher can send e-mails to players from different non-player game characters. This feature was implemented in order to form a feedback channel for tasks requiring creative content producing. Provided speech line templates and e-mail templates support teachers' communication with players. The template messages have been designed to trigger reflection in players and they also facilitate teachers' adoption of the roles of non-player game characters.

In order to be able to tutor players, the teacher needs to be aware about players' performance and progress in the game. Therefore, Media Detective includes also an observing tool. The teacher can grasp with one look the overall progress of the glass. Furthermore, teacher has also a possibility to check players' productions in real-time and publish them into the game world, if they are decently made. After the first pilot studies

also a trivia creation tool was embedded into the teacher's tool. Teachers requested this because they wanted to also test players' knowledge after the game. Most of the teachers thought that the production tasks were not adequate indicators of players' learning. In practice, a teacher can start the creation of a trivia from scratch or use or modify a trivia made by another teacher. When the trivia is published, the players can perform it after solving the game and finally the teacher can check player's performance from teacher's tool.

The observing tool makes it possible to use player-generated content also outside the game world. Such feature supports the integration of game content to other teaching. For example, a teacher can show someone's production task to whole glass and use it to raise discussion or deliver printed advertisements to students and ask them analyze them etc. As we can see quite simple tools provide a lot power and possibilities for a teacher. However, the integration of games into other teaching depends much on teacher's motivation and creativity.

Findings and Discussion

The results described in this section are based on authors' previous studies and general feedback that teachers have provided after using the game in teaching. The evaluation of Media Detective has indicated that the illusion of intelligence approach is a successful method that can be used to support teachers' work and facilitate players' experiences. In fact, many of the players have been impressed with the artificial intelligence of the game. For example, Matti stated that: "Hey, the artificial intelligence of the game was awesome. The author of the game should work for Remedy" (Remedy Entertainment is a game company that has published some very successful games). Naturally, Matti's enthusiasm was mainly the merit of the teacher who could create the kinds of messages that did not disturb the harmony of the game - teacher could act like a believable game character. On the other hand, the evaluation studies have showed that messages created by a teacher can also ruin the whole game. For, example one teacher used agent Silva to inform players that it was time for a lunch. After that, players did not know anymore how to interpret Silva's messages. Thus, the success of illusion of intelligence approach depends on teacher's skills to adapt the roles of different game characters so that the whole game forms a harmonious entity and the teacher-generated content does not stick out from other game content? This phenomenon relates to the concept of suspension of disbelief. According to Rollings and Adams (2003) suspension of disbelief reflects a mental state in which a player chooses, for a certain period of time, to believe that this pack of lies (the game) is current reality. It is important to realize that when suspension of disbelief is lost, it is extremely difficult to capture player's attention in such a way again. This is the thing that teachers should realize before they start to teach with games allowing them to create own content.

Overall, teachers have emphasized that guiding players is quite easy, but the real challenge lays in getting players to think more deeply. This is a real challenge also for the game designers. How the performance of the teacher can be supported so that the teacher can provide cognitive feedback for players? One thing is clear, the tempo of the tutoring have to be manageable in order that teachers have enough time to produce effective and constructive messages for players. However, the evaluation studies have revealed that in spite of some delay players seems to like the feedback system of Media Detective. The feedback provided with e-mails has experienced to be very effective, because it is contextualized. For example, one player said that, "I really liked the way how the game provided feedback from my tasks…It felt powerful because it game from real professionals." The player referred to e-mails generated by a teacher and send through non-player game characters. The results have shown that the feedback delivered through non-player game characters were more effective than the feedback that the teacher gave face-to-face. In other words players were more eager to modify for example their advertisement posters based on feedback that the CEO of advertisement agency provided. However, as mentioned before the success relays on teachers ability to maintain the suspension disbelief and the harmony of the game. To summarize, the illusion of intelligence seems to be a respectable approach to fulfilling the expectations of students as well as teachers and can be used to support reflection.

Integrating Games into Classroom: MAGOS Case

Due to social, economic, and technological changes in our society, creativity is nowadays seen as basic survival and success factor. It has been argued that innovation, creativity, and production of media should be emphasized also in the school of the future (Kangas, 2010). The gameplay of Media Detective involved content production tasks that support the development of such 21-century skills. Because user generated content approach, especially the game design task of Media Detective, motivated both students and teachers we decided to create better tools that allow non-programmers to create and share their own games.

First, we developed a 'Pelitehdas' tool that allowed students to create Tetris-based games. Although the tool was quite simple, it provided great possibilities for teachers to use learning by designing games method in different school subjects. The positive feedback and the usefulness of the game development approach motivated us to continue this work. In 2012, we started an EU funded project called MAGICAL in which we are now developing more open-ended game-authoring environment, called MAGOS, for non-programmers. We decided to present MAGOS shortly in this chapter, because it includes some game elements that are derived from Media Detective game and it supports the development of 21-century skills that will be emphasized in the curriculum of the future. Furthermore, learning by developing games approach may provide schools a cost-effective way to introduce game based learning in classrooms, because the game development environments are not bound to any single theme or subject.

Case Specific Background

The pedagogical strategy, Learning by Developing Games, is theoretically founded on Dewey's learning by doing approach (Dewey, 1938/1997) and Papert's learning by programming approach (Papert, 1980). The pedagogical idea behind Learning by Developing Games approach rely on an assumption that construction of artifacts helps children to reformulate their understanding of the subject and express their personal ideas and feelings about both the subject and the constructed artifacts (Kafai, 2006; Papert, 1980). Although the constructed artifacts motivate children a lot, they can be regarded only as by-products of learning. In its best the design and development of artifacts is creative teamwork, which supports reflective thinking, collaboration, problem solving, and co-construction of knowledge.

A distinction between game authoring and game programming approaches needs to be made. Game authoring is a process of creating, arranging, and structuring content and rules in an interactive game development environment whereas game programming is more advanced process of writing source code of a game. According to Yatim and Masuch (2007), an ideal development tool for children would scale in programming 'granularity' in order to grow in capability along with the user's programming skills. The Scratch is a good example of such visual programming language designed for children (Monroy-Hernández, et al., 2011). The idea of Scratch relies on Lego bricks—the Scratch grammar is based on a collection of graphical programming blocks that children can

snap together to create programs (Resnick, et al., 2009). In order to lower the starting floor, the blocks are designed such a way that they fit together only in ways that make syntactic sense. The aim of the MAGOS environment is to lower the starting floor even more and that way support the wider use of the learning by designing games approach.

Description and Learning Activities

The MAGOS game-authoring environment is targeted for children and teachers. We want to emphasize that we do not try to develop a new visual programming language like Scratch (Monroy-Hernández, et al., 2011), but a game-authoring environment that relies on dragging, selecting, clicking etc., but still provides wide possibilities to create different types of games. By selecting game-authoring approach instead of programming we want to make the adoption of the environment as easy as possible.

Unlike traditional game-authoring environments MAGOS is designed to support collaborative game development. Games can be developed individually or in small groups (2-4 persons). All developers of the group can modify the same game simultaneously. In practice, each user gets a spell set (certain game development tools). Spell sets include potion bottles that are used to add characteristics for game elements. Spells are activated by dragging the bottles on existing game elements, which activates a tool pane that can be used to modify spell's characteristics. Four different types of spell sets exist: artistic spells, sound spells, psychic spells, and mock-up spells. In the beginning, each user can select their spell set, but two persons cannot select the same. For example, the artistic spell set includes drawing tools, animation tools, etc. With dividing tools between different spell sets and users, we aim to facilitate discussion between users and make the user interface of the MAGOS as simple as possible—for the user it is easier to handle small set of tools at a time. In order to facilitate collaboration and development process, users are allowed to change the spell sets in the fly. For example, if the user with a psychic spell set has made an object and defined some collision rules, he can ask from the user owning sound spell set a possibility to interchange spell sets so that he can create and add a noise for a collision. If the user agrees the spell sets are interchanged. Communication and awareness tools are added to facilitate the collaboration between users. However, if only one user creates a game he or she can control all the spell sets.

The research has shown that the uses of existing materials inspire users and arouse creative ideas. In MAGOS we encourage and empower users to build on the work of those users who want their work to be reused. MAGOS allows users to share or publish their game projects in two different ways: 1) publish for only playing or 2) publish for playing and remixing. The authors of the games that are remixed will get credits of their original work and the credits can be used to buy licenses to remixable content.

Teacher's Role in MAGOS

In general, MAGOS provide wide possibilities for teachers to integrate game development into their teaching. However, the learning by developing games may first sound too complicated and challenging. Thus, the learning curve of the used tool or environment should be very steep and teacher's participation in students' game development processes should be facilitated at least in following ways.

First, teacher's lesson preparation activities should be supported. The use of game development as a pedagogical strategy may be challenging for teachers and they may need contextualized examples to perceive the possibilities that the strategy provides. Thus, MAGOS will include an example library for teachers that can be used in lesson preparation activities. Library includes

examples about teaching curriculum-based content with MAGOS environment and that tries to lower the starting floor.

Second, the previous research has shown that game design is very challenging for students (Kafai, 1995) and without teachers' support learning outcomes tend to be poor. Thus, in MAGOS a teacher can communicate with students through game design professors (wizards) included in the game-authoring environment. With such a feature teacher can guide students and give them feedback of their performance without breaking down the suspension of disbelief. This method provides opportunities to give feedback from creative production tasks that would be almost impossible to automate. However, in such solution the success depends also on teacher's abilities to adapt different roles in the environment and to collaborate with users as the results about Media Detective game have shown. Furthermore, in order to be able to give constructive feedback teachers need ways to follow students' game development processes.

Third, assessment should be supported. In general, the assessment is embedded into the projects created in MAGOS environment. If students create successful projects, it can be assumed that they have learned the subject matter. Nevertheless, the assessment of game projects is not always easy especially for teachers that are not fully familiar with games and thus we will create a framework that helps to succeed with the assessment. However, the end product is not always the only aspect that teachers are interested in. Thus, we have created also a spying tool that can be used to follow students' game development processes in real time. With this tool teacher has access to whole game design process if he or she wants to. Furthermore, a peer reviewing system will be included into MAGOS.

To conclude, if we try to integrate game development into the curriculum, it does not require a new subject into the curriculum, but using game development as a vehicle for teaching curriculum-based content and collaborative project work. We believe that learning by developing games will become more common teaching strategy and it will shape the classroom practices of the future.

Integrating Games into the Classroom: ALICE Case

A key notion behind the EU funded ALICE (Adaptive Learning via Intuitive/Interactive, Collaborative and Emotional Systems) project is that whilst technological selection should always be driven by pedagogical need, adequate support is essential in providing educators with the tools and resources they need to perform effective blending. ALICE exploits a close integration between game engine (Unity) and learning content management system (Intelligent Web Teacher) to provide educators with the tools to both analyze learner behavior and performance in-game, and exact a high degree of control over the environment. By allowing the game's developer to annotate pedagogically salient content, information on this content is in turn communicated to the educator who can compose individual scenarios be enabling, disabling, and grouping content objects. Tracking of learner performance via XML reporting on meaningful actions also allows the educator to reflect on both individual and group performance.

Game Description and Learning Activities

The specific scenario addressed by the prototype within ALICE focuses upon training evacuation skills in schoolchildren. The developed prototype allows a high degree of customisability by the educator, with evacuation signs, interactive objects such as the player's possessions, and game elements such as the evacuation timer being capable of external run-time configuration. This functionality can be used either for pedagogical objectives, for example configuring a specific scenario containing a given learning objective, or for repurposing, extracted, and converting game content to different localisations. Through the use of Web-based services such as Google Translate, this repurposing can be taken one step further, with multiple translations of game content being provided without the need for access to the game's development environment or source code. Furthermore, the externalisation allows the educator access to game content, being able to adjust scripts for characters and other text-based game content through a simple text editor.

Teacher's Role

It is important to note that game-based interventions are rarely promoted as a complete alternative to an existing method of teaching and learning. To support the relationship between teachers, learners and the learning components within a game-based learning environment, it is desirable for games to complement a more traditional or formal methods of instruction through careful blending with an existing curricula and technologies. The ALICE game initiative supporting an educational programme around the area of civil defence, and specifically building evacuation demonstrates a technical integration of a gaming engine with a proprietary Learning Content Management System (LCMS). This approach aims to promote rapid interchange of game-based learning objects, as well as the application of existing methods for assessment or content creation, drawing further on the representation of the game as a reusable learning object; demonstrating the potential of positioning teachers as key actors in managing the learning content.

Findings and Discussion

Preliminary evaluation of the ALICE platform (Dunwell et al., 2011) demonstrated both the feasibility of the approach, and validated the ability of the platform to provide a usable resource to educators. Ongoing research is investigating the pedagogical value of the integrated approach, and also identifying methods for addressing hardware availability and scalability. This is identified as a non-trivial issue: emerging generations of learners risk having far greater access to information technologies in their leisure time than in formal education, and both careful design and shifts in policy are required to address this. Furthermore, the notion of the "intuitive" learner is identified. Such learners learn by exploration, which can include deliberately performing incorrect actions; therefore, simply assessing the correctness of their in-game actions is of limited value in an assessment cycle. Models and methodologies facilitating a greater understanding of learners and how their behaviours correspond to levels of understanding and learning outcomes are thus a key area in future work.

FUTURE RESEARCH DIRECTIONS

Some teachers are said to avoid game based learning approaches because they are afraid to lose the control of the learning process. The approaches presented in this article are meant to strengthen and speed up teachers' opportunities to receive detailed information about the learning process and to integrate the gameplay effectively into daily classroom activities. With such solutions, teacher cannot only control the process, but he or she can use this information to master relatively large groups with numerous variances in skills. In future we should conduct robust research about the usefulness and effectiveness of game based learning solutions and clearly show how games can support learning as well as teachers work. For example, learning analytics will be a hot issue in the future and serious games provide engaging ways to collect the needed data and deliver it in understandable format to learners themselves, parents, and teachers as well as to actors that are considering reformation of the curriculum. So far, most of the analytics tools give usage reports, like times and frequencies. Such data sets are useful

for IT department in order to check what content is used and what content can be removed from learning management system. However, such data is not informative for pedagogic purposes: pupil needs to know his/her strengths and weaknesses, parents and teachers need information on how to support individual child and curriculum developer needs to now the breaking points in competence development. As the studies shows, this can be answered, but not in old fashioned way by giving only usage reports.

CONCLUSION

It has been argued that we are moving towards a new generation of educational use of games. The third generation educational games stress the meaning of the teacher in game based learning by expanding the scope of the games from just playing to learning and teaching. The aim of this paper was to uncover the opportunities that third generation educational games can provide and raise discussion about teacher's role in game based learning. In this paper, teacher's role has been approached from several perspectives. We described five game based learning solutions that have been designed according to learners' and teachers' needs. The examples show that there are both computational and non-computational methods that can be used to support learning and teachers' work in the game world.

Unfortunately, games that exclude the teacher from the game based learning process dominate the markets, which is of great concern. Thus, the aim of our research has been to study the use of novel game features that enable teachers to participate in game based learning events. The hope is that the research on the potential roles of teachers in game-based learning would awake the educational game community to take more user centered design approach. In fact, it has become evident that if we want to support the diffusion of game-based learning and maximize the effectiveness of educational games, we have to support both learners' and teachers' needs and goals.

However, the question still remains, why the teacher is usually neglected when designing educational games? Maybe one of the problems is that when game designers focus on fulfilling the demands of the curriculum, they try to make games that simply teach the subject without teacher's 'touch'. When a teacher is forgotten from the concept, we cannot expect that teachers take these games into the classrooms. Games just do not provide enough added value for them. On the other hand, the research has shown that one of the major barriers that have blocked the diffusion of educational games into schools is teachers' prejudices and negative perceptions about game based learning. Thus, it is not self-evident that although the games would rely on characteristics of the third generation educational games, they find their way into classrooms and are actually used in teaching. Thus, a lot of work is needed to change the negative attitudes and to win the trust of teachers. To achieve that, we need plenty of well-designed game examples, robust research about the effectiveness of game-based learning and good pedagogical models and support.

Finally, we argue that without binding games into the curriculum and highlighting the importance of the teacher the games will not be fully integrated into the classrooms. Eventually, the teacher decides whether the games are used in the school or not. In fact, the classrooms have not changed during the past century—teachers have: Teachers are more open to new ideas and solutions that support learning needs and pedagogical practices. Thus, the new teachership is about taking the advantage on new, and pedagogically meaningful, tools. The educational games have to master these two goals. Without a strong support to pedagogical use and evidence about learning outcomes, the educational games will not be integrated into classrooms or into the curriculum. Now, it is time to convince the educators about the possibilities that game based learning approach

provides—so teachers' can take a step towards a new teachership. Lastly, we want to stress that educational game community does not have too many chances left—maybe the next strike could be too much for game based learning.

ACKNOWLEDGMENT

This work is partially funded under the European Community Seventh Framework Programme (FP7/2007 2013), Grant Agreement nr. 258169, and supported by the European Commission under the Collaborative Project ALICE "Adaptive Learning via Intuitive/Interactive, Collaborative, and Emotional Systems," VII Framework Programme, Theme ICT-2009.4.2 (Technology-Enhanced Learning), Grant Agreement n. 257639.

REFERENCES

Amory, A., & Seagram, R. (2003). Educational game models: Conceptualization and evaluation. *South African Journal of Higher Education*, *17*(2), 206–217.

Dewey, J. (1997). *Experience and education*. New York, NY: Simon and Schuster.

Dunwell, I., de Freitas, S., & Jarvis, S. (2011). Four-dimensional consideration of feedback in serious games. In de Freitas, S., & Maharg, P. (Eds.), *Digital Games and Learning* (pp. 42–62). Continuum Publishing.

Egenfeldt-Nielsen, S. (2007). Third generation educational use of computer games. *Journal of Educational Multimedia and Hypermedia*, *16*(3), 263–281.

Garris, R., Ahlers, R., & Driskell, J. E. (2002). Games, motivation and learning. *Simulation & Gaming: An Interdisciplinary Journal of Theory. Practice and Research*, *33*(4), 43–56.

Gee, J. P. (2003). *What video games have to teach us about learning and literacy*. New York, NY: Palgrave Macmillan. doi:10.1145/950566.950595

Hall, V. C., Bailey, J., & Tillman, C. (1997). Can student-generated illustrations be worth ten thousand words? *Journal of Educational Psychology*, *89*(4), 667–681. doi:10.1037/0022-0663.89.4.677

Kafai, Y. B. (1995). *Minds in play: Computer game design as a context for children's learning*. Hillsdale, NJ: Lawrence Erlbaum Associates.

Kafai, Y. B. (2006). Playing and making games for learning: Instructionist and constructionist perspectives for game studies. *Games and Culture*, *1*(1), 36–40. doi:10.1177/1555412005281767

Kangas, M. (2010). Creative and playful learning: Learning through game co-creation and games in playful learning environment. *Thinking Skills and Creativity*, *5*(1), 1–15. doi:10.1016/j.tsc.2009.11.001

Ketamo, H. (2003). An adaptive AnimalClass for handheld devices. *Journal of Educational Technology & Society*, *6*, 83–95.

Ketamo, H. (2009). Semantic networks-based teachable agents in an educational game. *Transactions on Computers*, *8*(4), 641–650.

Ketamo, H. (2011). Sharing behaviors in games and social media. *International Journal of Applied Mathematics and Informatics*, *5*(1), 224–232.

Ketamo, H., & Kiili, K. (2010a). Conceptual change takes time: Game based learning cannot be only supplementary amusement. *Journal of Educational Multimedia and Hypermedia*, *19*(4), 399–419.

Ketamo, H., & Kiili, K. (2010b). Mining educational game data: Uncovering complex mechanisms behind learning. In *Proceedings of 4th European Conference on Games Based Learning*. Copenhagen, Denmark: IEEE.

Ketamo, H., & Suominen, M. (2008). AnimalClass: Social networks in gaming. In M. Kankaanranta & P. Neittaanmäki (Eds.), *Design and Use of Serious Games*, (pp. 143-154). Springer Science+Business Media B.V.

Ketamo, H., & Suominen, M. (2010). Learning-by-teaching in an educational game: The educational outcome, user experience and social networks. *Journal of Interactive Learning Research*, *21*(1), 75–94.

Kiili, K. (2005). Content creation challenges and flow experience in educational games: The IT-emperor case. *The Internet and Higher Education*, *8*(3), 183–198. doi:10.1016/j.iheduc.2005.06.001

Kiili, K. (2007). Foundation for problem-based gaming. *British Journal of Educational Technology*, *38*(3), 394–404. doi:10.1111/j.1467-8535.2007.00704.x

Kiili, K., & Ketamo, H. (2007). Exploring the learning mechanism in educational games. *Journal of Computing and Information Technology*, *15*(4), 319–324.

Kiili, K., Ketamo, H., & Lainema, T. (2011). Reflective thinking in games: Triggers and constraints. In Connolly, T. (Ed.), *Leading Issues in Games-Based Learning Research* (pp. 178–192). London, UK: Ridgeway Press.

Merenluoto, K., & Lehtinen, E. (2004). Number concept and conceptual change: Towards a systematic model of the processes of change. *Learning and Instruction*, *14*, 519–534. doi:10.1016/j.learninstruc.2004.06.016

Monroy-Hernández, A., Hill, B. M., González-Rivero, J., & boyd, d. (2011). Computers can't give credit: How automatic attribution falls short in an online remixing community. In *Proceedings of the 29th International Conference on Human Factors in Computing Systems (CHI 2011)*. IEEE.

Papert, S. (1980). *Mindstorms*. New York, NY: Basic Books.

Resnick, M., Maloney, J., Monroy-Hernandez, A., Rusk, N., Eastmond, E., & Brennan, K. (2009, November). Scratch: Programming for all. *Communications of the ACM.* doi:10.1145/1592761.1592779

Stern, E., & Aprea, C., & Ebner. (2003). Improving cross-content transfer in text processing by means of active graphical representation. *Learning and Instruction, 13*(2), 191–203. doi:10.1016/S0959-4752(02)00020-8

Sweller, J., van Merrienboer, J. J., & Paas, F. G. W. C. (1998). Cognitive architecture and instructional design. *Educational Psychology Review, 10*, 251–296. doi:10.1023/A:1022193728205

Virvou, M., Katsionis, G., & Manos, K. (2005). Combining software games with education: Evaluation of its educational effectiveness. *Journal of Educational Technology & Society, 8*, 54–65.

Vosniadou, S. (2007). Conceptual change approach and its re-framing. In Vosniadou, S., Baltas, A., & Vamvakoussi, X. (Eds.), *Re-Framing the Conceptual Change Approach in Learning and Instruction* (pp. 1–15). Oxford, UK: Elsevier Press.

Yatim, M. H. M., & Masuch, M. (2007). GA-TELOCK: A game authoring tool for children. In *Proceedings of the 6th International Conference on Interaction Design and Children*, (pp. 173–174). IEEE.

ADDITIONAL READING

Ketamo, H. (2009). Semantic networks -based teachable agents in an educational game. *Transactions on Computers, 8*(4), 641–650.

Ketamo, H. (2009). Teachable virtual characters in educational game. In *Proceedings of 1st International Open Workshop on Intelligent Personalization and Adaptation in Digital Educational Games*, (pp. 35-42). Graz, Austria: IEEE.

Ketamo, H. (2009). Teachable characters: Semantic neural networks in game AI. In *Proceedings of the 10th WSEAS International Conference on Neural Networks*, (pp. 11-17). Prague, Czech Republic: WSEAS.

Ketamo, H. (2010). Educational data mining: Tools to support learning 3.0. In *Proceedings of Online Educa Berlin 2010*. Berlin, Germany: Educa.

Ketamo, H. (2011). Sharing behaviors in games and social media. *International Journal of Applied Mathematics and Informatics, 5*(1), 224–232.

Ketamo, H., & Kiili, K. (2009). New teachership in game worlds. In *Proceedings of 3rd European Conference on Educational Game Based Learning*, (pp. 211-219). Graz, Austria: IEEE.

Ketamo, H., & Kiili, K. (2010). Conceptual change takes time: Game based learning cannot be only supplementary amusement. *Journal of Educational Multimedia and Hypermedia, 19*(4), 399–419.

Ketamo, H., & Kiili, K. (2010). Mining educational game data: Uncovering complex mechanisms behind learning. In *Proceedings of the 4th European Conference on Games Based Learning*, (pp. 151-159). Copenhagen, Denmark: IEEE.

Ketamo, H., & Suominen, M. (2006). AnimalClass – Animals that learn. In *Proceeding of Online Educa Berlin 2006*. Berlin, Germany: Educa.

Ketamo, H., & Suominen, M. (2007). Ways to support reflective thinking in educational games: Gaming strategies and learning. In *Proceeding of Online Educa Berlin 2007*. Berlin, Germany: Educa.

Ketamo, H., & Suominen, M. (2007). Learning by teaching: A case study on explorative behaviour in an educational games. In Ruokamo, Kangas, Lehtonen, & Kumpulainen (Eds.), *The Power of Media in Education*, (pp. 197-203). Rovaniemi, Finland: Academic Press.

Ketamo, H., & Suominen, M. (2008). AnimalClass: Social networks in gaming. In M. Kankaanranta & P. Neittaanmäki (Eds.), *Design and Use of Serious Games,* (pp. 143-154). Springer Science+Business Media B.V.

Ketamo, H., & Suominen, M. (2008). Learning-by-teaching in educational games. [Vienna, Austria: Ed-Media.]. *Proceedings of Ed-Media, 2008,* 2954–2963.

Ketamo, H., & Suominen, M. (2010). Learning-by-teaching in an educational game: The educational outcome, user experience and social networks. *Journal of Interactive Learning Research, 21*(1), 75–94.

Kiili, K. (2008). Reflection walkthrough method: Designing knowledge construction in learning games. In *Proceedings of European Conference on Game-Based Learning 2008.* Barcelona, Spain: IEEE.

Kiili, K. (2008). Teacher's role in media detective game: Communication through non-player game characters. In *Proceedings of World Conference on Educational Multimedia, Hypermedia and Telecommunications 2008,* (pp. 5248-5255). Chesapeake, VA: AACE.

Kiili, K., & Ketamo, H. (2007). Exploring the learning mechanism in educational games. *Journal of Computing and Information Technology, 15*(4), 319–324.

Kiili, K., & Ketamo, H. (2007). Exploring learning mechanism in educational games. In *Proceedings of the International Conference on Information Technology Interfaces,* (pp. 357-362). Cavtat, Croatia: IEEE.

Kiili, K., & Ketamo, H. (2009). Learning is not self-evident: Conceptual change demands time and support. In *Proceedings of 3rd European Conference on Educational Game Based Learning,* (pp. 227-233). Graz, Austria: IEEE.

Kiili, K., Ketamo, H., & Lainema, T. (2007). Reflective thinking in games: Triggers and constrains. In *Proceedings of European Conference on Game Based Learning,* (pp. 169-176). Paisley, UK: IEEE.

Kiili, K., Ketamo, H., & Lainema, T. (2011). Reflective thinking in games: Triggers and constraints. In Connolly, T. (Ed.), *Leading Issues in Games-Based Learning Research* (pp. 178–192). London, UK: Ridgeway Press.

KEY TERMS AND DEFINITIONS

Conceptual Change: Conceptual change is the phenomenon in which person's thinking changes radically.

Game Authoring: Game authoring is a process of creating, arranging, and structuring content and rules in an interactive game development environment that does not require programming.

Illusion of Understanding: In illusion of understanding a learner recognizes some familiar elements in the new phenomenon, but learner's knowledge is not adequate for paying attention to the novel aspects of phenomenon, which leads only to an enrichment of naïve thinking.

Learning by Developing Games: Learning by developing games is a pedagogical strategy in which students create their own games.

Teachable Agent: Teachable agent is an intelligent software component that is capable of learning.

Chapter 8
A Design Framework for Educational Exergames

Kristian Kiili
Tampere University of Technology, Finland

Arttu Perttula
Tampere University of Technology, Finland

ABSTRACT

This chapter presents a framework for understanding the elements of educational exergames that combine both cognitive and physical gameplay. The aim of the framework is to provide a foundation to develop engaging and effective educational exergames as well as to provide a blueprint to define reasonable research settings. By using the framework, designers can scrutinize their game designs, either in research or commercial settings, and reveal new ways to optimize learning effects, health effects, and user experience in educational exergames. The chapter describes a case study in which the framework was used to fine-tune an educational exergame called "Yammy Attack." The results showed that the framework was a useful tool to imagine and discover novel design solutions that would not necessarily otherwise emerge. Furthermore, the chapter discusses the usefulness of educational exergames and possibilities to incorporate them into the schools.

INTRODUCTION

The development of new educational methods is necessary to accelerate learning and to reach learner groups that are currently not reached by conventional techniques of learning. The potential use of games in educational settings is huge because a large and growing population is engaged with playing games. However, the popularity of games has also created problems. For example, obesity has become a big problem in many countries recently. According to Gorgu, O'Hare and O'Grady (2009), the reasons for obesity include a high calorie diet and a serious lack of physical activities in the daily lives of children. It has been argued that video games are one of the main reasons for physical inactivity (Vanderwater, Shim & Caplovitz, 2004; Sothern, 2004). Furthermore,

DOI: 10.4018/978-1-4666-3950-8.ch008

physical activity in schools has steadily declined since the 1970s. During this same period, the percentage of overweight children in the US, for example, has more than doubled (Hedley et al. 2004). The emerging exertion game genre tries to have an effect on this by encouraging players to perform physical movements during gameplay.

An adequate amount of physical activity is important for children because

1. Increased physical activity has the potential to improve fitness and decrease obesity, both of which positively impact cognitive functioning and academic achievement (Castelli, Hillman, Buck & Erwing, 2007),
2. Physical activity activates brains for enhanced learning and memory (e.g. Ratey & Hagerman, 2008; Hopkins, Nitecki, & Bucci, 2011), and
3. Good fitness potentially prevents troublesome behavior in schools (Ratey & Hagerman, 2008).

However, currently students spend the majority of their school time sitting in a classroom, which is not an optimal solution from both learning and health perspectives. We should find new ways to introduce good practices regarding the provision of regular physical activity in schools. Thus, this chapter considers exertion games as an alternative learning environment that could be applied on a day-to-day basis in elementary schools.

Although the possibilities that serious games can provide to schools have been recognized, still one of the biggest problems is the inadequate integration of education and game design principles (e.g. Arnab et al, 2011; Kiili, 2005a, Kiili, 2005b). According to Quinn (2005) it is a real challenge to design engagement that integrates with educational effectiveness. The challenge of the proposed approach is even higher, because an exertion dimension has been added to this problem space. A combination such as this, educational

exergames, is a new, unstudied branch of research in the era of serious games. In this chapter we propose a design framework for educational exergames. The aim of the framework is to provide foundation to develop engaging and effective educational exergames as well as to provide a blueprint to define reasonable research settings. First we shortly define exergames and consider bodily interaction. After that the initial structure of the design framework is presented and an educational exergame, Yammy Attack, is re-designed with the help of the framework. Finally, the possibilities and challenges that introduction of educational exergames provide for schools are discussed.

EXERGAMES AND BODILY INTERACTION

According to Mueller et al. (2011) exergames are an emerging form of computer games that aim to leverage the advantages of sports and exercise in order to support physical, social, and mental health benefits. An exergame is controlled with an input mechanism that requires a player to invest physical exertion. Exergaming is not a new phenomenon, but in recent years, the development of motion-based controllers has facilitated the advent of the exergame genre (Kiili, Perttula & Tuomi, 2010; Kiili & Merilampi, 2010). Currently, exergames are specifically associated with Nintendo Wii, Kinect and Playstation Move game consoles. Most commonly exergame movements are detected via motion sensors, cameras, pressure sensors or GPS sensors depending on the type of the game.

The Impacts of Exergaming

According to Staiano and Calfert (2011) exergame playing can lead in physical, social, and cognitive developments. Next, the major findings about the impacts of exergaming are shortly reviewed.

Physical Impacts

Many exergames can increase energy expenditure from sedentary or light levels to moderate levels (e.g. Papastergiou, 2009; Graf et al., 2009), but only few exergames result in vigorous levels of energy expenditure. Effectiveness has been mainly assessed according to the energy expenditure level that is not solely an adequate measure for exertion games targeted for children. In growing children the neuromuscular system is rapidly developing. The coordination of movements improves when they are exposed to different environments and various movement patterns during physical activities. Muscles need activity (Hamilton et al. 2007), and bones need impacts to become strong (Völgyi et al., 2010).

For example, Wii games rarely cause the needed impacts. Compare e.g. Wii Boxing with the actual boxing sport. Graves et al. (2007) found that playing the Wii uses significantly more energy than playing sedentary computer games. However, the energy used when playing active Wii games is not high enough to contribute towards the recommended daily amount of exercise in children. However, the playing styles affect greatly on energy expenditure; based on playing style some players expend more calories than the other. Nevertheless, according to Lieberman et al. (2011) as people become more involved and successful with exergames, they develop the skills that make it easier to engage in physical activity. They enjoy perceiving that their bodies are becoming more fit, and they experience more physical and emotional well-being. These rewards and benefits are motivating and can lead to more engagement in physical activity.

Papastergiou (2009) has conducted a survey based on Dance Dance Revolution, which is based on a platform interface that requires the player to step onto different parts of the platform, based on onscreen instructions. Results showed that intensity levels were just enough to fulfill the recommendations of the American College of Sports Medicine (ACSM), which indicate that exergames can be an effective form of exercise. Furthermore, Graf et al. (2009) demonstrated that energy expenditure during active video game play is comparable to moderate-intensity walking. On the other hand Daley (2009) criticizes the previous studies and calls for more extensive and methodologically robust research. He argues that, although studies have produced some encouraging results regarding the energy expenditure of exergames, active gaming is no substitute for real sports. All in all, whether the intensity is proper or not, players benefit from exergaming in some level; caloric expenditure, heart rate increment (Bailey & McInnis, 2012; Staiano & Calvert, 2011), and coordination skill developments (Staiano & Calvert, 2011).

Psychosocial Impacts

According to Staiano and Calfert (2011) exergaming may provide opportunities for social interaction that influence on friendship selection, self-esteem, moods, and motivation. In general, social aspect of gaming may reduce the risk of social isolation and loneliness (Mueller, Agamanolis, & Picard, 2003). The results have indicated that the social interaction and meeting of other players are important game playing motivators (Lieberman, 2006). For example, Kiili, Perttula, and Tuomi (2010) found that team-based multiplayer games motivated adolescent children a lot and team play facilitated also flow experience. Some studies have shown that exergaming can increase the self-esteem (e.g. Brubaker, 2006) and self-efficacy (e.g. Staiano et al., 2011) of overweight children. The nature of exergames may partly explain this; when playing exergames players usually directs their attention toward a screen instead of peers, which may reduce body self-consciousness during playing. Furthermore, Lieberman (2006) found that children and adolescents enjoyed and sustained exercise more after they began playing exergames. Thus, exergaming may motivate players to increase also real-world physical activities (Lieberman, et al 2011).

Cognitive and Academic Impacts

The major body of research studying the relation between cognitive impacts and physical activities has been conducted outside the school context and without exergaming dimension. For example, the results have indicated that increased physical activity has the potential to positively impact cognitive functioning, memory and academic achievement (Donnelly & Lambourne, 2011; Castelli, Hillman, Buck & Erwing, 2007). However, emerging research has also shown that exergame interventions in schools can improve academic performance, reduce classroom absenteeism, tardiness, and negative classroom behaviors (Lieberman, et al 2011). Furthermore, Lind, Welch and Ekkekakis (2009) have studied the effects of attentional association and dissociation on exertional, affective and physiological responses to exercise. The study states that shifting one's focus of attention towards environmental stimuli (dissociation) instead of one's body (association) has been theorized to enhance psychological responses and attenuate physiological stress (Lind et al. 2009). It suggests that exercising would facilitate learning by enhancing player's capability to respond while exercising.

Bodily Interaction

The ability to capture whole body interaction has arisen due to the developments in technology. For example miniaturized sensors and wireless networking enable unimpeded movements. In addition algorithms have been developed to model human kinematics (Corazza et al., 2006). England et al. (2009) have described whole body interaction as follows: *"The integrated capture and processing of human signals from physical,*

physiological, cognitive and emotional sources to generate feedback to those sources for interaction in a digital environment." The field of whole body interaction has recently emerged to take a more holistic view of Human Computer Interaction (HCI). It is a research, philosophical and engineering approach to combining several aspects of HCI. Whole body interaction involves input from and feedbacks via physical motion capture, physiological inputs such as pulse rate, the normal five senses plus, the sense of balance and proprioception, cognitive state, emotional state and social context (England, 2011).

Each bodily interaction application area, such as exergames, should have its own requirements as to accuracy of movement, the nature of any feedback and robustness of the system (England et al., 2009). As Ermi and Mäyrä (2005) pointed out sensory experience supports the engagement process by leading players to forget about the sensory input from the real world and focus on the sensory input from the virtual world. In movement-based games, movement is an important source of sensory feedback and therefore it is important that the interface provide believable movement feedback leading the player to feel part of the virtual world (Slater, Usoh, & Steed, 1995).

As shown by the Wii study (Bianchi-Berthouze, 2012), different levels of realism should be tailored to the player's fitness, coordination skills and knowledge of the simulated scenario. This is important not just from an engagement perspective but also from an ergonomics viewpoint. According to Bianchi-Berthouze (2012), if the difficulties are too high, participants may find workaround strategies that could cause injuries. In addition, as body movement has cognitive, affective and physiological effects on a player, traditional evaluation methods used for computer games need to be carefully applied to take such effects into account (Mueller and Bianchi-Berthouze, 2010).

Furthermore, body-movement itself is a key to the experience. Using video observations or full-body motion capture techniques can provide a better understanding of the experience of the player. As techniques to automatically analyze these data are becoming available (Camurri, Lagerlof, & Volpe, 2003; Koštomaj & Boh, 2009), a more thorough analysis of how the body is used in the game and how it supports the various components of engagement of the player could be carried to inform the design, as well as to better understand this important modality.

TOWARDS A DESIGN FRAMEWORK FOR EDUCATIONAL EXERGAMES

The positive impacts of exergaming indicate that bodily learning environments can provide engaging solutions also for schools. In some schools exergames are already integrated into physical education classes (e.g. Schiesel, 2007). Furthermore, according to Staiano and Calvert (2011) for example in United States, exergames like DDR are being incorporated not only into physical education classes, but also to recesses, lunchtimes, and after-school programs. Unfortunately, exergames are not always seen as appropriate activities for schools, because they do not clearly contribute to goals declared in the curriculum. Thus, bodily interactions should be merged into other learning activities such as educational games. Because the design of effective and useful educational exergames is challenging, we propose a design framework that support this ambition.

The framework for Exertion games (Mueller, et al., 2011), Dual flow model (Singlair, et al., 2007), Framework for sports engagement (Connolly's & Tenenbaum, 2010), Persuasive technology (e.g. Fogg, 2002), and Cognitive load theory (e.g. Sweller, Van Merriënboer, & Paas, 1998) form the foundation of the proposed Educational exergame framework (Figure 1). The aim of the framework is to provide theoretical means to balance the amount of physical, cognitive, and sensomotoric workloads in order to optimize learning and health

effects as well as describe ways to create more engaging exertion and learning experiences mediated by the technology.

In educational exergames the body and the mind plays the central role and in the framework we use those as lenses to consider other aspects of educational exergames. The overall structure of the design framework for educational exergames is modified from Mueller et al. (2011), who proposed four lenses that can be used to facilitate the designing of interactive exertion technology:

1. The responding body,
2. The moving body,
3. The sensing body, and
4. The relating body.

We extend this approach by adding lenses for learning interactions:

1. The sensing mind,
2. The processing mind,
3. The integrating mind, and
4. The relating mind.

Body and mind lenses provide means to consider game elements systematically and allow reflection of design solutions. In the framework a game is divided into rules, play and context dimensions that help designers to understand the formal structures of a game, the experiences of the people involved, and the larger context in which the game takes place.

Lenses for Exertion Interactions

The following body lenses are defined according to Mueller et al. (2011).

The lens of the responding body concerns how the body responds to exercise. The player can feel most of this response, but not directly control it—for example, a rise in heart rate or the occurrence of sweat. More and more sensor

Figure 1. A design framework for educational exergames (extended from the framework for exertion games proposed by Mueller, et al., 2011)

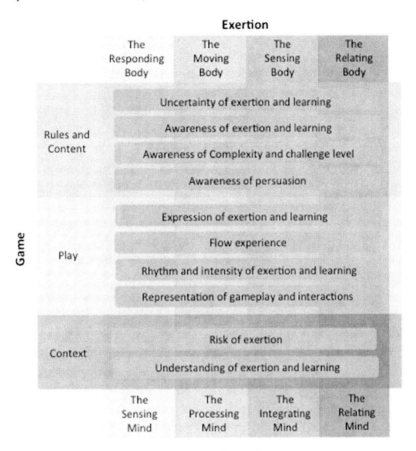

technologies emerge that can use this also as an input that creates new and interesting possibilities for game designers.

The lens of the moving body considers how the player's body parts are moving relative to one another. We can feel where our hand is in relation to our nose even when our eyes are closed. This lens highlights movement characteristics such as intensity (movement can carry "weight"), continuousness (movement exhibits preparatory and follow-through phases), and variety (the richness of human movement). The moving body also highlights the kinesthetic sense or proprioception.

The lens of sensing body describes how the body is sensing and experiencing the world and therefore aims to emphasize how the body interacts

with the world. Most traditional sports involve balls and equipment that affect the experience. In educational exergames equipment can be used to control the game and the game world can consist of both virtual and real object. For technology design, this might mean that instead of equipping users with sensors, we could put a sensor also into the ball. Furthermore, this lens highlights that playing in a big stadium is not the same as playing in the park, even though the pitch might be the same size.

The lens of relating body describes the ways in which bodies and people relate to one another through digital technology. For example, in "races" such as 100m sprints, the athletes do not interfere with one another bodily, they might try to intimidate one another with looks, etc., but they are not allowed to use their bodies to prevent one another from winning, which is very different to, for example, in football.

Lenses for Learning Interactions

The essential processes for active learning are selecting relevant material, processing selected material, integrating selected material with prior knowledge and sharing own understanding to others (e.g. Mayer, 2001).

The lens of the sensing mind emphasizes that humans cannot attend to all things at once, but have to select areas of interest from the world. Attention is used to focus our mental capacities of the sensory input so that the mind can successfully process the stimulus of interest (Duchowski, 2007). For the design of learning interactions, this means that we should ensure that learner selects most important content and elements from the learning material to be processed.

The lens of the processing mind addresses the limitations of human working memory. Working memory is very limited in both capacity and duration. According to Miller (1956), we can deal with no more than seven elements of information at a time without overloading the information processing capacity and decreasing the effectiveness of processing. Thus, According to (Sweller, Van Merriënboer, & Paas, 1998) any interactions between elements held in working memory themselves require working memory capacity, reducing the number of elements that can be dealt with simultaneously. When designing learning interactions we should remember that every element has a cognitive prize and they should be wisely used (Ketamo & Kiili, 2010).

The lens of integrating mind emphasizes the meaning of long-term memory in human intellectual skills. According to cognitive load theory, human intellectual ability relies on knowledge stored in long-term memory, because working memory is incapable of highly complex interactions involving novel content. Thus, we should carefully consider learner's' knowledge level when designing learning interactions—designs that require learners to engage in complex reasoning processes involving combinations of unfamiliar elements are likely to be deficient (Sweller, Van Merriënboer, & Paas, 1998).

The lens of the relating mind addresses the meaning of sharing your learning experiences with others. Socio-constructivist approach has turned out to facilitate learning and collaborative learning provides great possibilities also for educational exertion games.

Focus of Lenses

When the rules and content dimension, play dimension and context dimension are considered through exertion and learning interaction lenses several focus points that are crucial for designing educational exergames can be identified. Focus points are not mutually exclusive, but interrelated, offering different perspectives for designing educational exergames. Focus points highlight different aspects of game elements and provide conceptual guidance for design and analysis.

Focus Points of Rules and Content Dimension

Uncertainty of Exertion and Learning

Uncertainty is important element of engaging playing experiences. According to Mueller et al. (2011) uncertainty facilitates surprise in games through random or chance events. However, success should not be based truly on randomness and luck, but player's skills should be emphasized. In exergames player may be uncertain also about the relation between his movements and visualized game events. For example, if the player jumps one meter in the real world, how far does player's character jump in the virtual game world. Such uncertainty makes playing interesting while the player has to learn the characteristics of the game world and bodily interactions. However, if the player does not perceive the consequences of his physical actions in the virtual game world, the player may get confused. Thus, the learning curve of controlling of the game should be steep. In other words, the game controlling should be easy to learn, but hard to master. Furthermore, complex gameplay, pressure and the variety of bodily interactions can cause even simple actions to fail, which makes the experience more engaging. In general, designers should be aware and balance the uncertainty factors that are related to body, mind and virtual world in a way that the game experience is believable and engaging.

Awareness of Exertion and Learning

According to Mueller et al (2011), exergame players usually aim to overcome the limitations of their bodies, for example training longer periods or running faster. In educational exergames players additionally aim to learn new things during playing. Digital technology can be used to support these aims. For example, bodily information can be selectively hided from players as well as revealed so that the player can benefit either from increased or decreased awareness of their exertion. Similarly, information about knowledge and learning can be treated. On the other hand, the design can utilize also distractions such as playing music in supporting anti-awareness that dissociates the user from the discomfort that comes with strenuous physical activity (Karageorghis & Priest, 2008; Mueller et al 2011).

Also, the social aspect of games should be considered in the design. The related body and the related mind lenses emphasize the meaning of social interaction in creating engaging experiences. For example, awareness of the physical effort invested by players or learning achieved by players can be used to foster competition that may motivate players to invest even more effort

on playing and share their experiences. Furthermore, the awareness of exertion and learning can be used also in team formation and in balancing of challenge levels in multiplayer games.

Awareness of Persuasion

Designers have to determine to what extent and how the game tries to persuade players. Fogg's Behavior Model (FBM) explains the causes of behavior change and can be used to design persuasive aspects of the game (Fogg, 2002). According to the FBM, behavior is a product of three factors: motivation, ability, and triggers. The FBM argues that for a person to perform a certain target behavior, he or she must be sufficiently motivated, have the ability to perform the behavior, and be triggered to perform the behavior. Furthermore, all these three factors must occur at the same time, otherwise the behavior will not happen.

Thus, according to FBM a person that has increased motivation and increased ability will more likely perform the target behavior. Fogg (2002) has argued that people are fundamentally lazy and products that require people to learn new things routinely tend to fail. In order to increase user's ability to perform a task, designers should make the behavior easier to do. However, sufficient motivation and high ability to perform the task do not always lead to desired behavior. Thus, people need triggers that activate the target behavior. Fogg (2002) has distinguished three types of triggers: sparks, facilitators, and signals. A spark is a trigger that motivates behavior. A facilitator makes behavior easier and that way increases ability to perform the target behavior. On the other hand, a signal does not increase either motivation or ability, but it indicates or reminds the user about the target behavior.

Designers should use appropriate triggers to activate the target behavior. For example, suppose that we want to persuade a student to play a certain exergame during lesson breaks. The student likes similar games a lot and thus his playing motivation is high. The student has a required smartphone with GPS sensor and the user interface of the game client is easy to use. Although the motivation and ability seems to be above activation threshold of the target behavior, the student does not play the game during lesson breaks, because he has other interests and he does not even remember the possibility to play. In this kind of condition signal trigger is needed. For example, a student could get a notification SMS during lesson break or the exergame could be advertised in school's infoTV. Such triggers might persuade the student to play the game. On the other hand, for another student the low ability could be a stumbling block. For example, if the student does not have a required smartphone or money to buy one the task of the designer is more challenging. To conclude the FBM model provides designers the means to consider aspects that facilitate the use of games and helps designers to purposefully change player's behavior.

Awareness of Complexity

In general, complexity can be defined as a state of the system that involves numerous elements and numerous relationships among these elements. In educational exergames the complexity is composed from several factors such as the amount of bodily controls, the amount of simultaneous players, the type and the level of learning content, the audio-visual implementation of the game, the rules of the game, and of course the relationships between these factors.

When designing educational exergames we should remember the constraints of human cognition and thus design the gameplay according to target group's skills, characteristics, and knowledge. When playing educational exergames learners are challenged to extract relevant information from a game world, select corresponding parts of information and integrate all of these elements to coherent representation and at the same time track the state of the game, decide right movements to

carry out, possibly communicate with other players, and interpret bodily sensations. This requires a lot from the player, because the game world changes during playing, important information may be presented only a while, and thus it needs to be kept actively in working memory in order to integrate it to earlier presented information and relate it to one's actions. This may easily impose high cognitive load in learners' cognitive system and hinder learning and playing.

Thus, one expression and measurement of complexity is cognitive load. The purpose of cognitive load theory is to bridge the gap between information structures presented in the learning materials and human cognitive architecture so that learners can use their working memory more efficiently (Paas, Renkl, & Sweller, 2003). According to Kiili (2005a) one major problem of multimedia learning materials is that the working memory capacity of learners is often overloaded due to inappropriate ways of presentation. Because games usually consist of rich multimedia elements and exertion dimension bring in even more elements, applies this also to educational exergames.

Sweller, van Merrienboer, and Paas (1998) have identified three separate sources of cognitive load. Cognitive load may be affected by the intrinsic nature of the material (intrinsic cognitive load), the manner in which the material is presented (extraneous cognitive load), or the effort needed for the construction of schemata (germane cognitive load). Intrinsic cognitive load refers to the inherent nature of the task or the subject matter of the learning content. If the learning content consists of numerous elements that are related to one another, the intrinsic cognitive load is high. In contrast, if the material is simple, including only a few connections between elements, the intrinsic cognitive load is low. According to the cognitive load theory, instructional design cannot change the intrinsic cognitive load. Therefore, the most important aspects of the cognitive load theory for educational exergame designers are extraneous cognitive load and germane cognitive load.

From learning point of view extraneous cognitive load is unnecessary cognitive load and is determined by the instructional design. If the game is poorly designed, the extraneous cognitive load is high because learners have to engage in irrelevant cognitive processing. Mayer (2001) has primarily examined different presentation formats in order to reduce the extraneous cognitive load of learning materials. However, the reduction of the extraneous cognitive load by an ideal instructional format does not guarantee that all free cognitive resources will be allocated to a deeper knowledge construction process (Bannert, 2002). Unused working memory capacity should be used by optimizing the germane cognitive load, by stimulating the player to process the provided content more deeply. According to Kirschner (2002), the approach of encouraging learners to engage in appropriate cognitive processing can only work if the total cognitive load of instructional design is within working memory limits. If a learner's cognitive system is overloaded, it might impact negatively on learning and in this games also playing. In summary, cognitive load should be optimized in games by cutting down irrelevant multimedia elements, applying modality effect, providing usable user interface and challenges that support knowledge construction. The ways to decrease extraneous cognitive load are considered more deeply in Representation of gameplay and interactions focus point section.

In general, the complexity is related to challenge level of the game that is one of the most important dimensions of flow experience. Next, we consider the Flow experience focus point.

Focus Points of Play Dimension

Flow Experience

Games are designed to generate a positive effect in players and are most successful and engaging when they facilitate the flow experience (Kiili, 2005). Csikszentmihalyi (1975) introduced the flow state through the study of people involved in activities such as rock climbing, chess and dance. Flow describes a state of complete absorption or engagement in an activity and refers to the optimal experience (Csikszentmihalyi, 1990). During the optimal experience, a person is in a psychological state where he or she is so involved with the goal-driven activity that nothing else seems to matter. An activity that produces such experiences is so pleasant that the person may be willing to do something for its own sake, without being concerned with what he will get out of his action. Theoretically, flow consists of nine dimensions, but challenge-skill balance, immediate feedback, sense of control, loss of self-consciousness and clear goals are the most crucial dimensions that contribute to designing educational exergames. Because these dimensions provide a meaningful approach to embody engaging elements into educational exergames, they are considered more deeply.

When player's goals are clear he can more easily stay focused on the tasks that game provides. It is a good practice to provide a clear main goal in the beginning of the game. The main goal should be divided into sub-goals and provide them at an appropriate pace in order to create feelings of success (Kiili & Lainema, 2010). If the goals seem too challenging, the probability of experiencing flow is low. Furthermore, the goals should be related to the learning objectives of the game. If the learning objectives are discrete from gameplay the game may fail to produce educationally effective experiences.

The main purpose of the feedback is to inform the player about his performance and progression toward the goals and to monitor progress of game performance. In educational games, the feedback dimension can be divided into immediate feedback and cognitive feedback (Ketamo & Kiili, 2010). The immediate feedback keeps the player focused. If the player has to wait long before he can realize what effect his action caused, he will become distracted and lose the focus on the task. Additionally, the delayed feedback may create interpretation problems and in the worst-case even lead to misconceptions and negative learning transfer. The cognitive feedback provides the account for learning and cognitive immersion. The cognitive feedback aims to stimulate the player to reflect on his experiences and tested solutions in order to further develop his mental models and playing strategies. In other words, it focuses player's attention on information that is relevant for learning objectives and game strategy formation.

Focus of attention plays a central role in flow experience. During a flow experience, a person is totally focused on the activity and is able to forget all unpleasant things. Because flow-inducing activities require complete concentration of attention on the task at hand, there are no cognitive resources left over for irrelevant information and thoughts. Thus, self seems to disappear from awareness during flow. In other words, in flow there is no room for self-scrutiny and players are more willing to participate for example to public physical activities.

Challenge-skill balance and sense of control are often found to be most important factors that facilitate flow experience in educational games (e.g. Kiili & Lainema, 2010; Kiili & Lainema, 2008). Csikszentmihalyi (1990) has stated that

sense of control refers to possibility rather than to actuality of the control. It can be said that a person senses when he can develop sufficient skills to reduce the margin of error close to zero, which makes the experience enjoyable. In educational exergames challenge-skill balance and sense of control dimensions need to be considered from both cognitive and physical perspectives. The dual flow model forms the foundation for this consideration (Sinclair, Hingston & Masek, 2007).

In order to optimize the engagement and effectiveness of exergames Sinclair, Hingston, and Masek (2007) have proposed a dual flow model that extends the original three-channel flow model with a physiological dimension that reflects an intensity-fitness balance. Recently, Kiili and Perttula (2010) argued that the team-based gameplay facilitate achieving of flow in exergames and they added a team flow aspect into the dual flow model (Figure 2).

According to the extended dual flow model if the cognitive challenge is too low, a player tends to feel boredom and when the cognitive challenge is too high, a player tends to feel anxiety. Similarly, the intensity-fitness balance determines the effectiveness of the exertion. If the game is too intensive, a player will fail to play the game and is unable to continue exercising. On the other hand, if the intensity is too low compared to

Figure 2. An extended dual flow model for exergames (modified from Kiili & Perttula, 2010)

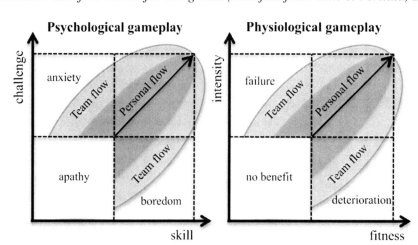

player's fitness level, a player will enter a state of deterioration. The optimal exergaming experience can be achieved when both the psychological and physiological aspects are in balance and a player is in the flow zone.

Boredom and anxiety are negative experiences that motivate the player to strive for the flow state. If the player is bored, the challenge needs to be increased. In contrast, if the player feels anxiety, the challenge must be decreased in order to get back to the flow state. Neither situations are stable states, because every now and then the player tends to either feel boredom or anxiety, which motivates him to strive for the flow state in order to feel enjoyment again. This dynamic feature explains why flow activities lead to growth and discovery. In general, the challenge of the game design is to keep the player in a flow state by balancing cognitive and physiological aspects of the game.

However, the balancing of educational exergames is not as straightforward as the balancing of traditional computer games. The basic balancing principle suggests that the difficulty level of a game can be gradually increased, because it is assumed that a player's skill level increases with playing time. Thus, for example, play testing can be used to balance the challenges for a certain target audience. Such a solution does not work properly in educational exergames. Although, a player's skills may increase during playing, in lengthy playing sessions the gradually increasing intensity will lead to exhaustion and failure. To overcome this problem, Sinclair, Hingston, and Masek (2007) have suggested that exergames should adapt dynamically to a player's performance, or they should be based on simple mechanics that focus more on input devices and exercise movements than on complex gameplay. However, when considering educational exergames, we cannot rely only on physical activities, but also the cognitive aspects have to be emphasized. Thus, we need new methods to balance the gameplay. The next focus point considers the balancing issue more deeply in terms of attentional strategies.

Rhythm and Intensity of Exertion and Learning

As the extended dual flow model argues physical and cognitive aspects of an exergame needs to be balanced. In educational exergames the balancing is even more important and challenging. The rhythm of gameplay and intensity of physical activities plays a central role in this. According to Tenenbaum (2001), exercise intensity impacts the focus of attention. Thus, the integration of learning content and exergame interfaces raises new design challenges. Research on sports has shown that when the physical workload increases, attention allocation shifts from dissociation to association (e.g. Tenenbaumb, & Connollya, 2008; Hutchinsona & Tenenbaum, 2007). Association can be defined as turning the focus inward and toward bodily sensations, while dissociation is focusing outward and away from body sensations (Scott, Scott, Bedic, & Dowd, 1999).

Such natural attention change disturbs processing of game elements and that way also learning and problem solving. In other words, this means that during high physical workload it is hard to concentrate on problem-solving and game stimuli designed to enhance learning. Thus, we should develop solutions that take into account player's physical and cognitive constraints and in the ideal case adapt to them. Figure 3 presents a starting point to conceptually model this phenomenon. Vertical axis describes the amount of cognitive workload and horizontal axis the amount of physical workload. The dashed diagonal line illustrates the constraint that combination of cognitive and physical workloads form on performing challenges of the game; what higher the sum of workloads is, the higher the possibility to fail in the game is. The model is illustrating only the relationship of the components rather than precise values for each. Thus, there are no units on the axis.

The balancing of workloads and adaptation to players' characteristics is very challenging, because the cognitive and physical workloads are composed from several factors as discussed as a

Figure 3. Conceptual model of cognitive and physical workloads in educational exergames

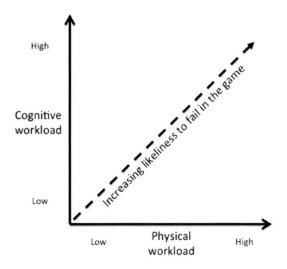

part of Complexity focus point. One solution to avoid cognitive or physical overload is to sequence the cognitive gameplay and physical gameplay. For example, players could first conceptually solve the puzzle and then perform the solution by controlling the game with physical movements.

Representation of Gameplay and Interactions

As the Complexity focus point stated the representation of game elements should be optimized in the way that players' working memory is not overloaded, but the game is still immersive and attractive. Game designers should be aware that every game element has it cognitive price (Kiili & Ketamo, 2010) and thus they need to decide whether the extraneous elements engage players so much that it is reasonable to include them into the game or not. Similarly, the fidelity of game elements should be considered. The weeding of the game is reasonable, because the research has clearly shown that multimedia presentations are more effective when irrelevant material is excluded (e.g. Mayer & Moreno, 2003).

Generally, the promise of multimedia learning and game based learning lays on modality effect, assuming that working memory capacity may be increased by the use of visual, auditory, and haptic information processing channels simultaneously. It is important to notice that graphics and sounds entice the player, but the gameplay keeps him or her there (Kiili, 2005b). Thus, the most challenging task of educational game design is to find a balance between attractive elements and educational objectives in order to optimize the possibility of players experiencing flow and then learn the relevant skills and information provided by the game.

In order to reduce extraneous cognitive load, the game designers should also consider the utilization of haptic feedback in educational exergames. The use of haptic technology can simulate cutaneous and kinesthetic sensations so that games not only look but also feel (McGee, 2002) and that way release working memory resources to other senses. Furthermore, haptics support immersion while learners can experience the game more realistically and pervasively.

Expression of Exertion and Learning

Performative expressions using the body is common in sports, often in the form of gestures directed to oneself or to the opponents, and celebratory dances after a score or a match. In educational exergames, there are four points to take into consideration when considering ways to support self-expression.

1. Similarly, like in sports, players' feelings are visible through body language. Although, expressions to other players might be different because of in sports players are usually in face-to-face situations and in exergames players interact more through the screen. Furthermore, there might be not such opportunities to bodily expressions during the nonstop gameplay.

2. The game can visualize players' state. For example, heart rate could be visible to co-players or success in the game is expressed via an avatar or rewards.

3. Players can be also considered as an audience, because they are usually watching the game events from.the screen. In sports for example celebratory dances are sometimes presented to the audience. Thus expressions may vary between sports and exergames.

4. According to Mueller et al. (2011) performative expressions consume bodily energy and hence one.might come to the conclusion that they do not support making progress towards the goal of the game, but because they can significantly contribute towards the experience, they are still performed.

Focus Points of Context Dimension

Risk of Exertion

As Mueller et al. (2009) have stated physical risk is an important aspect in order to understand exertion games. A risk to hurt other players is not always relevant, but it is possible for players to hurt themselves. In extreme cases, the engagement that exergames create have lead to injuries and doctors have even introduced Wiiitis (Bonis, 2007) and Wii shoulder (Cowley & Minnaar, 2008) conditions resulting from playing too much active Nintendo Wii games. Bonis (2007) has described the Wiiitis condition as follows: *If a gamer gets too engrossed, he may 'play tennis' on the video screen for many hours. Unlike in the real sport, physical strength and endurance are not limiting factors.* Pasch, Bianchi-Berthouze, van Dijk and Nijholt (2009) have assumed that the possible reason for such injuries is that gamers do not perceive exergaming as a sport and consequently do not worry about warming up before playing. One way to decrease the risk of hurting oneself is to take player's physical condition and playing behavior into account in the game design. For example, by utilizing heart rate monitors the level of exercise could be adjusted. Persuasive messages could be also used to warn players about risky playing performance.

There is also the risk caused by the surroundings or environment where game is played. For example, the game can take so much attention that the player stumbles or even hits something while watching the screen or other players. Thus, we argue that especially exergaming that includes cognitive tasks can increase the level of the risk, because the player is not completely aware of her body while thinking and reasoning. Furthermore, according to Mueller et al. (2011) physical risk can also contribute to a feeling of thrill. However, the risks of educational exergames are slightly different when compared to sports. Usually there are no such physical contacts in computer games. Compare for example boxing with a game controller with real boxing sports. Thus, also experiences might differ (Mueller et al., 2011).

Understanding the Exertion and Learning

This focus point refers to the potential of a game to support the development of kinesthetic literacy and knowledge about the learning content. For example, from exertion perspective a system could provide players with details about their heart rate changes during the game to help them understand their body better or information about the calories burned. This could be used to create novel experiences, for example, the winner is not the player with the most points, but who burnt the most calories. From learning perspective, the system could provide information for example about knowledge gains, progression towards goals, social interactions and shortages of skills. Equally, the winner could be the player who has gained most, not necessarily the player that has scored most points. The task of the designer is to determine how and what information is provided for players and consider how this information affect the gameplay.

EDUCATIONAL EXERGAME FRAMEWORK AS A DESIGN TOOL

Educational exergame framework can be used in several ways, for example, in concept generation, in optimizing learning and user experience or as the backbone of the whole design process. Thus, there are no detailed rules on how to apply framework in practice. Generally, the framework provides a common ground for designers to create novel and effective educational exergames and discuss about their designs. The focus points emphasized in the framework provide a systematic and structured way to consider the most important aspects of creating engaging educational exergames. However, it is noteworthy that not all focus points are appropriate for every game, but the use of focus points should be considered case sensitively. In this section we describe how we used the framework to fine-tune one of our game prototypes, Yammy Attack. In practice we kept a mind storming session, in which we utilized the framework to structure the session.

Description of Yammy Attack

Yummy Attack is an educational exergame targeted for small children. The game was built on our mobile exergame platform (Kiili, Perttula & Tuomi, 2010), which makes possible to develop games controlled with mobile phones and played in public spaces. Yummy Attack (Figure 4), deals with diet issues. In the game, player controls his or her game character by jumping. The main task of the player is to collect and eat healthy food that fly in the air in the game world. If the player eats junk food, his game character gets fatter, and it gradually loses its jumping power, which makes it harder to collect more food. In contrast, a fat game character loses weight, if it eats healthy food. Weight gaining was implemented to both visualize characters' eating habits and to provide players' a possibility to experience some consequences of weight gaining (e.g. more laborious movement).

Furthermore, each player's game character has a unique voice, which is used to provide feedback about the healthiness of the collected food items. When the player eats unhealthy food character sulks and makes a "yuck" sound. In contrast, when the player eats healthy food game character smiles and makes a "yippee" sound. Furthermore, character's teeth are also used to express the healthiness of eaten food—if the character eats too much unhealthy food its teeth starts to fall out. Finally, the game includes also some obstacles that disturb players' behavior. For example, a coke can occasionally flits from left to right. If the can collides with a character, the character cannot jump for a short period of a time. The black fishes swimming

Figure 4. Screenshot of the Yammy Attack game

in the water was implemented to warn players about an upcoming danger, a coke can. This gives players time to get ready for the danger.

Re-Designing a Yammy Attack Game

We used the framework and the results gathered from one focus group session to reveal game elements that disturb playing experience in Yammy Attack game. Next, we present revealed game design problems, solutions to these problems and discuss possible drawbacks of emerged solutions in accordance of appropriate focus points.

Uncertainty of Exertion and Learning

- **Problem:** In Yammy Attack the basic jumping power of the character is based on pre-determined constant and the weight of the game character affects this. However, the players tend to assume that their own jumping power is taken into account and they get confused because of the lack of this relationship.
- **Solution:** Jumping power should be determined according to magnitude of the acceleration vector detected from player's jump.
- **Problem:** The jump direction of the game character is not based on the jump direction of the player, but the stance of the game character (see Figure 4). This is problematic, because players tend to assume in the beginning that their jumps are simulated in the game world.
- **Possible solution:** The motion detection should be modified so that it takes the direction of player's jump into account.
- **Drawbacks:** In cheaper smartphones the processing of the direction takes too long and the delays disturb playing experience. Furthermore, according to Awareness of risks focus point players can collide with

each other and get hurt when they jump in different directions near other players.
- **Solution:** Because, in immersive game environment player does not have cognitive resources to follow co-players' behavior continuously and only few of game's target group own high-performance smartphones the original solution is kept.
- **Problem:** The coke can that is passing by now and then is hard to notice. This game element is important because it provide surprises for players and force players to be alert. However, the fishes that are running away from a can is not distinctive enough as a warning signal and coke can disturbs some of the players performance too much.
- **Solution:** According to the sensing mind lens we could use different media, for example sounds, to warn players about the approaching can. On the other hand, according to the sensing body, we could use mobile phone's vibrate feature to warn about the approaching can. We will implement the vibrate solution, because it fits better into the game world; Vibrate simulates the lateral line sense of the game character. Furthermore, sounds play an important role as a feedback channel and we do not want to risk that feature.

Awareness of Exertion and Learning

- **Problem:** Players are not aware of their characters or opponents jumping power and physical efforts invested. It is hard to evaluate the jumping power of others during the gameplay, because one has to concentrate on so many other game elements at the same time. Increment of awareness of exertion and learning would make the game strategically more interesting.
- **Solution:** Clouds or birds will be used to inform players about each player's average jumping power. Based on this information

players can strategically select jumping targets. Furthermore, calorie expenditures will be added into the result screen.

Rhythm and Intensity of Exertion and Learning

- **Problem:** The game testing has shown that the game tempo is too fast for young kids and they have problems to perceive the consequences of their actions. Furthermore, one game lasts too long and players get too exhausted, which disturbs goal-directed playing behavior. Players tend to occasionally jump even if their character is in the air. Such aimless behavior seems to increase when the playing time increases.
- **Solution:** We will slow down the movement speed of food items as well as the appearance interval of food items. We believe that the slower tempo will lead to more strategic playing behavior and provides time for reflecting own performance. Furthermore, a handicapping system will be implemented. If the game notices that a player has continuous difficulties to jump hard enough, player's jump power is slightly boosted in the virtual world.

Representation of Gameplay and Interactions

- **Problem:** As discussed above children have problems to perceive the consequences of their actions. The representation of game elements affects this. In particularly, the feedback mechanism is confusing and may even lead to formation of misconceptions.
- **Solution:** The slower game tempo partly solves the problem, but also other adjustments are needed. Each player has unique voice that gives verbal feedback. However, the voices are too similar and needs to be diversified, so that players clearly can per-

ceive their characters comments. Currently, player's character starts to spin when it has collected a food item and the player misses the face gestures of the character. Thus, the spinning effect is removed. Furthermore, the weight gaining of the player should be highlighted more, so that player perceives it more clearly.

Understanding the Exertion and Learning

- **Problem:** The game is about nutrition, but the game does not provide clear feedback about player's physical effort in terms of nutrition.
- **Solution:** As suggested earlier calorie expenditures of players will be added into the result screen and most calories burned player will get bonuses. In addition to calorie expenditure figures, the expenditure is visualized with graphical food items such as muffins and candies. Based on such information it is easier to understand the relationship between diet and physical exercises done.

CONCLUSION

In this chapter, the concept of educational exergames was introduced and the implementation scenarios were discussed. Educational exergames combine gameplay elements from educational games (cognitively challenging games) and exergames (physically challenging games). In general, educational exergames are a new and unstudied branch of research in the era of serious games. It has become evident that educational exergame design is hard to master because one has to understand a complex web comprised of education, sports, psychology, technology, art, business, and creativity. Thus, in this chapter a framework for designing educational exergames was proposed.

The aim of the framework is to clarify this complex web and its relations. However, the framework does not provide any magic bullet for design, but rather it provides a common ground and a structured tool for developers to build and fine-tune their designs on. By using the framework, designers can scrutinize their game designs, either in research or commercial settings, and reveal new ways to optimize learning, health effects and user experience. The framework provides means to identify existing problems in educational exergames that fail to achieve the intended outcomes. The identified problems can be solved with the help of the framework by considering the game elements systematically through body and mind lenses and the crucial focus points that the lenses create. Another benefit of using the educational exergame framework is creating a shared frame of reference for the design team. When the whole team has a common ground about educational exergames, the game design project can be conducted more efficiently.

Furthermore, in this chapter we reported a case study in which we used the framework to fine-tune one of our game prototypes, Yammy Attack. With the help of the framework, we could identify several weaknesses of the game and we were able to determine justifiable improvements. In general, the framework turned out to be a useful tool to imagine and discover novel and effective design solutions that would not necessarily otherwise emerged. However, the case showed that there are several focus points that are strongly related and this may confuse some designers. Although some of the focus points are parallel they all have their unique perspective resulting in more holistic analysis of the game elements. However, the understanding of such nuances requires a good theoretical knowledge about all the theories that the framework is based on. Thus, in future we are going to simplify the framework and condense the most crucial theoretical aspect into more easily absorbable format.

So far, we have discussed about the proposed framework that is targeted for designers and researchers. However, the teachers, educators, and policy makers play the crucial role that influences the adoption of educational exergames in schools. If we cannot convince all the stakeholders about the usefulness of educational exergames, they do not diffuse into the schools. In many countries, traditional exergames are already increasingly introduced into the physical education courses. However, only a little time is reserved for physical education and the use of exergames as a part of physical education does not really increase the overall amount of physical activity. Thus, the physical activities should be included also to other school subjects, which is problematic, because the demands of the curriculum and the overall time constraints make the introduction of exergames very challenging. However, educational exergames provide more appropriate solution for schools, because they have positive physiological, psychosocial, and cognitive impacts and they can be applied on a day-to-day basis in schools without interfering with the objectives of the curriculum. In general, incorporating educational exergames into schools and homes could promote students' healthier life style and combat against the emerging childhood obesity crisis. The aims of the proposed approach are convergent with the EU strategy for "Europe on Nutrition, Overweight and Obesity related health issues." One of the four pillars defined to tackle obesity is a clear reduction in high-risk behaviours, including lack of physical exercise and poor nutrition. According to this, the importance of introducing good practices regarding the provision of regular physical activity in schools should be emphasized.

To summarize, educational exergames have the potential to be integrated into the classrooms and even into the curriculum. However, good examples and research results about the usefulness of educational exergames in schools are needed. We hope that the proposed framework motivates researchers and game developers to start developing and studying educational exergames and possibilities that they provide for education. In the future, we are eager to study whether educational exergame home assignments could become one of the most popular, engaging, and health-promoting school activities of the twenty-first century or not.

ACKNOWLEDGMENT

This work is partially funded under the European Community Seventh Framework Programme (FP7/2007 2013), Grant Agreement nr. 258169 and FINNABLE 2020 project.

REFERENCES

Arnab, S., Bellotti, F., de Freitas, S., Kiili, K., Ott, M., & Gloria, D. (2011). Serious games in education: Linking pedagogy and game design. In *Proceedings of ECGBL 2011*. Athens, Greece: ECGBL.

Bailey, B., & McInnis, K. (2011). Energy cost of exergaming: A comparison of the energy cost of 6 forms of exergaming. *Archives of Pediatrics & Adolescent Medicine, 165*(7). doi:10.1001/archpediatrics.2011.15

Bannert, M. (2002). Managing cognitive load—Recent trends in cognitive load theory. *Learning and Instruction, 12*, 139–146. doi:10.1016/S0959-4752(01)00021-4

Bianchi-Berthouze, N. (2013). Understanding the role of body movement in player engagement. *Human-Computer Interaction*.

Bonis, J. (2007). Acute wiiitis. *The New England Journal of Medicine, 356*(23), 2431–2432. doi:10.1056/NEJMc070670

Brubaker, B. (2006, March 11). Teachers join the dance dance revolution: Educators begin training to use the exercise video game. *The Dominion Post*. Retrieved from http://www.redorbit.com/news/scifi-gaming/424434/teachers_join_the__dance_dance_revolution/index.html

Camurri, A., Lagerlof, I., & Volpe, G. (2003). Emotions and cue extraction from dance movements. *Journal of Human Computer Studies, 59*(1-2), 213–225. doi:10.1016/S1071-5819(03)00050-8

Castelli, D. M., Hillman, C. H., Buck, S. M., & Erwin, H. E. (2007). Physical fitness and academic achievement in third- and fifth-grade students. *Journal of Sport & Exercise Psychology, 29*, 239–252.

Connolly, C. T., & Tenenbaum, G. (2010). Exertion–attention–flow linkage under different workloads. *Journal of Applied Social Psychology, 40*(5), 1123–1145. doi:10.1111/j.1559-1816.2010.00613.x

Corazza, S., Muendermann, L., Chadhari, A., Demattio, T., Cobelli, C., & Andriacchi, T. (2006). A markerless motion capture system to study musculoskeletal biomechanics: Visual hull and simulated annealing approach. *Annals of Biomedical Engineering, 34*(6), 1019–1029. doi:10.1007/s10439-006-9122-8

Cowley, A. D., & Minnaar, G. (2008). Watch out for wii shoulder. *British Medical Journal, 336*, 110. doi:10.1136/bmj.39461.631181.BE

Csikszentmihalyi, M. (1975). *Beyond boredom and anxiety*. San Francisco, CA: Jossey-Bass.

Csikszentmihalyi, M. (1991). *Flow: The psychology of optimal experience*. New York, NY: Harper Perennial.

Daley, A. (2009). Can exergaming contribute to improving physical activity levels and health outcomes in children? *Pediatrics, 124*(2), 763–771. doi:10.1542/peds.2008-2357

Donnelly, J., & Lambourne, K. (2011). Classroom-based physical activity, cognition, and academic achievement. *Preventive Medicine, 52*(1), 36–42. doi:10.1016/j.ypmed.2011.01.021

Duchowski, A. T. (2007). *Eye tracking methodology - Theory and practice* (2nd ed.). Berlin, Germany: Springer.

England, D. (2011). Whole body interaction: An introduction. In *Whole Body Interaction* (pp. 1–6). Berlin, Germany: Springer. doi:10.1007/978-0-85729-433-3_1

England, D., Randles, M., Fergus, P., & Taleb-Bendiab, A. (2009). Towards and advanced framework for whole body interaction. In *Proceedings of 3rd International Conference on Virtual and Mixed Reality*. Berlin, Germany: Springer Verlag.

Ermi, L., & Mäyrä, F. (2005). Fundamental components of the gameplay experience: Analysing immersion. In *Proceedings of the DiGRA Conference Changing Views: Worlds in Play*, (pp. 15 – 27). DiGRA.

Fogg, B. J. (2002). *Persuasive technology: Using computers to change what we think and do*. San Francisco, CA: Morgan Kaufmann. doi:10.1145/764008.763957

Gorgu, L., O'Hare, G. M. P., & O'Grady, M. J. (2009). Towards mobile collaborative exergaming. In *Proceedings of the 2nd International Conference on Advances in Human-Oriented and Personalized Mechanisms, Technologies, and Services*, (pp. 61-64). Porto, Portugal: IEEE.

Graf, D. L., Pratt, L. V., Hester, C. N., & Short, K. R. (2009). Playing active video games increases energy expenditure in children. *Pediatrics, 124*(2), 534–540. doi:10.1542/peds.2008-2851

Graves, L., Stratton, G., Ridgers, N. D., & Cable, N. T. (2007). Comparison of energy expenditure in adolescents when playing new generation and sedentary computer games: Cross sectional study. *British Medical Journal, 335*, 1282–1284. doi:10.1136/bmj.39415.632951.80

Hamilton, M. (2007). Role of low energy expenditure and sitting in obesity, metabolic syndrome, type 2 diabetes, and cardiovascular disease. *Diabetes, 56*, 2655–2667. doi:10.2337/db07-0882

Hedley, A. A., Ogden, C. L., Johnson, C. L., Carroll, M. D., Curtin, L. R., & Flegal, K. M. (2004). Prevalence of overweight and obesity among US children, adolescents, and adults, 1999–2002. *Journal of the American Medical Association, 291*, 2847–2850. doi:10.1001/jama.291.23.2847

Hopkins, M. E., Nitecki, R., & Bucci, D. J. (2011). Physical exercise during adolescence versus adulthood: Differential effects on object recognition memory and brain-derived neurotrophic factor levels. *Neuroscience, 194*, 84–94. doi:10.1016/j.neuroscience.2011.07.071

Hutchinsona, J. C., & Tenenbaumb, G. (2007). Attention focus during physical effort: The mediating role of task intensity. *Psychology of Sport and Exercise, 8*(2), 233–245. doi:10.1016/j.psychsport.2006.03.006

Jackson, S., & Csikszentmihalyi, M. (1999). *Flow in sports: The keys to optimal experiences and performances*. Champaign, IL: Human Kinetics.

Karageorghis, C., & Priest, D.-L. (2008). Music in sport and exercise: An update on research and application. *The Sport Journal, 11*(3).

Ketamo, H., & Kiili, K. (2010). Conceptual change takes time: Game based learning cannot be only supplementary amusement. *Journal of Educational Multimedia and Hypermedia, 19*(4), 399–419.

Kiili, K. (2005a). *On educational game design: Building blocks of flow experience.* (Doctoral Thesis). Tampere University of Technology. Tempere, Finland.

Kiili, K. (2005b). Digital game-based learning: Towards an experiential gaming model. *The Internet and Higher Education, 8*(1), 13–24. doi:10.1016/j.iheduc.2004.12.001

Kiili, K., & Lainema, T. (2008). Foundation for measuring engagement in educational games. *Journal of Interactive Learning Research, 19*(3), 469–488.

Kiili, K., & Lainema, T. (2010). Power and flow experience in time-intensive business simulation game. *Journal of Educational Multimedia and Hypermedia, 19*(1), 39–57.

Kiili, K., & Merilampi, S. (2010). Developing engaging exergames with simple motion detection. In *Proceedings of the 14th International Academic MindTrek Conference: Envisioning Future Media Environments*, (pp. 103-110). Tampere, Finland: MindTrek.

Kiili, K., & Perttula, A. (2010). Exergaming: Exploring engagement principles. In *Proceedings of the Serious Games for Sports and Health*, (pp. 161-172). Darmstadt, Germany: IEEE.

Kiili, K., Perttula, A., & Tuomi, P. (2010). Development of multiplayer exertion games for physical education. *IADIS International Journal on WWW/Internet, 8*(1), 52-69.

Kirschner, P. (2002). Cognitive load theory: Implications of cognitive load theory on the design of learning. *Learning and Instruction, 12*, 1–10. doi:10.1016/S0959-4752(01)00014-7

Koštomaj, M., & Boh, B. (2009). Evaluation of user's physical experience in full body interactive games. *Lecture Notes in Computer Science, 5763*, 145–154. doi:10.1007/978-3-642-04076-4_16

Lieberman, D., Chamberlin, B., Medina, E., Franklin, B., Sanner, B., & Vafiadis, D. (2011). The power of play: Innovations in getting active summit 2011: A science panel proceedings report from the American heart association. *Circulation, 123*, 2507–2516. doi:10.1161/CIR.0b013e318219661d

Lieberman, D. A. (2006). What can we learn from playing interactive games? In Vorderer, P., & Bryant, J. (Eds.), *Playing Video Games: Motives, Responses, and Consequences* (pp. 379–397). Mahwah, NJ: Erlbaum.

Lind, E., & Welch, A., Ekkekakis, & Panteleimon. (2009). Do 'mind over muscle' strategies work? Examining the effects of attentional association and dissociation on exertional, affective and physiological responses to exercise. *Sports Medicine (Auckland, N.Z.), 39*(9), 743–764. doi:10.2165/11315120-000000000-00000

Mayer, R. E. (2001). *Multimedia learning.* Cambridge, UK: Cambridge University Press. doi:10.1017/CBO9781139164603

Mayer, R. E., & Moreno, R. (2003). Nine ways to reduce cognitive load in multimedia learning. *Educational Psychologist, 38*, 43–52. doi:10.1207/S15326985EP3801_6

McGee, M. R. (2002). *Investigating a multimodal solution for improving force feedback generated textures.* (PhD Thesis). University of Glasgow. Glasgow, UK.

Miller, G. (1956). The magical number seven, plus or minus two: Some limits on our capacity for processing information. *Psychological Review, 63*, 81–97. doi:10.1037/h0043158

Mueller, F., Agamanolis, S., & Picard, R. (2003). Exertion interfaces: Sports over a distance for social bonding and fun. In *Proceedings of the SIGCHI Conference on Human Factors in Computing Systems.* Ft. Lauderdale, FL: ACM.

Mueller, F., Agamanolis, S., Vetere, F., & Gibbs, M. R. (2009). A framework for exertion interactions over a distance. In *Proceedings of ACM SIGGRAPH 2009*. ACM.

Mueller, F., & Bianchi-Berthouze, N. (2012). Evaluating exertion games experiences from investigating movement-based games. In R. Bernhaupt (Ed.), *Evaluating User Experiences in Games*. Berlin, Germany: Springer. Retrieved from http://www.uclic.ucl.ac.uk/people/n.berthouze/MullerBerthouze2010

Mueller, F., Edge, D., Vetere, F., Gibbs, M. R., Agamanolis, S., Bongers, B., & Sheridan, J. G. (2011). Designing sports: A framework for exertion games. In *Proceedings of the SIGCHI Conference on Human Factors in Computing Systems*. Vancouver, Canada: ACM Press.

Paas, F. G. W. C., Renkl, A., & Sweller, J. (2003). Cognitive load theory: Instructional implications of the interaction between information structure and cognitive architecture. *Instructional Science*, *32*(1), 1–8. doi:10.1023/B:TRUC.0000021806.17516.d0

Papastergiou, M. (2009). Exploring the potential of computer and video games health and physical education: A literature review. *Computers & Education*, *53*, 603–622. doi:10.1016/j.compedu.2009.04.001

Pasch, M., Bianchi-Berthouze, N., van Dijk, B., & Nijholt, A. (2009). Movement-based sports video games: Investigating motivation and gaming experience. *Entertainment Computing*, *1*, 49–61. doi:10.1016/j.entcom.2009.09.004

Quinn. (2005). Engaging learning: Designing e-learning simulation games. San Francisco, CA: Pfeiffer.

Ratey, J., & Hagerman, E. (2008). *Spark: The revolutionary new science of exercise and the brain*. New York, NY: Little, Brown, and Company.

Schiesel, S. (2007, April 30). P.E. classes turn to video game that works legs, not thumbs. *The New York Times*. Retrieved March 5, 2009, from http://www.nytimes.com/2007/04/30/health/30exer.html

Scott, L. M., Scott, D., Bedic, S. P., & Dowd, J. (1999). The effect of associative and dissociative strategies on rowing ergometer performance. *The Sport Psychologist*, *13*, 57–68.

Sinclair, J., Hingston, P., & Masek, M. (2007). Considerations for the design of exergames. [Perth, Australia: GRAPHITE.]. *Proceedings of GRAPHITE*, *2007*, 289–295. doi:10.1145/1321261.1321313

Slater, M., Usoh, M., & Steed, A. (1995). Taking steps: The influence of a walking metaphor on presence in virtual reality. *ACM Transactions on Computer-Human Interaction*, *2*, 201–219. doi:10.1145/210079.210084

Sothern, M. (2004). Obesity prevention in children: Physical activity and nutrition. *Nutrition (Burbank, Los Angeles County, Calif.)*, *20*(7-8), 704–708. doi:10.1016/j.nut.2004.04.007

Staiano, A., & Calvert, S. (1998). Exergames for physical education courses: Physical, social, and cognitive benefits. *Child Development Perspectives*, *5*(2), 93–98. doi:10.1111/j.1750-8606.2011.00162.x

Sweller, J., Van Merriënboer, J., & Paas, F. (1998). Cognitive architecture and instructional design. *Educational Psychology Review*, *10*(3), 251–296. doi:10.1023/A:1022193728205

Tenenbaum, G. (2001). A social-cognitive perspective of perceived exertion and exertion tolerance. In Singer, R. N., Hausenblas, H., & Janelle, C. (Eds.), *Handbook of Sport Psychology* (pp. 810–820). New York, NY: Wiley.

Tenenbaumb, G., & Connollya, T. C. (2008). Attention allocation under varied workload and effort perception in rowers. *Psychology of Sport and Exercise*, *9*(5), 704–717. doi:10.1016/j.psychsport.2007.09.002

Vanderwater, E. A., Shim, M. S., & Caplovitz, A. G. (2004). Linking obesity and activity level with children's television and video game use. *Adolescence*, *27*(1), 71–85. doi:10.1016/j.adolescence.2003.10.003

Völgyi, E., Lyytikäinen, A., Tylavsky, F., Nicholson, P., Suominen, H., Alén, M., & Cheng, S. (2010). Long-term leisure-time physical activity has a positive effect on bone mass gain in girls. *Journal of Bone and Mineral Research*, *25*(5), 1034–1041.

ADDITIONAL READING

Johnston, H., & Whitehead, A. (2011). Pose presentation for a dance-based massively multiplayer online exergame. *Entertainment Computing*, *2*(2), 89–96. doi:10.1016/j.entcom.2010.12.007

Peng, W., & Hsieh, G. (2012). The influence of competition, cooperation, and player relationship in a motor performance centered computer game. *Computers in Human Behavior*, *28*(6), 2100–2106. doi:10.1016/j.chb.2012.06.014

Schrader, C., & Bastiaens, T. J. (2012). The influence of virtual presence: Effects on experienced cognitive load and learning outcomes in educational computer games. *Computers in Human Behavior*, *28*(2), 648–658. doi:10.1016/j.chb.2011.11.011

Vernadakis, N., Gioftsidou, A., Antoniou, A., Ioannidis, D., & Giannousi, M. (2012). The impact of Nintendo Wii to physical education students' balance compared to the traditional approaches. *Computers & Education*, *59*(2), 196–205. doi:10.1016/j.compedu.2012.01.003

KEY TERMS AND DEFINITIONS

Bodily Interaction: Bodily interaction is about utilization of human signals in a digital environment.

Cognitive Load: Cognitive load refers to the total amount of mental activity imposed on working memory at a certain time.

Complexity: Complexity is a state of the system that involves numerous elements and numerous relationships among these elements.

Educational Exergame: Educational exergame is a combination of educational game and exergame.

Exergame: An exergame is a game that is controlled with an input mechanism that requires a player to invest physical exertion.

Flow Experience: Flow describes a state of complete absorption or engagement in a goal-driven activity that is intrinsically rewarding.

Persuasive Technology: Persuasive technology describes design principles to change attitudes or behaviors of the users.

Chapter 9
Integrating Game-Enhanced Mathematics Learning into the Pre-Service Training of Teachers

Maria Meletiou-Mavrotheris
European University Cyprus, Cyprus

ABSTRACT

Mathematical literacy is a core literacy that functions as a critical gatekeeper for participation in many aspects of modern society. Research has shown that the way mathematics is taught at school is highly associated with students' achievement and interest levels. Declining interest in mathematics and the need to raise the educational standards of youth in this discipline set a critical agenda for the revision of pedagogical practices. Digital games hold a lot of promise as tools for improving mathematics instruction at the school level. This chapter reports the main insights gained from a study that implemented a game-enhanced learning environment for the training of pre-service elementary school teachers. Teachers experienced some of the ways in which online educational games could help students internalize key mathematical concepts across the school curriculum and build their problem-solving skills, while at the same time improving their attitudes towards the subject. The course also familiarized teachers with the design principles for constructivist gaming environments. Findings indicate a positive impact on teachers' competence in selecting, evaluating, and productively using online games as an instructional tool.

INTRODUCTION

In technology-based society, mathematics provides essential knowledge tools and the foundations for more advanced or specialized training either in higher education or through lifelong learning. Low proficiency in mathematics is highly correlated with low academic attainment, which leads to lower participation in the labour market and in lifelong learning activities after compulsory schooling (Commission of the European Communities, 2007). Despite, however, the fact that the development of mathematical knowledge and literacy is a fundamental requirement in

DOI: 10.4018/978-1-4666-3950-8.ch009

modern society, cross-national studies of student achievement (e.g. Trends in International Mathematics and Science Study [TIMSS], Programme for International Student Assessment [PISA]) indicate lack of mathematical competence for a considerable proportion of the student population around Europe and internationally. There is also well-documented evidence of declining interest in key science and mathematics topics, as well as in science careers (e.g. European Commission, 2007; U.S. Department of Education, 2000; Osborne & Collins, 2001; Adleman, 2004; Jenkins & Nelson 2005; Sjøberg & Schreiner, 2006; OECD, 2006). Students' low achievement and declining interest in mathematics is of concern given that mathematical literacy serves as one of the foundational areas of knowledge that drives scientific and technological advancement in knowledge-based economies (European Commission, 2004). Research suggests that students' mathematics identity is formed in the elementary grades and predicts their mathematics achievement in later years (Tate & Rousseau, 2002; Tate, 2005), and that pupils with poor quantitative skills are likely to have fallen behind by the age of ten (DfES, 2003). Thus, learning substantial mathematics is critical for young children, since the early years of schooling are especially important for children's mathematical development (Sarama & Clements, 2009).

Technology advances have provided the opportunity to create an entirely new learning environment in mathematics by significantly increasing the range and sophistication of possible classroom activities. Access to technology provides teachers and children with tools which, when constructively used, can create opportunities for enhanced learning of mathematics. Although traditional, teacher-centered approaches to mathematics instruction still dominate, there have been several attempts to improve mathematics instruction through the integration of learning technologies. One promising approach explored is the potential of computer games as tools for

supporting mathematics teaching and learning. The literature indicates strongly the educational value of using games within mathematics education (e.g. Resnick et al, 1996; Jonker & van Galen, 2004; Simpson et al., 2006).

The current article contributes to the emerging literature on game-enhanced mathematics teaching and learning. It reports on the main experiences gained from a study that aimed at providing a group of pre-service primary school teachers with the knowledge, skills, and confidence required to incorporate game-enhanced learning within the mathematics curriculum.

BACKGROUND

The formalist tradition has, in recent years, come under attack. A new paradigm has emerged, which views mathematics and science as meaning-making activities of a society of practitioners (Lakatos, 1976; Latour, 1987). Educational leaders and professional organizations in mathematics education (e.g. National Council of Teachers of Mathematics, 2000, Commission of the European Communities, 2007) have been advocating the adoption of more active learning environments that motivate learners, and encourage them through authentic inquiry to establish the relevance and meaning of mathematical concepts. These leaders stress the fact that the core of school mathematics should no longer be the teaching of techniques and calculations that computers can do much faster and more reliably, but the development of problem-solving skills that students will need to effectively live and function in a highly complex society. This shift is being reflected in most countries' educational policies and official curricula, which advocate pedagogical approaches that support inquiry-based, problem-solving learning of mathematics.

Despite the extensive calls for the uptake of learner-centered, inquiry-based pedagogical models, changing teaching practices is proving to be quite difficult. The research literature indicates a disconnection between curricula initiatives and calls for reform and actual classroom practice and suggests the persistence of traditional, teacher-centered approaches (European Commission, 2007; Barab et al., 2001; Klette, 2009; Klette et al., 2007; Tiberghien & Buty, 2007; Seidel & Prenzel, 2006). There is strong evidence that, in practice, inquiry-based teaching and learning of mathematics is not widely implemented (European Commission, 2007; Euler, 2011).

The methods of instruction have been identified as contributing to students' falling interest in mathematics (e.g. European Commission, 2004; European Commission 2007; Van Langen, 2005). Empirical classroom research over several decades shows that, with some notable exceptions, mathematics instruction has been characterized by traditional, abstract formulation which seems to be readily understood by only a small fraction of students (Mor et al., 2006). The teaching of mathematics is viewed as unappealing to the majority of students, as outdated and unconnected with their interests and experiences (Goodrum, Hackling & Rennie 2001). Ideas are presented in an overly theoretical and abstract manner without sufficient opportunities for students to engage in problem-solving and experimentation.

The connection between attitudes towards mathematics and the way it is taught sets a critical agenda for the revision of pedagogical practices at the school level. Many educational designers (e.g. Prensky, 2001; Shaffer et al., 2005; Shaffer, 2006) see computer games as a possible solution to the problem of the "Net Generation's" disengagement with traditional instruction. With international markets for computer games comparable with markets for movies and music, gaming has become a mainstream activity that has a prominent presence in students' daily life (Prensky, 2006; Lenhart et al., 2008). This increased popularity and proliferation of computer games, has led to a widespread interest in games as learning tools. Several mathematics educators have been experimenting with computer games, investigating the ways in which this massively popular worldwide youth activity could be brought into the mathematics classroom in order to capture students' interest and facilitate their learning of mathematics.

Digital games have many potential benefits for mathematics teaching and learning. One of the foremost qualities of digital games is their capacity to motivate, to engage and to immerse players (Felicia, 2009). Digital games can provide challenging experiences that promote players' intrinsic satisfaction, and keep them engaged and motivated. Research suggests that educational use of games is an effective means of improving students' attitudes towards mathematics (Lopez-Moreto & Lopez, 2007). It has been shown that educational games captivate students' attention, contributing to their increased motivation and engagement with mathematics (e.g. Squire, 2005; Young-Loveridge, 2005; Ke, 2008). Studies have also demonstrated that, in addition to providing an incentive for young people to engage in learning, games can also yield a potential increase in student learning outcomes. Although much of the research on the effectiveness of gaming on learning is inconclusive at this point (Fletcher & Tobias, 2006), there is strong evidence that appropriately designed educational games do have the potential to enhance children's learning of mathematics (e.g. Klawe, 1998; Bragg, 2007; McGivern et al., 2007; Kebritchi, Hirumi, & Bai, 2010). Games can also help to decrease the achievement gaps between students (Ketelhut et al., 2010; Cavanagh, 2008).

Research on teaching, learning and student cognition highlights that the process of teaching and learning in the sciences is complex and cannot be easily reduced to a set of algorithms and procedures (Leachm & Scott, 2000). The construction of meaningful understanding is supported by instruction that is collaborative, active, interactive, reflective, constructive and contextual (Bransford & Donovan, 2005). These characteristics of learning may be realized through a game-enhanced approach to mathematics instruction. Games offer immersive environments which are often impossible to access any other way, and which activate students' prior knowledge, provide immediate feedback and assessment of progress, require transfer of knowledge from other venues, and are naturally experiential (Ketelhut, & Schifter, 2011; Oblinger, 2004). Moreover, games are often social environments with communities of practice around the game, thus promoting collaborative learning through teaming up with other players (Ketelhut, & Schifter, 2011).

Games promote a constructivist approach to mathematics learning that can help students develop the types of skills suited to 21st century living and working (Wiliamson, 2009). Through the introduction of open-ended, challenging tasks that are meaningful for children and facilitate their interest in exploration, educational games can help focus mathematics instruction on conceptual understanding and problem-solving rather than on recipes and formal derivations (Koh et al., 2012). Using games, children can engage in authentic problem solving activities, build higher order critical thinking, and become reflective and self-directed learners (McFarlane, Sparrowhawk, & Heald, 2002; Bottino et al., 2007; Lenhart et al., 2008). When playing games, children have to diagnose problems, make conjectures, plan and carry out investigations to test their conjectures, distinguish alternatives, construct models, debate with peers, and form coherent arguments (Felicia, 2009). This supports the development of valuable skills such as logical and strategic thinking, planning, multi-tasking, self-monitoring, communication, negotiation, group decision-making, pattern recognition, accuracy, speed of calculation, and data-handling (Kirriemuir & McFarlane, 2004; Bottino et al., 2007; Miller & Robertson, 2010; Pratt et al., 2009). At the same time, games enable teachers to observe students' problem-solving strategies in action and assess their performance

(Koh et al., 2012). Thus, placing a focus on game-enhanced learning provides a powerful perspective that can contribute to transforming mathematics pedagogy at the school level.

One of the most important factors in any educational change is the change in teaching practices. The direct relationship between improving the quality of teaching and improving students' learning in mathematics is a common thread emerging from educational research (Stigler & Hiebert, 1999). For it is what a teacher knows and can do that influences how she or he/she organizes and conducts lessons, and it is the nature of these lessons that ultimately determines what students learn. Educational games' successful deployment in mathematics classrooms is highly dependent upon the knowledge, attitudes, and experiences of teachers with respect to games. Implementing game-enhanced learning in the classroom can be a challenge for teachers, requiring skills that are not necessarily addressed in current pre-service teacher education practices. Teachers need to be proactive, choosing high quality educational games, supporting and scaffolding pupils, and providing appropriate feedback. Thus, the provision of high quality teacher training on the educational applications of games is of paramount importance to their effective integration in classroom settings.

CASE DESCRIPTION

In the current study, a teaching experiment took place within an undergraduate mathematics education course targeting primary school teachers. The teaching experiment aimed at promoting, while at the same time also investigating, pre-service teachers' efficacy in effectively selecting and integrating digital games within the mathematics curriculum. This section provides an overview of the study design and of the main experiences gained from implementing the teaching experiment.

Methodology

Conceptual Framework

The design of the study was guided by the Technological Pedagogical Content Knowledge (TPACK) conceptual framework (Mishra & Koehler, 2006). The TPACK framework, which builds on Shulman's (1986) idea of Pedagogical Content Knowledge, emphasizes the importance of developing integrated and interdependent understanding of three primary forms of knowledge: technology, pedagogy, and content. The framework is based upon the premise that effective technology integration for pedagogy around specific subject matter requires developing understanding of the dynamic relationship between all three knowledge components. Thus, teacher ICT training cannot be treated as context-free, but should be accompanied with emphasis on how technology relates to the pedagogy and content. The aim is to move teachers beyond technocentric strategies that focus on the technology rather than the learning (Harris, Mishra, & Koehler, 2009).

Research Design: Scope and Context of Study

A case study design with mixed methods was employed in the study. The case studied consisted of a group of 13 pre-service primary school teachers (10 females, 3 males) enrolled in the undergraduate methods course *Integration of Modern Technology in the Teaching of Mathematics*, which includes a unit on game-enhanced learning. Students were mostly in the final year of their studies. The mean age of the course participants was 22 years.

Acknowledging the fact that teachers are at the heart of any educational reform effort, the course was designed to offer high-quality professional development experiences to these novice teachers that would enable them to effectively integrate technology with core curricular ideas. The emphasis was on enriching the participants'

Technological Pedagogical Content Knowledge (TPACK) of mathematics by providing them with opportunities to develop their knowledge, skills, and attitudes towards technology-enhanced mathematics learning.

The unit on game-enhanced learning, which lasted for three weeks (9 hours), introduced prospective teachers to the rational and context for employing digital games in mathematics classrooms. Teachers experienced some of the ways in which online educational games could help students internalize key mathematical concepts across the school curriculum while at the same time improving their attitudes towards the subject. The unit also familiarized teachers with the design principles for constructivist gaming environments (Munoz-Rosario & Widmeyer, 2009), and promoted the development of their skills in properly evaluating educational games available online, and in selecting games with pedagogically-sound design features.

Instruments, Data Collection and Analysis Procedures

Multiple forms of assessment were used to collect and document evidence of changes in teachers' Technological Pedagogical Content Knowledge (TPACK), and in their attitudes towards game-enhanced mathematics instruction as a result of participating in the course:

1. An open-ended pre-survey and a post-survey gathering pre-service teachers' perception of educational games before and after their participation in the course;
2. Individual interviews of selected pre-service teachers at the beginning of the course;
3. Video-records of group activities;
4. Samples of teacher work;
5. Classroom observations and artifacts.

Analysis of the collected data has provided rich insights into teachers' perspectives on game use and its effectiveness, and into the ways in which the course influenced these perceptive, as well as their confidence and ability to incorporate game-enhanced learning within the mathematics curriculum. The next section will share some of these insights.

Lessons Learned from Case Study

Prior Experiences and Attitudes towards Games

An online pre-survey completed in class by all course participants (*n=13*), and follow-up interviews of some of the participants (*n=5*), provided baseline information regarding the pre-service teachers' prior experiences and attitudes towards game-based mathematics learning.

The majority of the participants were quite facile with digital games. They had considerable experience with both single player games (e.g. Temple Run, Pro Evolution Soccer, Run Tekken, Soulcalibur), and with multiplayer games available on Facebook such as Diamond Dash and Bubble Island. This finding was not surprising given the prospective teachers' young age. All of them were "digital natives" who grew up surrounded by technology and who had been playing video games since the time they were little children.

Playing of games was an important leisure time activity for almost all of the pre-service teachers. Nine teachers reported playing games on a daily or weekly basis in their spare time, while two others reported playing games "a few times per month." Despite the small number of participants involved in the study, there was considerable breadth of game-based activity. Most of the teachers spent between 4-6 hours per week on games, but two of them were keen games players who spent at least 10 hours per week on games. At the same time, however, there were two teachers who reported rarely playing any games because they considered it to be *a waste of time*.

In the pre-survey and follow-up interviews, prospective teachers were asked to express their opinion regarding the use of digital games in mathematics education, and to state whether they would consider incorporating such games in their teaching in the future. All of the participants agreed that games should be considered as worthy of consideration in the classroom and indicated that they planned to utilize gaming in their teaching. Despite, however, their positive attitudes toward the use of games in education, teachers made comments which suggested very limited knowledge and experience with game-based instruction, and lack of appreciation of the potential of digital games to transform the nature of mathematics education provided to students. Teachers viewed games mainly as a useful aid for making mathematics instruction more joyful. The most commonly cited reasons for considering using games in the classroom were for increasing students' motivation and engagement. Responses such as the following were typical:

Games allow teachers to make their lessons more interesting and children to learn without getting bored.

It's more fun for children... They all love playing electronic games at home. Gaming in the classroom provides a strong incentive for children to actively participate in the learning process.

It's a powerful way to attract all children's attention and to help them learn mathematical concepts more easily.

When, in the follow-up interviews, teachers were prompted to identify opportunities for introducing games in the mathematics classroom, it became obvious that they had a very limited notion of game-based instruction. They viewed games as tools for practicing and/or evaluating acquired skills, and not as a powerful means of creating immersive learning experiences that would otherwise be impossible or too costly or too dangerous to provide to students (Mitchell & Savill-Smith, 2004):

I don't think it would be a good idea to use digital games for introducing a new concept or idea. I believe that games should be used at the completion of a unit for students to practice what they have been taught.

The teacher can use games at the completion of a lesson for summative evaluation purposes, in order to see whether his/her learning objectives have been achieved.

Teachers' restricted view of games seems to have stemmed from the fact that their past exposure to digital educational games in mathematics had been limited to drill-and-practice ones, as their comments indicated:

An example of a good educational game in mathematics education is one where children are asked to write the fraction corresponding to the highlighted portion of a shape.

Children can use games to practice doing addition, subtraction, multiplication and division.

None of the teachers had ever been exposed to a challenging, complex and scaffolded (Gee, 2003) educational game designed to help students build higher order mathematical problem-solving skills.

Nature of Teaching Experiment

Findings from the pre-survey and follow-up interviews pointed to the clear need for prospective teachers' professional training on effectively uses of digital games as a pedagogical tool. Despite their extensive prior experience and knowledge of playing games for their own leisure, par-

ticipants had very limited understanding of the educational potential of games, and of how to implement game-based mathematics instruction. The teaching experiment aimed at helping them develop a more sophisticated view regarding the benefits of gaming than their instrumental view of games as "providing the 'fun' incentive for young people to pay attention in lessons" (Williamson, 2009). Teachers were offered a critical introduction into the potential and challenges of using computer games in mathematics instruction, and into the ways in which purposefully selected games blended with carefully constructed learning experiences can be used to turn children into reflective and self-directed learners and to improve their learning of mathematics.

Pre-service teachers worked in group activities to explore a variety of mathematical concepts using online educational games. Through experimentation with a range of games platforms and software, feedback from each other and reflection, they gained better understanding of how digital games could be integrated into the mathematics curriculum. They also improved their ability to assess the educative power of different games, to properly identify their advantages and disadvantages.

In addition to computer activities, there were also discussions focusing on children's learning and what is required to involve them in learning about mathematics though use of educational games. These discussions provided the venue for pointing out the affordances and limitations of educational games, and for identifying design considerations and implementation strategies that promote the incorporation of online educational games in ways that motivate children, and help them build a solid foundation in their mathematics skills.

A characteristic example of the type of activities in which students engaged during the instructional experiment is the "Evaluation of Educational Games" task described next.

"Evaluation of Educational Games" Task

In this group activity, students worked together to compare and contrast different online educational games. They were provided with a long list of different educational games freely available online, from which they had to select two games: a good example of a high quality mathematics education game, and a poor example. Teachers had to write a report justifying the rationale for their choices. We describe next how two of the study participants, George and Anna, approached the task.

After experimenting with several educational games, George and Anna finally selected the game "Crack Hacker's Safe" as a good example of a high quality educational game. "Crack Hacker's Safe" can be found on Cyberchase, an award-winning, research-based website offered by Public Broadcasting Station (http://pbskids. org/cyberchase/math-games/crack-hackers-safe/), which has been designed for children ages 8 to 12 to *deliver positive messages about math by teaching concepts in a fun way that kids can understand.* The Cyberchase website has several dynamic web games packed with mystery, humor, and action that can help children build strong mathematics and problem-solving skills while exploring their world. In "Crack Hacker's Safe," the players "must help Digit crack the lock on Hacker's safe." They must complete a sequence of shape, number, and color patterns to crack the code on the hacker's safe and open the lock. The game aims at building students' algebraic reasoning through the identification of both growing and shrinking patterns. Children can play the game individually or with friends and classmates.

In their report, George and Anna gave several reasons for positively evaluating the specific game, including the following:

- The game interface is user-friendly, with well-designed graphics and easy to learn game functionalities.

- A Help section is available during the game to assist children that require extra help.

- **The game addresses important mathematical content and concepts:** The development of algebraic reasoning through pattern recognition.

- **The game has clear goals and objectives to be accomplished by the player in order to complete the game:** "Children aim at completing a series of shape, number, and color patterns to crack Hacker's safe."

- **The game has a good scenario:** "The game does not simply ask students to recognize some mathematical patterns. Children assume the role of a hacker and they try to find the right combinations to unlock the safe. This is an interesting and challenging scenario that can easily attract children's attention and increase their motivation."

- The game focuses on high-level mathematics learning rather than on factual recall, developing students' critical thinking, and problem solving skills.

- The game advances in a step-by-step fashion, providing a challenging problem-solving environment for children.

- Each student attempt is followed by appropriate feedback. If necessary, hints are provided to the player to help him/her solve the problem.

- **Players are recognized as winners only if important learning takes place:** "To find the right combination and open the safe, children need to decode complicated patterns that combine numbers, colors, and shapes. Thus winning cannot be the result of random selection, but has to be based on real understanding of the underlying patterns."

- **The game can support collaboration and group work:** "The teacher can ask children to play the game in pairs in order to promote interaction among students and teamwork."

- **The game can support competition:** "Although the game interface is not multi-player, if the game is played in class, then the teacher can increase students' motivation and help them develop their competition skills by asking them to work in pairs, with the winning team being the one that accomplishes to unlock the safe first."

The game selected by George and Anna as a poor example of an online educational game was "Tumbletown Mathletics" (http://www.tvokids.com/games/tumbletownmathletics). Tumbletown Mathletics is comprised of five "mini-games" which aim to help children develop their numeration and measurement skills by practicing mathematics "in a fun and exciting way." These games are based on the Ontario school curriculum. Children accumulate points through mathematical activities such as ordering numbers, finding fractions, adding and subtracting numbers, and making measurements using non-standard and standard units. The goal is for children to beat their last score.

George and Anna noted that although "Tumbletown Mathletics" does have a user-friendly and well designed interface, it is not a game they would introduce in their mathematics classroom. They gave several reasons to justify their negative evaluation of the game:

- **The game does not provide proper feedback:** "When the player gives a wrong answer, the system just lets them know that their answer is wrong. No other feedback is provided to help children understand why they are wrong."
- **The game is not based on any scenario:** "The game does not have any plot. All that the children do is to try to beat the score they got the previous they played the game."

- **The game is not challenging and engaging:** "The game is too easy. It is not motivating and children will get bored easily."
- The game can only be played individually, thus there is no opportunity for collaboration and/or competition among children.
- **It is a drill-and-practice game:** "The questions that students have to answer assess only procedural knowledge and not higher order thinking. The game can be used for drill-and-practice purposes, but not for building students' problem solving skills."
- **Finding the right answer can be based on random factors:** "The questions posed by the game are multiple choice questions with only two possible choices, so children can get the right answer by chance."

George and Anna based their evaluation of the two games on important technical and pedagogical considerations. Similarly to all of the other pre-service teachers participating in the study, while initially they tended to focus almost solely on the playfulness of games, they have now come to recognize the need for educational games to combine playfulness with instructional soundness (McDaniel & Telep, 2009).

DISCUSSION

Recognizing the central role of teachers in educational reform, the current study focused on initial teacher training. A teaching experiment took place within an undergraduate mathematics methods course, which aimed at empowering the participating pre-service primary teachers to effectively integrate digital games within the mathematics curriculum. The teaching experiment offered a critical introduction into the potential and challenges of game-enhanced mathematics instruction. Despite the tentative and non-generalizable nature of the study findings, it was still able to contribute some useful insights into the emerging literature on game-enhanced mathematics teaching and learning. Key conclusions from the analysis of the data collected during the study were that the course was quite successful in helping this group of young educators to improve their confidence and ability to integrate games within the mathematics curriculum.

In the survey administered at the completion of the course, teachers were again asked to express their opinion regarding the educational use of online games in mathematics education. Similarly to the pre-survey stage, teachers expressed very positive attitudes towards game-based mathematics learning. The teaching experiment further strengthened their belief that games are highly motivational, and can help create more active, student-centered learning environments. All of the teachers stressed that games motivate children to employ themselves in mathematics learning because they are an alternative way of teaching mathematics *which combines learning with fun,* and diverts instruction *from the typical classroom routine that fails to attract the attention of young learners, who grow up in a society full of action, images, and sounds.* Integration of games into the mathematics curriculum, they noted, *can capture students' attention for more extended periods of time and make them more perseverant."* Providing *"connections to children's recreational interests and experiences,* can enhance their enjoyment of mathematics, and help them develop positive attitudes towards the subject.

Unlike the pre-survey stage, in which pre-service teachers had focused on the playfulness of games, their responses to the post-survey indicate that the teaching experiment has helped them gain appreciation of the true potential of digital games to transform the nature of mathematics teaching and learning. All of the course participants emphasized the fact that the integration of games into the instructional process not only acts as a strong motivational tool for students, but can also lead to substantial gains in learning outcomes.

They stressed that games can offer a more active and effective learning context that promotes the construction of important mathematics knowledge and skills in ways that are difficult to achieve in a more traditional instructional setting.

Despite their enthusiasm and strong agreement regarding the usefulness of games as an educational tool, the prospective teachers recognized that games are not a panacea, and that their incorporation into the curriculum does not guarantee improved learning of mathematics. They made several recommendations regarding optimal ways of using computer games in schools so as to make a positive impact on students' engagement and learning. Their recommendations have generally supported the propositions of gaming researchers (e.g. Garris et al., 2002; Gee, 2003; Van Eck, 2006). In particular, the important role of the teacher in facilitating learning with digital games was stressed repeatedly by the pre-service teachers, who pointed out that games should not be employed as standalone applications, but as educational tools to be used in balance with other, educationally sound instructional strategies, in order to provide for a fuller learning experience.

To evaluate the applicability and success of the teaching experiment, teachers were asked to develop and submit on the last day of classes, a lesson plan incorporating digital games to help primary school students explore a new mathematics concept. They were required to consider the following in their lesson planning: national curriculum, the children's targeted grade level, lesson procedures, and possible facilitation strategies. Working individually, pre-service teachers selected a curriculum topic and a target grade level, and designed their lesson plan accordingly. Each lesson plan provided a description of the following elements: learning objectives, lesson sequence, and assessment strategies. All of the pre-service teachers submitted lesson plans of a very high quality, effectively applying the ideas they had learned in the course in their lesson design. All lesson plans included games with an attractive, user-friendly interface, and with clear game objectives. More importantly, teachers were careful to choose games that added real value to the effectiveness of the lesson by focusing on high-level mathematics learning, and on mathematical problem-solving. The selected games were also effectively integrated with the curriculum. The game goals and the stated learning objectives were well aligned in all of the lesson plans. Moreover, pre-service teachers ensured that they chose games that matched the targeted student age group competency level. The chosen games were within the learners' zone of proximal development (Vygotsky, 1978). They were challenging enough to keep children engaged for a long time, but not too difficult in order not to frustrate children with tasks that surpassed their abilities. Finally, game-based activities were accompanied with alternative pre-game and post-game instructional events, in order to ensure that children make the connection between gaming and learning

FUTURE RESEARCH DIRECTIONS

A drawback of this case study is the limited generalizability of its findings. The qualitative methodology used to research the case, the small scale of the study, and its limited geographical nature, means that generalizations to cases that are not very similar should be done cautiously as the specific classroom investigated might not be representative of all pre-service mathematics teacher-training classrooms. Additionally, although the rich insights gained from the instructional experiment suggest that digital games hold a lot of promise as a tool for reforming mathematics education, the research design of the present inquiry does not allow the drawing of generalizations.

More research is needed to advance our understanding of the ways in which games can be integrated into the mathematics learning process to maximize their learning potential. Future effect studies of digital games ought to take place in

regular classroom settings in order to determine the actual potential of games as learning tools (Van Eck, 2006). Research focusing on the integration of games in the mathematics classroom can shed light into both facilitating and inhibiting factors to the successful implementation of games in formal learning settings. It can provide useful insights to mathematics teachers on how to best utilize the affordances provided by digital games to motivate their students, and to scaffold and extend their mathematical reasoning.

A follow-up study currently planned by the author aims to enrich the initial insights gained from the instructional experiment described in this chapter. Some of the pre-service teachers that participated in the teaching experiment will be tracked into their teaching practice placements, in order to evaluate the effect of their experiences with game-enhanced mathematics learning on actual classroom performance. Guskey's hierarchical model (Guskey, 2002) will be used to guide the evaluation. According to this model, teacher professional development evaluation should move from the simple (reactions of participants), to the more complex (student learning outcomes), with data from each level building on the previous. Evaluation during the follow-up study will focus on how participants apply their new knowledge and skills in real classrooms. It will address "the bottom line" of professional development, which is the impact of professional development on student achievement, performance, attitudes, and self-efficacy (Abell et al., 2007). Evidence on this impact will come from pre- and post-testing of students, observations and videotaping of classroom episodes, interviewing of students, and samples of student work.

CONCLUSION

Mathematics literacy is among the key competencies that all individuals need in an information based society. Low proficiency in mathematics at school is highly correlated with low academic attainment, which leads to lower participation in the labor market and in lifelong learning activities after compulsory schooling (Commission of the European Communities, 2007). The current study represents an effort to address students' declining interest in mathematics, and to raise their educational standards in this discipline. It exploits the affordance of digital games in an effort to spark young children's interest in mathematics and to make mathematical concepts more accessible and attractive for all children.

One pervasive challenge in mathematics education at the school level is the identification and use of authentic contexts to motivate student inquiry. Games can be used as the machinery for students to engage in authentic problem solving activities that can help raise their intrinsic interest in mathematics, and promote the attainment of important competencies essential in modern society. They can support learning of the mathematics curriculum in educationally powerful and interactive ways that engage students and promote their growth. Game-enhanced learning activities incorporate important hands-on experiences and opportunities for children to see the relevance of mathematics, and can help them develop more interest in pursuing careers in mathematics and science-related fields (Van Langen, 2005). They can make the disciplines more accessible and attractive to all students, including those currently underrepresented in the sciences. By motivating a wide diversity of young people toward science and mathematics studies and career paths, games can increase learners' participation and success in these critically important aspects of society.

Teachers are the gatekeepers of what technological tools are used in their classrooms (Pastore & Falvo, 2010). The success of digital games as a tool for learning mathematics in formal situations will ultimately depend on the abilities of teachers to take full advantage of their educational potential (Becker, 2007). Findings from the current study corroborate with the research literature, which indicates that the majority of teachers do have positive attitudes towards the adoption games in instruction but lack appreciation of their true potential for transforming mathematics teaching and learning (e.g. Can & Cagiltay, 2006; Koh et al., 2012). Other researchers have also found that teachers lack the vision and the personal experience of what technology-enhanced teaching could look like (Redecker et al., 2009; Barbour & Evans, 2009; Ertzberger, 2009), and tend to view games as instructional tools to be mainly used for motivational purposes (Barab et al., 2005; Williamson, 2009; Ketelhut, Clarke, & Nelson, 2010).

Instructional integration of appropriate digital games can lead to improved learning of most topics included in the mathematics curriculum. However, the adoption of game-enhanced approaches to mathematics learning necessitates restructuring of the manner in which mathematics content is taught. It requires a move away from didactic teaching practices toward practices that engage students in autonomous, problem-solving activities, which culminate in the construction of deep knowledge and understandings of the discipline. In order to address teachers' limited assumptions and lack of knowledge about the educational applications of games, and to provide them to with the knowledge required to make gaming environments effective for teaching, there is an urgent need for high quality professional training at both the initial teacher training stage as well as through continuous professional development. Through their participation in gaming seminars, workshops, and conferences, teachers should be helped to move beyond their restricted views of digital games as tools to be used "for their own sake or for flimsily conceived incentivisation purposes" (Williamson, 2009). They should come to view games as powerful tools that can promote the construction of important mathematics knowledge and skills in ways, which are difficult to achieve through more traditional media or teaching approaches, and develop effective pedagogies for their successful integration into instructional settings.

Teacher professional development initiatives should pay special attention to the familiarization of teachers with the design principles for constructivist gaming environments. Although there are many online mathematics games available, most of them tend to be drill-and-practice games that address trivial facts and knowledge, and do not add any real value to the educational process. In order for teachers to provide challenging game-based environments that build children's mathematical reasoning, they should acquire the necessary skills for effectively assessing the educational potential and suitability of different digital games based on important technical and pedagogical considerations. Their professional development on game-based instruction should make them competent in selecting educationally sound games that include the elements of collaboration and competition, and promote authenticity of learning, inquiry learning, reflective thinking, and mathematical problem solving. Through experimentation with a variety of educational games for teaching different mathematical topics, teachers should also gain expertise in choosing games that fit well with their targeted grade level and curricular topic.

Learning outcomes achieved through educational games depend, to a large extent, on the instructional activities context that structures the way games are used in the classroom (Miller et al., 1999; Kaptelin and Cole, 2002). In addition to their critical role in choosing appropriate games to promote student learning, teachers also play a key role in planning classroom game-based activities, and in providing continued learner support. Educational gaming researchers (e.g., Garris et al., 2002; Gee, 2003) have shown that digital games are more effective when acting as adjuncts to traditional teaching methods rather than as standalone applications. They have also demonstrated that games should be incorporated within instructional settings that include debriefing and reflection as critical elements for game-based learning (Garris et al., 2002; Pivec & Pivec, 2009). Thus, training

teachers on how design suitable off-computer activities, and provide just-in-time guidance and scaffolding (Ke, 2008) is also an essential element for the successful integration of games into the instructional process.

REFERENCES

Abell, S. K., Lannin, J. K., Marra, R. M., Ehlert, M. W., Cole, J. S., & Lee, M. H. (2007). Multi-site evaluation of science and mathematics teacher professional development programs: The project profile approach. *Studies in Educational Evaluation, 33*, 135–158. doi:10.1016/j.stueduc.2007.04.003

Adleman, C. (2004). *Principal indicators of academic histories in postsecondary education: 1972-2000*. Washington, DC: U.S. Department of Education.

Barab, S., Thomas, M., Dodge, T., Carteaux, R., & Tuzun, H. (2005). Making learning fun: Quest Atlantis, a game without guns. *Educational Technology Research and Development, 53*(1), 86–107. doi:10.1007/BF02504859

Barab, S. A., Hay, K. E., Barnett, M. G., & Squire, K. (2001). Constructing virtual worlds: Tracing the historical development of learner practices/understandings. *Cognition and Instruction, 19*(1), 47–94. doi:10.1207/S1532690XCI1901_2

Barbour, M. K., & Evans, M. (2009). Making sense of video games: pre-service teachers struggle with this new medium. In *Proceedings of the 20th International Conference of the Society of Informational Technology and Teacher Education,* (pp. 1367–1371). Chesapeake, VA: AACE.

Becker, K. (2007). Teaching teachers about serious games. In C. Montgomerie & J. Seale (Eds.), *Proceedings of World Conference on Educational Multimedia, Hypermedia and Telecommunications 2007,* (pp. 2389-2396). Chesapeake, VA: AACE.

Bottino, R. M., Ferlino, L., Ott, M., & Tavella, M. (2007). Developing strategic and reasoning abilities with computer games at primary school level. *Computers & Education, 49*(4), 1272–1286. doi:10.1016/j.compedu.2006.02.003

Bragg, L. (2007). Students' conflicting attitudes towards games as a vehicle for learning mathematics: A methodological dilemma. *Mathematics Education Research Journal, 19*(1), 29–44. doi:10.1007/BF03217448

Bransford, J. D., & Donovan, M. S. (2005). Scientific inquiry and how people learn. In Donovan, M. S., & Bransford, J. D. (Eds.), *How Students Learn: Science in the Classroom* (pp. 397–420). Washington, DC: National Academies Press.

Can, G., & Cagiltay, K. (2006). Turkish prospective teachers' perceptions regarding the use of computer games with educational features. *Journal of Educational Technology & Society, 9*(1), 308–321.

Cavanagh, S. (2008). Playing games in class helps students grasp math. *Education Week*, 43–46.

Commission of the European Communities. (2007). *A coherent framework of indicators and benchmarks for monitoring progress towards the Lisbon objectives in education and training.* Retrieved September 15, 2012, from http://eur-lex.europa.eu/LexUriServ/site/en/com/2007/com2007_0061en01.pdf

DfES. (2003). *Excellence and enjoyment: A strategy for primary schools.* London, UK: DfES.

Ertzberger, J. (2009). An exploration of factors affecting teachers' use of video games as instructional tools. In *Proceedings of the 20th International Conference of the Society of Informational Technology and Teacher Education*, (pp. 1825–1831). Chesapeake, VA: AACE.

Euler (2011). *The PRIMAS project: Promoting inquiry-based learning (IBL) in mathematics and science education across Europe.* Retrieved September 15, 2012, from http://www.primasproject.eu/servlet/supportBinaryFiles?referenceId=8&supportId=1247

European Commission. Directorate -General for Research. (2007). *Science education now: A renewed pedagogy for the future of Europe: Report of the high-level group on science education.* Retrieved September 15, 2012, from http://ec.europa.eu/research/science-society/document_library/pdf_06/report-rocard-on-science-education_en.pdf

European Commission, Directorate-General for Education and Culture. (2004). *Working group D 'mathematics, science and technology' objective 1.4 "increasing recruitment to scientific and technical studies" Interim report.* Retrieved September 15, 2012, from http://ec.europa.eu/education/policies/2010/doc/math2004.pdf

Felicia, P. (2009). *Digital games in schools: A handbook for teachers.* Brussels, Belgium: European Schoolnet. Retrieved September 15, 2012, from http://games.eun.org/upload/GIS_handbook_en.pdf

Fletcher, J. D., & Tobias, S. (2006). Using games and simulations for instruction: A research review. In *Proceedings of New Learning Technologies 2006 Conference.* Warrenton, VA: Society for Applied Learning Technology.

Garris, R., Ahlers, R., & Driskell, J. E. (2002). Games, motivation, and learning: A research and practice model. *Simulation & Gaming, 33*(4), 441–467. doi:10.1177/1046878102238607

Gee, J. P. (2003). *What video games have to teach us about learning and literacy.* New York, NY: Palgrave/Macmillan. doi:10.1145/950566.950595

Goodrum, D., Hackling, M., & Rennie, L. (2001). *The status and quality of teaching and learning of science in Australian schools: A research report.* Canberra, Australia: Department of Education, Training and Youth Affairs.

Guskey, T. R. (2002). Does it make a difference? Evaluating professional development. *Educational Leadership, 59*(6), 45–51.

Harris, J., Mishra, P., & Koehler, M. (2009). Teachers' technological pedagogical content knowledge and learning activity types: Curriculum-based technology integration reframed. *Journal of Research on Technology in Education, 41*(4), 393–416.

Jenkins, E., & Nelson, N. W. (2005). Important but not for me: students' attitudes toward secondary school science in England. *Research in Science & Technological Education, 23,* 41–57. doi:10.1080/02635140500068435

Jonker, V., & van Galen, F. (2004). *KidsKount: Mathematics games for realistic mathematics education in primary school.* Paper presented at 10ᵗʰ International Conference on Mathematics Education (ICME). Kopenhagen, Denmark.

Kaptelin, V., & Cole, M. (2002). Individual and collective activities in educational computer game playing. In Kosmann, T., Hall, R., & Miyake, N. (Eds.), *g2057CSCL 2: Carrying Forward the Conversation* (pp. 303–316). Mahwah, NJ: Lawrence Erlbaum.

Ke, F. (2008). Computer games application within alternative classroom goal structures: Cognitive, metacognitive, and affective evaluation. *Educational Technology Research and Development, 56,* 539–556. doi:10.1007/s11423-008-9086-5

Kebritchi, M., Hirumi, A., & Bai, H. (2010). The effects of modern mathematics computer games on mathematics achievement and class motivation. *Computers & Education, 55*(2), 427–443. doi:10.1016/j.compedu.2010.02.007

Ketelhut, D. J., Clarke, J., & Nelson, B. (2010). The development of River City, a multi-user virtual environment-based scientific inquiry curriculum: Historical and design evolutions. In M. J. Jacobson & P. Reimann (Eds.), *Designs for Learning Environments of the Future,* (pp. 89-110). New York, NY: Springer Science + Business Media.

Ketelhut, D. J., Nelson, B., Clarke, J., & Dede, C. (2010). A multi-user virtual environment for building higher order inquiry skills in science. *British Journal of Educational Technology, 41*(1), 56–68. doi:10.1111/j.1467-8535.2009.01036.x

Ketelhut, D. J., & Schifter, C. C. (2011). Teachers and game-based learning: Improving understanding of how to increase efficacy of adoption. *Computers & Education, 56*(2), 539–546. doi:10.1016/j.compedu.2010.10.002

Kirriemuir, J., & Mcfarlane, A. (2004). *Literature review in games and learning.* Retrieved September 15, 2012, from http://hal.archives-ouvertes.fr/docs/00/19/04/53/PDF/kirriemuir-j-2004-r8.pdf

Klawe, M. (1998). *When does the use of computer games and other interactive multimedia software help students learn mathematics?* Paper presented at NCTM Standards 2000 Technology Conference. Washington, DC.

Klette, K. (2009). Challenges in strategies for complexity reduction in video studies: Experiences from the PISA+ study: A video study of teaching and learning in Norway. In Janik, T., & Seidel, T. (Eds.), *The Power of Video Studies in Investigating Teaching and Learning in the Classroom* (pp. 61–82). New York, NY: Waxmann Publishing.

Klette, K., Odegaard, M., & Arnesen, N. E. (2007). *Time scales and coding categories in video analysis.* Paper presented at ESERA 2007. New York, NY.

Koh, E., Kin, Y. G., Wadhwa, B., & Lim, J. (2012). Teacher perceptions of games in Singapore schools. *Simulation & Gaming*, *43*(1), 51–66. doi:10.1177/1046878111401839

Lakatos, I. (1976). *Proofs and refutations*. Cambridge, UK: Cambridge University Press. doi:10.1017/CBO9781139171472

Latour, B. (1987). *Science in action*. Cambridge, MA: Harvard University Press.

Lenhart, A., Kahne, J., Middaugh, E., Macgill, A. R., Evans, C., & Vitak, J. (2008). *Teens, video games and civics*. Retrieved September 15, 2012, from http://www.pewinternet.org/Reports/2008/Teens-VideoGames-and-Civics.aspx

Lopez-Moreto, G., & Lopez, G. (2007). Computer support for learning mathematics: A learning environment based on recreational learning objects. *Computers & Education*, *48*, 618–641. doi:10.1016/j.compedu.2005.04.014

McDaniel, R., & Telep, P. (2009). Best practices for integrating game-based learning into online teaching. *Journal of Online Learning and Teaching*, *5*(2), 424–438.

McFarlane, A., Sparrowhawk, A., & Heald, Y. (2002). *Report on the educational use of games*. Cambridge, UK: TEEM.

McGivern, R. F., Hilliard, V. R., Anderson, J., Reilly, J. S., Rodriguez, A., Fielding, B., & Shapiro, L. (2007). Improving preliteracy and premath skills of head start children with classroom computer games. *Early Childhood Services: An Interdisciplinary Journal of Effectiveness*, *1*, 71–81.

Miller, C. S., Lehman, J. F., & Koedinger, K. R. (1999). Goals and learning in microworlds. *Cognitive Science*, *23*(3), 305–336. doi:10.1207/s15516709cog2303_2

Miller, D. J., & Roberstson, D. P. (2010). Article. *British Journal of Educational Technology*, *41*(2), 242–255. doi:10.1111/j.1467-8535.2008.00918.x

Mishra, P., & Koehler, M. J. (2006). Technological pedagogical content knowledge: A framework for teacher knowledge. *Teachers College Record*, *108*(6), 1017–1054. doi:10.1111/j.1467-9620.2006.00684.x

Mitchell, A., & Savill-Smith, C. (2004). *The use of computer and video games for learning: A review of the literature*. London, UK: Learning and Skills Development Agency.

Mor, Y., Winters, N., Cerulli, M., & Björk, S. (2006). *Literature review on the use of games in mathematical learning, part I: Design. Report of the Learning Patterns for the Design and Deployment of Mathematical Games project*. Academic Press.

National Council of Teachers of Mathematics. (2000). *Principles and standards for school mathematics*. Reston, VA: National Council of Teachers of Mathematics.

Oblinger, D. (2004). The next generation of educational engagement. *Journal of Interactive Media in Education, 8*. Retrieved September 15, 2012, from http://jime.open.ac.uk/article/2004-8-oblinger/198

OECD. (2006). *Evolution of student interest in science and technology studies – Policy report*. Paper presented at the Global Science Forum. Paris, France.

Osborne, J. F., & Collins, S. (2001). Pupils' views of the role and value of the science curriculum: A focus-group study. *International Journal of Science Education*, *23*, 441–468. doi:10.1080/09500690010006518

Pastore, R. S., & Falvo, D. A. (2010). Video games in the classroom: Pre- and in-service teachers' perceptions of games in the K-12 classroom. *International Journal of Instructional Technology and Distance Learning*, *7*(12), 49–57.

Pivec, M., & Pivec, P. (2009). What do we know from research about the use of games in education? In Wastiau, P., Kearney, C., & van den Berghe, W. (Eds.), *How are Digital Games used in School* (pp. 123–156). Brussels, Belgium: European Schoolnet.

Pratt, D., Winters, N., Cerulli, M., & Leemkuil, H. (2009). A patterns approach to connecting the design and deployment of mathematical games and simulations. In Balacheff, N., Ludvigsen, S., de Jong, T., Lazonder, A., & Barnes, S. (Eds.), *Technology-Enhanced Learning: Principles and Products* (pp. 215–232). Dordrecht, The Netherlands: Springer. doi:10.1007/978-1-4020-9827-7_13

Prensky, M. (2001). *Digital game-based learning.* New York, NY: McGraw-Hill.

Prensky, M. (2006). *Don't bother me mom: I'm learning!* St. Paul, MN: Paragon House.

Redecker, C., Ala-Mutka, K., Bacigalupo, M., Ferrari, A., & Punie, Y. (2009). *Learning 2.0: The impact of web 2.0 innovations on education and training in Europe.* JRC Scientific and Technical Reports. Retrieved September 15, 2012, from http://ipts.jrc.ec.europa.eu/publications/pub.cfm?id=2899

Resnick, M., Bruckman, A., & Martin, F. (1996). Pianos not stereos: Creating computational construction kits. *Interaction, 3*(6).

Sarama, J., & Clements, D. H. (2009). Building blocks and cognitive building blocks: Playing to know the world mathematically. *American Journal of Play, 1*, 313–337.

Seidel, T., & Prenzel, M. (2006). Stability of teaching patterns in physics instruction: Findings from a video study. *Learning and Instruction, 16*, 228–240. doi:10.1016/j.learninstruc.2006.03.002

Shaffer, D. W. (2006). *How computer games help children learn.* New York, NY: Palgrave Macmillan. doi:10.1057/9780230601994

Shaffer, D. W., Squire, K. R., Halverson, R., & Gee, J. P. (2005). Video games and the future of learning. *Phi Delta Kappan, 87*(2), 104–111.

Shulman, L. S. (1986). Those who understand: Knowledge growth in teaching. *Educational Researcher, 15*(2), 4–14.

Simpson, G., Hoyles, C., & Noss, R. (2006). Exploring the mathematics of motion through construction and collaboration. *Journal of Computer Journal of Computer Assisted Learning, 22*, 114–136. doi:10.1111/j.1365-2729.2006.00164.x

Sjøberg, S., & Schreiner, C. (2006). How do learners in different cultures relate to science and technology? Results and perspectives from the project ROSE. *APFSLT: Asia-Pacific Forum on Science Learning and Teaching, 7*(1).

Squire, K. (2005). Changing the game: What happens when video games enter the classroom? *Innovate, 1*(6).

Stigler, M., & Hiebert, J. (1999). *The teaching gap.* New York, NY: Free Press.

Tate, W. F. (2005). *Access and opportunities to learn are not accidents: Engineering mathematical progress in your school.* Paper presented at the Southeast Eisenhower Regional Consortium for Mathematics Science at SERVE. Orlando, FL.

Tate, W. F., & Rousseau, C. (2002). Access and opportunity: The political and social context of mathematics education. In English, L. D. (Ed.), *Handbook of International Research in Mathematics Education* (pp. 271–299). London, UK: Erlbaum.

Tiberghien, A., & Buty, C. (2007). Studying science teaching practices in relation to learning: Times scales of teaching phenomena. In Pintó, R., & Couso, D. (Eds.), *ESERA Selected Contributions Book* (pp. 59–75). Berlin, Germany: Springer. doi:10.1007/978-1-4020-5032-9_5

U.S. Department of Education, National Center for Education Statistics. (2000). *Entry and persistence of women and minorities in college science and engineering education*. Washington, DC: NCES.

Van Eck, R. (2006). Digital game-based learning: It's not just the digital natives who are restless.... *EDUCAUSE Review, 41*(2).

Van Langen, A. M. L. (2005). *Unequal participation in mathematics and science education*. Antwerpen, Belgium: Garant-Uitgevers.

Vygotsky, L. S. (1978). *Mind in society: The development of higher psychological processes*. Cambridge, MA: Harvard University Press.

Williamson, B. (2009). *Computer games, schools, and young people: A report for educators on using games for learning*. London, UK: Futurelab.

Young-Loveridge, J. (2005). Students' views about mathematics learning: A case study of one school involved in the great expectations project. In Higgins, J., Irwin, K. C., Thomas, G., Trinick, T., & Young Loveridge, J. (Eds.), *Findings from the New Zealand Numeracy Development Project 2004* (pp. 107–114). Wellington, New Zealand: Ministry of Education.

ADDITIONAL READING

Aldrich, C. (2005). *Learning by doing: A comprehensive guide to simulations, computer games, and pedagogy in e-learning and other educational experiences*. San Francisco, CA: John Wiley & Sons.

Aldrich, C. (2009). *The complete guide to simulations and serious games*. San Francisco, CA: Jossey-Bass/Pfeiffer.

Amory, A., Naicker, K., Vincent, J., Adams, C., & McNaught, C. (1999). The use of computer games as an educational tool: Identification of appropriate game types and game elements. *British Journal of Educational Technology, 30*(4), 311–321. doi:10.1111/1467-8535.00121

Baek, Y. K. (2008). What hinders teachers in using computer and video games in the classroom? Exploring factors inhibiting the uptake of computer and video games. *Cyberpsychology & Behavior, 11*(6), 665–671. doi:10.1089/cpb.2008.0127

Becker, K. (2007). Digital game-based learning once removed: Teaching teachers. *British Journal of Educational Technology, 38*(3), 478–488. doi:10.1111/j.1467-8535.2007.00711.x

Bjorklund, D., Hubertz, M., & Reubens, A. (2004). Young children's arithmetic strategies in social context: How parents contribute to children's strategy development while playing games. *International Journal of Behavioral Development, 28*, 347–357. doi:10.1080/01650250444000027

Bogost, I. (2007). *Persuasive games: The expressive power of video games*. Cambridge, MA: The MIT Press.

Bokyeong, K., Hyungsung, P., & Youngkyun, B. (2009). Not just fun, but serious strategies: Using meta-cognitive strategies in game-based learning. *Computers & Education, 52*(4), 800–810. doi:10.1016/j.compedu.2008.12.004

Burguillo, C. J. (2010). Using game theory and competition-based learning to stimulate student motivation and performance. *Computers & Education, 55*(2), 566–575. doi:10.1016/j.compedu.2010.02.018

Cameron, B., & Dwyer, F. (2005). The effects of online gaming, cognition and feedback type in facilitating delayed achievement of different learning objectives. *Journal of Interactive Learning Research, 16*(3), 243–258.

Choy, D., Wong, A., & Gao, P. (2008). *Singapore's pre-service teachers' perspectives in integrating information and communication technology (ICT) during practicum.* Paper presented at the AARE 2008. Retrieved September 15, 2012, from http://www.aare.edu.au/08pap/cho08326.pdf

Chun-Yi, L., & Ming-Puu, C. (2009). A computer game as a context for non-routine mathematical problem solving: The effects of type of question prompt and level of prior knowledge. *Computers & Education, 52,* 530–542. doi:10.1016/j.compedu.2008.10.008

de Freitas, S., & Jarvis, S. (2009). Towards a development approach to serious games. In Connolly, T., Stansfield, M., & Boyle, L. (Eds.), *Games-Based Learning Advancements for Multi-Sensory Human Computer Interfaces: Techniques and Effective Practices* (pp. 215–231). Hershey, PA: IGI Global. doi:10.4018/978-1-60566-360-9.ch013

de Freitas, S., & Oliver, M. (2006). How can exploratory learning with games and simulations within the curriculum be most effectively evaluated? *Computers & Education, 46*(3), 249–264. doi:10.1016/j.compedu.2005.11.007

Dede, C. (2005). Planning for neomillenial learning styles. *EDUCAUSE Quarterly, 1,* 7–12.

Divjak, B., & Tomić, D. (2011). The impact of game-based learning on the achievement of learning goals and motivation for learning mathematics - Literature review. *Journal of Information and Organizational Sciences, 35*(1), 15–30.

Gee, J. (2004). Learning by design: Games as learning machines. *Interactive Educational Multimedia, 8,* 15–23.

Gee, J. P. (2005). *Why video games are good for your soul.* Victoria, Australia: Common Ground.

Graham, C. R. (2011). Theoretical considerations for understanding technological pedagogical content knowledge (TPACK). *Computers & Education, 57*(3), 1953–1960. doi:10.1016/j.compedu.2011.04.010

Hankaya, S., & Karamete, A. (2009). The effects of educational computer games on students' attitudes towards mathematics course and educational computer games. *Procedia Social and Behavioral Sciences, 1*(1), 145–149. doi:10.1016/j.sbspro.2009.01.027

Huang, W.-H., Huang, W.-Y., & Tschopp, J. (2010). Sustaining iterative game playing processes in DGBL: The relationship between motivational processing and outcome processing. *Computers & Education, 55,* 789–797. doi:10.1016/j.compedu.2010.03.011

Jenkins, H., & Squire, K. (2004). Harnessing the power of games in education. *Insight (American Society of Ophthalmic Registered Nurses), 3,* 5–33.

Kafai, Y. (1998). Game design as an interactive learning environment for fostering students' and teachers' mathematical inquiry. *International Journal of Computers for Mathematical Learning, 3,* 149–198. doi:10.1023/A:1009777905226

Kafai, Y. (2006). Playing and making games for learning: Instructionist and constructionist perspectives for game studies. *Games and Culture, 1*(1), 36–40. doi:10.1177/1555412005281767

Ke, F. (2008). A case study of computer gaming for math: Engaged learning from gameplay? *Computers & Education, 51,* 1609. doi:10.1016/j.compedu.2008.03.003

Ke, F., & Grabowski, B. (2007). Game playing for mathematics learning: cooperative or not? *British Journal of Educational Technology, 38*(2), 249–259. doi:10.1111/j.1467-8535.2006.00593.x

Kebretchi, M., & Hirumi, A. (2008). Examining the pedagogical foundations of modern educational computer games. *Computers & Education, 51,* 1729–1743. doi:10.1016/j.compedu.2008.05.004

Kennedy-Clark, S. (2011). Pre-service teachers' perspectives on using scenario-based virtual worlds in science education. *Computers & Education, 57,* 2224–2235. doi:10.1016/j.compedu.2011.05.015

Koehler, M. J., & Mishra, P. (2009). What is technological pedagogical content knowledge. *Technology and Teacher Education, 9*(1), 60–70.

Lach, T., & Sakshaug, L. (2004). The role of playing games in developing algebraic reasoning, spatial sense and problem solving. *Focus on Learning Problems in Mathematics, 26*(1), 34–42.

Lee, C. Y., & Chen, M. P. (2009). A computer game as a context for non-routine mathematical problem solving: The effects of type of question prompt and level of prior knowledge. *Computers & Education, 52*(3), 530–542. doi:10.1016/j.compedu.2008.10.008

Lim, C. P., Nonis, D., & Hedberg, J. (2006). Gaming in a 3-D multiuser virtual environment: Engaging students in science lessons. *British Journal of Educational Technology, 37*(2), 211–231. doi:10.1111/j.1467-8535.2006.00531.x

Liu, M., & Peng, W. (2009). Cognitive and psychological predictors of negative outcomes associated with playing MMOGs (massively multiplayer online games). *Computers in Human Behavior, 25,* 1306–1311. doi:10.1016/j.chb.2009.06.002

McDaniel, R., & Telep, P. (2009). Best practices for integrating game-based learning into online teaching. *Journal of Online Learning and Teaching, 5*(2), 424–438.

Michael, D., & Chen, S. (2006). *Serious games: Games that educate, train, and inform.* Boston, MA: Thomson Course Technology.

Munos-Rosario, R. A., & Widmeyer, G. R. (2009). An exploratory review of design principles in constructivist gaming learning environments. *Journal of Information Systems Education, 20*(3), 289–300.

Myers, D. (2005). Guest editorial: Video games: Issues in research and learning. *Simulation & Gaming, 36*(4), 442–446. doi:10.1177/1046878105282569

Nelson, B., Ketelhut, D. J., Clarke, J., Bowman, C., & Dede, C. (2005). Design-based research strategies for developing a scientific inquiry curriculum in a multi-user virtual environment. *Educational Technology, 45*(1), 21–27.

Oliver, M., & Pelletier, C. (2006). Activity theory and learning from digital games: Developing and analytical methodology. In Buckingham, D., & Willett, R. (Eds.), *Digital Generations: Children, Young People, and New Media* (pp. 67–88). Mahwah, NJ: Lawrence Erlbaum.

Papert, S. (1980). *Mindstorms: Children, computers and powerful ideas.* New York, NY: Basic Books.

Rosas, R. (2003). Beyond Nintendo: A design and assessment of educational video games for first and second grade students. *Computers & Education, 40,* 71–94. doi:10.1016/S0360-1315(02)00099-4

Salen, K., & Zimmerman, E. (2004). *Rules of play: Game design fundamentals.* Cambridge, MA: The MIT Press.

Shelton, B. E., & Wiley, D. A. (2007). *The design and use of simulation computer games in education.* Rotterdam, The Netherlands: Sense Publishers.

Sprague, D. (2004). Technology and teacher education: Are we talking to ourselves. *Contemporary Issues in Technology & Teacher Education, 3*(4), 353–361.

Tuzun, H., Yilmaz-Soylu, M., Karakus, T., Inal, Y., & Kizilkaya, G. (2009). The effects of computer games on primary school students' achievement and motivation in geometry learning. *Computers & Education*, *52*, 68–77. doi:10.1016/j.compedu.2008.06.008

Wastiau, P., Kearney, C., & Vanderberghe, W. (2009). *How are digital games used in schools?* Brussels, Belgium: European Schoolnet.

Winn, B. (2009). The design, play and experience framework. In Ferdig, R. E. (Ed.), *Handbook of Research on Effective Electronic Gaming in Education* (pp. 1010–1040). Hershey, PA: IGI Global.

Young-Loveridge, J. M. (2004). Effects on early numeracy of a program using number books and games. *Early Childhood Research Quarterly*, *19*, 82–98. doi:10.1016/j.ecresq.2004.01.001

Chapter 10
Using the Sims 3 for Narrative Construction in Secondary Education:
A Multimedia Experience in Language Classes

Natalia Monjelat
Universidad de Alcalá, Spain

Ana Belén García Varela
Universidad de Alcalá, Spain

Mirian Checa
Universidad de Alcalá, Spain

Héctor Del Castillo
Universidad de Alcalá, Spain

David Herrero
Universidad de Alcalá, Spain

ABSTRACT

In this chapter, the authors explore an innovative educational classroom scenario where commercial video games are used as an educational tool. They analyse an experiment involving students between the ages of 12 and 13, during the second semester of 2010, in a "Language and Literature" class of a Spanish Secondary School. The main aim of this chapter is to develop new literacies through new educational strategies. These relate commercial video games with the curriculum in order to improve students' specific cultural competences and social skills. The authors show how the social simulation video game "The Sims 3" can be used as a learning resource for students to create narratives and descriptions using a variety of media.

INTRODUCTION

In the context of today's participatory digital culture, schools need to find an educational application for many tools that may not have been originally designed with such a purpose in mind, but which are meaningful in the students' everyday life. In so doing, we approach popular culture through collaborative situations; learning to tell stories using both new and already consolidated technologies. In this regard, the educational potential of simulation games has become a subject for discussion and research (de Freitas & Oliver, 2006; Mitchell & Savill-Smith, 2004) and has en-

DOI: 10.4018/978-1-4666-3950-8.ch010

couraged us to develop different research projects in this area, taking a different approach from the perspective of 'serious gaming' (Djaouti, Alvarez & Jessel, 2011).

In this chapter, we explore an innovative classroom setting created through the use of a commercial video game as an educational tool. This investigation forms part of a larger research project, developed during the 2009/2010 school year by a group of researchers from the University of Alcalá and UNED (Universidad Nacional de Educación a Distancia) with members of the Culture, Technology and New Literacies Research Group (GIPI http://www.uah-gipi.org/). Research was carried out in collaboration with Electronic Arts, a leading company in video game design, within its corporate social responsibility program.

The whole project involved 204 students aged between 11 and 16, and their teachers, in a Secondary School in Coslada (Madrid, Spain). The students used a variety of commercial video games in workshops, coordinated by teachers, and were related to different subject areas: Biology, English, Spanish Literature, Physical Education and Sociolinguistics. These games were selected by researchers, teachers, and the students themselves, resulting in the following choices: Spore, The Sims 3, The Beatles Rock Band, FIFA 10, and NBA 10.

In this context, we are of the opinion that commercial video games can become learning tools when used in an educational context, although their original purpose is leisure. In our research, video games become an appropriate element of a comprehensive multimedia setting, in which the participants combine a variety of technologies such as digital cameras, software for audio/video edition, or the Internet.

During the project, each set of activities was organised as a workshop coordinated by the teachers. The teachers defined the learning objectives and shared them with the researchers and students. In each session, the design of classroom activities was divided into three stages: discussing a topic in relation to the learning objectives, playing with the video game in small groups, and teacher-lead, whole group sessions, where group members assessed the activities.

We analyse a trial where we show how some simulation video games, specifically The Sims 3, can be used as learning resources that help students create narratives and descriptions in the 'Language & Literature' class. The data for this trial comes from a specific workshop where the teacher used The Sims 3 to develop curricular content, such as descriptions and narratives, and also encouraged the students to create audio-visual productions using multimedia resources.

Basing our work on an ethnographical perspective (Hammersley & Atkinson, 1983/1995; Spindler & Hammond, 2006), we analyse how students working in small groups develop narratives when participating in situated learning activities. We use a sociocultural approach, based on the relationships between the context of the activity and the students' cognitive skills. Scribner (1976/1997) reflects on the relationship between the expression and development of cognitive skills, and how the cultural setting plays an important part in this (Jenkins, 2006). The use of participatory digital culture requires us to question which social and cultural competences young people need to master to be able to function fully in the new media landscape.

Everyone involved in preparing young people to go out into the world has contributions to make in helping students acquire the skills they need to become full participants in our society. Schools, afterschool programs, and parents have distinctive roles to play as they do what they can in their own spaces to encourage and nurture these skills (Jenkins, 2006, p. 4).

Our principal objective, then, is to develop new literacies through educational strategies, connecting commercial video games and the curriculum, in order to improve our students' specific cultural competences and social skills.

VIDEO GAMES AND NEW LITERACIES IN THE DIGITAL SOCIETY: A NEW APPROACH TO CURRICULAR CONTENTS

One of the most significant cultural phenomena of the second half of the twentieth Century was the communications revolution and its impact on social and institutional space and on people's private lives. Similarly, the structures of knowledge and symbolic appropriation of the world have changed.

The growth of digital media and Internet use has transformed the nature of communication in contemporary society (Castells, 2001). The increased digitisation of processes and communication over the last decade has brought about important changes beyond just communicative content; it affects other essential activities associated with the creation, production and dissemination of content (Tubella, 2008).

The development of new electronic technologies for data transmission and storage is one of the most complex and innovative processes found in our society. Media has become an ecosystem or an environment where, on the one hand, our lives develop and on the other, languages, knowledge, values and social orientations are formed (Leonard, Van Scotter & Pakdil, 2009).

Given this background new literacy requirements emerge, firstly for the digital technologies themselves and secondly, for social, economic, political and cultural changes. As Castells explained (2000, p. 60) this characterises the new technological paradigm organised around information technology.

Nowadays children and adolescents live in a "media universe." In this respect, Buckingham (2002) explains that the meaning of childhood in modern societies is created and defined through the children's interactions with electronic media. In many cases, adolescence is actively involved in what we call participatory culture (Jenkins, 2006), where members feel a high degree of social interconnection, engaging with each other to create and share their creations. Consequently, culture absorbs and responds to this explosion of new media technologies which enable consumers to write, circulate and archive media content in powerful new ways.

The ever-widening access to new technologies is not enough; we must also promote the skills and cultural knowhow necessary to use these tools for our own educational purposes. As an educator, Jenkins (2006) highlights the relevance of encouraging young people to develop skills, knowledge, ethical frameworks and the confidence to fully participate in contemporary culture. In this context, participatory culture is reworking the rules governing the school, cultural expression, and civic life.

Many authors have argued that this new participatory culture represents an ideal learning environment. As an example, Gee (2004) defines the concept of "affinity spaces" where people learn best when actively engaged and committed to popular culture. This author argues that with these new opportunities, people reach a higher degree of learning spaces as these are based on common effort regardless of age, class, gender, or education level.

In a technological society, schools cannot ignore the media presence, its effects or its uses. The school is an institution that has experienced the impact of the cultural changes that come as a result of media expansion and digitisation. However, the school is also an institution which resists these changes. More than a curriculum, what is required is the nurturing of a positive disposition towards changing the ways we learn, communicate, and produce content (Trahtemberg, 2000). This does not imply abandoning the traditional fields of learning, but accepting the fact that that young people live in a cultural world which has evolved (Mills, 2010).

Given that this is the media culture, children and adolescents need to be literate in it. In this way, Mills believes that literacy is the interpretation the individual makes of cultural products and the generation of ideas through this interpretation. Consequently, media needs to be interpreted and the school, educators, and researchers must be involved in such literacy processes.

More specifically, digital media literacy is one of the most significant educational challenges faced today (Squire, 2002): in an increasingly digital world, being competent in new practices must compete with new media and new ways of meaning and communication. Educational practices still are often designed for a society that has moved on and changed dramatically.

Today the school is a privileged setting to educate new generations as free citizens able to actively participate in the building of their future. To do this we must be literate in their languages and develop responsibility from participation, criticism, dialectics, etc. Education therefore, assumes the social responsibility to transform these challenges into possibilities (Mills, 2010).

Given this framework, it is essential to look closer at the concept of new literacies and point out those skills that, following Jenkins (2006), are necessary in today's society.

New Literacies in the Digital Society: New Skills for a Changing World

Today the concept of literacy and what it means to be literate in written culture is changing (Gee, 2001, 2000; Barton & Hamilton, 2005). On the one hand, different types of literacies have appeared alongside the traditional ones, these are more connected with technological culture and other elements from the information society. On the other, the Internet and new media (Manovich, 2001) modify the basic elements that play a part in the comprehensive reading processes (Coll, 2005) allowing new spaces for learning.

The definition of digital literacy can be taken from this framework. It is defined as a set of cultural practices that occur in a specific type of society based on intensive use of Information and Communication Technologies (ICT) (Hague & Williamson, 2009). This perspective leads us away from a naive view of literacy, which regards people as being literate because they use some technology in their daily life. We should understand digital literacy as an opportunity to learn and practice the internal dynamics of new media as everyday cultural tools (Mominó, Sigalés & Meneses, 2008). In this way, literacy processes give people the opportunity to develop the informational autonomy needed to function in new virtual spaces (Ortoll, 2007).

Scribner (1978) anticipated these ideas when she said: "as the technology of any society becomes more complex, the number and variety of tasks that must be applied to literacy also increases" (Scribner, 1978, p. 458). It is in this regard that we can talk about the "21st century literacies" defined by the "New Media Consortium" and quoted by Jenkins (2009) as the:

(...) Set of capabilities and skills where aural, visual and digital literacies overlap. These include the ability to understand the power of images and sounds, recognize and use that power, manipulate and transform digital media, distribute them penetrating and easily adapt to new media (cited in Jenkins et al, 2009, p. 19).

Following these ideas Gee (2004) also proposed the term "visual literacy" that refers to different communication systems which include language, images, symbols, graphs, diagrams, artefacts, etc. forming "multimodal texts" that require a "multimodal literacy". In the same way as this applies to images, it can also be applied to sound, movement, sensations, etc. New digital technologies can be thought of as instruments that require some understanding of these languages from the user, to comprehend the messages conveyed in all their complexity. In this framework, video games can introduce the students to this multimodal

183

world, since they combine different languages. It should be noted that neither Jenkins (2009) nor Gee (2004) rule out the use of traditional forms of literacy, but they propose expanding these more traditional skills to be better adapted to the new current situation. Considering these ideas, it is especially relevant to highlight some of the skills that are part of the 'package' needed to be literate in the digital society (Jenkins, 2009):

- **Play:** Posed as the ability to experiment with the environment as a way of solving problems through play activities. In this case, video games can be an important resource to develop this skill.
- **Simulation:** The ability to interpret and construct dynamic models of real world processes. In this way, new media provides new ways to represent and manipulate information. Jenkins (2009) notes that students who use learning simulations have greater flexibility when building and manipulating models. Regarding this, simulation video games can develop this skill since they offer virtual worlds, as described later.
- **Appropriation:** The ability to meaningfully sample and remix media content.
- **Cognitive Distribution:** Understood as the ability to interact with tools that expand our mental capacities, in this case by introducing video games and other media into the classroom. The term "distributed intelligence" emphasises the role that technologies play in this process, but is closely related to the social production of knowledge of what Jenkins refers to as "collective intelligence", which is another skill that the author promulgates.
- **Collective Intelligence:** Ability to pool knowledge and compare notes with others towards a common goal, as mentioned before this occurs when a group of people constitutes a community of practice.

These skills should be used in an integrated way to achieve actual literacy, as we defined literacy as the gradual acquisition of the skills. In this regard, video games can be used as an educational resource which allows students to approach the media context, developing some of the skills identified earlier, through play within an educational framework.

Video Games in the Classroom: New Ways of Approaching the Curriculum

We will now focus on video games as one type of media that currently has a special importance in the digital society, popular culture and the socialisation process of young people and adults (Buckingham, 2003). We will also examine why they can be used as learning tools in an educational setting.

Video games have some special characteristics that differentiate them from traditional games, creating a difference with respect to other new media that are currently also part of child and youth culture. They have created their own culture on websites, blogs, magazines, etc. With a fusion of music, technology in and simulated reality with effects and sounds, video games are technologically perfect for understanding the contemporary world. The players are not passive users of such games, rather they are active participants. Like a puzzle or other games, the video format requires the players to use their creativity to make a story or to win. Based on this, we can say that playing a game is an imaginary contract (Coleman and Dyer-Witheford, 2007).

According to Hernández (2008) some keys to the success of video games among the children and young people are:

- The attraction of the magical world of technology and machines.
- The constant action, overcoming challenges, competition, etc.

- The outcome (feedback) and immediate responses to actions.
- The aesthetic quality and variety of scenarios, characters, effects, etc.
- The originality of the stories or screenplays, engaging young audiences.
- The possibility of suddenly 'taking action.' The same game is designed to train and teach the players how to play by their own action.
- The culture that they generate. The language, symbols, trademarks, or magazines around which the video game players are grouped constitute an interesting attraction that allows them to be members of a group of peers and establish contacts and relationships based on similar interests.

Furthermore, as explained by Johnson (2005), video games can be a powerful resource, since they provide the same kind of rigorous mental training that is required for mathematical theorems and puzzles. We are "a species that solves problems" (Johnson, 2005) and that is one of the reasons we enjoy playing with them.

Taking part in these games is also a 'multiliterate' activity: it often involves interpreting complex three-dimensional visual environments, reading both on-screen and off-screen texts (such as games magazines and websites) and processing auditory information and committed acquisition of skills and knowledge (Buckingham, 2006).

Video games also have a motivational effect on students (Kong, 2009). Paras and Bizzocchi (2005) add that when people are intrinsically motivated to learn, they not only learn more but also have a more positive experience. These authors also note that virtual environments meet the characteristics of an effective environment for learning. In this regard, we can say that video games have the power to engage players in what is called "Flow" (Csikszentmihalyi, 1990) where players reach a state of perfect balance between challenge and

frustration and where the ultimate goal becomes so clear that obstacles disappear.

Moreover, Kirriemuir and McFarlane (2004) point out that instead of seeking an experience that superficially looks like a fun activity, we should understand the deep structures of the gaming experience that contribute to the state of "Flow" and build on these environments designed to support learning. However, a negative aspect of this experience is the lack of reflection, because even though players are developing skills, they may not be aware of it while in that state (Paras & Bizzocchi, 2005).

That is why the role of the adult, in this case the teacher/researchers is crucial, allowing the reflection needed to complete the learning process, selecting, accompanying and regulating the use that children make of video games. Moreover, Shaffer (2004) added that video games allow students to "learn by doing", where it is important to have the support of others who have already played and know the game. Sanford and Williamson (2005) agree with these ideas, emphasising the importance of "learning by playing."

Another point to consider is the possibility for the player to enter virtual worlds via video games. Shaffer (2004) points out that this is what makes video games a powerful tool for learning. These experiences in multiple contexts will enable learners to understand complex concepts without losing the connections between abstract ideas and real problems.

Turkle (1995) notes that the world of the video game shows actions free of the limitations of the physical world, such as flying, disappearing, etc. In this regard, the author includes simulation video games, which help students to actively think about complex phenomena related to dynamic systems.

Based on this, video games have a significant educational potential (Gee, 2007; Shaffer, 2006, Kirriemuir & McFarlane, 2004; Sanford & Williamson, 2005) and nowadays they represent the entry point for children into the virtual world and the culture of computers and simulation, giving them the skills needed to live in the digital society (Gros, 2002). Widely used by children and teenagers, video games are criticised for their content and used very little by educators (Gros, 1998).

Following these ideas, we need to consider the importance of the context if we plan to introduce video games into educational settings. The video game introduced in the school is transformed; it is no longer software to play with but a game that has an educational purpose, connecting the gaming experience with curricular content. In short, video games can be a means through which children acquire knowledge that contribute to developing the skills needed in today's society, as other types of games did in the past (Thomas, 2006).

Some of the most explored aspects of video games research are related to their ability to promote motivation (Prensky, 2001) or student involvement (Kafai, 1998). However, Squire (2002) stresses the need to carry out research in complex video games (mainly adventures and simulations) to examine how they can be used to support the learning of complex situations in formal and informal scenarios. Thus, in our research we were interested in video games as a resource to develop digital literacy skills and also contents specific to the Language and Literature subject in a formal educational setting.

Other studies have also focused on the use of video games in the school context to show how they can be used to teach specific content in a formal educational environment. (Lacasa et al, 2009; Watson et al, 2011; Squire, 2004, 2005; Sandford et al, 2006; Gros, 2008, 2004). Randel et al (1992) pointed out that subject matter areas where very specific content can be targeted and objectives precisely defined are more likely to show beneficial effects for gaming and especially from simulation games. These types of games have been among the most used in the school context as other studies proved (Sandford et al, 2006; Kirriemuir & McFarlane, 2003; Kirriemuir, 2002).

The use of virtual worlds, simulation and digital games might motivate learners to explore and play (Baek, 2010) while involving important learning principles (Gee, 2007) so it is natural to think that this could be a powerful learning resource. Also, simulation can integrate emotion, action and cognition, reproduce social life and have multiple rules (Hofstede et al, 2010). Furthermore, simulations have been playing an important part (Turkle, 1995) in different areas as diverse as military training (Smith, 2010), business teaching (Lin & Tu, 2012) or healthcare (Cannon-Bowers et al, 2011). To simulate is to model a system through a different system which maintains some of the behaviours of the original one. In this way simulation does not simply retain the characteristics of the object but it also includes a model of its behaviour, which reacts to certain stimuli (input data, pushing buttons, joystick movements) according to a set of conditions (Frasca, 2003). Based on that, a simulation game can be defined as a "simplified and dynamic model of a real or hypothetical system in which players are in position of competition or cooperation, rules structure the players actions, and the goal is to win" (Sauvé et al, 2009).

The Sims 3, the video game used in this study, comes under this category because it offers the model of a neighbourhood, where players can build their houses and create the virtual characters who are going to live in them. At the same time, players can choose the avatars' personalities and looks, controlling all their actions. This type of game is also called "Social Simulation", "Life Simulation" and even "God Game" (Sandford et al, 2006) since the players control a living creature and the entire associated environment.

The Sims saga has been present in many studies on games and education (Williamson, 2009; Gee, 2007; Hayes, 2011, 2009; Hayes & King, 2009; Panoutsopoulos & Sampson, 2012; Gee & Hayes, 2009; Lacasa, 2009). Furthermore, other studies also have shown how The Sims has the potential for language learning (Ranalli, 2008) for example. In our study we used The Sims 3 for a different purpose. The idea was to use the virtual environment presented in the game as a catalyst to motivate students to write, exploring literary resources and different narrative techniques which help them to structure a story. Playing with Sims 3 gave students topics to write about, offering a whole new world to describe and create narratives.

To summarise, the use of video games in school as a learning tool means a change in methodology and, consequently, also a change in the focus of learning. It is not only used to learn skills related to the use of technology and about specific content, but also the game develops competences related to negotiation skills, decision-making, communication and reflection (Gros, 2004).

Video Games and Narratives

One of the concepts that we could go more deeply into in the analyses of video games and cognitive skills is the development of narrative thinking. Bruner (1985, 1986, 1996) suggests that there are two complementary ways of understanding and thinking in which people organise and manage their perception of the world, each providing distinctive ways of ordering experience and constructing reality. One is what he called "paradigmatic or logico-scientific" and the other is "narrative". Thus, the first attempt to fulfil the ideal of a formal, mathematical system of descriptions and explanation, is based on the search for universal statements of truth and because of that, is more appropriate in natural and physical sciences. The second one is based on the assumption that the complicated and rich phenomena of life and experience are better presented in stories or narratives (Sheked, 2005).

Moreover, Bruner (1986) remarks that any attempt to reduce one mode to the other fail to capture the rich ways in which people know and describe situations around them. In relation to this, Carter (1993) adds that the richness of human events

and thoughts cannot be expressed in definitions, statements or facts or abstract propositions which are typical in a paradigmatic thinking, they need to be expressed through stories, also because an essential part of our mental lives is narratively organised in socially constituted systems of signs (Herman, 2011). Because of its importance, the Language & Literature subject usually addresses contents related to stories, teaching students how to create them from scratch. In our study, an innovative resource was introduced to mediate this process: the video game Sims 3 for PC.

Video games, because of their interactive character, have demonstrated their potential for increasing narrative stories, inviting the reader-player-narrator to make narrative choices involving them in developing stories (Esnaola, 2006). This first person experience makes the player participate in actions that are, in themselves, part of the script of their own game, as Gee (2004) explained is a mixture of four things:

- Decisions taken by the designers of the game (the authors).
- The way in which the player makes those decisions deployed in a specific case, with the order in which things are found.
- The actions the player has taken as one of the main characters in the story.
- The imaginative projection that the player makes about the characters, the plot, and the global story.

As a result of this, each player will build a different story, depending on how they combine these elements in their game. However, it is important to remember that the narrative structure of video games is similar to the structure of literary stories and that both involve a series of elements that bring the story to life. This how, despite the differences between the stories generated by the players, the basic elements: openness, conflict and its resolution are maintained (Propp, 1987). Literary narratives written in novel format allow us to explore the characteristics of the characters, their inner world, and their positions as the story unfolds. In contrast, staged narratives own a shared audio-visual discourse and allow us to explore the spatial characteristics of the action and movement of the characters in the scene. In this way, they encourage a recreational proposal to develop both real and virtual areas and inspire us to interfere with the unknown or enhance the known (Murray, 1997).

In this regard, video games will form part of what are called the "spatial stories" (Jenkins, 2002), where the key is not the construction of complex plots and characters but rather of spaces which can be explored, mapped and controlled. We can create our story of what happened in the game or invent what might have happened. When we build a story we can represent the past or enter in the world of imaginable, we request different alternatives and develop the imagination. Thus, from the video game we can learn to tell stories based on reality or create our own fantasy world. Therefore, the games' plots are influenced by the decisions and actions of the player, motivating and involving them in a way that is different to the stories told in literature or film. Gee (2004) called it stories personified, referring to all the perceptions, actions, decisions and mental simulations of action or dialogue. Thus, video games are presented as an interesting resource for working narrative construction in the classroom. Due to their nature, they offer students a specific medium on which to develop their own stories.

APPROACHING DIGITAL LITERACIES IN THE CLASSROOM

The study presented here was carried out following an ethnographic approach (Atkinson et al., 2001; Silverman, 2005), which helps us to understand the school as a cultural or institutional context in which the activity of individuals acquires meaning. This perspective has been focused on the study of literacy practices (e.g. Gee, 2004, 2008; Jenkins, 2006) that have emerged with the use of Information and Communication Technologies (ICT) and specifically video games.

The literacy practice that we investigated was the collaborative construction of audio-visual productions, using video games as learning tools, and based on a previous written text. It was carried out in the subject of "Language & Literature" by a class of Year 1 students in a secondary school in Coslada (Madrid, Spain). There were three main objectives in this project. The first one was to investigate how children could learn about a given curricular subject within this activity. The second objective was to investigate how children learned about the use of video games and ICT tools to construct new types of multimedia documents. In this case, we were particularly interested in looking at the ways children learned about creating narratives. The third objective was to investigate how cognitive skills were developed in social interaction through the use of video games in this particular literacy practice.

This project is part of a large research project developed by a group of researchers from the University of Alcalá and UNED, members of the "Culture, Technology and New Literacies Research Group." This large project involved 204 students aged between 11 and 16 and their teachers. Students used a variety of commercial video games in workshops coordinated by teachers and related to different subjects: Biology, English, Literature, Physical Education, and the Sociolinguistic Area. These games were selected among researchers, teachers, and students themselves, resulting in the following: Spore, The Sims 3, The Beatles Rock Band, FIFA 10, and NBA 10.

In order to plan this workshop, we worked with a secondary school teacher (Esther), who was happy to participate in this experience. We met several times to discuss ways to implement the programme in a way that would best suit the interests of both of us, as a teacher and researchers, respectively. In total, the project was comprised of seven 50-minutes weekly sessions. The activities carried out in all the sessions were agreed in advance in order to suit the needs for each session. We aimed to achieve the goal of having four groups of audio-visual productions constructed by the end of the project.

The participants in the specific workshop that we analysed in this chapter were 13 Year-1 secondary school students, 12-13 years old, working in groups of three (and one group of four), which were organised by the teacher using the criteria of mixed ability and mixed gender. Each group of students worked on one computer assigned to them with the video game The Sims 3.

The teacher was one of the main participants leading the activities through plenary sessions, providing support in small groups, and giving general advice about the different tasks that children were involved in. Thus, the teacher usually started with a brief whole class event where she introduced the goals of the session. After this, each group of children would go to their computer and work with the video game. Very often, the teacher moved around the room checking the progress of the students and reminding them about the tasks.

Researchers were also participant observers during all the sessions, filming and audio recording all the activities and providing technical assistance for the video game or the audio-visual editing software when required (del Castillo, et al. 2011; García Varela et al. 2011).

The data gathered in this project, as with any other project informed by an ethnographic methodological approach, came from several sources, providing insight into the phenomena under investigation from different perspectives. We used a number of instruments to register and analyse the information: audio and video files recorded, field notes and summaries of the sessions, the audio-visual productions of each group, diverse materials handled and generated by the participants in every session, 'activity cards' designed for the different tasks, etc. (see Table 1).

There were three main data sources within the above mentioned:

- Video files of whole class and small group activities. The whole class plenary sessions and one small group activity were video recorded.
- Ethnographic notes elaborated after every session with the field notes collected. We produced what we call 'summaries': narrative reconstructions of the sessions with the description of the activities and the interpretations and feelings of the researchers about what happened.
- Group responses to 'activity cards.' Students were required to write down information in them in relation to the main task of the workshop.

Table 1. Data collected

Sessions	Date	Summaries	Recorded video	Recorded Audio	Photos taken
1	2010 04 13	3	2 x 1 hour	6 x 33 minutes	109
2	2010 04 20	3	2 x 1 hour	3 x 15 minutes	106
3	2010 04 27	3	2 x 1 hour	6 x 27 minutes	124
4	2010 05 04	2	2 x 1 hour	3 x 5 minutes	69
5	2010 05 11	4	2 x 1 hour	4 x 23 minutes	44
6	2010 05 18	3	2 x 1 hour	5 x 4 minutes	54
7	2010 06 01	3	2 x 1 hour	-	64

All these resources were stored, organised, transcribed, and analysed using two software packages for qualitative research, Transana and NVivo, which helped us define the main categories for analysis and establish the relations and procedural sequences among them.

The Narrative of the Workshop: What, When, and How?

One of the most relevant points we had to take into consideration when trying to understand what happened during the workshops was identifying the context. Now we can present a narrative reconstruction of the workshop in which we describe the essential events.

The workshop covered seven weeks, and was held on Tuesdays while every Monday the students attended their usual 'Language and Literature' subject classes. The research team was present only in the classroom on Tuesdays when working on the activities with the video game, The Sims 3. However to understand the experience, it is necessary to contemplate all the 'Language and Literature' subject classes. Thus, the teacher linked the 'video game' sessions with the 'usual' classes by relating the activities in video games with the curricular content worked on the day before. Specifically, this happened during sessions 3, 4, and 5, where the students continued to develop their written narrative during the three sessions. Each Monday had the effect of 'continuing work in progress' from the earlier session and 'preparing and activating' the next session.

In addition to the students and the teacher, researchers were present in the classroom in all sessions. Their role was to manage digital media (video cameras, tape recorders, cameras) for data collection and support students and the teacher in the development of the session. This was done by explaining the specific aspects of the video game (options, controls, etc.) or the video editing software, or discussing with the teacher during

the development of the sessions and time spent on each task or phase of the workshop.

After analysing the data, and for a better understanding of the experience, sessions can be organised (see Figure 1) as follows:

- During the first two sessions (1 and 2) students became familiar with the new context in which they were working, with the people, the equipment and the new technology in the classroom, as well as the aims of the workshop.
- During the following two sessions (3 and 4) the students worked explicitly from the game written narrative. Thus, the academic curriculum was present through the descriptions drawn from the literary devices used, and the argument that they had come up with from their experience with the game.
- During the next two sessions (5 and 6) the students worked from their written productions. They had to transfer all these ideas (characters, places, situations, events, etc.) to another format. They used the 'Microsoft Movie Maker' software.
- In the last session (7) each group showed their productions to the classmates. In this session, after each projection, guided by the teacher, the students commented in narrative terms their own productions and those of other groups.

During the first three sessions, the exchange of experiences among students at the end of the activity was encouraged. They shared both the development of their own practices, with special attention to the elements on which then had to work (people, places, situations, events, etc.) and technical problems experienced through the use of these tools.

At the beginning of session 3 and the second part of the sessions 4 and 5, we can see (Figure

Figure 1. Workshop structure

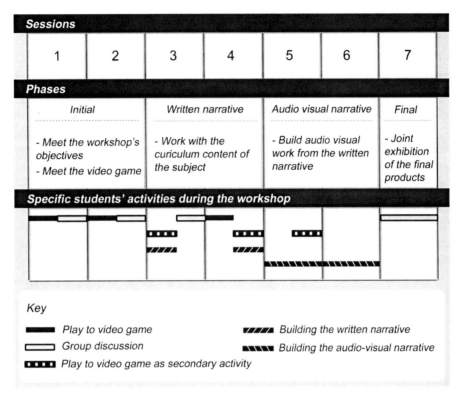

1) how there were two simultaneous activities: playing and working in the narrative (written -s3 and s4- and audio-visual -s5-). In all cases, the group sharing discussion (at the end of each session) started at the end of the game activity.

Considering the activities carried out during the sessions and the dynamics of the workshop, if we move to a higher level of abstraction related to the experience, we can say it was divided into 4 phases, previously shown in Figure 1.

- An initial phase of familiarisation with the goals, the game and the new situation in which they found themselves.
- A second phase of construction of a written narrative (composed of descriptions of the characters, places, events, etc.) that was where there was a very close link between the game and the subject curriculum.
- A third phase of story composition in audio-visual format.

- A final stage where they showed the results of their work, and analysed them in a large group discussion, guided by the teacher.

From this structure, we noticed that the most interesting phases for the purpose of this chapter are the second and the fourth. In both phases, the activities explicitly linked the video game to the curriculum content. Thus, our analysis will focus on the interaction events between teacher and students and among students.

ENHANCING THE PROCESS OF NARRATIVE BUILDING THROUGH THE SOCIAL SIMULATION VIDEO GAME THE SIMS 3

Having presented the chosen methodology, we can now examine the results of our study. To do this we will concentrate on the analysis of sessions 3, 4, and 7, as it is in these sessions that the curricular content of the "Language and Literature" subject area is related to building a narrative. Sessions 3 and 4 concentrate on the development of descriptions and narratives in small groups, while session 7 is dedicated to an idea-sharing session of the narratives created in the audio-visual workshops.

The Story-Building Process: From the Description to the Narration

Sessions 3 and 4 were the two sessions where more curricular content was worked on. It was in these moments where the students put into practice what they had worked on in the first two sessions.

Working towards Curricular Contents

The third session is an important one, as this is the one where the students start to work towards curricular content. They start out with some important language points during the language class, such as making descriptions, and work up to the construction of stories through the use of videogames.

At the start of the third session, the teacher suggested as an objective, that the students observe the characters in the video game and try to work on their descriptions. To help them in this task, the students were given a worksheet (Figure 2) to note down the traits of the Sims characters. After this stage of playing and observing the characters, we worked on putting together what each group had come up with; reading the descriptions and discussing aspects of the language curriculum that had been worked on. This session was carried out in a large group session.

The teacher asked the students in the first group to read their descriptions, while the others members listened and gave their opinions. The teacher's intention here is to get the children to be more critically aware, and to form their own opinions of their classmates' work (Mercer, 2000). Also, the students' learning environment is different to

the usual class setting, and the gaming experience is intrinsically motivating for them (Kong, 2009).

Teacher: OK, guys, let's stop. Leave it there and you can carry on next day. OK. The first group, can you read your descriptions out to us? Everybody pay attention, OK? So you can tell me what you think and if you think something is missing or could be improved on.

Text drafted by the first group:

María: She works snapping her fingers as a teacher. She also has a huge house that she shares with her friends from university.

Yanira: She works as a police officer and wants to have a child with Sergio although she says it's too soon.

Alicia: She doesn't have a job, she's looking for one. She's not in love with anyone. It's a boy (sic).

Sergio: He works as an organ donor and is in love with Yanira and wants a child with her

Yanira: She likes macaroni and cheese.

As we see in this example, the description of the group is fairly confused as it focuses on specific aspects which have no relation to each other. This is why the teacher continues the dialogue with students to help them improve on their descriptions, as shown below:

Teacher: Listen up, I think you can do this better. What things did I say that you needed to put in a description? What is being described?

Student 1 Group 2: A person.

Teacher: A person, but what about the person?

Student 1 Group 2: The clothes.

Teacher: The outfit, what else?

Student 1 Group 2: Hairstyle.

Teacher: Hairstyle...personality...

Student 1 group 1: What he likes.

Figure 2. Worksheet

VIDEO GAMES WORKSHOP. 1º ESO C

VIDEO GAME: *THE SIMS 3*

Group members:

Title of the Story:

Characters:

1.

2.

3.

4.

Surroundings (house)

Plot (important events)

Teacher: *Something about his life, if there is any detail. OK. In these descriptions, have you seen anything about their physical appearance?*

To make students think about their work, the teacher does not give answers but through guided participation (Rogoff, et al. 2001) she uses questions to point them in right direction. In this way the students share ideas to their classmates on how to improve their work. ("What is being described?", "What else?"). Here the role of the teacher is essential, encouraging the students to think about the learning process.

After using questioning to guide the students, the teacher reviews the traits they have come up with ("write something about the physical, something about the outfit, something about the personality") collaborating together, as we see in the next example:

Teacher: *You have to...write something about the physical, something about the outfit, something about the personality. Not so much about what he does, or who they are with, or what they intend to do, but what they are like on the outside, and how they are on the inside, OK? That is a description. And then remember what things can be added to make the description more interesting? We saw this yesterday.*

Students: *Details, comparisons.*

Teacher: *Details, metaphors.*

Students: *Exaggerations.*

Teacher: *Exaggerations, adjectives.*

Student Group 4: *Comparisons*

Thus, students learn to describe the characters for themselves, based on their gaming experience. From this point, the teacher tries to direct her questioning to include the curriculum descriptions that have been covered in the language class, such as literary figures. As shown in this and other examples, the teacher uses the potential of the Sims video game to enhance the learning of curriculum content related to the Language subject area (Ranalli, 2008).

The session continues with the reading of the description made by the second group, leading to a new dialogue between the teacher and students.

Peter Jackson: He is cool, arrogant, a bit of thug. He hates going outside. He is a vegetarian, has a strong personality, he is evil but at the moment of truth he acts like a coward. His favourite music is Indian style, his favourite food is autumn salad and favourite colour, turquoise. He works as a criminal, a thief.

Lock Morrison: He is a flirt, with a sense of humour. Easy to impress, friendly and likes to laze around. His favourite music is electronic, favourite food, the hamburger and his favourite colour is lilac. He works as a thief.

Olwen Beagarden: She is a good person, she has a quick temper but she is a hopeless romantic. She's usually a chatterbox and has a great gift for plants. Her favourite music is electronic, favourite food, sushi and her favourite colour is red. She is an actress.

Twisted Maddy: She is good, a perfectionist, she has innate culinary skills, she's a girl devoted to her family and is frugal. Her favourite music is electronic, favourite food is fruit pie and her favourite colour purple. Her job is an unconditional fan (sic).

Teacher: What can you tell this group?

Student: That it's OK.

Student: But the physical traits are not there.

Teacher: OK. You missed something about the physical description, but at least you have a lot more details. (...) Now, you have to improve it even more but try not to make it look like a list, OK? Don't follow the same structure as if it's all about accumulating traits. Maybe put in less features, but give

it more form. For example, if you say that he's a vegetarian then give him more life, 'he's a vegetarian, he's happy having a big salad while he watches TV and listens to indie music'. Something like that. If you bring the details together and group them, you can give a more complete picture. Do you understand what I'm saying?

In the dialogue with this group, the aim of the teacher goes beyond analysing whether they have been able to describe the characters in the video game. What the teacher does is try to encourage the students to make the description more complex, not only adding features but giving it structure ("Put in less features, but give him more form" "if you bring the details together and group them, you can give a more complete picture"). As we can see, the description is a part of the process that leads us to construct a narrative. The teacher's efforts focus on making students think about how to make the description more complex, to enrich the narrative.

To motivate the students, the teacher encourages them to explore figures of speech and different narrative techniques, to help them create their own narrative. In this way, we can appreciate the value of large group discussions, where the students are able to bring their ideas together and work with each other on how to their work, while receiving feedback from the teacher. In this respect, Shaffer (2004) explains how video games allow students to "learn by doing," where the important element is the support given by other people who have played with or are familiar with the video game.

Now the teacher wants the students to go beyond producing a description, and start working on a context suitable for creating the narrative, that Jenkins (2002) calls the construction of spatial stories. This is the most complicated part for the students; how to convert a few features into a character while at the same time integrating it into a specific context. To end this session, the last of the groups reads out their description.

Description Group 4:

Lock Morrison: *He is a podium polisher. He likes electronics and wants to be President. He's as blonde as the sun, with blue eyes like the sea.*

Olwen Beugarden: *She's a dark girl, specifically brown like chestnuts; she is thin and sometimes argues. She almost always wins. She wants to flirt. Occupation: a ballot paper counter.*

Peter Jackson: *He works as an organ donor; he's skilled in the kitchen, a vegetarian. He has a touch of childish cowardice. He likes Indian food and has a punk hair do.*

Twisted Maddy: *She's a dropout, very friendly. She is devoted to her family, has a great sense of humour, a perfectionist with cooking skills. Maddy seems to be such a hard worker that no one can get her away from her work. Her profession is unconditional fan, related to football.*

In the last of the above descriptions, the students have tried to go beyond the basic descriptions, but they do not find it easy. We can see how, as well as including the profession or the features provided by the video game, the students build up the characteristics which begin to relate to the setting (for example "is devoted to her family"). Below, is a discussion where students compare their work, focusing on the more important points of each example.

Teacher: *What can you say? Come on! Can anyone tell this group something?*

Student 1 Group 1: *That it's fine.*

Teacher: *That it's fine. It's the best. It's the best because it has...although it has less information, you (addressing group 2), for example, you have more information. But it's better because it has led to a more complete picture, right? Now, Juanjo (referring to student 2 from group 2).*

Student 2 Group 2: *Ours is more like a list...*

Teacher: *Yours was more like a list, and theirs is more like text, right? Also they used comparisons, which make it nicer. It was better. Well, that's all folks. Very good!*

In this example, we see how the teacher's key learning outcomes, as set out in the curriculum, are clearly stressed. For example, comparisons are included, as the students are learning to use them in the language class. In some cases they are a little overdone, but it requires an effort from the students to make sure they practice what they have seen in class. In this way, the game becomes a powerful learning tool; connecting game-play experiences with curricular content (Thomas, 2006). This final debate serves as an opportunity for the students to analyse how to put together their descriptions, both by doing it themselves and by comparing their work with their classmates' contributions.

Teaching Narrative Construction through Video Games

As the workshop progresses, we can see how in session 4 the teacher is still helping the students so that they are able to take ownership of the content they are working on. Specifically, the goal in this session is to continue working on the construction of a story.

The virtual world of the Sims offers different simulated scenarios which provide settings where each group's story unfolds. Students choose different routes through the video game, making decisions as they go which combine to form a unique plot for each student. In this way, the teacher encourages the students to pay close attention to what is happening on screen, so they can build their own narratives later. The story constructed in this session will serve to develop a video based on the story plot. Proceeding in small stages, the teacher asks students to write a description of the homes they have created, helping them by relating the activity to the curricular content. Following on from this, the teacher suggests they write down the most important events that occurred during play. To do this, they continue working on their worksheets where they have collected data in previous sessions.

Teacher: *During today's class what you have to do is play and be a little more aware of your story plot, which is what you will have to write later. You'll write at the end of the class and you'll be given time to write a description of your house, which many of you don't have yet, and the plot, the most important things that have happened in your story, OK? Your characters' stories. Yes? Some of you are looking at me with a confused look, do you understand?*

Student (off camera): *What argument? I mean, do we have to see what each one is doing?*

Teacher: *Let's see. What you are doing in the game is similar to a story, you have the characters, you have the house and it's assumed that something is happening between them, right? Then you have to tell that story.*

The extract above shows the teacher telling the students how to construct a story based on the video game. It also shows the importance of continuing their earlier work. The descriptions are based on the characters and now they have to do the same with the house descriptions.

The video game is used to encourage students to write. Specific details from the game form the basis of the written work, where they explain the decisions taken during the game. In this way, students develop their narratives from the free context provided by the video game.

Using this activity, we see how the teacher is interested in the way the students develop their narrative thinking (Bruner, 1996), through learning to retell events as a story. This is why the teacher emphasises the idea of the plot, as she wants the students to connect their actions to create a story with a beginning, a middle, and an end (Propp, 1987).

However, it would appear that the students do not manage to fully understand the concept of the plot, nor how they must combine their experiences in the game to make a story. As previously noted, the role of the teacher is crucial when working with video games, as the guidance of an adult is often required to help the students reflect on their experiences in the game. This is why when the teacher spots these problems; she looks for examples to clarify concepts and to guide the students towards their goal of creating an audio-visual production based on their work.

Teacher: *Everything that has happened. For example, 'they arrived at the house one day, I don't know, at first they got along very well but then there were problems, one day they burned the kitchen, whatever...' OK? You tell this here, the most important things, yes? What are we going to with this? For you to bear in mind. Next day we will begin to do the final work, which is a video... (...) In the video you have to tell the story, you have to put screenshots of the game, and also any other images you want to use, so the story is clear. Got that?*

Student: *(off camera) Yes.*

Teacher: *OK, we can show you a video which was made earlier so you can see how it's done. So you can see more or less what you must have in mind. What you are going to have to do is take some pictures of the game, these must make it very clear what the most important things are that have happened in the game, because that is what has to be in there, OK? If, for example, you say that: 'One day they arrived at the house', there should be a few words that say: 'One day they got home, and so on" and then you have an image of them coming into the house, OK? Then you'll say, "at first they didn't get along, bla, bla, bla," and you show a picture of them fighting, for example. OK? These are the images...*

With the above example, we can observe how the teacher tries to make the students relate the story plot to pictures from the video game. These images aim to show different moments in the story that will differ depending on the decisions and actions of each group member. This is a difficult task for the students, and they do not manage it as easily as the teacher expected. In the next extract, we see how the teacher tries to give the students some tips on how to transfer their personified stories (Gee, 2004) to an audio-visual format.

Teacher: Listen, for the plot, what matters is...you have to put the most important things that happened in order, and then tell the story. Just think when you make the video that the video you are making has to summarise all that happened, OK? So the video will start by saying: "First, there were some characters in a house", then you introduce the characters, taking pictures of them.

Student 1 group 2: Can we say that they met in college?

Teacher: Yes, "they met in college, and shared a house", OK? Then show some pictures of the house. "At first everything was going well and whatshisname gets to know whatshername", images of this, "then whatever happened...one day a ghost came", and the ghost appears. Do you understand the idea?

Student 1 Group 2: (nods)

Teacher: What you have to note here (points to the activity card), are the most important things that have been happening.

Student 1 Group 2: OK.

Teacher: So, here (pointing to the activity card), first you'd put "at first, this and that," then in the next script, "they kiss, and whatever" next script, "a ghost appears in the house."

In this fragment it can be seen how the teacher gives the students advice on how to write the narrative. To do this, she tells the students to observe the events that occur in their stories and note them down in chronological order. As seen in the previous example, the teacher shows them how to sequence the different moments they want to show, while relating them to each other using screen shots taken from the game. In the following sessions, they use these screen shots to make their video.

After these discussions with the teacher, the students start writing their stories while trying to keep in mind her advice. However, we can see how building a story becomes a complicated task. In Figures 3 and 4, we can observe how two of the groups have concentrated more on the introduction and descriptions of the characters, while the other two groups have developed further their stories but without managing to create the appropriate narrative structure.

In the first story in Figure 3, we can observe how the students present a series of events which have been important during the game. However we cannot claim they have created a story, as there is really no connection made between the different situations. On the other hand, the second story develops the introduction to the story but then it is not developed further. This is an improvement on the previous story, as a first step is taken towards building a narrative, giving the events some meaning and organising them chronologically.

The stories in Figure 4 are more complex and show a greater level of preparation when constructing the narrative.

The first story develops the events in the video game more fully, and establishes relationships between the different characters. It can be seen that the students have used the scenes in the video game to make up a story that happened in the past. They have reconstructed the situations which took place in the game but they have given them their own personal meaning. For example, the characters are given feelings and emotions (*Olwen is in love with Peter and he is with her, Olwen had a row with Peter for being so insistent about the baby*) related to their own value

197

Figure 3. Stories: groups 3 and 4: Translation (a): "When Mohame Yordan makes the dinner and suddenly she burns the kitchen because she can't cook. When Carlota Ramos goes for a shower and breaks the bath tap and she has to go to work. And when they see that the house is all flooded. When Sara Balbas and Mohame Yordan went to bed and you-know-what happens. And when we changed houses and we've put in a really big swimming pool." (b): "The four of us were friends at university and, with time, we became close friends. A year later the university split them up until through Facebook they got together again and decided to go and live together. Sergio and Yanira fell in love and now they want to have children together but Sergio doesn't want to."

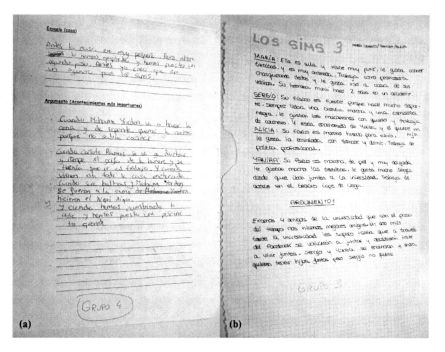

(a) (b)

judgements and their own way of interpreting the world and social relationships (*Peter is so absentminded that once he got home and went to bed in the same bed as Lock and when Maddy and Olwen got home they were stunned and thought the worst.*).

The second example however, is not a story set in the past but it begins at the start of the game. In this case, the students introduce the story and create a timeline for the events (*In the first place, later, a few days later, for the moment*). Likewise, they prepare the main plot of the story (*A few days later life carried on as usual but suddenly something magical happened*), although they do not manage to finish the ending and leave it somewhat

inconclusive. This is why the story appears to be similar to a serialised episode, where one episode is narrated in a specific time period, with little or no reference to events in the past, or in the future.

This analysis of the stories allows us to make two observations of relevance. On the one hand, having been given the same instructions by the teacher, each group has come up with a different piece of work depending on how they interpreted events in their games. On the other hand, the fact that each story is so different is remarkable, as all the groups played the same game from the start of the workshop. This indicates the potential a simulation video game has for developing creativity and narrative thinking.

Figure 4. Stories: groups 1 and 2. Translation (a): "They were neighbours when small, at primary school and high school they were classmates. Soon after buying the house the bath was broken by kicking the tap. Olwen is in love with Peter and he is with her. Peter wants to have a baby but Olwen thinks it's too soon. On the other hand, Lock is more focused on his work, until one day he meets a ghost who seduces him (it's one of Maddy's relatives), but he doesn't appear to be very interested in her. Meanwhile, Maddy stays in her world of football and never leaves it. Peter is so absentminded that once he came home and climbed into bed with Lock and when Maddy and Olwen got home they were stunned and thought the worst. Another day Peter was caught stealing and put in prison. Obviously nobody visited him because that day Maddy had a match. Olwen had a row with Peter for being so insistent about the baby and Lock met the love of his life (a ghost) and obviously he wanted to get her..." (b): "In this story no one has had a previous relation. Everything happens when the four meet. In the first place the characters meet, get together and have jobs, in some cases they changed them. They were fortunate enough to buy a red barbecue and Ivan wants to change some things in his room. Later they get to know Maddy Twisted better, she discovered she had a sister but unfortunately too late because she was already dead. A few days later, life carried on as usual but suddenly something magical happened; it was that special moment called love. Lock Morrison and Olwen Beugarden have fallen in love and are planning to have a baby boy or girl, who knows? For the moment this is all that has happened in the Twisted family."

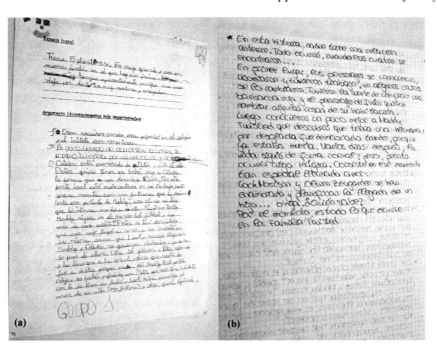

(a)   (b)

Taking these stories, in some cases just a rough sketch, while in others a more complete story, the students now tried to convert them from a written format to a visual format. To do this, sessions 5 and 6 were dedicated to editing their stories using Microsoft Movie Maker, using the images and video that they had captured while playing. As we will see next, in session 7 the students pooled together their ideas on their productions and revisited the ideas they developed earlier during the curricular content workshop.

From the Written Text to the Audio-Visual Narrative

The seventh and final session is dedicated to watching together the videos that they have made, and commenting on them. This session encourages the exchange of opinions on each of the videos, and helps the students revisit some of the ideas that they have been working with during the process. These are the ideas they covered in relation to curricular content and story building, as well as those skills related to using technology. We analyse the dialogues between the students and the teacher, after watching each video (see Figure 5).

First Group:

Teacher: *OK guys. There have been things that I liked and others that I didn't like. The things I liked a lot; I liked how you use music. That's very good. How you created effects and mystery with the Pink Panther theme was great. And that part with the ghost, I liked how it was made because it was quite a story. Could you see it? It followed the plot of the story. The characters were presented, where they live, what each one does ... and suddenly we arrived at the hall... pow!... the ghost! We had reached the heart of the story. But then what? From there on we were like... what now? What about the ghost? Then suddenly there are some people who go off in a balloon.*

Girl: *They leave things in half finished.*

Teacher: *Right?*

Girl: *And they said it'll be... (not understood)*

Boy: *But it's OK.*

Teacher: *You can tell you have worked hard and it has turned out very good. The mixture of...of images and music was very good. Just that. Note that it is telling a story even when you leave open endings. Listen, the end does not have to conclude in everything being sorted out. But the story has to follow a logical pattern so that someone watching it knows more or less where it's heading to and where it's leading to. Although in the end is whatever it is... bam!... but suddenly it's all over the place: Let's change the scenery, we're going to their work, then there are others in a car, right? It's a little confusing. But otherwise it is fine.*

The first video makes a good connection between the story, the music, and the images. For example, the students create a mysterious effect using music synchronised with the story and the images. The problem with this video, and as we will see, with the others too, is that it starts out introducing the story but this is neither developed nor concluded.

This first phase presenting the story is closely related to the development of the characters and the setting; material that was worked on most in the language class. However, building a story is a more complex process. We should also bear in mind that the video game does not provide a

Figure 5. Screenshots of the audio-visual project: group 1

- Sims' life - — Olwen is asleep - - Oh! a ghost! -

well-developed story with a clear ending; it is just a series of events that occur over time.

As defined by the term spatial stories (Jenkins, 2002), the video game is an action setting where a one participates with a character and through this character a narrative is constructed (see Figure 6).

Second video:

Teacher: *What do you think about this one?*
Children: *Good*
Teacher: *Have you seen how it is clearer, as it is less jumbled. You have been telling the whole story more clearly. I miss the...beginning, middle, end, right? There could have been story there, even though you had made it up. I told you. With those images you could have done more. Do you understand? Yes? (children agree) And about the ghost... and so on... and then there's something of a story, because you are in the beginning. You are setting the story, the four live there... very nice, and also you did the setting well! The four living (not understand) I liked that. A ghost appears and... OK, we have set the scene. And now what happens? What about the story? But OK, very good.*

The teacher suggests that they could have invented a storyline using the elements at their disposal. This idea arises because in their narratives the students have only described the events, without developing the narratives or bringing them to a conclusion. This brings us to the idea that the video game is a setting where the players can experiment with their environment and experience situations interactively. Along these lines, one of the essential skills Jenkins (2006) defines is precisely what he calls 'Play'; defined as the capacity to experiment with one's surroundings as a form of problem solving, or, in this case, a resource for creating a narrative. In the context of a video game such as The Sims, the character's story is not linear but is developed as the player recognises and uses the available resources from within the game. This way, it is the players who have to find a storyline which is not provided in the game, and it is the players who must build a story which makes some sense.

Another relevant point can be made in this example, and that is how one of the researchers, who was acting in the role of the teacher, encouraged the students to reflect on how to combine sound and images when making the audio-visual narratives. This went more deeply into the development of appropriation (Jenkins, 2006), understood as the ability to meaningfully sample and remix media content.

Researcher: *One thing that is very good in this video, so you can think about it when you make yours, is that when you use music in videos you can try...in this one it was a little by chance because we did it right now in a hurry. You can extend the images a couple of seconds or delay them...or make it a little shorter or whatever, so when a part of the*

Figure 6. Screenshots of the audio-visual project: group 2

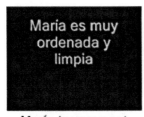 
- María is very neat and clean -

- Sergio is very clumsy -

music ends, you have silence. Why is it better? Because, for example in your one, that was playing the first song and then the Pink Panther started. Suddenly you're singing and then it cuts out...you can extend the picture so when you switch from one song to another, it will be in a part of the song where a verse is ending, so that the change seems a bit more natural. This is very cool in videos.

In this framework, we can observe how difficult it is to develop competences which connect different modalities of text. Jenkins (2006) defines this ability as 'transmedia navigation,' defined as the ability to deal with the flow of stories and information across multiple modalities. Following Jenkins, the strategy for students to learn about multimodality and transmedia navigation is based on three ideas (see Figure 7):

A. To spend time on focusing on how stories change as they move across different contexts of production and reception;
B. To consider the affordances and conventions of different media;
C. To learn to create using a range of different media tools.

Third Video:

Teacher: *OK, and this one, what would you say?*
Student group 1: *They got a bit carried away*

Teacher: *With the titles, yes? The titles were very slow...*
Student from another group: *And they told it very...*
Student 2 Group 2: *Very soon...*
Teacher: *OK, and then it's what Juanjo says (student 2 group 2), at the end it was like it was cut off, also, soon, suddenly... We lacked the introduction, because that was very good in these groups (referring to the two groups, 2 and 1), and in this one, for example, it was very nice, because, besides telling us what it's called, you also said something about it him, right? 'He was very lazy, this one was such a...' and that is what you do when you tell a story, start... Mary! Are you paying attention?*
Student group 1: *Yes*
Teacher: *Begin by introducing the characters, not just 'this one is called so and so, this one is called this', but describing a trait, something about them, a description, right? And here we missed that, introduce the characters. Then, it was good all that you showed about things that happened, but they should lead somewhere, the plot.*
Student Group 3: *In my opinion, we have been summing up the moments that we liked the most.*
Teacher: *Yes... Look, Aida (student group 3), with this same example. If at first you present the characters, yes? and you introduce them to*

Figure 7. Screenshots of the audio-visual project: group 3

- The best friends -   - Everyone was doing what they pleased -   - Making a new giant pool. Ah! -

us, because at first we don't know who they are, and then you set an ending, something that ends, something... even if you just say "and in the end they all turned out to be good friends and lived happily together forever," whatever, but put a few more little scenes, and those phrases, and you've got a story. OK?

Student Group 3: *Yes*

Teacher: *It's like that, I think, maybe you have not fully understood what it was you had to do, a story or a tale.*

Student group 3: *(off camera) I didn't.*

Teacher: *OK. At least in the end you understand.*

Researcher: *It's more like a description, right?*

Teacher: *Yes, you are making a description, yes. You have got stuck at the introduction, we saw that the other day. You made a chain story. Some wrote the introduction, you swapped them, then others wrote the middle part, you swapped again, and others wrote the outcome. So they could see what it was about. Well you got stuck at the introduction, you set up a story that could have been very good, but...*

Student: *(off camera) Yeah...*

In this case, the teacher does not give her opinion immediately but asks the students what they think. This way it is the students who analyse the work of their companions, thanks in part to the experience gained during this session dedicated to commenting the videos. In order to help the students reflect on their work, the teacher summarises what the other videos had compared to this one.

The three stories had one detail in common, and that was how none of them followed a storyline as the teacher intended. They just introduced the story but did not develop it. What this really reflects is what they have been working on in class, which is the presentation of the characters and their descriptions. Regarding this, it is interesting to note the commentary of one of the girls ("In my opinion, we have been summing up the moments that we liked the most.").

Making progress in the development of a story is not a simple process and it would have been better to go into this much more during the language classes. The teacher is aware that the students have not reached the learning objectives set ("maybe you have not fully understood what it was you had to do, a story or a tale"). However, in one of the language classes taught while the workshops were being run, they did successfully carry out a task set by the teacher on the subject of building narratives ("some wrote the introduction, you swapped them, others wrote the middle part, you swapped again, and others wrote the outcome"). This makes us think how a relatively common task using written texts requires the development of specific skills when working with digital media and audio-visual content. It reveals the importance of carrying out such work in the school, as students are faced with activities which allow them the use of different forms of expression and communication, responding to the needs of the digital society.

CONCLUDING REMARKS

This experience serves as an example of how new technologies, especially commercial video games, could be considered more than entertainment artifacts. It shows how they can be successfully introduced in schools, allowing teachers to promote new literacies (Buckingham, 2000; Prensky, 2004; Jewitt, 2008; Lacasa, 2011) and to introduce specific curricular contents in an innovative way.

We found that simulation video games can be used in different areas of formal education; they are a tool which helps teachers enhance curricular content through the use of technology in the classroom (Srinivasan, Butler-Purry & Pedersen, 2008). The simulation video games allow participants to experiment with different strategies without risk. This safe environment expands the situations that students can experience, thus enabling them to transfer these small episodes in the real world, and learning experiences. The causal maps developed from their participation in the game helps students to interpret and give meaning to their lives. In this study, we conclude that the use of The Sims 3 video game in the Language and Literature class can promote digital literacy by offering students a virtual world where they can develop their creativity to read and write stories in an innovative way (Black & Steinkuehler, 2009). Consequently, simulation video games provide their users with plenty freedom for action, the players are constantly taking decisions which open up a wide range of possibilities for creating stories. This game features make it a good resource to introduce in the classroom, since as the teacher mentioned in previous interviews, sometimes the students have some difficulties to write creatively. A simulated world that they can modify and rebuild as they want is then a good starting point that can help them to unfold their imagination.

Using a video game in a school context also involved the presence of the teacher, who has the role of connecting the game experience with the subject. In this respect, the teacher acts as a mediator between the video game and the curricular content, enhancing the learning process (Black & Steinkuehler, 2009). In this case, the teacher used the video game to introduce Language content in order to teach the students how to create narratives; the teacher encourages the students to focus their efforts on building a story, viewing it as a process that starts with the description of the characters and an appropriate setting. This is done by using the video game as the setting for the story providing the students with the elements necessary to create the stories. This process is based on what Jenkins (2002) called spatial stories, in this case each narrative evolves from simulation video games such as The Sims 3. The teacher is also the person who acts as a guide to what happens in the game, makes students aware of the development of the story and makes them think beyond what

happens on the screen. In this sense, the dialogue between the teacher and the students before and after the playtime is critical because together, they build the message they want to convey in the game, generating critical thinking. The teacher, based on the features display by the video game, encourage the students to reflect upon their own work recalling the use of different strategies to make the descriptions more complex and rich by introducing metaphors, comparisons, exaggerations and so on. These curricular contents were presented before during traditional classes and now are being explored in a practical way.

However, despite the efforts of the teacher, in their initial texts the students have difficulty getting beyond the descriptions. This could be related to the students' transition from an analytic mode of thinking to a more narrative thinking (Bruner, 1985, 1986, 1996). While the description of the characters and the environment requires them to be studied and analysed, the construction of a story requires an ability to develop this analysis based around a storyline. As a starting point, the teacher gets the students to describe what happens in the game and then make the switch to developing their narrative thinking abilities by learning to recount what happened in the form of short stories.

Analysis of the students' written work, which served as a starting point for the development of audiovisual narratives, reveals two important insights. Firstly, each group came up with something different depending on how they interpreted the events in the video game. This was despite the teacher's advice regarding curriculum content and story writing being the same for all students. Secondly, each storyline was very different even though all groups of students had identical characters at the start of the workshop. This makes us reflect on the enormous potential of video games that offer a free simulation environment as a resource for developing creativity and narrative thinking.

These findings reinforce the idea of the video game being a stage where players can develop the ability to experiment with their surroundings as a form of problem solving, or, in this case, a resource for creating a narrative (Jenkins, 2006). Depending on the strategies and alternatives chosen, the game will provide different options that can be used by students to create their own stories.

Therefore, in relation to the use of multimodal language in the classroom, we can state that the collective production of videos gives students opportunities to work together and work collaboratively in a way which. This experience provides students with a collaborative environment where they can develop critical thinking by providing arguments to their own narratives and to the opinions of their classmates. Also, the relationship between students and teachers becomes more symmetrical as the audiovisual language facilitates a more active participation of students in their own learning process. Thus, as a "curricular strategy", we have observed that neither the too limited and closed structures and work plans nor those which are too open and undefined are appropriate for collaborative work of video production (de Block, Buckingham & Banaji, 2005; Reid, et al., 2002).

In addition, with respect to the process of developing audiovisual products, we showed that it facilitates and enhances creative thought processes. It also contributes to the learning of the different phases and elements that form the creative process and enables an ideal scenario to build such social skills as negotiation, decision making and problem solving (Lacasa, 2011) alongside with the regular language curricula.

In this chapter we have shown that during the workshop students developed new literacies by working with different media (Manovich, 2001). The video game and its virtual world enhanced students' creativity regarding linguistic skills allowing the teacher to introduce basic narrative strategies in a more innovative way. For example, they were able to write descriptions of the characters created in the video game, using the possibilities and vocabulary offered within the game. Also, the stories enacted during the sessions gave them numerous ideas to come up with narratives,

both written and audio-visual. Together these processes illustrate the skill that Jenkins (2006) named "appropriation".

In addition, students come into contact with new forms of expression and communication through the creation of their multimodal texts. This allows them to improve the development of other fundamental new media skills such as transmedia navigation (Jenkins, 2006). One of the challenges of new media literacies is improving the ability to think across media, from a level of simple recognition (identifying the same content as it is translated across different modes of representation), to a level of narrative logic (understanding the connections between stories communicated through different media), or at the more complex level of rhetoric (learning to express an idea within a single medium or across the media spectrum). Thus, transmedia navigation involves the ability to both read and write across all available modes of expression, by processing new types of stories and arguments represented by the new media landscape.

In conclusion, after analysing how students approach the development of written and visual narratives, the challenge we now face is to develop strategies which provide opportunities for students to develop skills that will help them master different forms of expression through different media and supports.

REFERENCES

Atkinson, P., Coffey, A., Delamnont, S., Lofland, J., & Lofland, C. (2001). *Handbook of ethnography*. London, UK: Sage.

Baek, Y. (2009). Digital Simulation in Teaching and Learning. In D. Gibson & Y. K. Baek (Eds.), Digital Simulations for Improving Education: Learning Through Artificial Teaching Environments (pp. 25-51). Hershey, PA: Information Science Reerence. IGI Global.

Barton, D., & Hamilton, M. (2005). Literacy, reification and the dynamics of social interaction. In Barton, D., & Tusting, K. (Eds.), *Beyond Communities of Practice: Language, Power and Social Context*. Cambridge, UK: Cambridge University Press. doi:10.1017/CBO9780511610554.003

Black, R. W., & Steinkuehler, C. (2009). Literacy in virtual worlds. In Christenbury, L., Bomer, R., & Smagorinsky, P. (Eds.), *Handbook of Adolescent Literacy Research* (pp. 271–286). New York, NY: Guilford.

Bruner, J. (1985). Narratives and paradigmatics modes of thought. In Eisner, E. (Ed.), *Learning and Teaching the Ways of Knowing* (pp. 97–115). Chicago, IL: University of Chicago Press.

Bruner, J. (1986). *Actual minds, possible words*. Cambridge, MA: Harvard University Press.

Bruner, J. (1996). Frames for thinking: Ways of making meaning. In Olson, D. R., & Torrance, N. (Eds.), *Modes of Thought: Explorations in Culture and Cognition* (pp. 93–105). Cambridge, UK: Cambridge University Press.

Bruner, J. (2002). *Making stories: Law, literature, life*. Cambridge, MA: Harvard University Press.

Buckingham, D. (2000). *After the death of childhood: Growing up in the age of electronic media*. Cambridge, MA: Polity Press.

Buckingham, D. (2003). *Media education: Literacy, learning and contemporary culture*. Cambridge, MA: Polity Press.

Cannon-Bowers, J. A., Bowers, C., & Procci, J. (2011). Using video games as educational tools in healthcare. In Tobias, S., & Fletcher, J. D. (Eds.), *Computer Games and Instruction* (pp. 47–72). Hershey, PA: IGI Global.

Carr, D., Buckingham, D., Burn, A., & Schott, G. (2006). *Computer games: Text, narrative and play*. Cambridge, MA: Polity Press.

Carter, K. (1993). The place of story in the study of teaching and teacher education. *Educational Researcher, 22*(1), 5–18.

Castells, M. (2000). *La era de la información: La sociedad red*. Madrid, Spain: Alianza.

Castells, M. (2001). *The internet galaxy: Reflections on the internet, business, and society*. Oxford, UK: Oxford University Press.

Coiro, J., Knobel, M., Lankshear, C., & Leu, D. (2008). Central issues in new literacies and new literacies research. In Coiro, J., Knobel, M., Lankshear, C., Knobel, M., Lankshear, C., & Leu, D. (Eds.), *Handbook of Research on New Literacies*. New York, NY: Taylor & Francis.

Coleman, S., & Dyer-Witheford, N. (2007). Playing on the digital commons: Collectivities, capital and contestation in videogame culture. *Media Culture & Society, 29*(6), 934–953. doi:10.1177/0163443707081700

Coll, C. (2005). Lectura y alfabetismo en la sociedad de la información. *UOC Papers, 1*. Retrieved July 21, 2010, from http://www.uoc.edu/uocpapers/1/dt/esp/coll.pdf

Csikszentmihalyi, M. (1990). *Flow: The psychology of optimal experience*. New York, NY: Harper & Row.

de Block, L., Buckingham, D., & Banaji, S. (2005). *Children in communication about migration: Final report*. London, UK: University of London.

de Freitas, S., & Oliver, M. (2006). How can exploratory learning with games and simulations within the curriculum be most effectively evaluated? *Computers & Education, 46*(3), 249–264. doi:10.1016/j.compedu.2005.11.007

del Castillo, H., Herrero, D., Monjelat, N., García-Varela, A. B., & Checa, M. (2011). *Identity & performance: Developing innovative educational settings through sport videogames*. Madrid, Spain: IATED.

Djaouti, D., Alvarez, J., & Jessel, J.-P. (2011). Classifying serious games: The G/P/S model. In Felicia, P. (Ed.), *Handbook of Research on Improving Learning and Motivation through Educational Games: Multidisciplinary Approaches* (pp. 118–136). Hershey, PA: IGI Global. doi:10.4018/978-1-60960-495-0.ch006

Esnaola Horacek, G. (2006). *Claves culturales en la construcción del conocimiento: ¿Qué enseñan los videojuegos?* Buenos Aires, Argentina: Alfagrama.

Frasca, G. (2003). Simulation versus narrative: Introduction to ludology. In Wolf, M. J. P., & Perron, B. (Eds.), *The Video Game Theory Reader*. London, UK: Routledge.

García-Varela, A. B., del Castillo, H., Checa, M., Monjelat, N., & Herrero, D. (2011). *Learning to be digital producers: Writing a school newspaper*. Madrid, Spain: IATED.

Gee, J. P. (2000). The new literacy studies: From "socially situated" to the work of the social. In Barton, D., Hamilton, M., & Ivanic, R. (Eds.), *Situated Literacies: Reading and Writing in Context*. London, UK: Routledge.

Gee, J. P. (2001). *Literacy development, early and late: Ownership, identity, and discourse*. Paper presented at the International Literacy Conference: "Literacy and Language in Global and Local Settings: New Directions for Research and Teaching". New York, NY.

Gee, J. P. (2004). *Situated language and learning: A critique of traditional schooling*. New York, NY: Routledge.

Gee, J. P. (2007). *What video games have to teach about learning and literacy*. New York, NY: Palgrave Macmillan.

Gee, J. P. (2008). Video games and embodiment. *Games and Culture*, *3*(3-4), 253–263. doi:10.1177/1555412008317309

Gee, J. P., & Hayes, E. (2009). No quitting without saving after bad events: Gaming paradigms and learning in the Sims. *International Journal of Learning and Media*, *1*(3), 49–65. doi:10.1162/ijlm_a_00024

Gros, B. (1998). *Jugando con videojuegos: Educación y entretenimiento*. Bilbao, Spain: Desclée de Brouwer.

Gros, B. (2002). La dimensión socioeducativa de los videojuegos. *Edutec: Revista Electrónica de Tecnología Educativa, 12*.

Gros, B. (2004). *Pantallas, juegos y educación: La alfabetización digital en la escuela*. Bilbao, Spain: Desclée de Brouwe.

Gros, B. (2008). *Videojuegos y aprendizaje*. Barcelona, Spain: Graó.

Gros, B., & Silva, J. (2005). La formación del profesorado como docentes en los espacios virtuales de aprendizaje. *Revista Iberoamericana de Educación*, *36*, 2–16.

Hague, C., & Williamson, B. (2009). *Digital participation, digital literacy, and school subjects*. Bristol, UK: Futurelab.

Hammersley, M., & Atkinson, P. (1995). *Ethnography: Principles in practice* (2nd ed.). London, UK: Routledge.

Hayes, E. (2011). The Sims as a catalyst for girls' IT learning. *International Journal of Gender. Science and Technology*, *3*(1), 121–147.

Hayes, E. R., & King, E. M. (2009). Not just a dollhouse: What the Sims 2 can teach us about women's IT learning. *Horizon*, *17*(1), 66–69. doi:10.1108/10748120910936153

Herman, D. (2011). *Basic elements of narrative*. Singapore, Singapore: John Wiley & Sons.

Hernández, T. (2008). Los videojuegos. In López, F. (Ed.), *El Juego Como Estrategia Didáctica* (pp. 91–99). Barcelona, Spain: Graó.

Hofstede, G. J., Caluwé, L. D., & Peters, V. (2010). Why simulation games work—In search of the active substance: A synthesis. *Simulation & Gaming*, *41*(6), 824–843. doi:10.1177/1046878110375596

Jenkins, H. (2002). *Hop on pop: The politics and pleasures of popular culture*. Durham, NC: Duke University Press.

Jenkins, H. (2006). *Convergence culture: Where old and new media collide*. New York, NY: New York University Press.

Jenkins, H. (2009). *Confronting the challenges of participatory culture: Media education for the 21st century*. Washington, DC: MacArthur Foundation.

Jewitt, C. (2008). Multimodality and literacy in school classrooms. *Review of Research in Education*, *32*, 241. doi:10.3102/0091732X07310586

Johnson, S. (2005). *Everything bad is good for you: How today's popular culture actually making us smarter*. New York, NY: Riverhead Books.

Kafai, Y. (1998). Videogame designs by girls and boys: Variability and consistency of gender differences. In Cassell, J., & Jenkins, H. (Eds.), *From Barbie to Mortal Kombat* (pp. 90–117). Cambridge, MA: MIT Press.

Kemmis, S., & McTaggart, R. (2000). Participatory action research. In Denzin, N., & Lincoln, Y. (Eds.), *Handbook of Qualitative Research* (2nd ed., pp. 567–605). Thousand Oaks, CA: Sage.

Kemmis, S., & McTaggart, R. (2005). Participatory action research. In Denzin, N. K., & Lincoln, Y. S. (Eds.), *The Sage Handbook of Qualitative Research* (3rd ed., pp. 559–603). Thousand Oaks, CA: Sage.

Kirriemuir, J. (2002). *A survey of the use of computer and video games in classrooms. Internal Report for BECTA*. London, UK: British Educational Communications and Technology Agency.

Kirriemuir, J., & McFarlane, A. (2003). Use of computer and video games in the classroom. In *Proceedings of the Level Up Digital Games Research Conference*. Utrecht, The Netherlands: Universiteit Utrecht.

Kirriemuir, J., & McFarlane, A. (2004). *Literature review in games and learning*. Bristol, UK: Futurelab.

Kong, S. C., Ogata, H., Arnseth, H. C., Chan, C. K. K., Hirashima, T., Klett, F., et al. (2009). Mypet-my-quest: Utilizing game quests to scaffold students' goal setting for learning. In *Proceedings of the 17th International Conference on Computers in Education Hong Kong*. Pacific Society for Computers in Education.

Lacasa, P., & Gipi. (2006). *Aprendiendo periodismo digital: Historias de pequeñas escritoras*. Madrid, Spain: Machado Libros.

Lacasa, P., & Gipi. (2009). *Video games at the institute: Digital leisure as a learning tool*. Research Report. Madrid, Spain: Academic Press.

Lacasa, P. (2011). *Los videojuegos: Aprender en mundos reales y virtuales*. Madrid, Spain: Morata.

Leonard, K., Van Scotter, J., & Pakdil, F. (2009). Culture and communication: Cultural variations and media effectiveness. *Administration & Society*, *41*(7), 850–877. doi:10.1177/0095399709344054

Lin, Y.-L., & Tu, Y.-Z. (2012). The values of college students in business simulation game: A means-end chain approach. *Computers & Education*, *58*(4), 1160–1170. doi:10.1016/j.compedu.2011.12.005

Manovich, L. (2001). *The language of new media*. Cambridge, MA: MIT Press.

Mercer, N. (2000). *Words and mind: How we use language to think together*. New York, NY: Routledge. doi:10.4324/9780203464984

Mills, A. K. (2010). A review of the "digital turn" in the new literacies studies. *Review of Educational Research, 80*(2), 246–271. doi:10.3102/0034654310364401

Mitchell, A., & Savill-Smith, C. (2004). *The use of computer and video games for learning: A review of the literature*. London, UK: Learning and Skills Development Agency.

Mominó, J., Sigalés, C., & Meneses, J. (2008). *La escuela en la sociedad en red: Internet en la educación primaria y secundaria*. Barcelona, Spain: Ariel.

Murray, J. H. (1997). *Hamlet on the holodeck, the future of narrative in cyberspace*. New York, NY: The Free Press.

Ortoll, E. (Ed.). (2007). *La alfabetización digital en los procesos de inclusión social*. Barcelona, Spain: UOC.

Panoutsopoulos, H., & Sampson, D. G. (2012). A study on exploiting commercial digital games into school context. *Journal of Educational Technology & Society, 15*(1), 15–27.

Paras, B., & Bizzocchi, J. (2005). *Game, motivation and effective learning: And integrated model for educational game design*. Paper presented at the Changing Views--Worlds in Play. Vancouver, Canada.

Prensky, M. (2001). *Digital games-based learning*. London, UK: McGraw Hill.

Propp, V. (1987). *Morfología del cuento*. Madrid, Spain: Fundamentos.

Ranalli, J. (2008). Learning English with the Sims: Exploiting authentic computer simulation games for L2 learning. *Computer Assisted Language Learning, 21*(5), 441–455. doi:10.1080/09588220802447859

Randel, J., Morris, B., Wetzel, C. D., & Whitehill, B. (1992). The effectiveness of games for educational purposes: A review of recent research. *Simulation & Gaming, 23*, 261–276. doi:10.1177/1046878192233001

Reid, M., et al. (2002). *Evaluation report of the becta digital video pilot project*. Coventry, UK: Becta. Retrieved from http://www.becta.org.uk/research/reports/digitalvideo/

Sandford, R., Ulicsak, M., Facer, K., & Rudd, T. (2006). *Teaching with games: Using commercial off-the-shelf computer games in formal education*. Bristol, UK: Futurelab.

Sandford, R., & Williamson, B. (2005). *Games and learning*. Bristol, UK: Futurelab.

Sauvé, L., Renaud, L., & Kaufman, D. (2010). Games, simulations, and simulations games for learning: Definitions and distinctions. In Kaufman, D., & Sauvé, L. (Eds.), *Educational Gameplay and Simulation Environments: Case Studies and Lessons Learned* (pp. 1–26). Hershey, PA: IGI Global. doi:10.4018/978-1-61520-731-2.ch001

Scribner, S. (1997). Situating the experiment in cross-cultural research. In Tobach, E., Falmage, R. J., Parlee, M. B., Martin, L. M., & Scribner, A. (Eds.), *Selected Writings of Silvia Scribner* (pp. 94–105). Cambridge, UK: Cambridge University Press.

Scribner, S., & Cole, M. (1978). Literacy without schooling: Testing for intellectual effects. *Harvard Educational Review, 48*(4).

Shaffer, D. W. (2006). *How computer games help children learn*. New York, NY: Palmgrave Macmillan. doi:10.1057/9780230601994

Shaffer, D. W., Squire, K. R., Halverson, R., & Gee, J. P. (2004). *Video games and the future of learning*. Madison, WI: University of Wisconsin.

Sheked, A. (2005). *Multiple case narrative: A qualitative approach to studying multiple populations*. Amsterdam, The Netherlands: John Benjamins Publishing Company.

Silverman, D. (2005). *Doing qualitative research: A practical handbook* (2nd ed.). London, UK: Sage Publications.

Smith, R. (2010). The long history of gaming in military training. *Simulation & Gaming, 41*(1), 6–19. doi:10.1177/1046878109334330

Spindler, G., & Hammond, L. (2006). *Innovations in educational ethnography: Theory, methods and results*. New York, NY: LEA.

Squire, K. (2002). Cultural framing of computer/videogames. *Game Studies, 2*(1).

Squire, K. (2004). *Replaying history: Learning world history through playing civilization III*. Bloomington, IN: Indiana University.

Squire, K. (2005). Changing the game: What happens when video games enter the classroom?. *Innovate Journal of Online Education, 1*(6).

Squire, K. (2008). Open-ended video games: A model for developing learning for the interactive age. In Salen, K. (Ed.), *The Ecology of Games: Connecting Youth, Games and Learning* (pp. 167–198). Cambridge, MA: MIT Press.

Squire, K. (2011). *Video games and learning: Teaching and participatory culture in the digital age*. Cambridge, MA: Teachers College Press.

Srinivasan, V., Butler-Purry, K., & Pedersen, S. (2008). Using video games to enhance learning in digital systems. In *Proceedings of the 2008 Conference on Future Play Research Play Share Future Play*. (pp. 196-199). London, UK: ACM.

Steinkuehler, C. (2010). Video games and digital literacies. *Journal of Adolescent & Adult Literacy, 54*(1), 61–63. doi:10.1598/JAAL.54.1.7

Thomas, S. (2006). Pervasive learning games: Explorations of hybrid educational gamescapes. *Simulation & Gaming, 37*(1), 41–55. doi:10.1177/1046878105282274

Trahtemberg, L. (2000). El impacto previsible en las nuevas tecnologías en la enseñanza y la organización escolar. *Revista Iberoamericana de Educación, 24*. Retrieved from http://www.campus-oei.org/revista/ rie24a02.htm

Tubella, I., Tabernero, C., & Dwyer, V. (2008). *Internet i televisió: La guerra de les pantalles*. Barcelona, Spain: Editorial Ariel.

Turkle, S. (1995). *Life on the screen: Identity in the age of the internet*. New York, NY: Touchstone.

Watson, W. R., Mong, C. J., & Harris, C. A. (2011). A case study of the in-class use of a video game for teaching high school history. *Computers & Education, 56*, 466–474. doi:10.1016/j.compedu.2010.09.007

Williamson, B. (2009). *Computer games, schools, and young people: A report for educators on using games for learning*. Bristol, UK: Futurelab.

ADDITIONAL READING

Bransford, J. (2000). *The design of learning environments: How people learn: Brain, mind, experience, and school*. Washington, DC: National Academy of Sciences.

de Freitas, S., & Griffiths, M. (2008). The convergence of gaming practices with other media forms: What potential for learning? A review of the literature. *Learning, Media and Technology, 33*(1), 11–20. doi:10.1080/17439880701868796

del Castillo, H., & Dominguez, E. (2010). Escribir y pensar: Cuadernos, blogs y fotografías. *Cuadernos de Pedagogía, 398*.

Egenfeldt Nielsen, S., Smith, J. H., & Tosca, S. P. (2008). *Understanding video games: The essential introduction*. New York, NY: Routledge.

Frasca, G. (2003). Simulation versus narrative: Introduction to ludology. In Wolf, M. J. P., & Perron, B. (Eds.), *The Video Game Theory Reader* (pp. 221–236). London, UK: Routledge.

Gee, J. P. (2008). Video games and embodiment. *Games and Culture, 3*(3-4), 253–263. doi:10.1177/1555412008317309

Gros, B. (2008). *Videojuegos y aprendizaje*. Barcelona, Spain: Graó.

Herman, D. (2011). *Basic elements of narrative*. Singapore, Singapore: John Wiley & Sons.

Jenkins, H. (2009). *Confronting the challenges of participatory culture: Media education for the 21st century*. Washington, DC: MacArthur Foundation.

Juul, J. (2005). *Video games and classic game model: Half-real: Video games between real rules and fictional worlds*. Cambridge, MA: MIT Press.

Kirriemuir, J., & McFarlane, A. (2003). Use of computer and video games in the classroom. In *Proceedings of the Level Up Digital Games Research Conference*. Utrecht, The Netherlands: Universiteit of Utrecht.

Kirriemuir, J., & McFarlane, A. (2004). *Literature review in games and learning*. Bristol, UK: University of Bristol.

Lacasa, P., & Gipi. (2006). *Aprendiendo periodismo digital: Historias de pequeñas escritoras*. Madrid, Spain: Machado Libros.

Lacasa, P. (2011). *Los videojuegos: Aprender en mundos reales y virtuales*. Madrid, Spain: Morata.

Lave, J. (1997). The culture of acquisition and the practice of understanding. In Kirshner, D., & Whitson, J. A. (Eds.), *Situated Cognition: Social, semiotic and psychological perspectives* (pp. 17–36). Mahwah, NJ: Lawrence Erlbaum Associates.

McMahan, A. (2003). Immersion, engagement and presence. In Wolf, M. J. P., & Perron, B. (Eds.), *The Video Game Theory Reader* (pp. 67–86). New York, NY: Routledge.

Prensky, M. (2002). The motivation of gameplay: The real twenty-first century learning revolution. *On the Horizons, 10*(1), 5-11.

Prensky, M. (2002). *What kids learn that's positive from playing video games*. Retrieved from http://www.marcprensky.com/writing/

Salen, K., & Zimmerman, E. (2004). *Rules of play: Game design fundamentals*. Cambridge, MA: MIT Press.

Sandford, R., Ulicsak, M., Facer, K., & Rudd, T. (2006). *Teaching with games: Using commercial off-the-shelf computer games in formal education*. Bristol, UK: Futurelab.

Shaffer, D. W. (2006). *How computer games help children learn*. New York, NY: Palmgrave Macmillan. doi:10.1057/9780230601994

Squire, K. (2011). *Video games and learning: Teaching and participatory culture in the digital age*. Cambridge, MA: Teachers College Press.

Turkle, S. (1995). *Life on the screen: Identity in the age of the internet*. New York, NY: Touchstone.

Williamson, B. (2009). *Computer games, schools, and young people: A report for educators on using games for learning*. Bristol, UK: Futurelab.

KEY TERMS AND DEFINITIONS

Commercial Off The Shelf (COTS) Video Games: COTS games are computer or video games created almost entirely for entertainment purposes, yet some COTS games are not absent of intellectual challenges or content (Charsky & Mims, 2008). We can differentiate them from "serious games" term that refers to "a broad swath of video games produced, marketed, or used for purposes other than pure entertainment" (Egenfeldt Nielsen, Smith, & Tosca, 2008).

Digital Literacies: Set of cultural practices that occur in a specific type of society based on intensive use of Information and Communications Technologies (ICT). It is also considered the set of capabilities and skills where aural, visual, and digital literacies overlap (Hague & Williamson, 2009). These include the ability to understand the power of images and sounds, recognize and use that power, manipulate and transform digital media, distribute them penetrating and easily adapt to new media (Jenkins, 2009).

Narrative Thinking: Bruner (1985, 1986, 1996) suggest that there are two complementary ways of knowing and thinking in which people organize and manage their perception of the world, each providing distinctive ways of ordering experience and constructing reality. One is what he called "paradigmatic or logico-scientific" and the other is "narrative." Thus, the first attempt to fulfill the ideal of a formal, mathematical system of descriptions and explanation, is based on the search for universal statements of truth and because of that, is more appropriate in natural and physical sciences. The second one is based on the assumption that the complicated and rich phenomena of life and experience are better presented in stories or narratives (Sheked, 2005).

Play: Ability to experiment with one's surroundings as a form of problem solving. Through play, children try on roles, experiment with culturally central processes, manipulate core resources, and explore their immediate environments (Jenkins, 2009). As they grow older, play can motivate other forms of learning. Part of what makes play valuable as a mode of problem solving and learning is that it lowers the emotional stakes of failing: players are encouraged to suspend some of the real world consequences of the represented actions, to take risks and learn through trial and error. Games not only provide a rationale for learning: what players learn is put immediately to use to solve compelling problems with real consequences in the world of the game.

Sims 3: Is a 2009 strategic life simulation video game. It is the third release of the Sims franchise, which has been recognized for its appeal to a very wide audience, both male and female, and at any age. The game consists in create characters (Sims) and "build them" a life, meet their needs, achieve their aspirations and realize their dreams. Moods include emotional or physical events, like a good meal, comfort from sitting in a good chair. The game allows designing a house for the Sims and to supply it with all the objects that are required to meet their needs. In addition to the needs, Sims now have moods, which may be positive, negative or neutral. Sims live for a set duration of time (adjustable by the player) and advance through several stages (baby, toddler, child, teen, young adult, adult, and elder). Sims can die of old age or they can die prematurely from causes such as fire, starvation, drowning, electrocution, and a meteor. The main novelty of this sequel is the possibility to send your Sims out to explore new locations around town and meet other Sims in the neighborhood.

Simulation: Ability to interpret and construct dynamic models of real world processes. We learn through simulations by a process of trial and error: new discoveries lead researchers to refine their models, tweaking particular variables, trying out different contingencies (Jenkins, 2009). Educators have always known that students learn more through direct observation and experimentation than from reading about something in a textbook or listening to a lecture. Simulations broaden the kinds of experiences users can have with compelling data, giving us a chance to see and do things that would be impossible in the real world.

Simulation Videogames: A simulation game can be defined as a "simplified and dynamic model of a real or hypothetical system in which players are in position of competition or cooperation, rules structure players actions, and the goal is to win (Sauvé, et al., 2010). Another point to consider is the possibility for the player to enter virtual worlds through video games. Shaffer et al. (2004) points out that this is what makes games a powerful tool for learning. These experiences in multiple contexts will enable learners to understand complex concepts without losing the connections between abstract ideas and real problems.

Transmedia Navigation: Capacity to follow the flow of stories and information across multiple modalities. Transmedia stories at the most basic level are stories told across multiple media. At the present time, the most significant stories tend to flow across multiple media platforms. Each medium has its own affordances, its own systems of representation, its own strategies for producing and organizing knowledge. Participants in the new media landscape learn to navigate these different and sometimes conflicting modes of representation and to make meaningful choices about the best ways to express their ideas in each context (Jenkins, 2009). Kress (2003) mentioned that this tendency toward multimodality changes how we teach composition, because students must learn to sort through a range of different possible modes of expression, determine which is most effective in reaching their audience and communicating their message, and to grasp which techniques work best in conveying information through this channel.

Chapter 11
The Impact of International Management on Inclusion of Persons with Disabilities in the Workforce

George S. Mouzakitis
Educational Organization e-DEKA, Greece

Despoina Goutou
Educational Organization e-DEKA, Greece

ABSTRACT

Managers tend to recruit individuals of highest educational standards who deserve quality jobs and attractive remuneration. Equally, disabled persons should enjoy the same benefits. In our era of unprecedented technological development, education should be flexible in order to meet the contemporary demands and the needs of all persons. This chapter analyzes the use of aids, including educational games that can be helpful in supporting people with disabilities. Types of games and games for disabled persons are considered. A more active involvement of international managers in the use of games in educational/training courses for disabled persons is also proposed. Their duties must be amended to include participation in curricula design for any level of vocational/technical education.

INTRODUCTION

Curricula are key to an effective education and especially for effective course design. For decades, quite a few countries concluded to curricula drafted not on the basis of real market needs, but according to personal views of sociologists, educators,

psychologists. Their target was to establish norms in order to maintain a traditional form of school, with minor adjustments, and not a tool of preparing individuals for scientific and/or business careers or their integration onto society As a result, syllabuses have not attained the anticipated output. Though the syllabus is considered identical to curriculum both in meaning and value, the true is that it describes the content of a module, which

DOI: 10.4018/978-1-4666-3950-8.ch011

means, it is part of a curriculum and outlines the main points of a course of study.

Certain educationalists support the course delivery mode with teaching aids taking into consideration the classification of the memory capacity supported by Dale (2009) according to which we remember 20% of what we hear, 30% of what we see, 50% of what we hear and see and 80% of what we hear, see and do.

The use of games in the teaching process refers and takes into account also on this principle.

Historically, the first documented use of games for educational purposes dates back to mid-1800s. The Prussian army used simulated battles to train their officers. In the 1950s, the need to improve and professionalize business management led to the first non-military application of games. In 1956, the American Management Association published the first business game. In this simulation game, learners took a manager's role in the various functions of a company including events and challenges that confronted him.

Surprisingly enough, Plato had praised Egyptians for using games to develop learning experiences. The opinion of researches is that these games might become part of the school curriculum since they have significant value in education.

Managers may be useful in participating in educational issues such as design of curricula for vocational education/training, on the basis of their main role to plan, organize and control businesses at domestic level. These curricula should include a number of different tools, including those ICT based and in particular digital games.

Concerning the deployment of games and simulations of educational purposes, the general opinion is that they are important teaching tools in multiple environments. The prevailing belief is that educational games develop higher thinking skills and provide a learning environment appropriate to develop individuals ability to solve a wide range of problems and to support learning in a wide variety of subjects.

The chain sequence of instruction using games is a four- step-procedure which results to increased possibilities for employment (Figure 1). Educational games can be regarded as a medium suitable to sustain the instruction of persons with disabilities and thus their employment and inclusion in the workforce

In designating the year 1981 as the International Year of Disabled Persons, the UNO (1976) focused world attention, among others, to the growing commitment to protect the right of the disabled persons to enjoy equal opportunities in the workforce. According to the type of disability, 60 jobs are registered as possible positions and International Management has to play a decisive role in hiring disabled persons.

Today the duties of international Managers are multifarious not restricted to the coordination of the employees business activities.

They face difficult situations in their companies and make their best to satisfy clients and staff. A manager is considered international not only because he/she manages international subsidiaries but also because he/she has to hire "international staff" including disabled persons which will give them the opportunity to feel useful both to society and the work environment. International managers' role is not restricted to the evaluation of the employees qualifications, but is expected

Figure 1. The impact of use of games in instruction

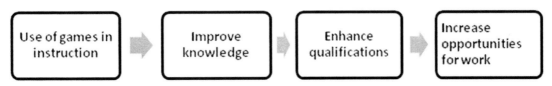

to identify specific impairments, which can be met through training via educational games. International managers should provide to people with disabilities:

- Special education and training programs.
- The use of adapted educational games

In order to match with the workforce capacities required by the company's strategies international managers should be open minded, flexible, able to see things differently and willing to include persons with disabilities in their workforce.

EDUCATION

General Overview

It is argued that education, despite its importance and contribution to economic growth, is still at low level as concerns attainment by disabled persons. In addition, illiteracy rates of Persons With Disabilities (PWD) remain quite higher than that of general population. School attendance for PWD is much lower than that of non-disabled persons.

Education is the driving force, which affects economic development and wealth acquisition. It delivers benefits to individuals and it is considered the most fundamental factors of development. It is important that economic strategies should be based on substantial investment in human capital.

Education is accepted to play crucial role in three major sectors of our contemporary lives, social, business and economy (Figure 2).

According to data, estimated by UNESCO (1990), of the 650 million people worldwide who suffer of a physical, sensory, intellectual or mental disability, 97% had "either never seen the inside of a classroom, or had left school, too early to have mastered basic literacy and numeracy skills."

Teaching disabled individuals the basic skills, instructors use games, mainly, through computers and/or multimedia. As an example, writing can be taught through intensive participation in writing instruction lasting 40 minutes per day. (Erickson, 2005). Statistics (EU Services, 2012) reveal that the percentage of women is higher than that of men in all three educational levels (Figure 3).

Educational Games and Visual Aids

Delivery of courses has been supported through the use of teaching aids as instructional devices to facilitate learning since 1880, though signs of their use dates back to as early as 150 B.C. with the Greeks.

Following the technological development there is a gradual shift from traditional aids to more effective and sophisticated ones, like games.

"Games have strong potential for bringing innovation to education, especially formal education. Nevertheless, their adoption calls for a radical rethinking of pedagogical approaches so that their potential can be leveraged and their effectiveness maximized" (de Freitas et al., 2011).

The teaching aids may be purchased from market resources or be constructed ad hoc. In the latter case, four factors are important for having effective games (Smith, 2012).

Figure 2. Educational dimensions

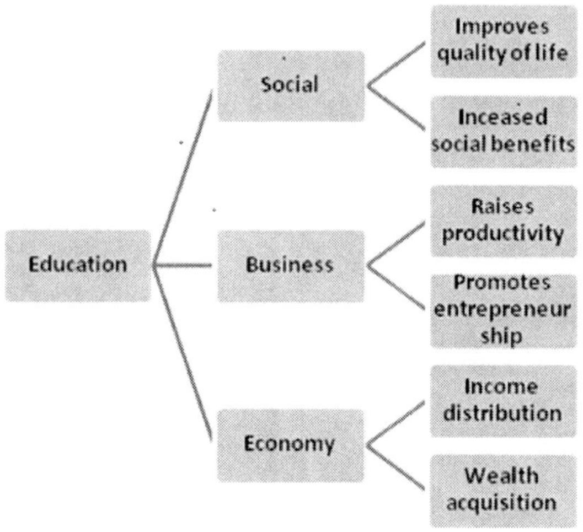

Figure 3. Prevalence of disability for working people of age 24-64 by education and gender (source: EU Statistics Services)

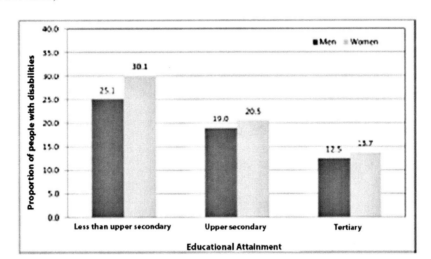

- Analysis of learners characteristics.
- Review of curriculum and syllabus elements.
- Comparison of games characteristics with the learners' skills.
- Survey of market materials and resources for development of aids.
- There are quite a lot of games that can be adopted to sustain, for instance, people with disabilities.

Examples of Educational Games for the Visually Impaired

Mathematical aids for the blind include, the *Cranmer abacus* (Figure 4). Each abacus has 13 rods. The joiner is used to allow the two abaci to be joined together to create one large 26-rod instrument. It is based on the Japanese Soroban Abacus with some tactile modifications. It is used by blind learners to set up and calculate problems without the use of calculator.

There are various systems which assist visual impaired persons in communicative and educational procedures such as *Megaword* Tactile and Braille Crossword Board (Figure 5).

Figure 4. Cranmer abacus

Figure 5. Braille crossword board

One of the most important and effective systems for teaching blind persons is the Braille system which represents the letters of the alphabet, numbers and other material with raised dots and users are asked to make new words. It is designed for the blind and visually impaired persons. All pieces, including the game board are Braille. Two to four persons can play the game.

As further example *Braille Sudoku*, a game of numerical strategy, introduced for the first time in Japan, allows blind people to exercise some math skills (Figure 6).

Speech can be facilitated by a rather recent innovation, the *Speech Plus Calculator*.

Talking calculators come in both standard and scientific models. Most will announce each key as it is pressed, and all read out each entry and result. Some models include a clock or have other added features, and most can be used with an earphone or headphone (Figure 7).

In addition, many talking calculators have tactile markings on the keys. They are used, also, for speech transmission as well as digital data, facsimile, telegraph transmission.

Optacon (Optical Tactile Converter) is an electromechanical device which can enable blind and deaf people to read printed material which is not transcribed into Braille (Figure 8).

Figure 7. Speech plus calculator

Figure 8. Optacon in use

Figure 6. Braille sudoku

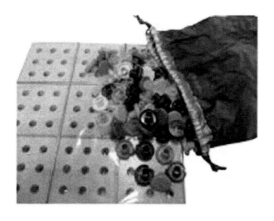

Solitaire Board Game. Solitaire is a popular card game (Figure 9). It enables visually impaired persons to use all their senses (Olson, 2010).

The solitaire board is not something new as a game from the blind or visual impaired. There have been reported samples even since 1779. As shown in Figure 10, there are six types of possible boards presenting differences in the shape and in the numbers of holes.

Braille Math Blocks (Figure 11) is a set of 16 blocks which present numbers and basic mathematical symbols with a corresponding Braille cell. In an easy way, it familiarizes blind persons with the math numbers and symbols

There are a lot of other games that can be adopted to train in human abilities (such as logical thinking or memory) of people with visual disabilities (Figure 12).

The object is a soft colored material of five varying sizes and colors. By size and thickness order the colors are: green, light blue, magenta, grey, and orange. The instructor delivers a piece at a time and while learner palpates it, he discloses the color The memory exercise helps learner to connect in his/her memory size and color.

Braille Talking Puzzle that enhances memorization (Figure 13).

Remove all the pieces and beginning to rebuild the USA map by finding the border states. When you place a piece in the correct space, a clear voice announces the name of the state and its capital.

Figure 9. Solitaire board

Examples of Educational Games for the Hearing Impaired

At this point we should mention board games adopted to teach the use of sign language as, for instance, jigsaw puzzles which make activities as visual as possible (Mackenzie, 2011).

The puzzle is divided into logic, mathematics, video games, word puzzles, (Figure 14) and specific topics are: brain teaser, optical illusion, problem solving.

This teaches hearing impaired persons to form words, distinguish ASL finger-spelling by having clues with words spelled using the manual alphabet. They read the fingerspelling and write the word in English in the clue boxes to create the English word.

Figure 10. Shapes of solitaire board games

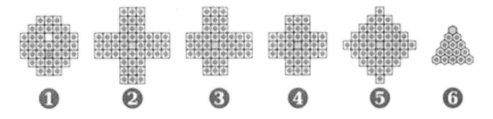

Figure 11. Braille math blocks

Figure 12. Brain memory puzzle

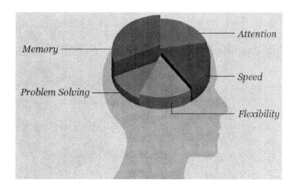

Figure 13. Map of USA in Braille talking instrument (independent living aids LLC)

One of the most important tools for teaching hearing impaired persons is actually the sign language. It is a way of communicating in all aspects of individuals everyday life activities. As an example we can refer to a game such as *Sign Language Puzzles*, a tool to teach American Sign Language (ASL), alphabet (Figure 15), numbers (Figure 16), and communication examples (Figures 17 and 18).

Many other games exist that can be adopted in the education of disabled persons (e.g. Physically Challenged, emotionally disturbed, Intellectually Disabled persons, or with learning disabilities).

Educational Games Integrated in the Curriculum

According to Beane (1995), curriculum integration is not simply an organizational device requiring cosmetic changes in lessons plans across various subject areas. Rather, it is a way of thinking about what schools are for, about the sources of curriculum and about the uses of knowledge. Curriculum integration begins with the idea that the sources of curriculum ought to be problems, issues, and concerns posed by life itself. Integration is a philosophy of teaching in which content is drawn from several subject areas to focus on a particular topic.

In the process of curriculum design priority should be given to the real needs of the market and the reason education/training process should be followed (Figure 19).

Once identified the learners' needs, the objectives of the courses must be set. For example, the intended leaning outcome should be described as follows: "At the end of the course, the learners will be able to explain, to analyze, to apply, to describe, to demonstrate...."

Figure 14. Jigsaw puzzle

Figure 15. American sign language

In the teaching/learning strategies we have to consider factors such as:

1. The teachers qualifications,
2. The learners aptitude rate, and
3. The effectiveness of the teaching mechanisms.

Finally, the purpose of the evaluation is to trace whether the envisaged goals have been met.

Naturally, under the contemporary conditions, the involvement of international managers is, almost, a *sine qua non* condition since, due to the content of the courses of their studies, the extended relationships with international companies, the ad hoc network, can contribute not only to the design of an effective curriculum, but, also, to the production of teaching aids and particularly education games which render the course delivery more effective.

SOLUTIONS AND RECOMMENDATIONS

The issues raised in this chapter mainly refer to the use of games in the instruction of persons with disabilities.

The solution of these multidimensional problems requires a series of structured initiatives with short- and long-term targets. Areas of immediate priority include economics and finance, education with emphasis on curricula design and use of educational games, sociology in terms of developing

Figure 16. Numbers in the US sign language

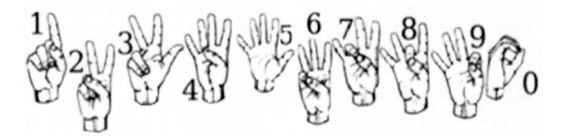

Figure 17. Question in sign language

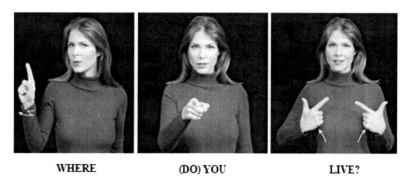

WHERE   (DO) YOU   LIVE?

Figure 18. Answer in sign language

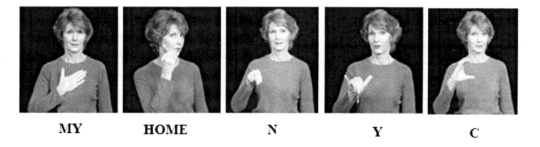

MY   HOME   N   Y   C

sense of responsibility to citizens and equal concern for the workforce of disabled persons and the sustained involvement of managers, particularly of international orientation, in conducing market researches, designing curricula, and planning the appropriate courses delivery (syllabus).

Figure 19. Factors to be considered for the design of curricula

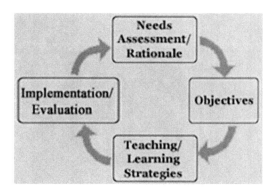

A chain mechanism is recommended, to deal successfully with the difficult situations which have a major effect on our lives.

Thus, the Educational courses content and delivery should change drastically by means of a workable curriculum to meet the market demands in a globalization era, based on a reliable market research, conducted jointly by researches and business manager and providing, the use of educational games in the instruction process.

The sense of responsibility should be enhanced by introducing courses of relative quality in the teaching-learning program at all levels of schooling. In parallel, ways of inclusion of disabled individuals in ordinary schools and work environments will be beneficial for the communities as a whole.

Managers should contribute to the phases of market research, the curriculum design and the selection of prospective learners after evaluation of their background, aptitude score, motivation

Managers, mainly with major in international aspects, are qualified to navigate individuals in the pathway of the required professional experience due to their industry knowledge, ability to seek staff demonstrating a willingness to learn (Uthalsangchai, 2011).

According to Prof. DR Ingo Boeckenholt (International School of Management, Dortmund, 2011), "Globalization calls for a broader management education appropriate to the requirements of working in an international environment."

For this reason, employees have to develop an extraordinary sensitivity for cultural differences and familiarize themselves with information and communication technologies.

CONCLUSION AND FUTURE RESEARCH DIRECTIONS

The innovative proposal concerning the contribution of international managers in the design of curricula and syllabi for Vocational/Technical Education raises some disputes as concerns

A. The effectiveness of this procedure,
B. The willingness of international managers to get involved in a task that might be considered other people's duties, and
C. The reaction of researchers and educators to share with international managers the responsibilities of designing curricula.

However, as per the recent research we have conducted among 20 university faculty members and 16 instructors of HTI instructors a majority of 44.44% agreed to a joint committee with the participation of managers, the sample cannot considered representative.

Therefore, three research projects are planned to be carried out with representative samples of educators, managers, and researchers.

From the perspective of the chapter focus, we are planning to proceed to a model teaching courses using educational games in order to evaluate their effectiveness in teaching persons with disabilities. Finally, a survey will be conducted among enterprises employing persons with disabilities to assess their performance.

For decades, curricula have been designed by educational planners and policy makers on the basis of personal views instead of the findings of market research. Partially, this is the reason of the failure of educational programs, paving the way for economic recession, though there are other causes that the economic theories like capitalism, deregulation, liberalization etc, even supported by renowned economists, have failed to attain the anticipated results. This failure is attributed to economic, psychological, demographic sectors, which have been overlooked by the economic theorists.

An important concern is the inclusion of disabled persons in school classes at any level and their employment in equal terms with others, since more than 60 professions can be joined by them.

Our proposal for participation of qualified managers, preferably international, due to globalization, in the basic educational factors, like curriculum design and courses content, we trust will improve the situation and increase employability of persons either disabled or non-disabled. The expertise of these persons, their knowhow of the market demands globally, their opinions about the required qualifications per se can outweigh any unwanted outcomes.

REFERENCES

Aberdeene, T. (2011). *Games for kids with learning disabilities*. Retrieved on March 15, 2012 from http://www.livestrong.com/article/214918-games_for_kids_with-learn

Able Trust. (1993). *Florida governor's alliance to the employment of disabled citizens, employer research kit*. Retrieved on March 5, 2012 from http://www.abletrust.org

Alba, J. W., & Hashler, L. (1983). Is memory schematic? *Psycological Bulletin, 93*.

Allen, J., & Walker, M. (1991). Training employees with disabilities: Strategies from corporate training. *The Journal for Vocational Special Needs Education, 18*(3), 105–108.

American Psychological Association. (2012). *Learning and memory*. Retrieved on September 18, 2012 from www.apa.org/topics/learning/index.aspx

American School in Japan. (2011). *Pros and cons of globalization*. Retrieved on February 21, 2012 from http://www.asij.ac.jp/highscholl/academic/ss/Economics/2nd semester

Arjunan, N. K. (2010). *Philosophical and sociological foundation in education*. Palakkad, India: Yuga Publications. Retrieved on February 23, 2012 from http/wiki.answers.com,Q

Asia e University. (2012). *Learning theories-cognitive learning theories. Asia e University, Knowledge Center*. AEU.

Ausubel, D. (1969). *Meaningful learning*. Retrieved on September 12, 2012 from http://www.problemlearn.homestead.com/beduc/chapter_5.pdf

Bella, N., & Belkachla, S. (2000). *Impact of demographic trends on the achievement of the millenium development and goal of universal primary education*. Geneva, Switzerland: UNESCO.

Bloom, B. (1987). *The closing of the American mind*. New York, NY: Simon and Schuster.

Boeckenhoft, I. (2012). *Qualifications in international management*. Retrieved on March 15, 2012 from http://www.sm/de

Bowers, H. (2006). *Curriculum design in vocational education*. Paper presented at the Conference of the Australian Associations for research in Education. Adelaide, Australia.

Bureau of Labour Statistics. (2011). *Occupational employment statistics of 2010*. Retrieved on February 18, 2012 from www.blsr.gov/oes/current/oes_net.htm

Careers for People with Disabilities. (2012). *Opening the door to new opportunities*. Retrieved on March 10, 2012 from http://www.careersfor-peoplewith disabikities.org/employe

Chtaini, M. (2011). Has the Keynesian economic theory failed? *MoroccoBoard News Service*. Retrieved on February 21, 2012 from http://www.moroccoboard.com/home

Colceag, F. (2001). *The relationship between education, economy and social systems*. Retrieved on February 23, 2012 from http://www.austega.com/florin/

Coobs, N. (1989). *Education for persons with physical disabilities*. Paper presented at a Meeting. Milton Keynes, UK.

Dale, E. (2009). *How much do we remember? Guide to student success*. San Luis Obispo, CA: Cuesta College.

de Freitas, S. (2012). *New pedagogical approaches in game enhanced learning: Curriculum integration*. Hershey, PA: IGI Global.

Douglass, J. A. (2010). *Higher education budgets and the global recession*. Retrieved on February 23, 2012 from http://cshe.berkeley.edu/

EU-SILK. (2011). *The situation of working age people with disabilities across the EU*. Geneva, Switzerland: EU-SILK.

European Commission. Eurostat. (2010). *Percentage of rates of low educational attainment per age*. Geneva, Switzerland: Eurostat.

Eurostat. (2011). *Unemployment statistics.* Geneva, Switzerland: Eurostat.

Frost, G. (2008). *What is memory retention?* Retrieved from http://ezinearticles.com/?What-is-Memory-Retention?&id=996416

Habschick, M., Seldi, B., & Evers, J. (2007). *VT Markt/2006/26-H-with cooperation of Doreen Klose and Yoshua Parsian.* Final report on survey of financial literacy schemes.

Hag, M. (2011). *Intellectual disability activities.* Retrieved on March 20, 2012 from http://www.ehow.com/info_8028431_intellectual-disability-activities

Hagenbach, S. (2011). *Teaching children responsible behaviour, human kinetics.* Retrieved on February 28, 2012 from http://www.humankinetics.com

Hlebowitsh, P. S. (2011). *The College of Idaho, John Dewey and the idea of experimentalism.* Retrieved on March 5, 2012 from http://www.edu301fall.wikispaces.com/.../John dewey

Institute for Statistics. (2012*). Website.* Retrieved on February 26, 2012 from www.un.org/esa/.../06_UNESCO.pdf

Institute of Neeurosciences. (2012). *Mental health and addiction (NMHA).* Retrieved on September 11, 2012 from http://www.thebrain.megill.co/flash/d/d_07_p/d-O7_p_tra.html

Kaufman, R. (2010). The manager's role in service education. *UP Your Service.* Retrieved on September 10, 2012 from http://www.upyourservice.com/blog/service-education/the-managers-role-in-service-education/

Keynes, J. M. (1936). *General theory of employment, interest and money.* New York, NY: Harcourt, Brace and Co. Retrieved on February 15, 2012 from www.marxists.org/reference/subject/economics/keynes/general theory/

Laabs, J. J. (1991). The golden arches provide golden opportunities. *The Personnel Journal, 70*(7), 52–57.

Lean, E. (1983). Learning disabled trainees: Finding and helping the "hidden handicapped". *Training and Development Journal, 37*(9), 56–62.

Leinhart & Byrness. (1996). *Schemata serve several functions in learning, categorizing, remembering, comprehending and problem solving.* Academic Press.

Mackenzie, A. (2011). *Games for deaf kids.* Retrieved on March 20, 2012 from www.ehow.com/list_6399398_games-deaf-kids.html

Miller, G. (1992). Making training accessible to people with disabilities. *Training (New York, N.Y.), 92*(8), 94.

Mote, D. (2011). Management. In *Encyclopedia of Business* (2nd ed). Retrieved on March 15, 2012 from http://www.referenceforbusiness.com/encyclopedia/Kor-kids-with-learn

Musafiri, E. (2011). *Maters program-responsible management and sustainable economic development.* Kigala, Rwanda: Natural University.

NAMI. (2011). *Website.* Retrieved on April 5, 2012 from www.nami.org//template.clm?section=about_mental_illness

Olsen, A. (2010). *Educational games for the visual impaired.* Retrieved on March 20, 2012 from www.brighthub.com/education/special/articles/65405.aspx

Patrick, J. J. (1991). *Teaching the responsibilities of citizens.* Bloomington, IN: ERIC Clearinghouse for Social Studies/Social Sciences Education.

Pearson, H. H. (2009). *Idealism and education.* Retrieved on February 29, 2012 from pearsonhighered.com/.../0132540746.p

Peavler, R. (2012). *What is capitalism?* Retrieved from http://www.about.com

Prince, A. (2011). *Games for emotionally disturbed children.* Retrieved on March 20, 2012 from http://www.ehow.com/info_81.007533_games-emotionally-disturbed

Prospects.Net. (2011). *The impact of higher education on employment prospects and earnings.* Retrieved on February 15, 2012 from http://ww2-prospects.ac.uk/cms/ShowPage

Sengupta, S. (2011). *Causes of unemployment.* Retrieved on February 18, 2012 from www.buzzle.com/articles/causes-of-unemployment.html

Sharma, A. (2011). What is the relationship between education and education and psychology? *Preserve Articles.* Retrieved on February 23, 2012 from www.preservearticles.com/about_preserve-darticles.com.html

Smith, A. (1776). *The wealth of nations.* Retrieved on February 18, 2012 from www.bibliomania.com/2/1/65/112/frameset.html

Smith, J. (2012). *How to develop teaching materials.* Retrieved on March 10, 2012 from www.ehom.com/how_6592423_develop_teaching-materials.html

UNESCO. (2006). *Report on education for all: Literacy for life.* Retrieved on February 26, 2012 from www.uis.unesco.org/Library/Documents/gmr06.en.pdf

United Nations. (1976). *General assembly resolution 31/123 – The international year of disabled persons, 1981.* Geneva, Switzerland: United Nations.

United Nations. (1993). *General assembly, standard rules on the equalization of opportunities for persons with disabilities.* Retrieved on March 5, 2012 from www.un.org/documents/ga/res/48/ar096.htm

University of Nottingham. (2012). *Corporate social responsibility.* Retrieved on February 29, 2012 from http://pgstudy.nottingham.ac.uk/postgraduate-courses

Uthalsangchai, P. (2011). *Qualities of a successful international manager.* Retrieved on March 15, 2012 from www.bangkokbank.com

Walker, J. (2010). Being a responsible citizen. *Responsible Citizen Co.* Retrieved on February 28, 2012 from www.resposblecitizen.co.uk/being-a-responsible-citizen.html

Wiles, J., & Bondl, J. (1979). *Curriculum development-A guide to practice.* Columbus, OH: Chales E. Merril Publishing Company.

Wilson, L. O. (2005). *Curriculum index.* Retrieved on March 5, 2012 from www4.uwsp.edu/education/Wilson.index

KEY TERMS AND DEFINITIONS

Curriculum: Is a systematic set of courses description which aims to provide knowledge and skills to learners, at all levels, for academic and professional purposes.

Deregulation: Refers to an economic system according to which governmental influence and restrictions on economic activities is reduced. Normally, it affects specific industrial production aiming at increasing competition among particular industries.

Educational Games: Are constructed under cognitive, social, behavioral and pedagogical principles in order to facilitate the courses delivery, knowledge acquisition and skills development to learners with and without disabilities.

Globalization: Is probably the most fashionable economic term, which, though it is highly disputed for its effectiveness. In fact it covers a wide range of political, economic, social and cultural trends. The concept is to cover every phase of human activities without considering geographic and political barriers, linked to the growth of social intercourse.

Illiteracy: Originally referred to inability of individuals to read and write. The contemporary meaning of the term is used to described people of low or zero educational level.

Inclusion: Is a pedagogical principle which provides the opportunity of persons with disabilities to attend courses in the same classroom with children without disabilities.

Persons with Disabilities: Individuals who have physical, mental or combination of characteristics deviating from normal situation. There are six distinctive categories of persons with disabilities: Visual Impaired, Hearing Impaired, Physical Disabilities, Emotionally Disturbed, Intellectually Disabled, Persons with Learning Disabled.

Recession: Is an economic term denoting a general slowdown in economic activities such as employment, industrial production, investments, income, business profits.

Responsibility: is a term of social and psychological concern used to express an obligation to obey to laws and behave according to accepted ethic patterns.

Unemployment: Is an economic term used to describe the condition of persons in the working range of ages 15-64 years who do not have a job. The main reason seems to be the technological development under which there is a demand of skillful workforce without providing alternative work positions for persons unskilled or not meeting the current requirements. Other reasons refer to recession, low educational levels and lack of experience. Unemployment rates refer to the number of unemployed persons divided by total labor force. In EU27 the unemployed rate as of 2010 in the ages 15-24 was 20.5%.

Chapter 12
Games in Higher Education:
Opportunities, Expectations, Challenges, and Results in Medical Education

Cláudia Ribeiro
Technical University of Lisbon, Portugal

Sofia Corredoura
Centro Hospitalar Lisboa Ocidental, Portugal

Micaela Monteiro
Centro Hospitalar Lisboa Ocidental, Portugal

Fernanda Candeias
Stand Clear, Lda., Portugal

João Pereira
Technical University of Lisbon, Portugal

ABSTRACT

Medical knowledge has increased exponentially in the last decades. Healthcare professionals face a lifetime challenge in keeping abreast with current medical education. Continuing Medical Education (CME) is an ongoing challenge. Traditional adult education, largely used in medical training, shows little effectiveness. Problem-based-learning has been proposed as a student-centred pedagogy to overcome failure of traditional medical instruction. In this chapter, the authors review the status quo of medical education, certification, and recertification in Europe. A summary of the history of simulation in medical education is presented. In recent years, there has been a growing interest in using video games for educational purposes. This is also true for medical education. The use of serious games in medical education is reviewed, and its integration in medical curricula is discussed. The efforts to raise awareness of policy makers are described. Finally, a critical assessment of the strengths and weaknesses of these technologies as well as a proposal to overcome some of its limitations are made.

INTRODUCTION

Given the far-reaching economic and political impact of healthcare policy, it is considered a priority sector by political decision makers worldwide. Medical knowledge is expanding quantitatively and qualitatively. Healthcare professionals face a life-time challenge in keeping abreast with current medical education from what they learnt right from the beginning of medical school. Many of these professionals need practical experience without endangering themselves and others. This principle holds for many medical areas, such as medical

DOI: 10.4018/978-1-4666-3950-8.ch012

decision-making, behavioural training, and other areas involving dynamism and complexity.

Medical schools and residencies are currently facing a shift in their teaching paradigm. The increasing amount of medical information and research makes it difficult for medical education to stay current in its curriculum. Educators have faced these challenges by restructuring curricula, developing small-group sessions, and increasing self-directed learning and independent search. Nevertheless, it has been widely recognized that students have been ill prepared for their roles as young doctors. In addition to the well documented deficiencies in a range of skills, there have been reports of stress resulting from inadequate preparation for their roles. These skill deficiencies have occurred along a changing pattern of health care delivery, which has seen significant changes pertaining to the clinical experience of undergraduates. In the postgraduate arena, working time restrictions have raised concerns towards a more streamlined, shorter duration of higher professional training and also caused concern about the amount of direct clinical experience it is possible to provide.

In the light of decreasing time available for higher training, the case has been made for planned exposure to simulated cases to ensure that sufficient material is covered. The use of simulations in not new in medical education, in fact, it spans the centuries. Low-fidelity and high fidelity simulation is used across different areas of medical education to teach different levels of skills and as an evaluation tool to assess knowledge gaps. Another trend in medical education is Game-Based Learning (GBL). GBL is also expanding and in the last decade several research works have studied the impact of the application of such technologies in medicine and healthcare training and highlighted that GBL could provide new approaches and opportunities. However, most of this work is isolated and focuses on a particular problem with very little possibilities for generalization. This presents an important limitation

as medical procedures are reviewed/updated in relatively short time intervals which would result in making the games becoming obsolete very fast and thereby very costly to maintain.

In this chapter, we report the challenges in medical education, for continuing medical education for undergraduates and postgraduates. Also, a description of how certification and recertification works both in Europe and USA is provided. Certification and recertification presents both an opportunity and a challenge to the introduction of serious games in medical education. In part two of this chapter a summary of the history of simulation in medical education is described. This review ranges from the use of mannequin-based simulation to software and virtual reality based simulation. Next, we turn to serious games and its uses to promote both health education and also create awareness amongst policy makers.

A critical description of the current strengths and weaknesses of both, simulation and serious games, and a proposal to overcome these limitations are also presented. Towards the concluding part we point to the future scope for applicability and development in this area with potentially wide-ranging economic and social implications.

MEDICAL EDUCATION

Society has changed dramatically in the last decades. Medicine is no exception. Medical knowledge has experienced an exponential growth. New diseases emerge and treatment is in permanent change with new drugs and treatment strategies being developed. Evidence-based state-of-the-art guidelines are updated every few years. For a student, what is current medical practice at the beginning of medical faculty may be completely obsolete when leaving it. Technology sets new standards in a vertiginous rhythm. Globalization is almost omnipresent and the Internet and its web 2.0 have changed the way people communicate, interact and perceive the world. As Prensky (Prensky, 2001) stated, rising generations are active and not passive, privilege graphics and animation over text, view technology as part of their lives and work as play and play as work.

Therefore medical education must not stick. It has to change. Traditional medical education, mainly teacher centred and based on reading, listening or watching, has now proven insufficient in adult education and not adequate for teaching either technical or soft skills. There is also an increasing consciousness about the importance of approximating the learning environment to real life by simulation and immersive realities, especially in a safety critical area like medicine.

Universities have to create flexible curricula, harmonized within the global medical community. Teaching methods and learning environments must adapt. Lifelong learning has become not only an ethical obligation but also a demand of an empowered society in order to guarantee state-of-the art medical assessment and treatment.

Pre-Graduate Medical Education in Europe

There have been strong efforts to harmonize medical school curricula across Europe in order to promote mobility, changing society needs and employability.

In the year 1999, Education Ministers of 29 European countries signed the Bologna Declaration with the goal of making academic degrees comparable and mutually recognized. The Bologna Process started. In this context the TUNING Educational Structures in Europe Project[1] was created in 2000. Its aim is "to contribute significantly to the elaboration of a framework of comparable and compatible qualifications in each of the signatory countries of the Bologna process, which should be described in terms of workload, level, learning outcomes, competences, and profile." Within the TUNING Project the MEDINE Network[2] works on converging the medical curricula, making them transparent, comparable and consistent. A Euro-

pean Credit Transfer and Accumulation System (ECTS) credit system was created to encourage and facilitate students' mobility across European medical faculties.

There are several initiatives, like the CHARME Project[3], a common project of European Universities and other medical organizations, for the modernization of the medical curriculum. The mEducator Best Practice Network[4] "aims to implement and critically evaluate existing standards and reference models in the field of e-learning in order to enable specialized state-of-the-art medical educational content to be discovered, retrieved, shared, and re-used across European higher academic institutions."

Since 2005, basic medical training is automatically recognized throughout the EU, entitling to work in any EU country (EU Directives, 2012).

Post-Graduate Medical Education in Europe

Harmonisation and mutual recognition of academic diplomas was already pointed out as an important issue in the early days of the political processes that lead to the existing European Union. The Treaty of Rome, concerned with creating the conditions for the free exchange of persons, services, goods, and capital within the European Community, foresaw it as a goal in 1957. In 1958, the Union of European Medical Specialists (UEMS) was founded in order to bring together the medical specialities of the member states so that a consensus on content and quality of medical specialist training and practice could be reached (UEMS Continuing Medical Education). In 1993, the European Community Directive 93/16/EEC specified that "Each Member State shall recognize the diplomas, certificates and other evidence of formal qualifications in specialized medicine awarded to nationals of Member States by the other Member States". In the same year UEMS issued the "Charter on Training of Medical Specialists in the European Community" (UEMS, 1993).

Despite these efforts post-graduate medical education remains very heterogeneous across Europe.

After medical school, doctors start a three to six year long training to become specialists. In some countries, like Germany, there is a common root for certain specialities (Berlin Chamber of Physicians). To become a cardiologist, for example, doctors must first do a three year training in internal medicine and, after three more years of specific cardiology training, they will become a "specialist in internal medicine with a main focus in cardiology". In other countries, such as Portugal (Cardiologia Port 46, 2001), cardiology is an independent speciality that includes one year of training in internal medicine and another four in cardiology.

This period of specialization is structured by specific learning curricula and terminates with an exam. Curricula contents and final examination are defined on a country level or, like in some federal countries, even regional level by organisms of the national or regional medical boards, and may vary significantly from country to country or even region to region.

Despite all the national differences there are clear efforts to move towards automatic recognition of specialist doctors' qualification by the EU member states (EU Directives, 2012) in order to respond to the challenges and needs of the 21st century labour market.

Lifelong Learning, Continuing Medical Education, Continuing Professional Development, and Recertification

Lifelong learning is without doubt an imperative for healthcare professionals. This is recognized at almost all levels. The UEMS calls it an "ethical obligation" (UEMS Continuing Medical Education). The American Board of Medical Specialties states:

The measure of physician specialists is not merely that they have been certified, but how well they keep current in their specialty (ABMS).

Therefore it created the ABMS Maintenance of Certification ® and defined six core competences for Quality Patient Care:

- **Professionalism:** Demonstrate a commitment to carrying out professional responsibilities, adherence to ethical principles and sensitivity to diverse patient populations.
- **Patient Care and Procedural Skills:** Provide care that is compassionate, appropriate and effective treatment for health problems and to promote health.
- **Medical Knowledge:** Demonstrate knowledge about established and evolving biomedical, clinical and cognate sciences and their application in patient care.
- **Practice-Based Learning and Improvement:** Able to investigate and evaluate their patient care practices, appraise and assimilate scientific evidence and improve their practice of medicine.
- **Interpersonal and Communication Skills:** Demonstrate skills that result in effective information exchange and teaming with patients, their families and professional associates (e.g. fostering a therapeutic relationship that is ethically sounds, uses effective listening skills with nonverbal and verbal communication; working as both a team member and at times as a leader).
- **Systems-Based Practice:** Demonstrate awareness of and responsibility to larger contexts and systems of healthcare. Be able to call on system resources to provide optimal care (e.g. coordinating care across sites or serving as the primary case manager when care involves multiple specialties, professions or sites).

These core competences clearly transcend the idea of Continuing Medical Education (CME), defined as "expanding the knowledge and skill base required by doctors" (American Board of Medical Specialities) evolving it to the concept of Continuing Professional Development (CPD) defined by the UEMS' Basel Declaration on Continuing Professional Development Policy as "educative means of updating, developing and enhancing how doctors apply the knowledge, skills and attitudes required in their working lives." (Basel Declaration) The goal of CPD is outcome centred: "to improve all aspects of a medical practitioner's performance in his/her work."

The ABMS created a four-part Process for Continuous Learning to put CPD into practice. The four-part Maintenance of Competence (MOC) Process includes:

- **Part 1– Licensure and Professional Standing:** Medical specialists must hold a valid, unrestricted medical license in at least one state or jurisdiction in the United States, its territories or Canada.
- **Part 2– Lifelong Learning and Self-Assessment:** Physicians participate in educational and self-assessment programs that meet specialty-specific standards that are set by their member board.
- **Part 3– Cognitive Expertise:** They demonstrate, through formalized examination, that they have the fundamental, practice-related and practice environment-related knowledge to provide quality care in their specialty.
- **Part 4– Practice Performance Assessment:** They are evaluated in their clinical practice according to specialty-specific standards for patient care. They are asked to demonstrate that they can assess the quality of care they provide compared to peers and national benchmarks and then apply the best evidence or consensus recommendations to improve that care using follow-up assessments (American Board of Medical Specialities).

In the US all Member Boards received approval of their ABMS MOC program plans in 2006 and are now in the process of implementation. In Europe, the CPD landscape varies substantially[5]. While there is mandatory recertification in the UK or in Slovakia, in Germany there are mandatory CME requirements that may lead to sanctions if not accomplished but will not withdraw specialists' certifications. In other countries CME is voluntary, like in Finland or Portugal. However, it seems clear that also in Europe the implementation of a consistent and convergent CDP policy is inevitable and only a question of time.

CME Credits

Organizers of educational activities in the field of continuing medical education can apply for CME credits that are conferred to its attendees. Doctors need these credits to fulfill their CME/CPD obligations.

The American Medical Association Physician's Recognition Award authorizes CME credits in the US. In Europe, the European Accreditation Council for Continuing Medical Education (EACCME) established by the UEMS in 1999 sets itself as the central link between the National Accreditation Authorities, the UEMS Specialist Sections and Boards, the European Specialty Accreditation Boards and the providers of CME activities and ensures within Europe the international mutual recognition of quality assessments of CME/CPD activities. There is an agreement between the American Medical Association and the EACCME for mutual conversion of AMA and European CME Credits since 1999.

CME credits are thereby comparable to an international currency for CME/CPD activities.

Methods in Medical Education

Undergraduate medical education is still predominantly lecture-based and teacher-centred. But more and more medical schools have started a smooth transition to a student-centred paradigm.

They are "changing their educational programs and teaching strategies to ensure that students have active responsibility for their learning process and are prepared for life-long, self-directed learning" (Rendas et al., 2006). Problem-Based-Learning (PBL), a method developed in the late 1960s at the medical school at McMaster University in Canada, has been proposed as a student-centred strategy. It is progressively being established as pedagogical base of a real-life-teaching approach at medical faculties. PBL is problem centred, integrates different areas of knowledge, trains skills and competences, encourages problem-solving strategies and motivates. The teacher is a facilitator who guides the learning process.

Most of the post graduate training, such as specialization, is done "on job" accompanied by reading textbooks and medical journals, as well as attending to congresses and participating in practical courses, mostly on a voluntary basis. With exception of the latter, concrete objectives of these learning activities, a careful design or the evaluation of outcomes are generally missed. Curricula, such as the ISCP General Surgery Curriculum (ISCP, 2010), explain exhaustively skills and competences to be achieved but there is hardly any emphasis on the very learning process. Junior doctors learn from senior doctors, who often do not have specific preparation for teaching or training.

Newer learning tools such as simulation labs are still an exception.

The courses on Advanced Life Support[6] provided by the European Resuscitation Council are therefore an example. Small groups of trainees simulate with mannequins in a role-play scenario resuscitations of patients in cardiac arrest under the guidance of tutors.

Most of the existing e- and b-learning programmes already overcome distance and time schedule issues by providing bibliography, slide presentations, videos and podcasts. They permit communication with tutors/ educators and classmates and give remote access to live sessions and evaluation tools like written tests. However they often do not explore its whole potential of creating simulation environments or engage by a high interactive design of its learning contents. The offer of such programmes, unfortunately, is also still very limited. An example of a very interesting approach in this area is the UK's Department of Health project "e-Learning for Healthcare"[7] (http://www.e-lfh.org.uk/news_video.html). By defining learning objectives and disseminating it through the whole British NHS, this programme not only answers individual education needs but also creates a powerful tool to set standards and homogenize good medical practice throughout the country.

Medical education is clearly much more than acquiring knowledge. It has a social responsibility. It has to train skills and competences like time-critical decision-making, dealing with risk and uncertainty, communication with peers, patients and relatives, to deal with error and failure and techniques of problem-solving. In conclusion: it must enable doctors to know, to put knowledge successfully into practice and to develop appropriate behaviour in order to accomplish their mission.

But how this goal can best be accomplished, given the time constraints faced by physicians, has challenged the profession and medical educators since the early 1900s (Manning, 2005, p. 3).

It is amazing to me that in the modern age, when we have technologies like the Internet and the hand-held and the computers and the computer games, we are still teaching inside four walls, where all the information is coming from within those walls and where all students, regardless of the amount of preparation they have, are sitting together (Foreman, 2004, p. 53).

Therefore continuing professional development has not only to incorporate the principles of adult learning, shift from passive to active learning, adapt to individual needs but also has to take into account the new opportunities offered by the new technologies as well as important cognitive style changes of the new generation of trainees, the so called "digital natives," Prensky (2001) describes them as:

- Operate at twitch speed rather than conventional speed
- Are parallel processors, not linear processors
- Privilege graphics and animation over text
- Are random accessors of information
- Prefer connected to stand-alone
- Are active, not passive
- Expect pay-off for effort
- See work as play, and play as work
- Expect fantasy and reality in equal measure
- View technology as life, and not a separate activity

The introduction of videogames, so called "Serious Games," into undergraduate education and CMD has attracted a lot of interest in the last years, as these games appear to have a number of characteristics to answer these challenges.

SIMULATIONS, SERIOUS GAMES AND DIGITAL STORYTELLING IN MEDICAL EDUCATION

In the past, the technology used in simulators was only available to high-end expensive industrial and military systems (Hughes, 1990), since they made use of the extensive computational capabilities of high-performance computers. Simulation technology was also used in non-real-time systems

for running computationally intensive models of real-world systems, for example, analytic simulators (Hughes, 1990) and weather simulation (Johnson, 1996). The evolution of technology, the affordability of computer hardware and the advent of the Personal Computer (PC) have made possible to run simulation technology in low-end computers such as the PC and also introduced the possibility of new application for running simulations. Some of those applications are the robotics simulator (Worspace, 2005), the electronics simulator (Workbench, 2005) and simulation games (Narayanasamy, 2006). Also, this interchange of technology between high-end simulations and simulation technology for PCs has resulted in the development of hybrid simulation applications that integrate some of the high-fidelity simulation features (Narayanasamy, 2006). Among these, are applications that have been used for "serious" training purposes as well as for entertainment (Narayanasamy, 2006). Serious games (de Freitas, 2007) are a result of applying simulation technology to non-entertainment (mostly training) purposes, while simulation games (Aldrich, 2009) are a result of applying simulation technology for entertainment purposes.

In recent years, as a result of this technology diffusion, simulation games, serious games, and training simulators have become popular (Aldrich, 2004, 2009; Smith, 2009). Serious game and virtual-based environments are an important response from the education technologist to the "digital natives" (Squire, 2005), a generation of students who were raised on interactive games and expect the same kind of interactive experiences from their education media. Indeed, it may be incorrect to call the use of serious games in education a novelty, since by nature young children begin to learn through games during their earliest years (Rieber, 1996). Due to their characteristics, games can introduce clear advantages in supporting complex learning processes and knowledge transfer. Through games it is possible to simulate environments and systems allowing learners to experience situations that are impossible in the real world for reasons of safety, cost and time (Corti, 2007; Jenkins, 2004). Games and virtual simulations are often referred to in literature as experiential exercises (Gredler, 1994) in which people *"learn by doing"* avoiding *"mimicry learning"* (Turkle, 1984). They in fact increase greatly the learning outcomes since they easily change our mood towards the learning of specific topics (Mc Gonigal, 2012). As Savill-Smith argue (Savill-Smith, 2004), games can support the development of a number of different competences such as: analytical and spatial skills, strategic skills and insight learning, recollection capabilities, psychomotor skills, visual selective attention, showing promising results when compared to traditional methods (Szezurek, 1982; VanSickle, 1986; Randel, 1992; Van Eck, 2006). Also, in serious games human actors are the active decision makers whose actions will affect the future state of the simulation run. This active role of human players separates simulation games from pure simulations (Martin, 2000). Pure simulations use static rules to calculate the outcome of the situation. Human players are unpredictable; therefore, they might choose to do things that extend the possibilities taken into account by the original designer.

The use of serious games in an education context is not a distant concept, they were adopted long time ago by organizations in a wide range of sectors, nowadays no pilot will ever pilot an airplane without an intensive training using simulation and games, no power plant manager will ever run a nuclear plant without an intensive training using simulation and games (Aldrich, 2004). The same kind of examples can be found in medical education where simulators and simulation games have been used to improve the level of knowledge and practice of medical professionals in different levels of education (undergraduate, graduate, or postgraduate) (Lane, Slavin, & Ziv, 2001; Bradley, 2006; Okuda, et al., 2009; McGaghie, Issenberg, Petrusa, & Scalese, 2010). Namely, Medical researchers and surgeons are increasingly trying out

operating techniques on a virtual patient before testing or using them on real patients. In the next sub-sections, an account of how simulation and games have evolved and been used in medical education is described.

Simulation in Medical Education

Medical simulation in primitive forms has been practiced for centuries. Physical models of anatomy and disease were constructed long before the advent of modern plastic or computers. The representation of medical signs and symptoms in literature or theatre can be imagined as the precursors or nontechnical simulation (Rosen, 2008).

The modern era of medical simulation has its origins in the second half of the 20th century (Bradley, 2006). Since different movements have evolved and with it the technologic contributions to simulation in medical education. These different movements incorporate simulators that range from low-tech, simple plastic models to realistic high-tech simulators that have been incorporate in medical curriculum to teach and evaluate three levels of skills that range from basic, unidirectional, individual skills through higher level, multidimensional, individual skills to very complex, multidimensional, team work skills (Lane, Slavin, & Ziv, 2001; Teteris, Fraser, Wright, & McLaughlin, 2012).

It started with the work developed by Laerdal, a Norwegian publisher and a toy manufacturer. Working with anaesthetists, he developed the Resusci-Anne, a part-task trainer that was to revolutionise resuscitation training through the widespread availability of a low-cost, effective training model (Christensen, Heffernan, & Barach, 2001). The prototype focused on airway management and basic life support techniques, and it paved the way for the new generation of high-tech simulators (Lane, Slavin, & Ziv, 2001). The latest Rescusi Anne Model is computer driven, has a cardiac rhythm generator, and is used worldwide as the standard simulation for teaching and evaluating life support skills (Lane, Slavin, & Ziv, 2001). At the same time Rescui Anne was being developed, Sim 1 was being developed at the University of Southern California (Denson & Abrahamson, 1969). Sim 1 was also intended for training anaesthetists but it included more sophisticated simulators dedicated to reproduce aspects of the human patient, namely heartbeat, temporal and carotid pulse and blood pressure; open and close mouth; blink eyes; and responded to four intravenously administrated drugs and two gases (oxygen and nitrous oxide) administrated through mask or tube (Bradley, 2006).

After these early simulators, a new wave of simulation technology made its way to the market and also in medical curricula. These new simulators, denominated task-specific simulators, appeared as a response to the increase complexity of some clinical tasks and two known examples of such simulators are the CathSim and the Ultrasim. The Cathsim is used for phlebotomy and IV insertion training[8]. The environment includes patented force feedback technology that simulates the feel of vascular access procedures, including "pop" of venepuncture. Ultrasim[9], an ultrasound simulator developed by MedSim in 1996, operates like an actual ultrasound system allowing the students/ residents to practice performing sonographic examinations on a mannequin while viewing real-time sonographic images. Both these simulators are still used worldwide and are continually being improved. Other relevant simulators are the MIST VR (Gallagher, McClure, McGuigan, Crothers, & Browning, 1999; Taffinder, Russell, Manus, et al., 1998) and Cinemed[10] used for laparoscopic surgery training. A part from simulators, simulation environments have also been developed separately and later integrated in new releases of some of these simulators, like the Comprehensive Anaesthesia Simulation Environment (CASE) developed by the group led by David Gaba and the Gainesville Anaesthesia Simulator (GAS) developed by Michael Good and J. S. Gravenstein (Lane, Slavin,

& Ziv, 2001). Finally, the Anaesthesia Crisis Resource Management (ACRM) was developed at Stanford University and focused significantly on the development of team-based working in realistic simulation environments (Barach, Satish, & Streufert, 2001; Gaba, Howard, Fish, Smith, & Sowb, 2001).

Besides the mannequin-based simulation, other important trends are the software-based simulation and Virtual Reality (VR). Smith and colleagues at the University of California, San Diego developed the first known software-based simulation, the Sleeper. It was based on sophisticated multi-compartment modelling of physiology and pharmacology. After this attempt many followed from which some of the most referenced are, the BodySim software (Cooper & Taqueti, 2004; Fukui & Smith, 1981), Anaesthesia Simulator (Cooper & Taqueti, 2004), Gas Man (Philip, 1986), MicroSim (Perkins, Green, Farquharson, et al., 2006).

Foundations of modern VR began in the 1950s and 1960s. The first product was the sensorama constructed by Norton Heilig. The apparatus projected images, vibration, sound, smell and wind to deliver five different immersive experiences (Hamit, 1993). The CAVE at the University of Michigan broke new ground with the triage and management of patients in a virtual environment. Medical simulations began to appear in Second Life in 2007 in the community know as Ann Myers Medical Centre. In the future, a proposed fusion between Second life and the Wii remote may further enhance training options (Rosen, 2008).

Serious Games in Medical Education

There has been a vast research for the last two decades on the value of Digital Game-Based Learning (DGBL) as effective educational tool. It is not difficult to agree that DGBL fits educational concepts and theories. Richard van Eck argues:

Games embody well-established principles and models of learning. For instance, games are effective partly because the learning takes place within a meaningful (to the game) context. What you must learn is directly related to the environment in which you learn and demonstrate it; thus, the learning is not only relevant but also applied and practiced within that context. Learning that occurs in meaningful and relevant contexts is more effective than learning that occurs outside of those contexts, as is the case with most formal instruction. Researchers refer to this principle as situated cognition and have demonstrated its effectiveness in many studies over the last fifteen years…Interacting with a game requires a constant cycle of hypothesis formulation, testing, and revision. This process happens rapidly and often while the game is played, with immediate feedback (Van Eck, 2006).

Videogames are accessible at any time and from any place (whenever-wherever availability) to a virtually unlimited audience. They can be played at individual rhythms and repeated as often as necessary. They may be played alone or in a multi-player setting. But it is important to remember that a barrier to successful learning is not to analyse the learner's profile, to assume it equal for all, forgetting that different people need different education strategies. Videogames have to adapt to learners and to educational purposes.

On the other hand, teachers/tutors must understand the nature of instructional videogames in order to know how and when to use them. Only thereby maximum advantage of this tool can be taken.

Medicine, like aviation, is an area where safety is a central issue. Therefore, knowledge, competences, and skills should be trained without endangering trainees or patients. Simulation is a powerful tool and videogames can create engaging virtual simulation environments. In theory, DGBL is very appealing as long as it is carefully designed, with clear learning goals, final debrief-

ing and with a goal oriented learning result evaluation. Herz resumes the potential of this DGBL approach when he states,

What games allow you to do that lectures don't is to explore the solution space and ask, 'What if I did this'? (Foreman, 2004).

Two important aspects must not be forgotten if DGBL is to become a successfully and consensually established learning tool: it must entertain and be fun, usually by being challenging and awarding, otherwise it cannot be called a game and will certainly loose much of its attraction and motivating power. Therefore, serious games must show a careful equilibrium between instructional design and game design. On the other hand, instructional videogames must prove that their players achieve set learning goals. Validation of videogames as effective learning tools is a major challenge for DGBL proponents as it will be decisive for its acceptance by the education community and its inclusion in learning curricula.

The use of serious games for medical education can be considered a relative recent topic. Although there has been a lot effort to develop serious games that address and help overcome some of the difficulties and issues dealt by medicine, most of these games are directed to patients and general individuals or groups and not for training medical undergraduates, graduates, or postgraduates. This trend is connected to the idea that prevention can, in many cases, avoid sickness and also promote a better quality of life and longer life span. In this context games such as Pomp and Circumstance and the Encounters Family of Simulations have been developed (Greenblat, 2001). The Pomp and Circumstance game is an abstract two-person risk-taking exercise modelling the circumstances leading to premarital pregnancy. It was designed to be played by groups of up to 30 participants for sex education and to sensitize adults to some of the reasons for ineffective use of contraception by sexually active adolescents. The Encounters

Family of Simulations is a role-play that exercises dealing with communications related to HIV issues. More recently prototypes of serious games for lifestyle change (Nauta & Spil, 2011), for children with psychological special needs (Szczesna, Grudzinski, Grudzinski, Mikuszewski, & Debowski, 2011), to improve seniors citizens life quality (Portela, Fonseca, Correia, & Andrade, 2011), and to raise awareness to diseases, proper food and sleeping habits have been developed.

Regarding medical education, although there are a limited number of examples, some of the issues addressed by this trend are training medical personnel disregarding the graduate or professional level of the learner and to raise awareness of policy makers. In this context games such as the Haemophilia Planning Game and the Blood Money (Greenblat, 2001) have been developed. The Haemophilia Planning Game is targeted at medical personnel and policy makers working in haemophilia care. The goal of the game is to work as a vehicle to ain in the more effective integration of individuals looking at and working on haemophilia care from different perspectives: care, education and training, payment sectors. The Blood Money game is targeted at the general public, policy makers, physicians and nurses in training or practice. The focus of this game is to provide a highly interactive gaming simulation of the social psychological world of the haemophiliac and general issues in health care delivery. More recent examples include serious games for training medical professional about insulin management for treatment of diabetes mellitus (Diehl, et al., 2011), Magnetic Resonance Imaging (MRI) (Valente, Kozlova, & Lima, 2011) and advance life support training (Monteiro, Corredoura, Candeias, Morais, & Diniz, 2011).

There are also examples of videogames in medical education that confer CME credits. Recently The Stanford School of Medicine edited an online accessed videogame called "Septris" (http://cme.stanford.edu/septris/). It trains the management of patients with suspected Sepsis, a prevalent

infectious condition with a high mortality. It is based on international practice guidelines. Doctors/Players who successfully conclude the game will get CME credits.

"Burn Centre™" (https://www.burncenter-training.com/) is a videogame that creates a simulation environment where healthcare professionals are trained in mass-scale casualty burn treatment. It also awards correct accomplishment with CME and Continuous Nursing Education (CNE) credits.

On its website "The American Association of Medical Colleges" draws attention to the fact that "medical schools around the country are creating video games with the expressed goal of improving medical education"[11]. It makes reference to "3DiTeams," a project of Duke University, which creates a "game environment for training healthcare team coordination skills"[12]. This game recreates very realistic scenarios. The Florida State University Medical College, on the other hand, developed a videogame that teaches geriatric concepts to medical students immerging them into a fantasy adventure world like Zelda or Alice in Wonderland (http://www.youtube.com/watch?v=YertjfCoWhg).

The Imperial College of London Medical School created a virtual hospital in "Second Life", an online virtual world where users can interact with each other through avatars. It designs "game-based learning activities for the delivery of virtual patients that can drive experiential, diagnostic, and role-play learning activities supporting patients' diagnosis, investigation, and treatment."[13] These activities can be played at home or in the very classroom, oriented by teachers/tutors complementing other education techniques within a learning curriculum.

Interactive Storytelling

When compared to traditional videos-games, serious games due to the characteristics tend to be significantly more complex in the organization and structuring of their pedagogical content. This constitutes probably one of the most relevant limitations in the development and maintenance of such games. This is the reason why most of the serious games previously presented focus on training specific skills or protocols, being extremely limited in their scope. The cause of such limitation stems from the complexity of the content itself and the process through which the content is transferred from real life into a computer-based experience.

In recent years a new research field has emerged, proposing the adoption of complex narrative structures in the creation of interactive drama experiences similar to movies, books or theatre plays, called Interactive Storytelling (IS). Storytelling per se, is appreciated by many people, as both tellers and audience, having evolved through drama writing, books, films, and recently television. Yet stories typically place the audience in a passive role, thereby limiting their interaction. In this context, Interactive Storytelling emerges as a way of offering a world where the participant can have a real interaction with the drama he/she is experiencing. This factor can bring clear benefits when associated with serious games, facilitating the creation of more dense and complex experience, increasing the player's level of immersion in a story and allowing the creation of personalized experiences based on the pedagogical goal of each player (Ribeiro, 2011).

Although Interactive Storytelling finds potential as digital entertainment and art, several authors present it as a possible solution to deliver effectively pedagogical content through serious games. Research in psychology has argued that narrative is central to how we understand the world and communicate that understanding (Bruner, 1990), and of course, the engrossing, motivational nature of story is unmistakable. This naturally raises the interest in associating Interactive Storytelling with pedagogical goals. This association is commonly referred in the literature as interactive pedagogical drama (Marsella, 2003) or narrative-centered environments (NLEs) (Mott, 1999; Callaway, 2002), with applications as diverse as training leader-

ship (Hill, 2001; Riedl, 2006), strategic thinking (Marsella, 2003), business soft-skills (Oliveira, Andersen, Pereira, Seager, & Ribeiro, 2011) and microbiology (Rowe, Shores, Mott, & Lester, 2010). The use of these environments has proven to have the potential for offering constructivist learning, learning by doing and enable learners to be co-constructors of narrative, promoting the deep connection-building meaning-making activities that define constructivist learning (Mott, 1999).

The use of Interactive Storytelling in educational contexts exploit the edifying power of story while promotes active learning, immersing the learner in an engaging, evocative story where he/she interacts openly with realistic characters. The learner makes decisions or takes actions on behalf of a character in the story, and sees the consequences of his/her decisions. The learner identifies with and assumes responsibility for the characters in the story, while the control afforded to the learner enhances intrinsic motivation (Lepper, 2000). Moreover, this approach usually allows the existence of multiple interacting characters, enabling embed learning in a social context (Vygotskiǐ, 1978).

The effective use of Interactive Storytelling demands the creation of good stories, achieving pedagogical goals and allowing the player sense control over the story while maintaining high artistic standards. Balancing correctly these factors is extremely difficult; a good story demands a dramatic tension; pacing and integrity of both story and characters. Pedagogical goals require the design of a pedagogically-appropriate "gaming" space with appropriate consequences for learner choices and a style of play appropriate to the learner's skill and age. To provide learner control, an interaction framework must be developed to allow the learner's interactions to impact story and the pedagogical goals. And many times these various demands can be in conflict, for example, pedagogically appropriate consequences can conflict with dramatic tension and learner control can impact pacing and story integrity. Despite of not taking into account interactivity, drama theories can point out solutions that minimize those conflicts and limitations. Therefore, it can be a valuable source of information regarding narrative structuring and analysis.

The possibility of interaction within a story implies making available a variety of alternatives story lines that are chosen based on the player's decisions. If the author needs to write out all the variations, this naturally leads to a combinatorial explosion of possibilities that become impractical to maintain as soon as the user is offered more than a handful of meaningful alternatives. This is the differentiating factor between Interactive Storytelling and traditional videos-games that contain a story component, where narrative is often static and linear leading to a limited user experience.

Understanding this limitation, most of the authors proposed the use of a procedural way to represent these variations as a function of user interaction where several strategies were proposed. One of the proposals is to make sure that different storylines end up at the same future point. Another is limiting the authoring to "cut off" choices by making sure that while some continue the story, others lead to a quicker ending. The story authoring may therefore vary from complete off-line story generation in order to produce a rich enough branching narrative (Riedl, 2006), to online moment-to-moment decision making to create pieces of a story, without needing to know about the player choices beforehand (Thue, Bulitko, & Spetch, 2008).

Despite its limitations, the Interactive Storytelling authoring process can bring several advantages to serious games since it can split the game development between software developers and pedagogical experts. If proper authoring tools are available, new storylines can be developed by experts and dynamically added to the game without the need of software development. Existing storylines can be adapted so they can be updated taking into account the present context, thereby dramatically increasing the life cycle of a game. Furthermore, the game development process can be focused on the player experience rather than on specific technologic factors, thus allowing the development of more complex and dense experiences thus approaching the real-life experience.

INTEGRATION OF SERIOUS GAMES IN MEDICAL EDUCATION

As described previously in this chapter, traditional medical education, mainly teacher centred and based on reading, listening or watching, has now proven insufficient in adult education. The medical learner at any stage—undergraduate, graduate, or postgraduate—is truly an adult learner. An adult learner, as defined by many education theorists, learns by different methods and for different reasons in contrast to earlier stages of his/her education. Bryan et al. (Bryan, Kreuter, & Brownson, 2009) described 5 adult principles that apply to medical learner:

1. Adult learners need to know why they are learning.
2. Adult learners are motivated by the need to solve problems.
3. The previous experiences of adult learners must be respected and build upon
4. The educational approach should match the diversity and background of adult learners.
5. Adults need to be involved actively in the process

Nevertheless, a disconnection still exists between the classroom and the clinical environment. Many students feel that they are inadequately trained in history taking, physical examination, diagnosis, and management. Medical simulation has been proposed as a technique to bridge this educational gap. Okuda (Okuda, et al., 2009) has conducted a literature review regarding the evidence for utility of simulation in medical education, from which we summarize the findings in the following paragraphs. Residents trained on laparoscopic surgery simulators showed improvement in procedural performance in the operating room. Other studies showed that residents trained on simulators were more likely to adhere to the advanced cardiac life support protocol than those who received standard training for cardiac arrest patients. In other areas of medical training, simulation has been demonstrated to lead to improvements in medical knowledge, comfort in procedures, and improvements in performance during retesting in simulated scenarios. Simulation has also been shown to be a reliable tool for assessing learners and for teaching topics such as teamwork and communication. Only a few studies have shown direct improvements in clinical outcomes form the use of simulation for training. Multiple studies have demonstrated the effectiveness of simulation in teaching basic science and clinical knowledge, procedural skills, teamwork, and communication as well as assessment at the undergraduate and graduate medical education levels.

As showed by recent results modern simulation has come a long way, but there are still major barriers to its use in health care education. Fidelity and validity issues still justify the sceptical delay in implementation (Day, 2006). Cost of equipment, personnel, and programs only recently have been overcome by expansion of large collaborative simulation centres (Rosen, 2008). These partnerships support the projection of increases in multidisciplinary, inter-professional, and multimodal simulation training (Bradley, 2006). Despite these problems, worldwide acceptance of this type of training is growing (Kurrek & Fish, 1996; Ridley, Wilks, & Freeman, 1997). The debate over the use of mannequin-based simulation for competency testing is quite active and promising in terms of results and conclusions (Forrest & Taylor, 1998; Kapur & Steadman, 1998). Surgical specialities are moving rapidly forward with incorporating simulation into competency requirements during residency and licensure. Anaesthesiology predicts that simulation will be part of maintenance of certification process after 2008. The American college of Surgeons has begun to offer a process of certification for multidisciplinary simulation centres. In November 2007, the American Society of Anaesthesiologists posted applications to offer a similar credential on its Web site (Rosen, 2008).

Regarding serious games, although they prove to have promising results on training, the introduction of serious games in medical education still faces major challenges. Medical procedures are constantly being updated as a result of evolving cultural contexts and to incorporate the latest research. This is the reason why healthcare professionals are obligated to maintain lifelong learning, through recertification, courses and participation in conferences. This implies a constant change in healthcare training curriculums obviously affecting the content lectured, a fact, which may have a strong impact on the life span of curricular tools such as serious games. Typically, serious games are not designed to support adaptations, meaning that, in the presence of a curriculum change there is a strong likelihood of not being possible to re-use the same games. This factor limits the investment in the development of such tools since they can be rapidly outdated (Greenblat, 2001).

The game design process is also of critical importance, serious games frequently provide a limited vision over healthcare procedures not allowing replicating real-life environments adequately. Although players are free to develop their own gaming strategies, often they cannot establish the parallel between elements in the game and the real world. In order to overcome this limitation, a facilitator is often required to promote discussion and reflection over used strategies, as well as to establish the link with real-life examples. Facilitators also play a key role in giving support to technical issues and assisting the players overcoming difficulties in using the game, presenting the game play, and giving an insight on how to play.

Healthcare procedures differ from country to country requiring an adaptation over the training curriculums as well as in pedagogical tools. Serious games are often developed for a particular context hindering their use as a cross curriculum tool. Nevertheless, some games provide different game scenarios depending on the chosen context allowing the support for different languages. Although this can increase the adoption of such game in different curriculums, it may also have a meaningful impact on development and maintenance costs.

The limitations previously discussed suggest the need for a content-centred approach to game design, allowing the decoupling of pedagogical content from the game technology therefore allowing the content adaptation based on context and on healthcare procedures revisions. This content-centred approach can be achieved through the use of Interactive Storytelling, allowing not only the development of several storylines but also the adaption of the existing ones based on procedures revisions. If proper authoring tools are available content can be developed by healthcare experts, providing a greater autonomy in the use of such tools and on their adaption to particular curriculums. This flexibility translates also into an increase on the tools time span, therefore reducing the development and maintenance costs.

CONCLUSION

Medicine is expanding (quantitatively and qualitatively). This is due partly to growth in world population, partly to increased awareness of health issues, partly to aging of some societies, and partly to medical progress. This resulted in an exponential growth of medical knowledge in the last decades. Therefore, professionals face a life-time challenge in medical education right from the beginning of medical school. Many of these professionals need practical experience without endangering themselves and others.

Simulation methodology, namely serious games is also expanding and in the last decade several research works have been developed that study the impact of the application of such technologies in medicine and healthcare training, stating that serious games could provide new approaches and opportunities. Nevertheless, most of this works are isolated and focus on a particular problem with very little possibilities for generalization. This presents an important limitation due to the fact that medical procedures are reviewed in relatively short time intervals which would result in making the games obsolete very quickly or very costly to maintain. In order for this approach to succeed in this application area it is mandatory that fundamental methods are developed and tested. Narrative structures, authoring and interactive storytelling systems should be developed in order to support the development of these kinds of games without the intervention of programmers and focus on the specification of medical algorithms. This would greatly reduce the required investment and time of development.

REFERENCES

ABMS. (2012). *Website.* Retrieved May 1, 2012, from http://www.abms.org/Maintenance_of_Certification/ABMS_MOC.aspx

Aldrich, A. (2009). *The complete guide to simulations and serious games: How the most valuable content will be created in the age beyond Gutenberg to Google.* New York, NY: Pfeiffer.

Aldrich, C. (2004). *Simulations and the future of learning: an innovative (and perhaps revolutionary) approach to e-learning.* New York, NY: Pfeiffer.

American Board of Medical Specialities. (2012). *Website.* Retrieved May 1, 2012, from http://www.abms.org/Maintenance_of_Certification/MOC_competencies.aspx

Ann Myers Medical Centre. (2012). *Website.* Retrieved May 1, 2012, from http://ammc.wordpress.com/

Barach, P., Satish, U., & Streufert, S. (2001). Healthcare assessment and performance: Using simulation. *Simulation & Gaming.* Retrieved from http://sag.sagepub.com/content/32/2/147.abstract

Basel Declaration. (2012). *Website.* Retrieved May 1, 2012, from http://admin.uems.net/uploadedfiles/35.pdf

Berlin Chamber of Physicians. (2012). *Website.* Retrieved May 1, 2012, from http://www.aerztekammer-berlin.de/60englisch/index.html

Bradley, P. (2006). The history of simulation in medical education and possible future directions. *Medical Education, 40*(3), 254–262. doi:10.1111/j.1365-2929.2006.02394.x

Bruner, J. (1990). *Acts of meaning.* Boston, MA: Harvard University Press.

Bryan, R., Kreuter, M., & Brownson, R. (2009). Integrating adult learning principles into training for public health practice. *Health Promotion Practice, 10*(4), 557–563. doi:10.1177/1524839907308117

Callaway, C. B. (2002). Narrative prose generation. *Artificial Intelligence, 139*(2), 213–252. doi:10.1016/S0004-3702(02)00230-8

Cardiologia Port 46. (2001). *Website.* Retrieved May 1, 2012, from https://www.ordemdosmedicos.pt/?lop=conteudo&op=3cf166c6b73f030b4f67eeaeba301103&id=dd055f53a45702fe05e449c30ac80df9

Christensen, U., Heffernan, D., & Barach, P. (2001). Microsimulators in medical education: An overview. *Simulation & Gaming, 32*(2), 250–262. doi:10.1177/104687810103200212

Continuing, U. E. M. S. Medical Education. (2012). *Website.* Retrieved May 1, 2012, from http://admin.uems.net/uploadedfiles/174.pdf

Cooper, J., & Taqueti, V. (2004). A brief history of the development of mannequin simulators for clinical education and training. *Quality & Safety in Health Care, 13,* 11–18. doi:10.1136/qshc.2004.009886

Corti, K. (2006). *Gamesbased learning a serious business application.* Retrieved from http://202.119.101.57/upload/2006_09/06091415525749.pdf

Day, R. (2006). Challenges of biological realism and validation in simulation-based medical education. *Artificial Intelligence in Medicine, 38,* 47–66. doi:10.1016/j.artmed.2006.01.001

de Freitas, S., J. S. (2007). Serious games—Engaging training solutions: A research and development project for supporting training needs. *British Journal of Educational Technology, 38*(3), 523–525. doi:10.1111/j.1467-8535.2007.00716.x

Denson, J., & Abrahamson, S. (1969). A computer controlled patient simulator. *Journal of the American Medical Association, 208*(3), 504–515. doi:10.1001/jama.1969.03160030078009

Diehl, L., Lehmann, E., Souza, R., Alves, J., Esteves, R., & Gordan, P. (2011). A serious game prototype for education of medical doctors and students about insulin management for the treatment of diabetes mellitus. In *Proceedings of the IEEE 1st International Conference on Serious Games and Applications for Health,* (pp. 70-73). IEEE Press.

Directives, E. U. (2012). *The EU single market.* Retrieved May 1, 2012, from http://ec.europa.eu/internal_market/qualifications/directive_in_practice/automatic_recognition/doctors/index_en.htm

Foreman, J. (2004). Game-based learning: How to delight and instruct in the 21st century. *EDUCAUSE Review, 39*(5), 50–66.

Forrest, F., & Taylor, M. (1998). High level simulators in medical education. *Hospital Medicine (London, England), 59,* 653–655.

Fukui, Y., & Smith, N. (1981). Interaction among ventilation, the circulation, and the uptake and distribution of halothane—Use of a hybrid computer multiple model: I: The basic model. *Anesthesiology, 54,* 107–118. doi:10.1097/00000542-198102000-00003

Fukui, Y., & Smith, N. (1981). Interaction among ventilation, the circulation, and the uptake and distribution of halothane—Use of a hybrid computer multiple model: II: Spontaneous vs. controlled ventilation and the effects of CO2. *Anesthesiology, 54,* 199–224.

Gaba, D., Howard, S., Fish, K., Smith, B., & Sowb, Y. (2001). Simulation-based training in anesthesia crisis resource management (ACRM): A decade of experience. *Simulation & Gaming, 32*(2), 175–193. doi:10.1177/104687810103200206

Gallagher, A., McClure, N., McGuigan, J., Crothers, I., & Browning, J. (1999). Virtual reality training in laparoscopic surgery: A preliminary assessment of minimally invasive surgical trainer virtual reality (MIST VR). *Endoscopy, 31*(4), 310–313. doi:10.1055/s-1999-15

Gas Man. (2012). *Website.* Retrieved May 1, 2012, from http://www.gasmanweb.com/

Gredler, M. (1994). *Designing and evaluating games and simulations.* Gulf Professional Publishing.

Greenblat, C. (2001). The design and redesign of gaming simulations on health care issues. *Simulation & Gaming, 32*(3), 315–330. doi:10.1177/104687810103200303

Hamit, F. (1993). *Virtual reality and the exploration of cyberspace.* Indianapolis, IN: Sams Publishing.

Hill, R. A. (2001). Toward the holodeck: Integrating graphics, sound, character and story. In *Proceedings of the Fifth International Conference on Autonomous Agents,* (pp. 409-416). IEEE.

Hughes, R. (1990). Simulation for design, test and evaluation, and training - Reconciling the differences. In *Proceedings of the 1990 Winter Simulation Conference,* (pp. 231-236). IEEE.

ISCP. (2010). *General surgery curriculum.* Washington, DC: General Medical Council.

Johnson, H. C. (1996). Stochastic weather simulation: Overview and analysis of two commonly used models. *Journal of Applied Meteorology, 35,* 1878–1896. doi:10.1175/1520-0450(1996)035<1878:SWSOAA>2.0.CO;2

Kapur, P., & Steadman, R. (1998). Patient simulator competency testing: Ready for take-off? *Anesthesia and Analgesia, 86,* 1157–1159.

Kurrek, M., & Fish, K. (1996). Anaesthesia crisis management training: An intimidating concept, a rewarding experience. *Canadian Journal of Anaesthesia, 43,* 430–434. doi:10.1007/BF03018101

Lane, J., Slavin, S., & Ziv, A. (2001). Simulation in medical education: A review. *Simulation & Gaming, 32*(3), 297–314. doi:10.1177/104687810103200302

Lepper, M. R. (2000). Turning "play" into "work" and "work" into "play": 25 years of research on intrinsic versus extrinsic motivation. In Sansone, C., & Harackiewicz, J. M. (Eds.), *Intrinsic and Extrinsic Motivation The Search for Optimal Motivation and Performance* (pp. 257–307). San Diego, CA: Academic Press. doi:10.1016/B978-012619070-0/50032-5

Manning, P. (2005). Continuing medical education 1906-1975: How the past influences the present. *Almanac, Alliance for CME, 27*(12).

Martin, A. (2000). The design and evolution of a simulation/ game for teaching information systems development. *Simulation & Gaming, 31*(4), 445–463. doi:10.1177/104687810003100401

McGaghie, W., Issenberg, B., Petrusa, E., & Scalese, R. (2010). A critical review of simulation-based medical education research: 2003–2009. *Medical Education, 44*(1), 50–63. doi:10.1111/j.1365-2923.2009.03547.x

McGonigal, J. (2012). *Reality is broken: Why games make us better and how they can change.* New York, NY: Random House.

MicroSim. (2012). *Website.* Retrieved May 1, 2012, from http://www.laerdal.com/docid/5899175/MicroSim

Mitchell, A., & Savill-Smith, C. (2004). *The use of computer and video games for learning: A review of the literature.* Learning and Skills Development Agency.

Monteiro, M., Corredoura, A., Candeias, M., Morais, P., & Diniz, J. (2011). Central hospital - Master of resuscitation: An immersive learning approach. In *Proceedings of the IEEE 1st International Conference on Serious Games and Applications for Health,* (pp. 74-77). IEEE Press.

Mott, B. W. (1999). Towards narrative-centered learning environments. In Proceedings of the Narrative Intelligence Symposium, AAAI 1999 Fall Symposium Series. AAAI.

Narayanasamy, V. (2006). Distinguishing games and simulation games from simulators. *Computers in Entertainment, 4*(2), 9. doi:10.1145/1129006.1129021

Nauta, H., & Spil, T. (2011). Change your lifestyle or your game is over: The design of a serious game for diabetes. In *Proceedings of the IEEE 1st International Conference on Serious Games and Applications for Health,* (pp. 62-68). IEEE Press.

Okuda, Y., Bryson, E., DeMaria, S. Jr, Jacobson, L., Quinones, J., Shen, B., & Levine, A. (2009). The utility of simulation in medical education: What is the evidence? *The Mount Sinai Journal of Medicine, New York, 76*(4), 330–343. doi:10.1002/msj.20127

Oliveira, F., Andersen, B., Pereira, J., Seager, W., & Ribeiro, C. (2011). The use of integrative framework to support the development of competences. In *Proceedings of the Second International Conference on Serious Games Development and Applications,* (pp. 117-128). Berlin, Germany: Springer-Verlag.

Perkins, G., Green, C., & Farquharson, W. (2006). Microsim: A new tool for advanced life support training. *Resuscitation, 69,* 54.

Philip, J. (1986). Gas man: An example of goal oriented computer-assisted teaching which results in learning. *Journal of Clinical Monitoring and Computing, 69,* 387–394.

Portela, F., Fonseca, J., Correia, R., & Andrade, J. (2011). Wii therapy on seniors: Effects on physical and mental domains. In *Proceedings of the IEEE 1st International Conference on Serious Games and Applications for Health,* (pp. 84-88). IEEE Press.

Prensky, M. (2001). *Digital game-based learning.* New York, NY: McGraw Hill.

Randel, J. M. (1992). The effectiveness of games for educational purposes: A review of recent research. *Simulation & Gaming, 23*(3), 261–276. doi:10.1177/1046878192233001

Rendas, A. (2006). Towars meaningful learning in undergraduate medical education using concept maps in a PBL pathophysiology course. *Advances in Physiology Education, 30*(1), 23–29. doi:10.1152/advan.00036.2005

Ribeiro, C., Fernandes, J., & Pereira, J. (2011). Didactical competence modeller: Dynamic story creation for serious games. In *Proceedings of KMEL 2011: The 1st International Symposium on Knowledge and E-Learning.* Springer.

Ridley, R., Wilks, D., & Freeman, J. (1997). Anaesthetists' attitudes towards an anesthesia simulator: A comparative survey: USA and Australia. *Anaesthesia and Intensive Care, 25,* 514–519.

Rieber, L. (1996). Seriously considering play: Designing interactive learning environments. *Educational Technology Research and Development, 44*(2), 43–58. doi:10.1007/BF02300540

Riedl, M. O. (2006). Believable agents and intelligent story adaptation for interactive storytelling. In Proceedings of the 3rd International Conference on Technologies for Interactive Digital Storytelling and Entertainment (TIDSE06), (pp. 1-12). TIDSE.

Rosen, K. (2008). The history of medical simulation. *Journal of Critical Care, 23*, 157–166. doi:10.1016/j.jcrc.2007.12.004

Rowe, J., Shores, L., Mott, B., & Lester, J. (2010). Integrating learning and engagement in narrative-centered learning environments. In *Proceedings of the 10th International Conference on Intelligent Tutoring Systems,* (pp. 166-177). IEEE.

Smith, R. (2009). *Military simulation & serious games: Where we came from and where we are going.* Modelbenders Press.

Squire, K., & Jenkins, H. (2004). Harnessing the power of games in education. *Insight (American Society of Ophthalmic Registered Nurses), 3*(1), 5–33.

Squire, K. A. (2005). From users to designers building a self-organizing game-based learning. *TechTrends, 49*(5), 32–42. doi:10.1007/BF02763688

Stacy, C. Marsella, W. L. (2003). Interactive pedagogical drama for health interventions. In *Proceedings of the Eleventh International Conference on Artificial Intelligence in Education,* (pp. 341-348). IEEE.

Szczesna, A., Grudzinski, J., Grudzinski, T., Mikuszewski, R., & Debowski, A. (2011). The psychology serious game prototype for preschool children. In *Proceedings of the IEEE 1st International Conference on Serious Games and Applications for Health,* (pp. 58-61). IEEE Press.

Szezurek, M. (1982). *Meta-analysis of simulation games effectiveness for cognitive learning.* Bloomington, IN: Indiana University.

Taffinder, N., Russell, R., & Manus, I. (1998). An objective assessment of laparoscope psychomotor skills: The effect of a training course on performance. *Surgical Endoscopy, 12*, 493.

Teteris, E., Fraser, K., Wright, B., & McLaughlin, K. (2012). Does training learners on simulators benefit real patients? *Advances in Heath Sciences Education, 17*(1), 137–144. doi:10.1007/s10459-011-9304-5

Thue, D., Bulitko, V., & Spetch, M. (2008). Making stories player-specific: Delayed authoring in interactive storytelling. In *Proceedings of the 1st Joint International Conference on Interactive Digital Storytelling: Interactive Storytelling,* (pp. 230-241). IEEE.

Turkle, S. (1984). *Video games and computer holding power.* The New Media Reader.

UEMS. (1993). *Charter on training of medical specialists in the European community.* European Union of Medical Specialists.

Valente, J., Kozlova, V., & Lima, C. (2011). Virtual tutor in MRI learning. In *Proceedings of the IEEE 1st International Conference on Serious Games and Applications for Health,* (pp. 37-41). IEEE Press.

Van Eck, R. (2006). Digital game-based learning: It's not just the digital natives who are restless. *EDUCAUSE Review, 41*, 16–30.

VanSickle, R. L. (1986). A quantitative review of research on instructional simulation gaming: A twenty-year perspective. *Theory and Research in Social Education, 14*(3), 245–264. doi:10.1080/00933104.1986.10505525

Vygotski, L. A. (1978). *Processes, mind in society: The development of higher psychological.* Boston, MA: Harvard University Press.

Workbench, E. (2005). *Electronics workbench - A national instruments company.* Retrieved May 1, 2012, from http://www.electronicsworks.com/

Worspace. (2005). *Workspace 5 PC based robotic simulation software.* Retrieved May 1, 2012, from http://www. workspace5.com/

ENDNOTES

1   http://www.unideusto.org/tuningeu/
2   www.medine2.com
3   www.charite.de/charme
4   www.meducator.net
5   http://www.continuingmedicaleducation-europe.com/
6   https://www.erc.edu/index.php/als_over-view/en/
7   http://www.e-lfh.org.uk/about_elfh.html#
8   http://www.immersion.com/
9   http://www.medsim.com/
10 http://cine-med.com/
11 https://www.aamc.org/newsroom/reporter/june2011/250894/games.html
12 http://simcenter.duhs.duke.edu/3DiTeams.html
13 http://www1.imperial.ac.uk/medicine/teaching/elearning/secondlife/game-basedlearning/

Chapter 13
Time Factor in the Curriculum Integration of Game-Based Learning

Margarida Romero
Universitat Ramon Llull, Spain

Mireia Usart
Universitat Ramon Llull, Spain

ABSTRACT

From primary and secondary educational levels to higher education and lifelong learning, the use of games for educational purposes has become a focus of increasing interest for instructional designers, teachers, and researchers. To ensure the achievement of learning objectives and competency in the use of games for educational purposes, the use of Game-Based Learning (GBL) in the curriculum should be considered in terms of its learner-centred characteristics, game dynamics, and interactional requirements. A dimension that involves all these characteristics is the time factor. Time is considered in this chapter from three different points of view: learner's psychological time; temporal gameplay; and the "interaction tempo" required for successfully including games in the curriculum. This chapter describes four typologies of the time factor: time-on-task; temporal perspectives of learners; temporal gameplay; and interaction tempo. Finally, the chapter proposes practical ideas for game designers and teachers when using GBL in face-to-face and online contexts.

THE TIME FACTOR IN EDUCATION

Time is one of the most polysemic words in every language. From objective time to the subjective perception of time at individual and collaborative levels, the concept of time may be defined and perceived in many forms. In educational contexts, the time factor is an implicit transversal perspective that some approaches have tried to make explicit by defining different typologies of academic time. The time factor and time quality are important aspects in the understanding of learning activities (Gros, Barberà & Kirschner, 2010; Romero, 2010). This is especially true in active learning

DOI: 10.4018/978-1-4666-3950-8.ch013

methodologies such as Game Based Learning (GBL), where students have a central role – and time represents an important factor when including games in the curriculum.

In this chapter, we aim to characterise the time factor from a variety of perspectives: the learner's perspective; the game based learning task as proposed to the learner; the tempo of the interaction of the learner with other learners; and the learner with the game. Figure 1 shows an overview of the typologies of time that will be addressed in this chapter and the relationships between these different concepts of time.

THE TIME FACTOR IN GAME BASED LEARNING

Learner Time in Game-Based Learning

Learner time can be considered from a time use perspective to identify temporal resources and time management competencies; as time (self, co-, and socially shared) regulation of academic time; and also from the psychological perspective—such as a student's temporal perspectives and orientation to multitasking.

The Time-on-Task Approach

In this approach, time is considered as a learner resource that can be allocated to GBL or other concurrent activities. The learner time-on-task allocation and regulation in the context of GBL is an important factor in understanding the learner's level of achievement and temporal pressure during the game (Usart & Romero, 2012). To characterise the time-on-task in GBL, we analyse student time according to the ALT model. The ALT model has been designed to characterise the different typologies of time: including *scheduled time* (e.g., the academic semester in which the course using the game is scheduled); a teacher's *allocated time* for starting and finishing the game (i.e., the game duration); *engaged time* or *time-on-task* (i.e., the time in which the learner is playing the game); and *effective learning time* (i.e., the specific moments when the student is learning through playing). The ALT model was designed for assessing new or beginning teachers. The model distinguishes different types of time in the process of teaching and learning and the relationships between them, including both hierarchical and interactional relationships. Firstly, *effective learning time* is considered, including the time in which the student is 'effectively' learning. *Effective learning time* is found within the time devoted to the task

Figure 1. The time factor in game based learning

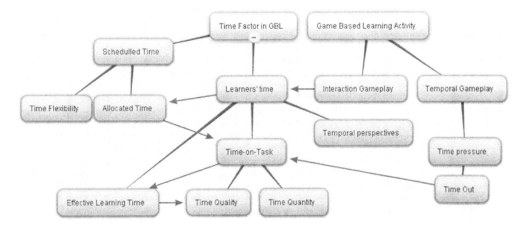

Figure 2. Academic learning time (ALT) model in face-to-face contexts (beginning teacher evaluation study, Fisher, et al., 1980)

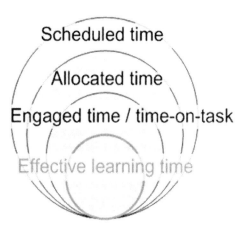

or *time-on-task*, which also includes a period of time in which the student is doing other elements of the task—such as organisation. The time defined by the teacher for the task is considered as the *allocated time* (Figure 2).

Within the ALT model, students can devote more or less time to the learning activity (*time-on-task*) within the bounds of *allocated time*, and within this time period they have a certain amount of *effective learning time*. Figure 3 shows an example of the allocated time defined by a

teacher in a GBL activity—between the 9th and the 13th (deadline).

Figure 4 shows an example of a student's Time-On-Task (TOT) within the allocated time, and the part of this time-on-task that he is allocating effectively to the game activity learning objectives (e). The *effective learning time* (e) is found within the time-on-task allocated by the student on Saturday 10th. In this example, the time-on-task also includes a period of time during which the student is not effectively learning. Effective learning time is therefore less than the total amount of time-on-task.

We should consider a learner's Effective Learning Time (ELT) as the amount of time a learner devotes to relevant academic tasks and successfully performs those tasks. In GBL, the ELT corresponds to the time the learner is successfully engaged in activities oriented towards learning objectives and competencies development. Games with educational purposes, also known as Serious Games (SG), should reduce the time allocated to non-educational objectives and increase the time allocated to activities that ensure the learner's achievement of the learning objectives and the development of competencies.

Figure 3. Example of an instructor's allocated time for a GBL activity: between the 9th and the 13th (deadline) of the month

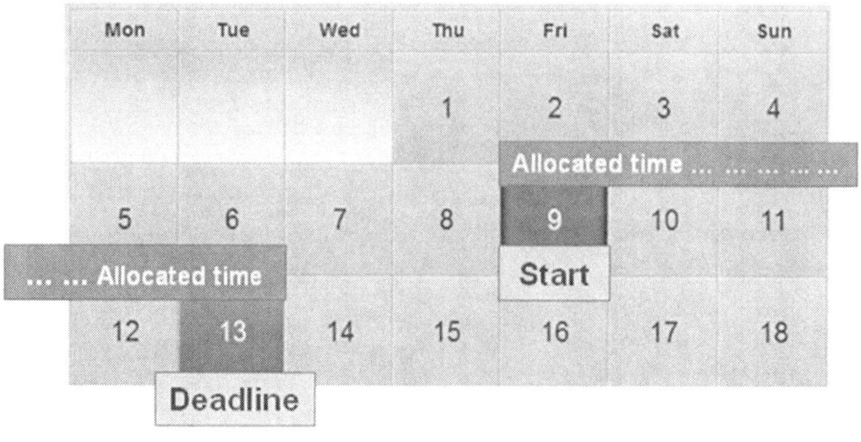

Mon	Tue	Wed	Thu	Fri	Sat	Sun
			1	2	3	4
				Allocated time		
5	6	7	8	9	10	11
... ... Allocated time				Start		
12	13	14	15	16	17	18
	Deadline					

Figure 4. Example of GBL effective learning time (e) within the time-on-task in the allocated time

Time-on-Task Quality and Effective Learning Times

A similar concept to Effective Learning Time (ELT) is the quality of learner's time. Time quality ensures the time-on-task allocated to the GBL activity is good enough to favour *effective learning time*. In other words, a student's time quality increases the *effective learning time* within the total amount of the *allocated time-on-task*. In GBL, time quality is made up of attributes related to the quality of a student's time-on-task. The quality of a student's learning time is considered to be cognitive, an attribute that facilitates success in the learning processes involved in learning activities (Romero & Barberà, 2011) such as GBL. Learner time quality is influenced by the learning task difficulty and daily time.

Some researchers have analysed the degree of alertness by monitoring physiological indicators as they change during the day. The early work of Blake (1967) suggested that alertness changes depending on the time of day and introduced the term 'post-lunch dip' to describe the diminished attention observed after lunch. In academic settings, Lewis and his colleagues (1988) observed

that concentration levels were highest at 7 p.m. among undergraduates at Cambridge University. However, physiological indicators of actual alertness and alertness as perceived by the subjects may differ. In their study, subjects stated that their alertness was highest at 11 a.m. and 3 p.m., while physiological indicators pointed to higher alertness at 7 a.m. and 9 p.m. These studies were carried out among individuals engaged in a single, primary activity (professional or academic). In distance education, adult learners have professional, social, or family responsibilities, and distance studies are considered to be secondary. We might therefore expect students to engage in learning time after their primary activity, at a time of day when alertness is lower, because of the time of day and the fatigue caused by the primary activity; assuming that, in general terms, the evening and night are times when cognitive quality is diminished and the morning and weekends are times with the highest cognitive quality because of the absence of a previous activity.

The quality of student learning time is also influenced by whether the learning activity is individual or collaborative. In collaborative learning tasks, students need to regulate their own time-on-task—in terms of quantity, quality, and synchronicity—according to the learning times of their fellow students (Capdeferro & Romero, 2012; Romero, 2010). Time zone differences within different members of a group could be a challenge for the organisation of group activity (Rutkowski, Saunders, Vogel & Genuchten, 2007). Collaborative online games involving a certain degree of synchronicity should be organised taking into account the time zones of the learners and their time availability both in terms of quantity and quality. Time quality in multiplayer games will depend on the quality of the different players' time qualities. For this reason, a higher number of learners could increase the risk of introducing students with a low level of quality time for the GBL activity, and so decrease the overlapping joint quality time availability for the time-on-task allocated to the game.

Time-on-Task Flexibility

Most of the individual games used in educational settings can be played on demand and so can be considered as time independent and offering the highest level of time flexibility for the learner. In this case, the learner has a certain degree of flexibility when deciding how much time to allocate to playing the game. Playing with (or against) another learner reduces this flexibility by introducing the

need to coordinate the temporal availabilities of two or more learners. In the following paragraphs, we develop the concept of time flexibility in GBL for both individual and collaborative settings according to the time typologies of the ALT model (Beginning Teacher Evaluation Study, Fisher et al., 1980).

In the context of GBL, we define student time flexibility as a student's ability to regulate the *time-on-task* allocated to the GBL activity according to learning time availability, instructional time requirements, and the flexibility of the GBL activity. In the context of GBL temporal flexibility, there is no assurance of the quantity and quality of a learner's time-on-task because *instructional-time* and *allocated-time* flexibility leads the learner to regulate his or her own time-on-task quantity and quality. The degree of flexibility that is available at each level (student, teacher, and institution) will shape the scope for action of each of these actors in the planning and regulation of their teaching and learning times.

An example of this temporal flexibility is the case of the individual GBL activities that are proposed to students as autonomous activities out of the classroom. The *allocated-time* includes a start and end day, but students can spend *time-on-task* on different days and at different moments of the day. Figure 5 shows an example of temporal flexibility in an individual game, where the instructor has

Figure 5. Example of temporal flexibility to play the game between the 9th and 13th (deadline) of the month

defined a flexible allocated time between the 9th and 13th (deadline). Student 1 chooses to allocate her time-on-task to the GBL activity on Saturday at midday; while student 2 chooses to allocate his time-on-task on Monday morning.

In other contexts, the instructor introduces a higher level of constraint and schedules the time for playing the game: the student cannot choose the time to allocate and has no temporal flexibility in the GBL time-on-task.

Time flexibility will be highly influenced by the learning modality, and reflect the face-to-face, blended learning, or online modality used. We observed a major difference in the temporalities of the face-to-face modality and the online learning modality. In a face-to-face class, 'a group of people starts at the same time, studies the same materials at the same pace, and ends at the same time' (Downes, 1998, p. 1). In online learning, temporal flexibility is higher than in face-to-face contexts. Nevertheless, time flexibility in formal online learning is less important than the initial expectations of the online learners (Levinson, 2006). Collis and Moonen (2001) consider temporal flexibility in terms of: institutional constraints; instructional design characteristics; and the pace of the students. Despite all the advantages of temporal flexibility in GBL, this high degree of temporal self-regulation could cause the less regulated students to fail to devote enough time-on-task, so reducing their effective learning times and performance (Romero, 2010).

In multiplayer GBL, the temporal flexibility will depend on the synchronous or asynchronous nature of the game. In asynchronous games, learners should coordinate their time-on-task in turns, but be more flexible in their *time-on-task* allocation than learners playing collaborative synchronous games that require the other player to be playing at the same moment. As discussed previously, the learner time zones and quantity and quality of time availability should be also considered in the organisation of multiplayer activities. Playing together for learning requires an adequate level of joint cognitive time quality, which could be difficult to achieve in online learning contexts where time flexibility allows a higher degree of temporal flexibility for the distributed learning teams engaged in GBL activities.

Time-on-Task and Performance in GBL

Time-on-task has been considered in educational studies because of the relevance this factor is supposed to have in relation to learning performance. The intuitive conception of most learners and instructors is that a larger amount of time-on-task will lead to a better performance. Nevertheless, this is not always the case, and investing a large amount of time-on-task does not guarantee Effective Learning Times (ELT) according to the ALT model. We can understand that a learner who is devoting 10 hours to playing an educational game is perhaps only learning during a much shorter period of time, e.g. 40 minutes. The time-on-task that is not effective learning time could be engaged in understanding the game mechanics (extrinsic cognitive load), enjoying the game without learning, playing the game even if the learning objectives have already been achieved, and the many other ways of engaging a time-on-task that do not contribute effectively to the learning objectives. In this section, we consider studies that have analysed the relationship between the time-on-task and performance in learning activities generally, and specifically GBL, following the literature review developed by Romero and Usart (2012). They analysed the studies analysing the time factor in relation to the academic performance, observing a focus on the relation between time-on-task and academic performance, especially in the context of face-to-face education homework assignments.

Wagner, Schober, and Spiel (2008) show a positive relationship between performance and the quantity of time allocated by postsecondary learners (N = 824). Using the German PISA data set in primary education (N = 24,273), Trautwein (2007) observes that the frequency of homework is even more relevant in academic performance than the amount of time it takes to complete assignments. Other studies on time quantity and academic performance provide variable results, with a slight positive relationship between the quantity of study time and performance (Allen, Lerner, and Hinrichsen, 1972, r =.23; Hinrichsen, 1972, r =.32; Wagstaff and Mahmoudi, 1976, r =.31) and indicate a negative relationship in some cases (Greenwald and Gillmore, 1997, r = -.15). The analysis made by Schuman et al. concluded that 'there is at best only a very small relationship between amount of studying and grades' (1985, p. 945). Observing a group of 120 college students in an online pharmacist program, Wellman and Marcinkiewicz (2004) found that time spent online by learners was only weakly correlated with learning. In Game-Based Learning (GBL), Lewis (2007, p. 918) observes that 'time-on-task' is one of the great general truisms of educational interventions: the longer one spends learning, generally, the more one learns. However, he claims that the influence of time-on-task is subject to the relevance of the learning objectives addressed by the game. Let us look at the level of efficiency and consider a student's time-on-task in relation to an increase in learning performance. Games may facilitate an (enormous) increase in time-on-task because of their engagement and so improve some learning performances, but does increasing the time-on-task efficiently increase learning performance? Gee (2003) argues that a well-designed SG may increase the time-on-task by students by creating an environment that fosters practice, but that this time-on-task does not directly relate to a better learning performance. The Horizon Report released by the New Media Consortium and EDUCAUSE (2011) foresees that in a three-year horizon Massively Multiplayer Online (MMO) games designed for learning will make players dedicate enormous amounts of time-on-task pursuing collaborative problem-solving goals. However, the report does not predict an increase in learning performances and efficiency. Moreover, study dur-

ing the time-on-task and learning performance is sometimes not analysed as a casual relationship, as in SG DimensionM (2010). This SG has been designed to teach algebra. An analysis of the use of SG DimensionM shows an increase in student time-on-task and a parallel increase in student performance and knowledge transfer" (Romero & Usart, 2012, p. 426).

The relationship between the time-on-task and performance in GBL should be further analysed to help game designers conceive games that increase the Effective Learning Time (ELT) and reduce the time allocated to activities that are not contributing to learning objectives. To analyse the qualitative aspect of learner's time, in the following sections we focus on the intrapsychological times—with particular emphasis on the learner's time perspective.

The Learner's Psychological Time Approach

Time is not only an objective factor. Because of the subjective dimension of time, temporal perception and temporal perspectives can be experienced by each subject in a different manner. The intrapsychological factors of time perception and perspectives have been analysed by psychologists and sociologists in recent decades (Block, 1974; Zakai, 1989; Zimbardo & Boyd, 1999). The intrapsychological approximation of learner time can be approached from the study of different individual variables related to the concept of time, and how it is perceived by humans. Nuttin and Lens (1985) defined four individual constructs as the generators of so-called psychological time: orientation to multitasking or polychronism, time attitude, time orientation, and time perspective (TP; Zimbardo & Boyd, 1999). Although these constructs have been studied in relation to cognitive and learning aspects, TP is probably the aspect of psychological time that has historically been most related to learning processes and outcomes in formal education (Schmidt & Werner, 2007).

However, despite the wide corpus of research on TP and learning, as far as the authors are aware, little research has focused on TP in game based learning (Usart, & Romero, 2012). A key issue of TP in GBL environments is the fact that the GBL approach is based on the active role of the student. This scenario has not been studied before in relation to student TPs, but it could presumably show differing results when compared to instructivist methodologies (Usart & Romero). In this section, we will begin with the definition and measurement of individual TPs. The role of this individual construct will then be further explained, especially in relation to learning performance. After presenting a general overview, we will focus on game based learning and analyse the results of student TP in relation to performance in the MetaVals game, designed by the ESADE Learning Innovation Unit (Romero, Usart & Almirall, 2011; Usart, Romero & Almirall, 2011). Finally, we will examine the future needs for study in this field.

Time Perspective Definition and Measurement

TP has been defined and measured from a wide range of approaches and using many methods. Studies on TP and learning have sometimes produced ambiguous results (Sejts, 1998). The authors of this chapter do not disagree with other definitions, but choose to focus on the definition and corresponding measurement process given by Zimbardo, Keough, and Boyd (1997): namely, that time perspective is 'the manner in which individuals, and cultures, partition the flow of human experience into distinct temporal categories of past, present and future,' (Keough and Boyd, 1997, p. 1008). From this definition, TP can be understood as a cognitive construct that can be operationalised through the use of Zimbardo and Boyd's (1999) measuring instrument, the Zimbardo Time Perspective Inventory (hereinafter ZTPI). The test independently measures an individual's orientation towards

past-negative, past-positive, present-fatalistic, present-hedonistic, and future time perspectives. This technique consists of 56 items or statements such as: 'It upsets me to be late at appointments'. Each statement has to be rated by using a 5-point Likert scale (1 = *strongly disagree*, to 5 = *totally agree*). The self-reported test provides researchers with a quantitative value for an individual's TP. It has been tested by different authors in various contexts and results have shown it to be reliable when used in Western cultures (Apostolidis & Fieulaine, 2004; Díaz-Morales, 2006).

In this operationalisation of TP, the past, present, and future temporal frames are subdivided into five subscales or factors: present hedonism; present fatalism; past positivism; past negativism; and future time perspective (Figure 6). Researchers in the field of TP and learning have focused specifically on two of these factors. Present hedonism (defined as seeking immediate pleasure, with little regard to risk or concern for consequences) and future time perspective (FTP; characterised by delay of reward, as a result of the desire to achieve specific long-term goals). As we will show hereafter, these two temporal orientations seem to be strongly related to learning. To be specific, present-oriented individuals have shown lower academic achievement when compared to future-oriented students (Adelabu, 2007), while future-oriented individuals tend to engage more in learning activities (Adelabu, 2007; Simons, Vansteenkiste, Lens, & Lacante, 2004).

Time Perspective and Learning

There is a significant research background in the field of TP and learning. Education has historically been defined as future-oriented (Leonardi, 2007) and ideally seeks a significant acquisition of learning. Education demands that students plan their learning process and set short and long-term goals for evaluation and results. Furthermore, education demands a degree of gratification delay (Mischel, 1974). Due to the future orientation of

Figure 6. Intrapsychological division of the temporal frame according to Zimbardo and Boyd TP theory

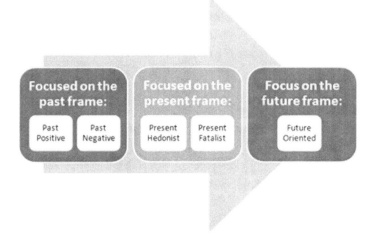

education itself, there has been a wide corpus of research focused on studying the possible relationship between the future factor of TP and learning. In particular, FTP has been related to academic achievement by Adelabu (2007) in a study of 232 low-income, urban African-American adolescents. The study measured positive and significant relationships for academic achievements (operationalised as the cumulative Grade Point Average [GPA] in four subjects), FTP, sense of school belonging, and school acceptance. The results showed a negative, significant relationship between academic achievement and present time perspective. Zimbardo and Boyd (1999) studied the TP in 31 university students in relation to their GPAs. Results indicated a significant positive relation between ZTPI future subscale scoring and student GPAs. Using the ZTPI, Ozcetin, and Eren (2010) studied the relationship between TP and academic achievement in 1061 vocational students (measured as the final exam grade) in an English course. Results showed that future-oriented student attitudes regarding English classes were not significantly different from those of present and past-oriented students, yet the effect of the future-oriented student graded performances in English class was noticeable.

Despite results described in the previous paragraph which indicate that future-oriented students tend perform better than their present-oriented counterparts, in the next section we will see that studies in GBL reveal very different tendencies for individual with differing TPs when performing SG activities.

Time Perspective and Performance in Game-Based Learning

Education, as stated earlier, can be defined as a future-oriented process that requires students to accept a considerable delay in gratification (de Bilde, Vansteenkiste, & Lens, 2011). Nevertheless, the inclusion of SGs in curricula adds a present-oriented learning methodology and provides students with instant rewards (Zimbardo & Boyd, 1999). This active learning approach involves competition and social interaction and obliges students to think about the future—but also focus on instant rewards (Bateman & Boon, 2006). It may therefore be supposed that GBL leverages the performances of present-oriented individuals.

Despite a general lack of studies on TP and GBL, there are various studies in educational and social psychology focused on TP in social and instant feedback situations. Brown and Jones (2004) showed how present-oriented individuals have a higher engagement in social activities. The authors used a self-reported questionnaire, the Temporal Orientation Scale (TOS) to measure TP. Results on African-American high school students indicate that past and present-oriented students tended to engage in social activities more than academic activities. In the same study, Brown and Jones observed that future-oriented individuals saw education as useful for future success in life. In the same vein, Wassarman's (2002) thesis on TP and gambling behaviour points to present-oriented adults engaging more in gambling activities than past and future-oriented individuals. These results could be explained by various underlying causes. Firstly, as studied by Moreno-Ger et al. (2008), the mix of fun and learning introduced by the GBL methodology could neutralise the heterogeneous learning outcomes expected from the results seen in classical learning activities. Focusing on motivation, present-oriented students prefer instant-reward activities (Wassarman, 2002), while future focused individuals can foresee investment in learning as a source of future rewards.

According to these studies, there are empirical and theoretical reasons to affirm that no significant differences in performance should be observed in a GBL scenario between present and future-oriented participants (see Figure 7). Nevertheless, these results point to specific aspects of games, such as social activities and gambling. There is still a lack of research on TP in SG activities. With

the aim of approaching these intrapsychological temporal aspects, not previously targeted in the field of GBL, Usart and Romero (2012) designed the study described below. A total of 24 adult students in a master's course at ESADE formed the sample of our case study (9 women and 15 men, age $M = 31.90$, $SD = 4.09$). A classification game, MetaVals, was implemented in the introductory finance course. The research scenario was set by an online pre-test of financial literacy, together with face-to-face SG activity, (where students played a web-based SG to classify assets and liabilities) and an online post-test. Students were rated, according to the ZTPI, as future or present-oriented.

The ANOVA analysis for this study confirmed the central hypothesis: there were no significant differences in game performance among different TP profiles. Nevertheless, due to the lack of previous studies in the field of GBL and TP, more research needs to be done to confirm the tendency of future-oriented students to score higher than balanced and present-oriented individuals. Similar results shown among students with different TPs support the theory that a mix of fun and learning introduced by GBL methodology neutralises the different learning performances found in classical learning activities. Present-oriented individuals approach a GBL activity as an entertaining and challenging activity. However, future-oriented students may be engaging in GBL activity not for fun—but for the learning and future outcomes of playing in an educational context.

Figure 7. Time perspectives and the learning performances of students

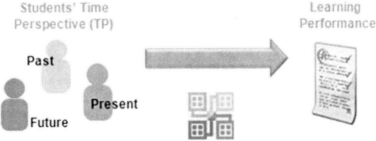

However, there are still different aspects of the role of student TPs in educational games that need to be approached. One of the factors to be studied is the social aspect of collaborative GBL (Romero et al., 2012). TP studies have only focused on individual learning activities; and little is known about how differently oriented individuals behave when collaborating or competing with other students. Since SGs feature increasingly in current learning trends in adult formal education, research on TP should now study how student time perspectives could be related to student interactions, motivations, and learning outcomes in collaborative SGs. Furthermore, very little is known about past-oriented student performance in GBL environments; in order to fill this gap, there is a need for future research to focus on samples that may include past-oriented students.

In conclusion, we may assume that student intrapsychological time in general, and TP in particular, play a role in performance in GBL environments. These scenarios may help students who are not future-oriented in terms of knowledge acquisition (and less engaged in learning activities) but are attracted to SGs. Therefore, TP must be taken into account when deciding on the implementation of SGs in the curriculum. As an individual and cultural construct, TP is related to motivation and learning performance in GBL.

The Temporal Gameplay in Game-Based Learning Contexts

Games in general, and Serious Games (SGs) in particular, can be defined as activities with a certain level of engagement that should allow players to achieve objectives within a certain time duration, temporal modality, and time pressure.

Games may last minutes, hours, days, weeks or they may even be pervasive permanent universes (such *The Sims*) that exist beyond the time-on-task devoted by the player. In terms of Zagal and Mateas (2010, p. 848), time duration corresponds to gameworld time and 'events within

the represented gameworld, including events associated with gameplay actions.' In GBL we should consider the game's duration according to the instructional tempo and the time that can be devoted to the achievement of the learning objectives and competencies development.

In relation to duration and the need for time to complete the task, we should consider time pressure. Time pressure is a subjective state related to a student's perception that the allocated learning time, and the possible time-on-task within this allocated time, is shorter than the time required to achieve the task objectives (Romero, Hyvönen, & Barberà, 2012). Time pressure in GBL could be considered as a stressful condition that supplements the apprehension induced by the threat of the negative consequences of not achieving the learning objectives in the allocated playing time. Time pressure could increase the gameplay if the level of pressure allows the learner to achieve the learning objectives in the proposed GBL. Excessive time pressure in GBL could be counterproductive and prevent learners from achieving the educational objectives. According to Harteveld, Guimarães, Mayer, and Bidarra (2007) 'too much information, time pressure or other factors inside a game environment could lead to cognitive overload or lead a person to filtering out critical information' (2007, p. 131). Both in individual and collaborative contexts, time pressure is identified as a factor in explaining poor performance by decision-making groups (Karau & Kelly, 1992; Kerstholt, 1994; Linehan, Lawson, Doughty & Kirman, 2009; Linehan et al., 2012). The balance between the level of difficulty and time pressure leads to the state described by Csikszentmihalyi (1997) as the flow state, in which 'the sense of duration of time is altered; hours pass by in minutes, and minutes can stretch out to seem like hours' (Csikszentmihalyi, 1997, p. 49). Csikszentmihalyi (1997) identifies game playing as one of the activities that help individuals 'achieve an ordered state of mind that is highly enjoyable' (Csikszentmihalyi, 1997, p. 72).

In SGs, instructors can use the level design to regulate the correct level of difficulty, and time duration and time-outs are specific mechanisms for regulating time pressure. In the MetaVals game, time pressure can be regulated by the instructor in the initial settings of the game (Figure 8). Usually, students are given one minute to classify by completing each of the six items. In the next release, MetaVals could advance with respect to personalisation and associate the time-out duration to the level of prior knowledge assessed in the first stage of the game.

The Interaction Tempo in Collaborative Game-Based Learning

SGs in general and collaborative serious games in particular are characterised by an interaction tempo. Interaction tempo includes the concept of coordination time proposed by Zagal and Mateas (2010, p. 848), which relates to the 'events that coordinate the actions of players and agents'. This variable is defined as the pace (slow or fast) of human communication (Auer, Couper-Kuhlen, & Muller, 1999). Interaction tempo should be

considered from the perspective of two different levels in GBL environments. The first level can be defined as the very interaction of players with the game context itself (hereinafter *learner-context* interaction tempo). This first level should only be considered as relevant for computer-based games, as face-to-face board games are based on a stable physical interface that does not depend on time (Juul, 2005). The second level is defined as the pace of time experienced during learner interaction in the gameplay (*learner-learner* interaction tempo). On the assumption that computer mediated communication (CMC) in learning environments differs from face-to-face communication (St. Amant & Kelsey, 2011), the *learner-learner* interaction tempo is also expected to vary, depending on the digital or face-to-face nature of the game.

In the field of digital GBL, positive and negative factors have been related to the *learner-context* interaction tempo. Well designed games can engage learners through the use of a hypnotic accelerating tempo, as observed in the classic game *Space Invaders* (Crawford, 1984). Nevertheless, this positive effect can be countered if the interface response is slow and deficient (Lemay, 2007).

Figure 8. Screenshot of the time-out feature in MetaVals

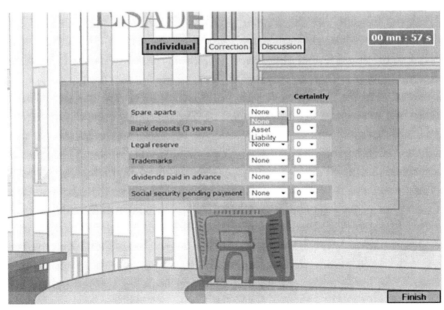

The author claims that intense and pleasurable activities are those involving focused attention and immediate feedback. There is also a second factor outlined by Lemay, namely the matching of the game to the player's skills. In particular, the ICT competence of a player may impact on the *learner-context* interaction tempo. Poorly skilled ICT students may spend more time learning how to interact with the game interface. According to Kiili (2005), the intended optimal tempo (flow effect) in SGs could disappear due to an over-loading of the learner's working memory as a consequence of too many multimedia elements. The solution to this problem could be to design SGs with less information. This could help players reach a balanced and optimal rhythm of gameplay in digital GBLs.

Focusing on the aspects related to *learner-learner* interaction tempo, different variables can be identified. Computer based games can be played individually (including games against a virtual player) or involve collaboration and competition (Romero, et al., 2012). Collaborative GBL requires participants to monitor and adapt their interaction tempo, via their temporal competence, to the changes in their motivational state (Azevedo, 2008).

In face-to-face games, *learner-learner* interaction tempo presents the same characteristics as the pace of time in natural human interaction. According to Hedenbro, Shapiro, and Gottman (2006), natural interaction is not due to external sources, but emerges from the dynamics of the participants; therefore, interaction in collaborative games depends on the social interaction rules defined by the context of each game. In collaborative SGs, participants do not totally depend on the natural interaction factor, and their participation and communication with other players is constrained by the type of communication the game settings allow. According to the collaborative game dynamics, it is also important to consider the interaction tempo for intragroup cooperation

(need for time for knowledge elicitation, sharing, and discussion) and the interaction tempo for intergroup competition, limited by the time pressure for competing between different teams involved in a GBL (Romero, et al., 2012).

Despite the lack of studies specifically focused on interaction tempo in digital GBL, when these contexts allow two or more individuals to interact, they rely on human-human interactions. Based on studies of CMC interaction, we could state that a temporal delay of feedback among students during gameplay could hamper the interaction tempo between game peers. In the field of game design, Talin (1998) highlights the fact that games providing a large number of pre-programmed events, such as narrative SGs, could also slow interaction tempo, as players have to pay attention to narration and spend more time passively studying instructions than interacting with other game characters (Mallon & Webb, 2005). Furthermore, de Freitas et al. (2010) studied how negative learning transfer may occur when players in GBL contexts do not meet their expectations in high fidelity environments. This aspect could also be slowing tempos in interaction due to feelings of being lost in an unknown context.

CONSIDERATIONS FOR GAME AND INSTRUCTIONAL DESIGNERS, TEACHERS, AND LEARNERS

By drawing on the analyses of the time factor in GBL (addressed in detail in the previous sections), we offer recommendations for game designers, teachers, and learners. These recommendations are followed by further suggestions for teachers and practitioners that are focused on aspects of including games in the curriculum. The theories, studies, and results outlined in this chapter reflect the importance of different temporal aspects in GBL—both external and intrapsychological. When deciding how to include SG activities in the curriculum, time-on-task, time perspective, and interaction tempo must be taken into account, especially if the aim is to optimise learner time and help improve knowledge acquisition.

Before including SGs in the curriculum, game designers, and instructional designers should start conceiving an educational game according to both the instructional tempo and the learners' use of time. When designing and implementing a game in class, they should also consider the intrapsychological time factor, specifically, the learners' temporal orientation and the TP profiles of the students. A student's ability to multitask could help designers in the adaptation of GBL for formal learning contexts. The setting of a game should therefore start with its design and/or adaptation, which in turn, determines the implementation of the class dynamics and the temporal aspects of the game. Instructional designers should consider the Academic Learning Times model (Beginning Teacher Evaluation Study, Fisher et al., 1980) for defining the flexibility of the allocated time as this may help teachers engage students in a certain amount and quality of time-on-task through the gameplay. Furthermore, interaction tempo must be considered when designing both individual and collaborative SGs. We have learnt that in the case of both individual and team-based games, a slow interaction tempo between the player and the game interface could go against the learning process by increasing student stress. In contrast, an optimised interaction tempo could allow students to focus on gameplay. If the SG has a collaborative phase, designers should also provide a 'natural tempo' scenario for player interaction. It has been observed that games that do not feel real can hamper student engagement and performance in the game.

TEACHING WITH GAMES: RECOMMENDATIONS FOR TEACHERS AND PRACTITIONERS

Firstly, instructors could take into account the Academic Learning Times model (Beginning Teacher Evaluation Study, Fisher et al., 1980) for redefining, if needed, the flexibility of the allocated time and allow learners a given amount and quality of time-on-task. Beyond time-on-task quantity, learners should be aware that their time-on-task quality will be related to their effective learning times (Romero & Barberà, 2012). Furthermore, research on student TPs points towards the importance of including GBL activities in formal education. These educational tools provide instant rewards to players; and this fact could counterbalance the future-orientation of formal education by helping present-oriented individuals engage more fully in learning activities. Including educational games in the curriculum could help reduce the current differences in performance, particularly those observed between present and future-oriented learners.

Secondly, teachers should regulate the time-on-task of learners during GBL activity and adapt their external regulation according to the intra-psychological factors apparent in their students (temporal perspectives, polychronicity, circadian rhythms, etc.). The results of various studies on learner TPs and performance in GBL indicate that a teacher's knowledge of the temporal perspectives of students should help them decide when to include a SG activity. In this way, teachers can help students manage their learning processes in terms of performance and engagement. Furthermore, teachers play a key role in the regulation of interaction tempos. When teachers are guiding a GBL activity, they should be able to monitor and use different teaching tools to counteract, if needed, the possible delays in student interaction tempo in both face-to-face and online learning activities.

Finally, through the use of SGs, students could learn to regulate their GBL time-on-task and ensure the quality of the time they devote to GBL activity. Time pressure management through the use of different time-out and time management features in individual and multiplayer games could help learners develop time regulation skills and transfer these skills to other aspects of their lives. SGs could also help students with different orientations perform equally when learning. Understanding the psychological times of students could help in the process of guiding them in active learning environments. Moreover, given the intrinsic value SGs could have in the development of time regulation skills, and the value they could have in supporting the various temporal perspectives of learners, there is a need to develop games that support time-on-task regulation or the development of time management skills.

In summary, this chapter has sought to reveal the different requirements on quantitative and qualitative time involved in the processes of playing and learning in formal and educational contexts. In the first sections of the chapter, time in GBL has been defined and tackled from three different approaches that define the temporal scenario: the use of time by learners; the psychological time perspective; and finally, temporal gameplay and interaction tempo. In the second part of the chapter, the instructional design process was discussed with regard to both internal and external time variables. External regulation by teachers and self-regulation by learners should set a scenario that enables all the actors to make successful use of games for educational purposes. Due to all the previously stated, time is an aspect that should be further studied in the years ahead.

REFERENCES

Adelabu, D. H. (2007). Time perspective and school membership as correlates to academic achievement among African American adolescents. *Adolescence*, *42*(167), 525–538.

Allen, G. J., Lerner, W. M., & Hinrichsen, J. J. (1972). Study behaviors and their relationships to test anxiety and academic performance. *Psychological Reports*, *30*, 407–410. doi:10.2466/pr0.1972.30.2.407

Apostolidis, T., & Fieulaine, N. (2004). Validation franc¸aise de l'e'chelle de temporalite´: The Zimbardo time perspective inventory. *European Review of Applied Psychology*, *54*, 207–217. doi:10.1016/j.erap.2004.03.001

Auer, P., Couper-Kuhlen, E., & Muller, F. (1999). *Language in time: The rhythm and tempo of spoken interaction*. Oxford, UK: Oxford University Press.

Azevedo, R. (2008). The role of self-regulation in learning about science with hypermedia. In Robinson, D., & Schraw, G. (Eds.), *Recent Innovations in Educational Technology that Facilitate Student Learning* (pp. 127–156). Academic Press.

Bateman, C. M., & Boon, R. (2006). *21st century game design*. Hingham, MA: Charles River Media.

Belmont, J. M., & Butterfield, E. C. (1971). Learning strategies as determinants of memory deficiencies. *Cognitive Psychology*, *2*(4), 411–420. doi:10.1016/0010-0285(71)90024-7

Berliner, D. (1984). The half-full glass: A review of research on teaching. In Hosford, P. (Ed.), *Using What We Know about Teaching*. Alexandria, VA: Association for Supervision and Curriculum Development.

Blake, M. J. F. (1967). Relationship between circadian rhythm of body temperature and introversion-extroversion. *Nature*, *215*, 896–897. doi:10.1038/215896a0

Block, R. A. (1974). Memory and the experience of duration in retrospect. *Memory & Cognition*, *2*, 53–160. doi:10.3758/BF03197508

Bluedorn, A. C., & Denhardt, R. B. (1988). Time and organizations. *Journal of Management*, *14*, 299–320. doi:10.1177/014920638801400209

Brown, W. T., & Jones, J. M. (2004). The substance of things hoped for: A study of the future orientation, minority status perceptions, academic engagement, and academic performance of black high school students. *The Journal of Black Psychology, 30*(2), 248–273. doi:10.1177/0095798403260727

Caldwell, J. H., Huitt, W. G., & Graeber, A. O. (1982). Time spent in learning: Implications from research. *The Elementary School Journal, 82,* 471–480. doi:10.1086/461282

Capdeferro, N., & Romero, M. (2012). Are online learners frustrated with collaborative learning experiences. *International Review of Research in Open and Distance Learning, 13*(2), 26–44.

Collins, B., & Moonen, J. (2001). *Flexible learning in a digital world.* London, UK: Kegan Page Ltd.

Crawford, C. (1984). *The art of computer game design.* Berkeley, CA: Osborne/McGraw-Hill.

Csikszentmihalyi, M. (1997). *Creativity: Flow and the psychology of discovery and invention.* New York, NY: Harper Collins.

de Bilde, J., Vansteenkiste, M., & Lens, W. (2011). Understanding the association between future time perspective and self-regulated learning through the lens of self-determination theory. *Learning and Instruction, 21*(3), 332–344. doi:10.1016/j.learninstruc.2010.03.002

de Freitas, S., Rebolledo-Mendez, G., Liarokapis, F., Magoulas, G., & Poulovassilis, A. (2010). Learning as immersive experiences: Using the four dimensional framework for designing and evaluating immersive learning experiences in a virtual world. *British Journal of Educational Technology, 41*(1), 69–85. doi:10.1111/j.1467-8535.2009.01024.x

Díaz-Morales, J. F. (2006). Estructura factorial y fiabilidad del inventario de perspectiva temporal de Zimbardo. *Psicothema, 18*(3), 565–571.

Dimension, M. (2010). *Tabula digita video games add up fast: One million DimensionM games played by math students.* New York, NY: DimensionM.

Downes, S. (1998). *The future of online learning.* Paper presented at the NAWeb 1998 meeting. Fredericton, Canada.

Fisher, C., Berliner, D., Filby, N., Marliave, R., Cahen, L., & Dishaw, M. (1980). Teaching behaviors, academic learning time, and student achievement: An overview. In Denham, C., & Lieberman, A. (Eds.), *Time to Learn.* Washington, DC: National Institute of Education.

Gee, J. P. (2003). *What video games have to teach us about learning and literacy.* New York, NY: Palgrave Macmillan. doi:10.1145/950566.950595

Greenwald, A. G., & Gilmore, G. M. (1997). No pain, no gain? The importance of measuring course workload in student ratings of instruction. *Journal of Educational Psychology, 89*(4), 743–751. doi:10.1037/0022-0663.89.4.743

Gros, B., Barberà, E., & Kirschner, P. (2010). Time factor in e-learning: Impact literature review. *eLC Research Paper Series, 0,* 1-32.

Hall, E. T., & Hall, M. R. (1987). *Hidden differences: Doing business with the Japanese.* Garden City, NY: Anchor Books Doubleday.

Harteveld, C., Guimarães, R., Mayer, I., & Bidarra, R. (2007). Balancing pedagogy, game and reality components within a unique serious game for training levee inspection. *Lecture Notes in Computer Science, 4469,* 128–139. doi:10.1007/978-3-540-73011-8_15

Hedenbro, M., Shapiro, A. F., & Gottman, J. M. (2006). Play with me at my speed: Describing differences in the tempo of parent-infant interactions in the Lausanne triadic play paradigm in two cultures. *Family Process, 45*(4), 485–498. doi:10.1111/j.1545-5300.2006.00184.x

Hinrichsen, J. J. (1972). Prediction of grade point average from estimated study behaviors. *Psychological Reports, 31*(3), 974–975. doi:10.2466/pr0.1972.31.3.974

Juul, J. (2005). *Half-real: Video games between real rules and fictional worlds*. Cambridge, MA: MIT Press.

Karau, S. J., & Kelly, J. R. (1992). The effects of time scarcity and time abundance on group performance quality and interaction process. *Journal of Experimental Social Psychology, 28*(6), 542–571. doi:10.1016/0022-1031(92)90045-L

Kaufman-Scarborough, C., & Lindquist, J. D. (1999). Time management and polychronicity: Comparisons, contrasts, and insights for the workplace. *Journal of Managerial Psychology, 14*(3-4), 288–312. doi:10.1108/02683949910263819

Kersholt, J. H. (1994). The effect of time pressure on decision making behaviour in a dynamic task environment. *Acta Psychologica, 86*, 89–104. doi:10.1016/0001-6918(94)90013-2

Kiili, K. (2005). Digital game-based learning: Towards an experiential gaming model. *The Internet and Higher Education, 8*, 13–24. doi:10.1016/j.iheduc.2004.12.001

Kobasigawa, A., & Metcalf-Haggert, A. (1993). Spontaneous allocation of study time by first- and third-grade children in a simple memory task. *The Journal of Genetic Psychology, 154*, 223–235. doi:10.1080/00221325.1993.9914736

Kose-Bagci, H., Dautenhahn, K., & Nehaniv, C. L. (2008). Emergent dynamics of turn-taking interaction in drumming games with a humanoid robot. In *Proceedings of the 17th IEEE International Symposium on Robot and Human Interactive Communication*. Munich, Germany: IEEE Press.

Kramer, A. F., Hahn, S., Irwin, D. E., & Theeuwes, J. (2000). Age differences in the control of looking behavior: Do you know where your eyes have been. *Psychological Science, 11*, 210–217. doi:10.1111/1467-9280.00243

Lemay, P. (2007). Developing a pattern language for flow experiences in video games. In *Proceedings of DiGRA 2007 Conference*. DiGRA.

Levinsen, K. (2006). Collaborative on-line teaching: The inevitable path to deep learning and knowledge sharing. *Electronic Journal of E-Learning, 4*(1), 41–48.

Lewis, G., Robertson, I., Watson, P., & Datta, A. (1998). Circadian rhythm of sleepiness and vigilance studied in man. *The Journal of Physiology, 27*(1), 506.

Lewis, M. W. (2007). Analysis of the roles of serious games in helping teach health-related knowledge, skills, and in changing behavior. *Journal of Diabetes Science and Technology, 1*(6).

Linehan, C., Lawson, S., Doughty, M., & Kirman, B. (2009). There's no "I" in "emergency management team": Designing and evaluating a serious game for training emergency managers in group decision making skills. In *Proceedings of the 39th Conference of the Society for the Advancement of Games & Simulations in Education and Training*, (pp. 20-27). IEEE.

Linehan, C., Lawson, S., Doughty, M., Kirman, B., Haferkamp, L., & Krämer, N. C. … Nigrelli, M. L. (2012). Teaching group decision making skills to emergency managers via digital games. In A. Lugmayr, H. Franssila, P. Näränen, O. Sotamaa, J. Vanhala, & Z. Yu (Eds.), *Media in the Ubiquitous Era: Ambient, Social and Gaming Media*. Hershey, PA: IGI Global.

Mallon, B., & Webb, B. (2005). Stand up and take your place: Identifying narrative elements in narrative adventure and role-play games. *Computers in Entertainment, 3*(1).

Moreno-Ger, P., Burgos, D., Martínez-Ortiz, I., Sierra, J., & Fernández-Manjón, B. (2008). Educational game design for online education. *Computers in Human Behavior, 24,* 2530–2540. doi:10.1016/j.chb.2008.03.012

New Media Consortium & EDUCAUSE. (2011). *The horizon report.* Austin, TX: The New Media Consortium.

Ozcetin, N., & Eren, A. (2010). The effects of perceived instrumentality and future time perspective on students' graded performance and attitudes regarding English class. *International Journal on New Trends in Education and Their Implications, 1*(4), 5.

Peetsma, A., & Thea, T. D. (1999). Future-time perspective: Analysis of a facet-designed questionnaire. *European Journal of Psychological Assessment, 15*(2), 99–105. doi:10.1027//1015-5759.15.2.99

Pivec, M., Dziabenko, O., & Schinnerl, I. (2003). Aspects of game-based learning. In *Proceedings of I-KNOW 2003.* Graz, Austria: UCS.

Romero, M. (2010). *Gestion du temps dans les activités projet médiatisées à distance.* Editions Européenes Universitaires.

Romero, M. (2011). Distance learners' work life balance. *Journal of Instructional Technology and Distance Learning, 8*(5), 43–47.

Romero, M., & Barberà, E. (2011). Quality of e-learners' time and learning performance beyond quantitative time-on-task. *International Review of Research in Open and Distance Learning, 12*(5), 122–135.

Romero, M., Hyvönen, P., & Barbera, E. (2012). Creativity in collaborative learning across the life span. *Creative Education, 3*(4), 422–429. doi:10.4236/ce.2012.34066

Romero, M., & Lambropoulos, N. (2011). Internal and external regulation to support knowledge construction and convergence in CSCL. *Electronic Journal of Research in Educational Psychology, 9*(1), 309–330.

Romero, M., & Usart, M. (2012). Game based learning time-on-task and learning performance according to students' temporal perspective. In *Proceedings of ECGBL,* (pp. 424-431). Cork, Ireland: ECGBL.

Romero, M., Usart, M., & Almirall, E. (2011). Serious games in a finance course promoting the knowledge group awareness. *Proceedings of EDULEARN, 2011,* 3490–3492.

Romero, M., Usart, M., Ott, M., Earp, J., de Freitas, S., & Arnab, S. (2012). Learning through playing for or against each other? Promoting collaborative learning in digital game based learning. In *Proceedings of the 20th European Conference on Information Systems.* Barcelona, Spain: ESADE.

Rutkowski, A. F., Saunders, C., Vogel, D., & van Genuchten, M. (2007). Is it already 4am in your time zone: Focus immersion and temporal dissociation in virtual teams. *Small Group Research, 38*(1), 98–129. doi:10.1177/1046496406297042

Schmidt, J. T., & Werner, C. H. (2007). Designing online instruction for success: Future oriented motivation and self-regulation. *The Electronic Journal of e-learning, 5*(1), 69-78.

Schuman, H., Walsh, E., Olson, C., & Etheridge, B. (1985). Effort and reward: The assumption that college grades are affected by quantity of study. *Social Forces, 63*(4), 945–966.

Simons, J., Vansteenkiste, M., Lens, W., & Lacante, M. (2004). Placing motivation and future time perspective theory in a temporal perspective. *Educational Psychology Review, 16*(2), 121–139. doi:10.1023/B:EDPR.0000026609.94841.2f

St. Amant, K., & Kelsey, S. (2011). *Computer mediated communication: Issues and approaches in education*. Hershey, PA: IGI Global.

Trautwein, U. (2007). The homework-achievement relation reconsidered: Differentiating homework time, homework frequency, and homework effort. *Learning and Instruction, 17*(3), 372–388. doi:10.1016/j.learninstruc.2007.02.009

Ulicsak, M., & Wright, M. (2010). *Games in education: Serious games*. Bristol, UK: Futurelab. Retrieved from http://www.futurelab.org

Usart, M., & Romero, M. (2012). Students' time perspective and its effects on game based learning. In *Proceedings of the 8th International Scientific Conference eLearning and Software for Education*. Bucharest, Romania: IEEE.

Usart, M., Romero, M., & Almirall, E. (2011). Impact of the feeling of knowledge explicitness in the learners' participation and performance in a collaborative game based learning activity. *Lecture Notes in Computer Science, 6944*, 23–35. doi:10.1007/978-3-642-23834-5_3

Wagner, P., Schober, B., & Spiel, C. (2008). Time students spend working at home for school. *Learning and Instruction, 18*, 309–320. doi:10.1016/j.learninstruc.2007.03.002

Wagstaff, R., & Mahmoudi, H. (1976). Relation of study behaviors and employment to academic performance. *Psychological Reports, 38*, 380–382. doi:10.2466/pr0.1976.38.2.380

Wassarman, H. S. (2002). The role of expectancies and time perspectives in gambling behaviour. *The Sciences and Engineering, 62*(8B), 3818.

Wellman, G. S., & Marcinkiewicz, H. (2004). Online learning and time-on-task: Impact of proctored vs. un-proctored testing. *Journal of Asynchronous Learning Networks, 8*(4), 93–104.

Zagal, J. P., & Mateas, M. (2010). Time in video-games: A survey and analysis. *Simulation & Gaming, 41*(6), 844–868. doi:10.1177/1046878110375594

Zakay, D. (1989). Subjective time and attentional resource allocation: An integrated model of time estimation. In Levin, I., & Zakay, D. (Eds.), *Time and Human Cognition: A Life-Span Perspective* (pp. 365–397). Amsterdam, The Netherlands: North-Holland. doi:10.1016/S0166-4115(08)61047-X

Zhang, Y., Goonetilleke, R. S., Plocher, T., & Liang, S.-F. M. (2005). Time-related behaviour in multitasking situations. *International Journal of Human-Computer Studies, 62*, 425–455. doi:10.1016/j.ijhcs.2005.01.002

Zimbardo, P. G., & Boyd, J. N. (1999). Putting time in perspective: A valid, reliable individual-differences metric. *Journal of Personality and Social Psychology, 77*, 1271–1288. doi:10.1037/0022-3514.77.6.1271

Zimbardo, P. G., Keough, K. A., & Boyd, J. N. (1997). Present time perspective as a predictor of risky driving. *Personality and Individual Differences, 23*, 1007–1023. doi:10.1016/S0191-8869(97)00113-X

Compilation of References

Abell, S. K., Lannin, J. K., Marra, R. M., Ehlert, M. W., Cole, J. S., & Lee, M. H. (2007). Multi-site evaluation of science and mathematics teacher professional development programs: The project profile approach. *Studies in Educational Evaluation, 33*, 135–158. doi:10.1016/j.stueduc.2007.04.003

Aberdeene, T. (2011). *Games for kids with learning disabilities*. Retrieved on March 15, 2012 from http://www.livestrong.com/article/214918-games_for_kids_with-learn

Able Trust. (1993). *Florida governor's alliance to the employment of disabled citizens, employer research kit*. Retrieved on March 5, 2012 from http://www.abletrust.org

ABMS. (2012). *Website*. Retrieved May 1, 2012, from http://www.abms.org/Maintenance_of_Certification/ABMS_MOC.aspx

Achtenhagen, L., & Johannisson, B. (2011). *Blogs as learning journals in entrepreneurship education – Enhancing reflexivity in digital times*. Paper presented at the Scandinavian Academy of Management Conference (NFF). Stockholm, Sweden.

Achtenhagen, L., & Johannisson, B. (2013b). The making of an intercultural learning context for entrepreneuring. *International Journal of Entrepreneurial Venturing*.

Achtenhagen, L., & Johannisson, B. (2013a). Context and ideology of teaching entrepreneurship in practice. In Weber, S., Oser, F., & Achtenhagen, F. (Eds.), *Entrepreneurship Education: Becoming an Entrepreneur*. Rotterdam, The Netherlands: SensePublishers.

Adelabu, D. H. (2007). Time perspective and school membership as correlates to academic achievement among African American adolescents. *Adolescence, 42*(167), 525–538.

Adleman, C. (2004). *Principal indicators of academic histories in postsecondary education: 1972-2000*. Washington, DC: U.S. Department of Education.

Alba, J. W., & Hashler, L. (1983). Is memory schematic? *Psycological Bulletin, 93*.

Aldrich, A. (2009). *The complete guide to simulations and serious games: How the most valuable content will be created in the age beyond Gutenberg to Google*. New York, NY: Pfeiffer.

Aldrich, C. (2004). *Simulations and the future of learning: an innovative (and perhaps revolutionary) approach to e-learning*. New York, NY: Pfeiffer.

Aldrich, C. (2009). *Learning online with games, simulations, and virtual worlds: Strategies for online instruction*. San Francisco, CA: Jossey-Bass.

Alexander, R. (2008). *Essays on pedagogy*. London, UK: Routledge.

Allen, G. J., Lerner, W. M., & Hinrichsen, J. J. (1972). Study behaviors and their relationships to test anxiety and academic performance. *Psychological Reports, 30*, 407–410. doi:10.2466/pr0.1972.30.2.407

Allen, J., & Walker, M. (1991). Training employees with disabilities: Strategies from corporate training. *The Journal for Vocational Special Needs Education, 18*(3), 105–108.

Alvesson, M., & Willmott, H. (1996). *Making sense of management: A critical introduction*. London, UK: Sage.

American Board of Medical Specialities. (2012). *Website*. Retrieved May 1, 2012, from http://www.abms.org/Maintenance_of_Certification/MOC_competencies.aspx

American Psychological Association. (2012). *Learning and memory*. Retrieved on September 18, 2012 from www.apa.org/topics/learning/index.aspx

American School in Japan. (2011). *Pros and cons of globalization*. Retrieved on February 21, 2012 from http://www.asij.ac.jp/highscholl/academic/ss/Economics/2nd semester

Amory, A. (2007). Game object model version II: A theoretical framework for educational game development. *Educational Technology Research and Development, 55*, 51–77. doi:10.1007/s11423-006-9001-x

Amory, A., Naicker, K., Vincent, J., & Adams, C. (1999). The use of computer games as an educational tool: Identification of appropriate game types and game elements. *British Journal of Educational Technology, 30*(4), 311–321. doi:10.1111/1467-8535.00121

Amory, A., & Seagram, R. (2003). Educational game models: Conceptualization and evaluation. *South African Journal of Higher Education, 17*(2), 206–217.

Ananiadou, K., & Claro, M. (2009). 21st century skills and competences for new millenniumm learners in OECD countries. EDUWorking paper no. 41. *Organization for Economic Cooperation and Development*. Retrieved from http://www.oecd-ilibrary.org/education/21st-century-skills-and-competences-for-new-millennium-learners-in-oecd-countries_218525261154

Ann Myers Medical Centre. (2012). *Website*. Retrieved May 1, 2012, from http://ammc.wordpress.com/

Apostolidis, T., & Fieulaine, N. (2004). Validation franç̧aise de l'e'chelle de temporalite´: The Zimbardo time perspective inventory. *European Review of Applied Psychology, 54*, 207–217. doi:10.1016/j.erap.2004.03.001

Arjunan, N. K. (2010). *Philosophical and sociological foundation in education*. Palakkad, India: Yuga Publications. Retrieved on February 23, 2012 from http/wiki.answers.com,Q

Arnab, S., Bellotti, F., de Freitas, S., Kiili, K., Ott, M., & Gloria, D. (2011). Serious games in education: Linking pedagogy and game design. In *Proceedings of ECGBL 2011*. Athens, Greece: ECGBL.

Arnab, S., Berta, R., Earp, J., de Freitas, S., Popescu, M., & Romero, M. (2012). Framing the adoption of serious games in formal education. *Electronic Journal of E-Learning, 10*(2), 159–171.

Asia e University. (2012). *Learning theories-cognitive learning theories. Asia e University, Knowledge Center*. AEU.

Atkinson, P., Coffey, A., Delamnont, S., Lofland, J., & Lofland, C. (2001). *Handbook of ethnography*. London, UK: Sage.

Atkinson, P., & Housley, W. (2003). *Interactionism: An essay in sociological amnesia*. London, UK: SAGE.

Auer, P., Couper-Kuhlen, E., & Muller, F. (1999). *Language in time: The rhythm and tempo of spoken interaction*. Oxford, UK: Oxford University Press.

Ausubel, D. (1969). *Meaningful learning*. Retrieved on September 12, 2012 from http://www.problemlearn.homestead.com/beduc/chapter_5.pdf

Azevedo, R. (2008). The role of self-regulation in learning about science with hypermedia. In Robinson, D., & Schraw, G. (Eds.), *Recent Innovations in Educational Technology that Facilitate Student Learning* (pp. 127–156). Academic Press.

Baek, Y. (2009). Digital Simulation in Teaching and Learning. In D. Gibson & Y. K. Baek (Eds.), Digital Simulations for Improving Education: Learning Through Artificial Teaching Environments (pp. 25-51). Hershey, PA: Information Science Reerence. IGI Global.

Bailey, B., & McInnis, K. (2011). Energy cost of exergaming: A comparison of the energy cost of 6 forms of exergaming. *Archives of Pediatrics & Adolescent Medicine, 165*(7). doi:10.1001/archpediatrics.2011.15

Bannert, M. (2002). Managing cognitive load—Recent trends in cognitive load theory. *Learning and Instruction, 12*, 139–146. doi:10.1016/S0959-4752(01)00021-4

Barab, S. A., Hay, K. E., Barnett, M. G., & Squire, K. (2001). Constructing virtual worlds: Tracing the historical development of learner practices/understandings. *Cognition and Instruction, 19*(1), 47–94. doi:10.1207/S1532690XCI1901_2

Barab, S., Pettyjohn, P., Gresalfi, M., Volk, C., & Solomou, M. (2012). Game-based curriculum and transformational play: Designing to meaningfully positioning person, content, and context. *Computers & Education, 58*(1), 518–533. doi:10.1016/j.compedu.2011.08.001

Barab, S., Thomas, M., Dodge, T., Carteaux, R., & Tuzun, H. (2005). Making learning fun: Quest Atlantis, a game without guns. *Educational Technology Research and Development, 53*(1), 86–107. doi:10.1007/BF02504859

Barach, P., Satish, U., & Streufert, S. (2001). Healthcare assessment and performance: Using simulation. *Simulation & Gaming*. Retrieved from http://sag.sagepub.com/content/32/2/147.abstract

Barbour, M. K., & Evans, M. (2009). Making sense of video games: pre-service teachers struggle with this new medium. In *Proceedings of the 20th International Conference of the Society of Informational Technology and Teacher Education,* (pp. 1367–1371). Chesapeake, VA: AACE.

Barbour, M., Rieber, L. P., Thomas, G., & Rauscher, D. (2009). Homemade powerpoint games: A constructivist alternative to webquests. *TechTrends, 53*(5), 54–59. doi:10.1007/s11528-009-0326-2

Barth, F. (2002). An anthropology of knowledge. *Current Anthropology, 43*(1), 1–18. doi:10.1086/324131

Barton, D., & Hamilton, M. (2005). Literacy, reification and the dynamics of social interaction. In Barton, D., & Tusting, K. (Eds.), *Beyond Communities of Practice: Language, Power and Social Context*. Cambridge, UK: Cambridge University Press. doi:10.1017/CBO9780511610554.003

Basel Declaration. (2012). *Website*. Retrieved May 1, 2012, from http://admin.uems.net/uploadedfiles/35.pdf

Bateman, C. M., & Boon, R. (2006). *21st century game design*. Hingham, MA: Charles River Media.

Baumol, W. J. (1990). Entrepreneurship: Productive, unproductive, and destructive. *The Journal of Political Economy, 98*(5), 893–921. doi:10.1086/261712

Becker, K. (2007). Teaching teachers about serious games. In C. Montgomerie & J. Seale (Eds.), *Proceedings of World Conference on Educational Multimedia, Hypermedia and Telecommunications 2007,* (pp. 2389-2396). Chesapeake, VA: AACE.

Becker, K. (2007). Digital game-based learning once removed: Teaching teachers. *British Journal of Educational Technology, 38*(3), 478–488. doi:10.1111/j.1467-8535.2007.00711.x

Becker, K. (2008). Video game pedagogy: Good games = good pedagogy. In Thomas Miller, C. (Ed.), *Games: Purpose and Potential in Education* (pp. 73–125). New York, NY: Springer.

Bedwell, W. L., & Salas, E. (2010). Computer-based training: Capitalizing on lessons learned. *International Journal of Training and Development, 14*(3), 239–249. doi:10.1111/j.1468-2419.2010.00355.x

Belanich, J., Sibley, D. E., & Orvis, K. L. (2004). *Instructional characteristics and motivational features of a PC based game*. Washington, DC: US Army Research Institute for the Behavioral & Social Sciences.

Bella, N., & Belkachla, S. (2000). *Impact of demographic trends on the achievement of the millenium development and goal of universal primary education*. Geneva, Switzerland: UNESCO.

Bellotti, F., Berta, R., & De Gloria, A. (2010). Designing effective serious games: Opportunities and challenges for research. *International Journal of Emerging Technologies in Learning, 5,* 22–35.

Belmont, J. M., & Butterfield, E. C. (1971). Learning strategies as determinants of memory deficiencies. *Cognitive Psychology, 2*(4), 411–420. doi:10.1016/0010-0285(71)90024-7

Berglund, K., Johannisson, B., & Schwarz, B. (Eds.). (2013). *Societal entrepreneurship – Positioning, penetrating, promoting*. Cheltenham, UK: Edward Elgar.

Berglund, K., & Johansson, A. W. (2013). Dark and bright effects of a polarized entrepreneurship discourse … and the prospects of transformation. In Berglund, K., Johannisson, B., & Schwarz, B. (Eds.), *Societal Entrepreneurship – Positioning, Penetrating, Promoting*. Cheltenham, UK: Edward Elgar.

Berlekamp, E. (2000). *The dots-and-boxes game: Sophisticated child's play*. Boston, MA: A. K. Peters.

Berlin Chamber of Physicians. (2012). *Website*. Retrieved May 1, 2012, from http://www.aerztekammer-berlin.de/60englisch/index.html

Berliner, D. (1984). The half-full glass: A review of research on teaching. In Hosford, P. (Ed.), *Using What We Know about Teaching*. Alexandria, VA: Association for Supervision and Curriculum Development.

Bianchi-Berthouze, N. (2013). Understanding the role of body movement in player engagement. *Human-Computer Interaction*.

Biddle, B. J. (1997). Recent research on the role of the teacher. In Biddle, B. J., Good, T. L., & Goodson, I. (Eds.), *International Handbook of Teachers and Teaching* (pp. 499–520). New York, NY: Springer.

Biesta, G. (2010). *What is education for? Good education in an age of measurement: Ethics, politics, democracy*. Boulder, CO: Paradigm Publishers.

Biesta, G., & Burbules, N. (2003). *Pragmatism and educational research*. Lanham, MD: Rowman & Littlefield.

BinSubaih, A., Maddock, S., & Romano, D. (2006). A serious game for traffic accident investigators. *International Journal of Interactive Technology and Smart Education*, *3*(4), 329–346. doi:10.1108/17415650680000071

Black, R. W., & Steinkuehler, C. (2009). Literacy in virtual worlds. In Christenbury, L., Bomer, R., & Smagorinsky, P. (Eds.), *Handbook of Adolescent Literacy Research* (pp. 271–286). New York, NY: Guilford.

Blake, M. J. F. (1967). Relationship between circadian rhythm of body temperature and introversion-extroversion. *Nature*, *215*, 896–897. doi:10.1038/215896a0

Block, R. A. (1974). Memory and the experience of duration in retrospect. *Memory & Cognition*, *2*, 53–160. doi:10.3758/BF03197508

Bloom, B. (1987). *The closing of the American mind*. New York, NY: Simon and Schuster.

Bloomfield, P. R., & Livingstone, D. (2009). Multi-modal learning and assessment in second life with quizHUD. In *Proceedings of the 2009 Conference in Games and Virtual Worlds for Serious Applications*, (pp. 217-218). IEEE.

Bluedorn, A. C., & Denhardt, R. B. (1988). Time and organizations. *Journal of Management*, *14*, 299–320. doi:10.1177/014920638801400209

Boeckenhoft, I. (2012). *Qualifications in international management*. Retrieved on March 15, 2012 from http://www.sm/de

Bonis, J. (2007). Acute wiiitis. *The New England Journal of Medicine*, *356*(23), 2431–2432. doi:10.1056/NEJMc070670

Botermans, J. (2008). *The book of games: Strategy, tactics & history*. New York, NY: Sterling Publishing Co., Inc.

Bottino, R. M., Ferlino, L., Ott, M., & Tavella, M. (2007). Developing strategic and reasoning abilities with computer games at primary school level. *Computers & Education*, *49*(4), 1272–1286. doi:10.1016/j.compedu.2006.02.003

Bottino, R. M., & Ott, M. (2006). Mind games, reasoning skills, and the primary school curriculum. *Learning, Media and Technology*, *31*(4), 359–375. doi:10.1080/17439880601022981

Bourgonjon, J., & Hanghøj, T. (2011). What does it mean to be a game literate teacher? Interviews with teachers who translate games into educational practice. In *Proceedings for the 5th European Conference on Games Based Learning*, (pp. 67-74). Reading, MA: Academic Publishing Limited.

Bowers, H. (2006). *Curriculum design in vocational education*. Paper presented at the Conference of the Australian Associations for research in Education. Adelaide, Australia.

Bradley, P. (2006). The history of simulation in medical education and possible future directions. *Medical Education*, *40*(3), 254–262. doi:10.1111/j.1365-2929.2006.02394.x

Bragg, L. A. (2006). *The impact of mathematical games on learning, attitudes, and behaviours*. (Doctoral Thesis). La Trobe University. Melbourne, Australia.

Bragg, L. (2007). Students' conflicting attitudes towards games as a vehicle for learning mathematics: A methodological dilemma. *Mathematics Education Research Journal*, *19*(1), 29–44. doi:10.1007/BF03217448

Bransford, J. D., & Donovan, M. S. (2005). Scientific inquiry and how people learn. In Donovan, M. S., & Bransford, J. D. (Eds.), *How Students Learn: Science in the Classroom* (pp. 397–420). Washington, DC: National Academies Press.

Brown, W. T., & Jones, J. M. (2004). The substance of things hoped for: A study of the future orientation, minority status perceptions, academic engagement, and academic performance of black high school students. *The Journal of Black Psychology, 30*(2), 248–273. doi:10.1177/0095798403260727

Brubaker, B. (2006, March 11). Teachers join the dance dance revolution: Educators begin training to use the exercise video game. *The Dominion Post*. Retrieved from http://www.redorbit.com/news/scifi-gaming/424434/teachers_join_the__dance_dance_revolution/index.html

Bruner, J. (1985). Narratives and paradigmatics modes of thought. In Eisner, E. (Ed.), *Learning and Teaching the Ways of Knowing* (pp. 97–115). Chicago, IL: University of Chicago Press.

Bruner, J. (1986). *Actual minds, possible words*. Cambridge, MA: Harvard University Press.

Bruner, J. (1990). *Acts of meaning*. Cambridge, MA: Harvard University Press.

Bruner, J. (1996). Frames for thinking: Ways of making meaning. In Olson, D. R., & Torrance, N. (Eds.), *Modes of Thought: Explorations in Culture and Cognition* (pp. 93–105). Cambridge, UK: Cambridge University Press.

Bruner, J. (1996). *The culture of education*. Cambridge, MA: Harvard University Press.

Bruner, J. (2002). *Making stories: Law, literature, life*. Cambridge, MA: Harvard University Press.

Bryan, R., Kreuter, M., & Brownson, R. (2009). Integrating adult learning principles into training for public health practice. *Health Promotion Practice, 10*(4), 557–563. doi:10.1177/1524839907308117

Buckingham, D. (2000). *After the death of childhood: Growing up in the age of electronic media*. Cambridge, MA: Polity Press.

Buckingham, D. (2003). *Media education: Literacy, learning and contemporary culture*. Cambridge, MA: Polity Press.

Buckingham, D., & Scanlon, M. (2005). Selling learning: towards a political economy of edutainmnet media. *Media Culture & Society, 27*(1), 41–58. doi:10.1177/0163443705049057

Bureau of Labour Statistics. (2011). *Occupational employment statistics of 2010*. Retrieved on February 18, 2012 from www.blsr.gov/oes/current/oes_net.htm

Buttori, L., & Loh, C. S. (2009). Once upon a game: Rediscovering the roots of games in education. In Miller, C. T. (Ed.), *Games: Purpose and Potential in Education* (pp. 1–22). New York, NY: Springer. doi:10.1007/978-0-387-09775-6_1

Caillois, R. (1990). *Os jogos e os homens*. Lisboa, Portugal: Cotovia.

Caldwell, J. H., Huitt, W. G., & Graeber, A. O. (1982). Time spent in learning: Implications from research. *The Elementary School Journal, 82*, 471–480. doi:10.1086/461282

Callaway, C. B. (2002). Narrative prose generation. *Artificial Intelligence, 139*(2), 213–252. doi:10.1016/S0004-3702(02)00230-8

Camurri, A., Lagerlof, I., & Volpe, G. (2003). Emotions and cue extraction from dance movements. *Journal of Human Computer Studies, 59*(1-2), 213–225. doi:10.1016/S1071-5819(03)00050-8

Can, G., & Cagiltay, K. (2006). Turkish prospective teachers' perceptions regarding the use of computer games with educational features. *Journal of Educational Technology & Society, 9*(1), 308–321.

Cannon-Bowers, J. A., Bowers, C., & Procci, J. (2011). Using video games as educational tools in healthcare. In Tobias, S., & Fletcher, J. D. (Eds.), *Computer Games and Instruction* (pp. 47–72). Hershey, PA: IGI Global.

Capdeferro, N., & Romero, M. (2012). Are online learners frustrated with collaborative learning experiences. *International Review of Research in Open and Distance Learning, 13*(2), 26–44.

Cardiologia Port 46. (2001). *Website*. Retrieved May 1, 2012, from https://www.ordemdosmedicos.pt/?lop=conteudo&op=3cf166c6b73f030b4f67eeaeba301103&id=dd055f53a45702fe05e449c30ac80df9

Careers for People with Disabilities. (2012). *Opening the door to new opportunities*. Retrieved on March 10, 2012 from http://www.careersforpeoplewithdisabikities.org/employe

Carr, D., Buckingham, D., Burn, A., & Schott, G. (2006). *Computer games: Text, narrative and play*. Cambridge, MA: Polity Press.

Carter, K. (1993). The place of story in the study of teaching and teacher education. *Educational Researcher, 22*(1), 5–18.

Castelli, D. M., Hillman, C. H., Buck, S. M., & Erwin, H. E. (2007). Physical fitness and academic achievement in third- and fifth-grade students. *Journal of Sport & Exercise Psychology, 29*, 239–252.

Castells, M. (2000). *La era de la información: La sociedad red*. Madrid, Spain: Alianza.

Castells, M. (2001). *The internet galaxy: Reflections on the internet, business, and society*. Oxford, UK: Oxford University Press.

Castro, J. P., & Rodrigues, M. (2008). *Sentido de número e organização de dados: Textos de apoio para Educadores de Infância*. Lisboa, Portugal: DGIDC, ME.

Catarino, I. (2007). O metromachia, um jogo geométrico. *Boletim da Sociedade Portuguesa de Matemática*, 105-122.

Cavanagh, S. (2008). Playing games in class helps students grasp math. *Education Week*, 43–46.

Charness, N., Reingold, E. M., Pomplun, M., & Stampe, D. M. (2001). The perceptual aspect of skilled performance in chess: Evidence from eye movements. *Memory & Cognition, 29*(8), 1146–1152. doi:10.3758/BF03206384

Charsky, D., & Ressler, W. (2011). Games are made for fun: Lessons on the effects of concept maps in the classroom use of computer games. *Computers & Education, 56*, 604–615. doi:10.1016/j.compedu.2010.10.001

Chen, P. Y., & Popovich, P. M. (2002). *Correlation: Parametric and nonparametric measures*. Thousand Oaks, CA: Sage.

Christensen, U., Heffernan, D., & Barach, P. (2001). Microsimulators in medical education: An overview. *Simulation & Gaming, 32*(2), 250–262. doi:10.1177/104687810103200212

Christmann, E. P., & Badgett, J. L. (2009). *Interpreting assessment data: Statistical techniques you can use*. Washington, DC: NSTA Press.

Chtaini, M. (2011). Has the Keynesian economic theory failed? *MoroccoBoard News Service*. Retrieved on February 21, 2012 from http://www.moroccoboard.com/home

Churces, A. (2008). *Bloom's taxonomy*. Retrieved from http://edweb.sdsu.edu/courses/EDTEC470/sp09/5/bloomstaxanomy.html

Clandinin, D. J., & Connelly, F. M. (1992). Teacher as curriculum maker. In Jackson, P. (Ed.), *Handbook of Curriculum Research* (pp. 363–401). New York, NY: MacMillan.

Clidière, M. (1968). *Le guide marabout des jeux de société*. Verviers, Belgium: Editions Gérard & C°.

Cohen, L., & Manion, L. (1989). *Research methods in education* (3rd ed.). London, UK: Routledge.

Coiro, J., Knobel, M., Lankshear, C., & Leu, D. (2008). Central issues in new literacies and new literacies research. In Coiro, J., Knobel, M., Lankshear, C., Knobel, M., Lankshear, C., & Leu, D. (Eds.), *Handbook of Research on New Literacies*. New York, NY: Taylor & Francis.

Colceag, F. (2001). *The relationship between education, economy and social systems*. Retrieved on February 23, 2012 from http://www.austega.com/florin/

Coleman, S., & Dyer-Witheford, N. (2007). Playing on the digital commons: Collectivities, capital and contestation in videogame culture. *Media Culture & Society, 29*(6), 934–953. doi:10.1177/0163443707081700

Coll, C. (2005). Lectura y alfabetismo en la sociedad de la información. *UOC Papers, 1*. Retrieved July 21, 2010, from http://www.uoc.edu/uocpapers/1/dt/esp/coll.pdf

Collins, B., & Moonen, J. (2001). *Flexible learning in a digital world*. London, UK: Kegan Page Ltd.

Commission of the European Communities. (2007). *A coherent framework of indicators and benchmarks for monitoring progress towards the Lisbon objectives in education and training*. Retrieved September 15, 2012, from http://eur-lex.europa.eu/LexUriServ/site/en/com/2007/com2007_0061en01.pdf

Connolly, C. T., & Tenenbaum, G. (2010). Exertion–attention–flow linkage under different workloads. *Journal of Applied Social Psychology, 40*(5), 1123–1145. doi:10.1111/j.1559-1816.2010.00613.x

Continuing, U. E. M. S. Medical Education. (2012). *Website*. Retrieved May 1, 2012, from http://admin.uems. net/uploadedfiles/174.pdf

Coobs, N. (1989). *Education for persons with physical disabilities*. Paper presented at a Meeting. Milton Keynes, UK.

Cooper, J., & Taqueti, V. (2004). A brief history of the development of mannequin simulators for clinical education and training. *Quality & Safety in Health Care, 13*, 11–18. doi:10.1136/qshc.2004.009886

Corazza, S., Muendermann, L., Chadhari, A., Demattio, T., Cobelli, C., & Andriacchi, T. (2006). A markerless motion capture system to study musculoskeletal biomechanics: Visual hull and simulated annealing approach. *Annals of Biomedical Engineering, 34*(6), 1019–1029. doi:10.1007/s10439-006-9122-8

Corti, K. (2006). *Game-based business and management skill development*. Retrieved from http://www.pixelearning.com/docs/games_basedlearning_pixelearning.pdf

Corti, K. (2006). *Gamesbased learning a serious business application*. Retrieved from http://202.119.101.57/upload/2006_09/06091415525749.pdf

Cowley, A. D., & Minnaar, G. (2008). Watch out for wii shoulder. *British Medical Journal, 336*, 110. doi:10.1136/bmj.39461.631181.BE

Crawford, C. (1984). *The art of computer game design*. Berkeley, CA: Osborne/McGraw-Hill.

Csikszentmihalyi, M. (1975). *Beyond boredom and anxiety*. San Francisco, CA: Jossey-Bass.

Csikszentmihalyi, M. (1991). *Flow: The psychology of optimal experience*. New York, NY: Harper Perennial.

Csikszentmihalyi, M. (1997). *Creativity: Flow and the psychology of discovery and invention*. New York, NY: Harper Collins.

Cunliffe, A. L. (2004). On becoming a critically reflective practitioner. *Journal of Management Education, 28*(4), 407–426. doi:10.1177/1052562904264440

Dale, E. (2009). *How much do we remember? Guide to student success*. San Luis Obispo, CA: Cuesta College.

Daley, A. (2009). Can exergaming contribute to improving physical activity levels and health outcomes in children? *Pediatrics, 124*(2), 763–771. doi:10.1542/peds.2008-2357

Day, R. (2006). Challenges of biological realism and validation in simulation-based medical education. *Artificial Intelligence in Medicine, 38*, 47–66. doi:10.1016/j.artmed.2006.01.001

de Bilde, J., Vansteenkiste, M., & Lens, W. (2011). Understanding the association between future time perspective and self-regulated learning through the lens of self-determination theory. *Learning and Instruction, 21*(3), 332–344. doi:10.1016/j.learninstruc.2010.03.002

de Block, L., Buckingham, D., & Banaji, S. (2005). *Children in communication about migration: Final report*. London, UK: University of London.

de Freitas, S. (2012). *Learning in immersive worlds: A review of game-based learning JISC e-learning programme*. Retrieved from http://www.jisc.ac.uk/media/documents/programmes/elearninginnovation/gamingreport_v3.pdf

de Freitas, S. (2012). *New pedagogical approaches in game enhanced learning: Curriculum integration*. Hershey, PA: IGI Global.

de Freitas, S., J. S. (2007). Serious games—Engaging training solutions: A research and development project for supporting training needs. *British Journal of Educational Technology, 38*(3), 523–525. doi:10.1111/j.1467-8535.2007.00716.x

de Freitas, S., & Oliver, M. (2006). How can exploratory learning with games and simulations within the curriculum be most effectively evaluated? *Computers & Education, 46*(3), 249–264. doi:10.1016/j.compedu.2005.11.007

de Freitas, S., Rebolledo-Mendez, G., Liarokapis, F., Magoulas, G., & Poulovassilis, A. (2010). Learning as immersive experiences: Using the four dimensional framework for designing and evaluating immersive learning experiences in a virtual world. *British Journal of Educational Technology, 41*(1), 69–85. doi:10.1111/j.1467-8535.2009.01024.x

del Castillo, H., Herrero, D., Monjelat, N., García-Varela, A. B., & Checa, M. (2011). *Identity & performance: Developing innovative educational settings through sport videogames*. Madrid, Spain: IATED.

Denson, J., & Abrahamson, S. (1969). A computer controlled patient simulator. *Journal of the American Medical Association, 208*(3), 504–515. doi:10.1001/jama.1969.03160030078009

Derryberry, A. (2007). *Serious games- Online games for learning.* Retrieved from http://www.adobe.com/products/director/pdfs/serious_games_wp_1107.pdf

DeSantis, N. (2012). *A boom time for education start-ups.* Retrieved from http://chronicle.com/article/A-Boom-Time-for-Education/131229/

Devlin, K. (1997). *Mathematics: The science of patterns.* New York, NY: Scientific American Library.

Dewey, J. (1916). *Democracy and education: An introduction to the philosophy of education.* New York, NY: The Free Press.

Dewey, J. (1922). *Human nature and conduct: An introduction to social psychology.* New York, NY: Cosimo Classics.

Dewey, J. (1997). *Experience and education.* New York, NY: Simon and Schuster.

DfES. (2003). *Excellence and enjoyment: A strategy for primary schools.* London, UK: DfES.

DGIDC. (2007). *Programa de matemática do ensino básico.* Retrieved January 4, 2008 from http://sitio.dgidc.min-edu.pt/PressReleases/Paginas/ProgramadeMatematicadoEnsinoBasico.aspx

Díaz-Morales, J. F. (2006). Estructura factorial y fiabilidad del inventario de perspectiva temporal de Zimbardo. *Psicothema, 18*(3), 565–571.

Diehl, L., Lehmann, E., Souza, R., Alves, J., Esteves, R., & Gordan, P. (2011). A serious game prototype for education of medical doctors and students about insulin management for the treatment of diabetes mellitus. In *Proceedings of the IEEE 1st International Conference on Serious Games and Applications for Health*, (pp. 70-73). IEEE Press.

Dimension, M. (2010). *Tabula digita video games add up fast: One million DimensionM games played by math students.* New York, NY: DimensionM.

Directives, E. U. (2012). *The EU single market.* Retrieved May 1, 2012, from http://ec.europa.eu/internal_market/qualifications/directive_in_practice/automatic_recognition/doctors/index_en.htm

Dixon, B. (2011). *When will educators get serious about gaming?* Retrieved from http://blogs.hbr.org/innovations-in-education/2011/03/when-will-educators-get-seriou.html

Djaouti, D., Alvarez, J., & Jessel, J. P. (2011). *Classifying serious games: The G/P/S model.* Hershey, PA: IGI Global. doi:10.4018/978-1-60960-495-0.ch006

Donnelly, J., & Lambourne, K. (2011). Classsroom-based physical activity, cognition, and academic achievement. *Preventive Medicine, 52*(1), 36–42. doi:10.1016/j.ypmed.2011.01.021

Dorn, J. (1989). Simulation games: One more tool on the pedagogical shelf. *Teaching Sociology, 17*(1), 1–18. doi:10.2307/1317920

Douglass, J. A. (2010). *Higher education budgets and the global recession.* Retrieved on February 23, 2012 from http://cshe.berkeley.edu/

Downes, S. (1998). *The future of online learning.* Paper presented at the NAWeb 1998 meeting. Fredericton, Canada.

Dreyfus, H. L., & Dreyfus, S. E. (1986). *Mind over machine: The power of human intuition and expertise in the era of the computer.* New York, NY: The Free Press.

Driskell, J. E., & Dwyer, D. J. (1984). Microcomputer videogames based training. *Educational Technology Research and Development, 44*(2).

Duchowski, A. T. (2007). *Eye tracking methodology - Theory and practice* (2nd ed.). Berlin, Germany: Springer.

Dunwell, I., de Freitas, S., & Jarvis, S. (2011). Four-dimensional consideration of feedback in serious games. In de Freitas, S., & Maharg, P. (Eds.), *Digital Games and Learning* (pp. 42–62). Continuum Publishing.

Dzinory, M. (2005). *Ids digital game-based learning (DGL) situated learning?* Austin, TX: University of Texas.

Egenfeldt-Nielsen, S. (2005). *Beyond edutainment, exploring the educational potential of computer games.* (Unpublished Dissertation). IT University of Copenhagen. Copenhagen, Denmark.

Egenfeldt-Nielsen, S. (2004). Practical barriers in using educational computer games. *Horizon, 12*(1), 18–21. doi:10.1108/10748120410540454

Egenfeldt-Nielsen, S. (2007). Third generation educational use of computer games. *Journal of Educational Multimedia and Hypermedia, 16*(3), 263–281.

England, D., Randles, M., Fergus, P., & Taleb-Bendiab, A. (2009). Towards and advanced framework for whole body interaction. In *Proceedings of 3rd International Conference on Virtual and Mixed Reality.* Berlin, Germany: Springer Verlag.

England, D. (2011). Whole body interaction: An introduction. In *Whole Body Interaction* (pp. 1–6). Berlin, Germany: Springer. doi:10.1007/978-0-85729-433-3_1

Ermi, L., & Mäyrä, F. (2005). Fundamental components of the gameplay experience: Analysing immersion. In *Proceedings of the DiGRA Conference Changing Views: Worlds in Play,* (pp. 15 – 27). DiGRA.

Ertzberger, J. (2009). An exploration of factors affecting teachers' use of video games as instructional tools. In *Proceedings of the 20th International Conference of the Society of Informational Technology and Teacher Education,* (pp. 1825–1831). Chesapeake, VA: AACE.

Ertzberger, J. (2010). *Everybody wins: A teacher's guide to customizing games for any curriculum.* Retrieved October 13, 2011, from http://www.uncw.edu

Esnaola Horacek, G. (2006). *Claves culturales en la construcción del conocimiento: ¿Qué enseñan los videojuegos?* Buenos Aires, Argentina: Alfagrama.

Euler (2011). *The PRIMAS project: Promoting inquiry-based learning (IBL) in mathematics and science education across Europe.* Retrieved September 15, 2012, from http://www.primasproject.eu/servlet/supportBinaryFiles ?referenceId=8&supportId=1247

European Commission, Directorate-General for Education and Culture. (2004). *Working group D 'mathematics, science and technology' objective 1.4 "increasing recruitment to scientific and technical studies" Interim report.* Retrieved September 15, 2012, from http://ec.europa.eu/education/policies/2010/doc/math2004.pdf

European Commission. Directorate-General for Research. (2007). *Science education now: A renewed pedagogy for the future of Europe: Report of the high-level group on science education.* Retrieved September 15, 2012, from http://ec.europa.eu/research/science-society/document_library/pdf_06/report-rocard-on-science-education_en.pdf

European Commission. Eurostat. (2010). *Percentage of rates of low educational attainment per age.* Geneva, Switzerland: Eurostat.

Eurostat. (2011). *Unemployment statistics.* Geneva, Switzerland: Eurostat.

EU-SILK. (2011). *The situation of working age people with disabilities across the EU.* Geneva, Switzerland: EU-SILK.

Facer, K. (2003). *Computer games and learning: Why do we think it's worth talking about computer games and learning in the same breath?* London, UK: Futurelab.

Fang, D., & Nuefeld, Y. (2007). The role of information technology in technology-mediated learning: A review of the past for the future. *Journal of Information Systems Education, 18*(2), 183–192.

Fayolle, A., & Matley, H. (Eds.). (2010). *Handbook of research on social entrepreneurship.* Cheltenham, UK: Edward Elgar.

Felicia, P. (2009). *Digital games in schools: A handbook for teachers.* Brussels, Belgium: European Schoolnet. Retrieved September 15, 2012, from http://games.eun.org/upload/GIS_handbook_en.pdf

Ferreira, D., & Palhares, P. (2009). The ability to identify patterns. In *Proceedings of the Elementary Mathematics Education,* (pp. 209-216). Braga, Portugal: AEME.

Ferreira, D., & Palhares, P. (2008). Chess and problem solving involving patterns. *The Montana Math Enthusiast, 5*(2-3), 249–256.

Filguth, R. (2007). *A importância do xadrez.* Porto Alegre, Brazil: Artmed.

Fisher, C., Berliner, D., Filby, N., Marliave, R., Cahen, L., & Dishaw, M. (1980). Teaching behaviors, academic learning time, and student achievement: An overview. In Denham, C., & Lieberman, A. (Eds.), *Time to Learn.* Washington, DC: National Institute of Education.

Fletcher, J. D., & Tobias, S. (2006). Using computer games and simulations for instruction: A research review. In *Proceedings of the Society for Advanced Learning Technology Meeting.* Orlando, FL: IEEE.

Fogg, B. J. (2002). *Persuasive technology: Using computers to change what we think and do.* San Francisco, CA: Morgan Kaufmann. doi:10.1145/764008.763957

Foreman, J. (2004). Game-based learning: How to delight and instruct in the 21st century. *EDUCAUSE Review, 39*(5), 50–66.

Forrest, F., & Taylor, M. (1998). High level simulators in medical education. *Hospital Medicine (London, England), 59*, 653–655.

Frasca, G. (2003). Simulation versus narrative: Introduction to ludology. In Wolf, M. J. P., & Perron, B. (Eds.), *The Video Game Theory Reader*. London, UK: Routledge.

Friedrich, R., Peterson, M., & Koster, A. (2011). *The rise of generation C.* Retrieved from http://www.strategy-business.com/article/11110

Frost, G. (2008). *What is memory retention?* Retrieved from http://ezinearticles.com/?What-is-Memory-Retention?&id=996416

Fukui, Y., & Smith, N. (1981). Interaction among ventilation, the circulation, and the uptake and distribution of halothane—Use of a hybrid computer multiple model: I: The basic model. *Anesthesiology, 54*, 107–118. doi:10.1097/00000542-198102000-00003

Fukui, Y., & Smith, N. (1981). Interaction among ventilation, the circulation, and the uptake and distribution of halothane—Use of a hybrid computer multiple model: II: Spontaneous vs. controlled ventilation and the effects of CO2. *Anesthesiology, 54*, 199–224.

Futurelab. (2009). *NFER teacher voice omnibus February 2009 survey: Using computer games in the classroom.* London, UK: Futurelab.

Gaba, D., Howard, S., Fish, K., Smith, B., & Sowb, Y. (2001). Simulation-based training in anesthesia crisis resource management (ACRM): A decade of experience. *Simulation & Gaming, 32*(2), 175–193. doi:10.1177/104687810103200206

Gallagher, A., McClure, N., McGuigan, J., Crothers, I., & Browning, J. (1999). Virtual reality training in laparoscopic surgery: A preliminary assessment of minimally invasive surgical trainer virtual reality (MIST VR). *Endoscopy, 31*(4), 310–313. doi:10.1055/s-1999-15

García-Varela, A. B., del Castillo, H., Checa, M., Monjelat, N., & Herrero, D. (2011). *Learning to be digital producers: Writing a school newspaper.* Madrid, Spain: IATED.

Garris, R., Ahlers, R., & Driskell, J. E. (2002). Games, motivation, and learning: A research and practice model. *Simulation & Gaming, 33*(4), 441–467. doi:10.1177/1046878102238607

Gas Man. (2012). *Website.* Retrieved May 1, 2012, from http://www.gasmanweb.com/

Gee, J. (2004). *Learning by design: Games as learning machines.* Paper presented at the Game Developers Conference. San Jose, CA.

Gee, J. P. (2001). *Literacy development, early and late: Ownership, identity, and discourse.* Paper presented at the International Literacy Conference: "Literacy and Language in Global and Local Settings: New Directions for Research and Teaching". New York, NY.

Gee, J. P. (2000). The new literacy studies: From "socially situated" to the work of the social. In Barton, D., Hamilton, M., & Ivanic, R. (Eds.), *Situated Literacies: Reading and Writing in Context*. London, UK: Routledge.

Gee, J. P. (2004). *Situated language and learning: A critique of traditional schooling.* New York, NY: Routledge.

Gee, J. P. (2007). *What video games have to teach about learning and literacy.* New York, NY: Palgrave Macmillan.

Gee, J. P. (2008). Video games and embodiment. *Games and Culture, 3*(3-4), 253–263. doi:10.1177/1555412008317309

Gee, J. P. (2011). Reflections on empirical evidence on games and learning. In Tobias, S., & Fletcher, J. D. (Eds.), *Computer Games and Instruction* (pp. 223–232). Albany, NY: State University of New York.

Gee, J. P., & Hayes, E. (2009). No quitting without saving after bad events: Gaming paradigms and learning in the Sims. *International Journal of Learning and Media, 1*(3), 49–65. doi:10.1162/ijlm_a_00024

Gershenfeld, A. (2011). From player to designer. *Educational Gaming, 40*(1), 55–59.

Goffman, E. (1961). Fun in games. In *Encounters*. Indianapolis, IN: Bobbs-Merrill Company.

Goffman, E. (1974). *Frame analysis: An essay on the organization of experience.* New York, NY: Harper & Row.

Goodrum, D., Hackling, M., & Rennie, L. (2001). *The status and quality of teaching and learning of science in Australian schools: A research report.* Canberra, Australia: Department of Education, Training and Youth Affairs.

Gorgu, L., O'Hare, G. M. P., & O'Grady, M. J. (2009). Towards mobile collaborative exergaming. In *Proceedings of the 2nd International Conference on Advances in Human-Oriented and Personalized Mechanisms, Technologies, and Services,* (pp. 61-64). Porto, Portugal: IEEE.

Graf, D. L., Pratt, L. V., Hester, C. N., & Short, K. R. (2009). Playing active video games increases energy expenditure in children. *Pediatrics, 124*(2), 534–540. doi:10.1542/peds.2008-2851

Granström, H. (2010). *Det barnsliga manifestet.* Stockholm, Sweden: Ink bokförlag.

Graves, L., Stratton, G., Ridgers, N. D., & Cable, N. T. (2007). Comparison of energy expenditure in adolescents when playing new generation and sedentary computer games: Cross sectional study. *British Medical Journal, 335,* 1282–1284. doi:10.1136/bmj.39415.632951.80

Gray, D. E. (2007). Facilitating management learning: Developing critical reflection through reflective tools. *Management Learning, 38*(5), 495–517. doi:10.1177/1350507607083204

Gredler, M. (1994). *Designing and evaluating games and simulations.* Gulf Professional Publishing.

Greenblat, C. (2001). The design and redesign of gaming simulations on health care issues. *Simulation & Gaming, 32*(3), 315–330. doi:10.1177/104687810103200303

Greenwald, A. G., & Gilmore, G. M. (1997). No pain, no gain? The importance of measuring course workload in student ratings of instruction. *Journal of Educational Psychology, 89*(4), 743–751. doi:10.1037/0022-0663.89.4.743

Gregory, G., & Chapman, C. (2007). *Differentiated instructional strategies: One size doesn't fit all* (2nd ed.). San Francisco, CA: Corwin Press.

Gros, B. (2002). La dimensión socioeducativa de los videojuegos. *Edutec: Revista Electrónica de Tecnología Educativa, 12.*

Gros, B., Barberà, E., & Kirschner, P. (2010). Time factor in e-learning: Impact literature review. *eLC Research Paper Series, 0,* 1-32.

Gros, B. (1998). *Jugando con videojuegos: Educación y entretenimiento.* Bilbao, Spain: Desclée de Brouwer.

Gros, B. (2004). *Pantallas, juegos y educación: La alfabetización digital en la escuela.* Bilbao, Spain: Desclée de Brouwe.

Gros, B. (2008). *Videojuegos y aprendizaje.* Barcelona, Spain: Graó.

Gros, B., & Silva, J. (2005). La formación del profesorado como docentes en los espacios virtuales de aprendizaje. *Revista Iberoamericana de Educación, 36,* 2–16.

Gudmunsen, J. (2006). *Movement aims to get serious about games.* Retrieved from http://www.usatoday.com/tech/gaming/2006-05-19-serious-games_x.htm

Guskey, T. R. (2002). Does it make a difference? Evaluating professional development. *Educational Leadership, 59*(6), 45–51.

Habschick, M., Seldi, B., & Evers, J. (2007). *VT Markt/2006/26-H-with cooperation of Doreen Klose and Yoshua Parsian.* Final report on survey of financial literacy schemes.

Hag, M. (2011). *Intellectual disability activities.* Retrieved on March 20, 2012 from http://www.ehow.com/info_8028431_intellectual-disability-activities

Hagenbach, S. (2011). *Teaching children responsible behaviour, human kinetics.* Retrieved on February 28, 2012 from http://www.humankinetics.com

Hague, C., & Williamson, B. (2009). *Digital participation, digital literacy, and school subjects.* Bristol, UK: Futurelab.

Hainey, T., Connolly, T., Baxter, G., Boyle, L., & Beeby, R. (2012). Assessment integration in games-based learning: A preliminary review of the literature. In *Proceedings of the 6th European Conference on Games-Based Learning.* IEEE.

Hall, E. T., & Hall, M. R. (1987). *Hidden differences: Doing business with the Japanese.* Garden City, NY: Anchor Books Doubleday.

Hall, V. C., Bailey, J., & Tillman, C. (1997). Can student-generated illustrations be worth ten thousand words? *Journal of Educational Psychology, 89*(4), 667–681. doi:10.1037/0022-0663.89.4.677

Hamilton, M. (2007). Role of low energy expenditure and sitting in obesity, metabolic syndrome, type 2 diabetes, and cardiovascular disease. *Diabetes, 56*, 2655–2667. doi:10.2337/db07-0882

Hamit, F. (1993). *Virtual reality and the exploration of cyberspace.* Indianapolis, IN: Sams Publishing.

Hammersley, M., & Atkinson, P. (1995). *Ethnography: Principles in practice* (2nd ed.). London, UK: Routledge.

Hamza-Lup, F., & Stănescu, I. A. (2010). The haptic paradigm in education: Challenges and case studies. *The Internet and Higher Education, 13*, 78–81. doi:10.1016/j.iheduc.2009.12.004

Hanghøj, T., & Magnussen, R. (2010). *The role of the teacher in facilitating educational games: Outline of a game pedagogy.* Paper presented at the 2nd Designs for Learning Conference. Stockholm, Sweden.

Hanghøj, T., & Meyer, B. (2010). How to study something that does not exist: Making design interventions with educational games. In *Proceedings of the 4th European Conference on Games Based Learning,* (pp. 123-130). Reading, MA: Academic Publishing Limited.

Hanghøj, T. (2011a). *Playful knowledge: An explorative study of educational gaming.* Saarbrücken, Germany: Lambert Academic Publishing.

Hanghøj, T. (2011b). Emerging and clashing genres: The interplay of knowledge forms in educational gaming. *Designs for Learning, 4*(1), 22–33.

Hanghøj, T. (Ed.). (2013). *Spil i undervisningen.* Aarhus, Denmark: Aarhus University Press.

Hanghøj, T., & Brund, C. E. (2011). Teachers and serious games: Teacher roles and positionings in relation to educational games. In Meyer, B., Sørensen, B. H., & Egenfeldt-Nielsen, S. (Eds.), *Serious Games in Education* (pp. 125–136). Aarhus, Denmark: Aarhus University Press.

Harris, J., Mishra, P., & Koehler, M. (2009). Teachers' technological pedagogical content knowledge and learning activity types: Curriculum-based technology integration reframed. *Journal of Research on Technology in Education, 41*(4), 393–416.

Harteveld, C., Guimarães, R., Mayer, I., & Bidarra, R. (2007). Balancing pedagogy, game and reality components within a unique serious game for training levee inspection. *Lecture Notes in Computer Science, 4469,* 128–139. doi:10.1007/978-3-540-73011-8_15

Hayes, E. (2011). The Sims as a catalyst for girls' IT learning. *International Journal of Gender. Science and Technology, 3*(1), 121–147.

Hayes, E. R., & King, E. M. (2009). Not just a dollhouse: What the Sims 2 can teach us about women's IT learning. *Horizon, 17*(1), 66–69. doi:10.1108/10748120910936153

Hays, R. T. (2005). *The effectiveness of instructional games: A literature review and discussion.* Washington, DC: Naval Air Warfare Center.

Hedenbro, M., Shapiro, A. F., & Gottman, J. M. (2006). Play with me at my speed: Describing differences in the tempo of parent-infant interactions in the Lausanne triadic play paradigm in two cultures. *Family Process, 45*(4), 485–498. doi:10.1111/j.1545-5300.2006.00184.x

Hedley, A. A., Ogden, C. L., Johnson, C. L., Carroll, M. D., Curtin, L. R., & Flegal, K. M. (2004). Prevalence of overweight and obesity among US children, adolescents, and adults, 1999–2002. *Journal of the American Medical Association, 291,* 2847–2850. doi:10.1001/jama.291.23.2847

Henriksen, D. T. (2010). *A little more conversation, a little less action, please: Rethinking learning games for organisational development and adult education.* Saarbrücken, Germany: Lambert Academic Publishing.

Herlitz, W., Ongstad, S., & van de Ven, P.-H. (Eds.). (2007). *Research on mother tongue education in a comparative international perspective: Theoretical and methodological issues.* Utrecht, The Netherlands: Rodopi.

Herman, D. (2011). *Basic elements of narrative.* Singapore, Singapore: John Wiley & Sons.

Hernández, T. (2008). Los videojuegos. In López, F. (Ed.), *El Juego Como Estrategia Didáctica* (pp. 91–99). Barcelona, Spain: Graó.

Hill, R. A. (2001). Toward the holodeck: Integrating graphics, sound, character and story. In *Proceedings of the Fifth International Conference on Autonomous Agents*, (pp. 409-416). IEEE.

Hinrichsen, J. J. (1972). Prediction of grade point average from estimated study behaviors. *Psychological Reports*, *31*(3), 974–975. doi:10.2466/pr0.1972.31.3.974

Hirumi, A., Appelman, B., Rieber, L., & Eck, R. V. (2010a). Preparing instructional designers for game-based learning: Part I. *TechTrends*, *54*(3), 27–37. doi:10.1007/s11528-010-0400-9

Hjorth, D., & Johannisson, B. (2007). Learning as an entrepreneurial process. In Fayolle, A. (Ed.), *Handbook of Research in Entrepreneurship Education: A General Perspective* (pp. 46–66). Cheltenham, UK: Edward Elgar.

Hjorth, D., Johannisson, B., & Steyaert, C. (2003). Entrepreneurship as discourse and life style. In Czarniawska, G., & Sevon, G. (Eds.), *Northern Light – Organization Theory in Scandinavia* (pp. 91–110). Malmö, Sweden: Liber.

Hlebowitsh, P. S. (2011). *The College of Idaho, John Dewey and the idea of experimentalism*. Retrieved on March 5, 2012 from http://www.edu301fall.wikispaces.com/.../John dewey

Hofstede, G. J., Caluwé, L. D., & Peters, V. (2010). Why simulation games work—In search of the active substance: A synthesis. *Simulation & Gaming*, *41*(6), 824–843. doi:10.1177/1046878110375596

Hogle, J. G. (1996). *Considering games as cognitive tools: In search of effective "edutainment"*. Retrieved October 13, 2011, from http://twinpinefarm.com/pdfs/games.pdf

Holland, Jenkins, & Squire. (2003). Theory by design. In *Video Game Theory*. New York, NY: Routledge.

Hong, J. C., Cheng, C. L., Hwang, M. Y., Lee, C. K., & Chang, H. Y. (2009). Assessing the educational values of digital games. *Journal of Computer Assisted Learning*, *25*, 423–437. doi:10.1111/j.1365-2729.2009.00319.x

Honig, B. (2004). Entrepreneurship education: Toward a model of contingency-based business planning. *Academy of Management Learning & Education*, *3*(3), 258–273. doi:10.5465/AMLE.2004.14242112

Honig, B., & Karlsson, T. (2004). Institutional forces and the written business plan. *Journal of Management*, *30*(1), 29–48. doi:10.1016/j.jm.2002.11.002

Hopkins, M. E., Nitecki, R., & Bucci, D. J. (2011). Physical exercise during adolescence versus adulthood: Differential effects on object recognition memory and brain-derived neurotrophic factor levels. *Neuroscience*, *194*, 84–94. doi:10.1016/j.neuroscience.2011.07.071

Hughes, R. (1990). Simulation for design, test and evaluation, and training - Reconciling the differences. In *Proceedings of the 1990 Winter Simulation Conference*, (pp. 231-236). IEEE.

Huizenga, J., Admiral, W., Ackerman, S., & Dam, G. T. (2009). Mobile game-based learning in secondary education: Engagement, motivation and learning in a mobile city game. *Journal of Computer Assisted Learning*, *25*, 332–344. doi:10.1111/j.1365-2729.2009.00316.x

Huizinga, J. (1955). *Homo ludens: A study of the play element in culture*. Boston, MA: Beacon Press.

Hutchinsona, J. C., & Tenenbaumb, G. (2007). Attention focus during physical effort: The mediating role of task intensity. *Psychology of Sport and Exercise*, *8*(2), 233–245. doi:10.1016/j.psychsport.2006.03.006

Institute for Statistics. (2012). *Website*. Retrieved on February 26, 2012 from www.un.org/esa/.../06_UNESCO.pdf

Institute of Neeuroscinces. (2012). *Mental health and addiction (NMHA)*. Retrieved on September 11, 2012 from http://www.thebrain.megill.co/flash/d/d_07_p/d-07_p_tra.html

ISCP. (2010). *General surgery curriculum*. Washington, DC: General Medical Council.

Jackson, S., & Csikszentmihalyi, M. (1999). *Flow in sports: The keys to optimal experiences and performances*. Champaign, IL: Human Kinetics.

Jarzabkowski, P., & Wilson, D. C. (2006). Actionable strategy knowledge: A practice perspective. *European Management Journal*, *24*(5), 348–367. doi:10.1016/j.emj.2006.05.009

Jenkins, E., & Nelson, N. W. (2005). Important but not for me: students' attitudes toward secondary school science in England. *Research in Science & Technological Education, 23,* 41–57. doi:10.1080/02635140500068435

Jenkins, H. (2002). *Hop on pop: The politics and pleasures of popular culture.* Durham, NC: Duke University Press.

Jenkins, H. (2006). *Convergence culture: Where old and new media collide.* New York, NY: New York University Press.

Jenkins, H. (2009). *Confronting the challenges of participatory culture: Media education for the 21st century.* Washington, DC: MacArthur Foundation.

Jewitt, C. (2008). Multimodality and literacy in school classrooms. *Review of Research in Education, 32,* 241. doi:10.3102/0091732X07310586

Joas, H. (1993). *Pragmatism and social theory.* Chicago, IL: University of Chicago Press.

Johannisson, B. (1991). University training for entrepreneurship: Swedish approaches. *Entrepreneurship and Regional Development, 3*(1), 67–82. doi:10.1080/08985629100000005

Johannisson, B. (2000). Networking and entrepreneurial growth. In Sexton, D., & Landström, H. (Eds.), *Handbook of Entrepreneurship* (pp. 368–386). London, UK: Blackwell.

Johannisson, B. (2010). In the beginning was entrepreneuring. In Bill, F., Bjerke, B., & Johansson, A. W. (Eds.), *De)mobilizing the Entrepreneurship Discourse: Exploring Entrepreneurial Thinking and Action* (pp. 201–221). Cheltenham, UK: Edward Elgar.

Johannisson, B. (2011). Towards a practice theory of entrepreneuring. *Small Business Economics, 36*(2), 135–150. doi:10.1007/s11187-009-9212-8

Johnson, H. C. (1996). Stochastic weather simulation: Overview and analysis of two commonly used models. *Journal of Applied Meteorology, 35,* 1878–1896. doi:10.1175/1520-0450(1996)035<1878:SWSOAA>2.0.CO;2

Johnson, S. (2005). *Everything bad is good for you: How today's popular culture actually making us smarter.* New York, NY: Riverhead Books.

Jonker, V., & van Galen, F. (2004). *KidsKount: Mathematics games for realistic mathematics education in primary school.* Paper presented at 10th International Conference on Mathematics Education (ICME). Kopenhagen, Denmark.

Juul, J. (2005). *Half-real: Video games between real rules and fictional worlds.* Cambridge, MA: MIT Press.

Kafai, Y. (1998). Videogame designs by girls and boys: Variability and consistency of gender differences. In Cassell, J., & Jenkins, H. (Eds.), *From Barbie to Mortal Kombat* (pp. 90–117). Cambridge, MA: MIT Press.

Kafai, Y. B. (1995). *Minds in play: Computer game design as a context for children's learning.* Hillsdale, NJ: Lawrence Erlbaum Associates.

Kafai, Y. B. (2006). Playing and making games for learning: Instructionist and constructionist perspectives for game studies. *Games and Culture, 1*(1), 36–40. doi:10.1177/1555412005281767

Kafai, Y. B., Franke, M. L., Ching, C. C., & Shih, J. C. (1998). Game design as an interactive learning environment for fostering students' and teachers' mathematical inquiry. *International Journal of Computers for Mathematical Learning, 3*(2), 149–184. doi:10.1023/A:1009777905226

Kamisah, O., & Nurul, A. B. (2011). *Implementation of educational computer games in Malaysian chemistry classroom: Challenges for game designers.* Paper presented at the 10th WSEAS International Conference on Education and Educational Technology (EDU 2011). Penang, Malaysia.

Kangas, M. (2010). Creative and playful learning: Learning through game co-creation and games in playful learning environment. *Thinking Skills and Creativity, 5*(1), 1–15. doi:10.1016/j.tsc.2009.11.001

Kapp, K. M. (2012). *The gamification of learning and instruction: Game-based methods and strategies for training and education.* San Francisco, CA: Pfeiffer.

Kaptelin, V., & Cole, M. (2002). Individual and collective activities in educational computer game playing. In Kosmann, T., Hall, R., & Miyake, N. (Eds.), *g2057CSCL 2: Carrying Forward the Conversation* (pp. 303–316). Mahwah, NJ: Lawrence Erlbaum.

Kapur, P., & Steadman, R. (1998). Patient simulator competency testing: Ready for take-off? *Anesthesia and Analgesia, 86*, 1157–1159.

Karageorghis, C., & Priest, D.-L. (2008). Music in sport and exercise: An update on research and application. *The Sport Journal, 11*(3).

Karau, S. J., & Kelly, J. R. (1992). The effects of time scarcity and time abundance on group performance quality and interaction process. *Journal of Experimental Social Psychology, 28*(6), 542–571. doi:10.1016/0022-1031(92)90045-L

Katz, J. A. (2003). The chronology and intellectual trajectory of American entrepreneurship education. *Journal of Business Venturing, 18*, 283–300. doi:10.1016/S0883-9026(02)00098-8

Kaufman, R. (2010). The manager's role in service education. *UP Your Service.* Retrieved on September 10, 2012 from http://www.upyourservice.com/blog/service-education/the-managers-role-in-service-education/

Kaufman-Scarborough, C., & Lindquist, J. D. (1999). Time management and polychronicity: Comparisons, contrasts, and insights for the workplace. *Journal of Managerial Psychology, 14*(3-4), 288–312. doi:10.1108/02683949910263819

Kebritchi, M., & Hirumi, A. (2008). *Examining the pedagogical foundations of modern educational computer games.* Paper presented at the International Technology, Educational, Research. Orlando, FL.

Kebritchi, M., Hirumi, A., & Bai, H. (2010). The effects of modern mathematics computer games on mathematics achievement and class motivation. *Computers & Education, 55*(2), 427–443. doi:10.1016/j.compedu.2010.02.007

Ke, F. (2008). Computer games application within alternative classroom goal structures: Cognitive, metacognitive, and affective evaluation. *Educational Technology Research and Development, 56*, 539–556. doi:10.1007/s11423-008-9086-5

Keitt, T. J., Daley, E., & Iqbal, R. (2009). *Predictions 2010: What's in store for serious games and B2B virtual worlds?* Boston, MA: Forrester Research.

Kelley, J. A. (1999). *Great book of dominoes games.* New York, NY: Sterling Publishing Co., Inc.

Kemmis, S., & McTaggart, R. (2000). Participatory action research. In Denzin, N., & Lincoln, Y. (Eds.), *Handbook of Qualitative Research* (2nd ed., pp. 567–605). Thousand Oaks, CA: Sage.

Kemmis, S., & McTaggart, R. (2005). Participatory action research. In Denzin, N. K., & Lincoln, Y. S. (Eds.), *The Sage Handbook of Qualitative Research* (3rd ed., pp. 559–603). Thousand Oaks, CA: Sage.

Kerstholt, J. H. (1994). The effect of time pressure on decision making behaviour in a dynamic task environment. *Acta Psychologica, 86*, 89–104. doi:10.1016/0001-6918(94)90013-2

Ketamo, H., & Kiili, K. (2010b). Mining educational game data: Uncovering complex mechanisms behind learning. In *Proceedings of 4th European Conference on Games Based Learning.* Copenhagen, Denmark: IEEE.

Ketamo, H., & Suominen, M. (2008). AnimalClass: Social networks in gaming. In M. Kankaanranta & P. Neittaanmäki (Eds.), *Design and Use of Serious Games,* (pp. 143-154). Springer Science+Business Media B.V.

Ketamo, H. (2003). An adaptive AnimalClass for handheld devices. *Journal of Educational Technology & Society, 6*, 83–95.

Ketamo, H. (2009). Semantic networks-based teachable agents in an educational game. *Transactions on Computers, 8*(4), 641–650.

Ketamo, H. (2011). Sharing behaviors in games and social media. *International Journal of Applied Mathematics and Informatics, 5*(1), 224–232.

Ketamo, H., & Kiili, K. (2010). Conceptual change takes time: Game based learning cannot be only supplementary amusement. *Journal of Educational Multimedia and Hypermedia, 19*(4), 399–419.

Ketamo, H., & Suominen, M. (2010). Learning-by-teaching in an educational game: The educational outcome, user experience and social networks. *Journal of Interactive Learning Research, 21*(1), 75–94.

Ketelhut, D. J., Clarke, J., & Nelson, B. (2010). The development of River City, a multi-user virtual environment-based scientific inquiry curriculum: Historical and design evolutions. In M. J. Jacobson & P. Reimann (Eds.), *Designs for Learning Environments of the Future,* (pp. 89-110). New York, NY: Springer Science + Business Media.

Ketelhut, D. J., Nelson, B., Clarke, J., & Dede, C. (2010). A multi-user virtual environment for building higher order inquiry skills in science. *British Journal of Educational Technology, 41*(1), 56–68. doi:10.1111/j.1467-8535.2009.01036.x

Ketelhut, D. J., & Schifter, C. C. (2011). Teachers and game-based learning: Improving understanding of how to increase efficacy of adoption. *Computers & Education, 56*(2), 539–546. doi:10.1016/j.compedu.2010.10.002

Keynes, J. M. (1936). *General theory of employment, interest and money.* New York, NY: Harcourt, Brace and Co. Retrieved on February 15, 2012 from www.marxists.org/reference/subject/economics/keynes/general theory/

Kickmeier-Rust, & Albert, D. (2010). Micro-adaptivity: Protecting immersion in didactically adaptive digital educational games. *Journal of Computer Assisted Learning, 26,* 95–105. doi:10.1111/j.1365-2729.2009.00332.x

Kickmeier-Rust, M. D., & Dietrich, A. (2012). A domain model for smart 21st century skills training in game-based virtual worlds. In *Proceedings of ICALT 2012.* ICALT.

Kiili, K. (2005a). *On educational game design: Building blocks of flow experience.* (Doctoral Thesis). Tampere University of Technology. Tampere, Finland.

Kiili, K., & Merilampi, S. (2010). Developing engaging exergames with simple motion detection. In *Proceedings of the 14th International Academic MindTrek Conference: Envisioning Future Media Environments,* (pp. 103-110). Tampere, Finland: MindTrek.

Kiili, K., & Perttula, A. (2010). Exergaming: Exploring engagement principles. In *Proceedings of the Serious Games for Sports and Health,* (pp. 161-172). Darmstadt, Germany: IEEE.

Kiili, K., Kiili, C., Ott, M., & Jönkkäri, T. (2012). Towards creative pedagogy: Empowering students to develop games. In *Proceedings ECGBL 2012.* ECGBL.

Kiili, K., Perttula, A., & Tuomi, P. (2010). Development of multiplayer exertion games for physical education. *IADIS International Journal on WWW/Internet, 8*(1), 52-69.

Kiili, K. (2005). Content creation challenges and flow experience in educational games: The IT-emperor case. *The Internet and Higher Education, 8*(3), 183–198. doi:10.1016/j.iheduc.2005.06.001

Kiili, K. (2005b). Digital game-based learning: Towards an experiential gaming model. *The Internet and Higher Education, 8*(1), 13–24. doi:10.1016/j.iheduc.2004.12.001

Kiili, K. (2007). Foundation for problem-based gaming. *British Journal of Educational Technology, 38*(3), 394–404. doi:10.1111/j.1467-8535.2007.00704.x

Kiili, K., & Ketamo, H. (2007). Exploring the learning mechanism in educational games. *Journal of Computing and Information Technology, 15*(4), 319–324.

Kiili, K., Ketamo, H., & Lainema, T. (2011). Reflective thinking in games: Triggers and constraints. In Connolly, T. (Ed.), *Leading Issues in Games-Based Learning Research* (pp. 178–192). London, UK: Ridgeway Press.

Kiili, K., & Lainema, T. (2008). Foundation for measuring engagement in educational games. *Journal of Interactive Learning Research, 19*(3), 469–488.

Kiili, K., & Lainema, T. (2010). Power and flow experience in time-intensive business simulation game. *Journal of Educational Multimedia and Hypermedia, 19*(1), 39–57.

Kirchhoff, B. A., & Phillips, B. D. (1988). The effect of firm formation and growth on job creation in the United States. *Journal of Business Venturing, 3*(4), 261–272. doi:10.1016/0883-9026(88)90008-0

Kirkland, K., & Williamson, B. (2010). Play-school: Linking culture and curriculum through games-based learning in schools. In *Proceedings for the 4th European Conference on Games Based Learning,* (pp. 168-176). Reading, MA: Academic Publishing Limited.

Kirriemuir, J., & McFarlane, A. (2003). Use of computer and video games in the classroom. In *Proceedings of the Level Up Digital Games Research Conference.* Utrecht, The Netherlands: Universiteit Utrecht.

Kirriemuir, J. (2002). *A survey of the use of computer and video games in classrooms. Internal Report for BECTA.* London, UK: British Educational Communications and Technology Agency.

Kirriemuir, J., & McFarlane, A. (2004). *Literature review in games and learning.* Bristol, UK: Futurelab.

Kirschner, P. (2002). Cognitive load theory: Implications of cognitive load theory on the design of learning. *Learning and Instruction, 12,* 1–10. doi:10.1016/S0959-4752(01)00014-7

Klabbers, J. H. G. (2009). *The magic circle: Principles of gaming and simulation* (3rd ed.). Rotterdam, The Netherlands: Sense Publishers.

Klamer, A. (2011). Cultural entrepreneurship. *The Review of Austrian Economics, 24*, 141–156. doi:10.1007/s11138-011-0144-6

Klawe, M. (1998). *When does the use of computer games and other interactive multimedia software help students learn mathematics?* Paper presented at NCTM Standards 2000 Technology Conference. Washington, DC.

Klette, K., Odegaard, M., & Arnesen, N. E. (2007). *Time scales and coding categories in video analysis.* Paper presented at ESERA 2007. New York, NY.

Klette, K. (2009). Challenges in strategies for complexity reduction in video studies: Experiences from the PISA+ study: A video study of teaching and learning in Norway. In Janik, T., & Seidel, T. (Eds.), *The Power of Video Studies in Investigating Teaching and Learning in the Classroom* (pp. 61–82). New York, NY: Waxmann Publishing.

Klimmt, C. (2009). Key dimensions of contemporary video game literacy: Towards a normative model of the competent digital gamer. *Eludamos: Journal for Computer Game Culture, 3*(1), 23–31.

Kobasigawa, A., & Metcalf-Haggert, A. (1993). Spontaneous allocation of study time by first- and third-grade children in a simple memory task. *The Journal of Genetic Psychology, 154*, 223–235. doi:10.1080/00221325.1993.9914736

Koh, E., Kin, Y. G., Wadhwa, B., & Lim, J. (2012). Teacher perceptions of games in Singapore schools. *Simulation & Gaming, 43*(1), 51–66. doi:10.1177/1046878111401839

Kolb, D. (1984). *Experiential learning: Experience as the source of learning and development.* Englewood Cliffs, NJ: Prentice Hall.

Kong, S. C., Ogata, H., Arnseth, H. C., Chan, C. K. K., Hirashima, T., Klett, F., et al. (2009). My-pet-my-quest: Utilizing game quests to scaffold students' goal setting for learning. In *Proceedings of the 17th International Conference on Computers in Education Hong Kong.* Pacific Society for Computers in Education.

Kose-Bagci, H., Dautenhahn, K., & Nehaniv, C. L. (2008). Emergent dynamics of turn-taking interaction in drumming games with a humanoid robot. In *Proceedings of the 17th IEEE International Symposium on Robot and Human Interactive Communication.* Munich, Germany: IEEE Press.

Koštomaj, M., & Boh, B. (2009). Evaluation of user's physical experience in full body interactive games. *Lecture Notes in Computer Science, 5763*, 145–154. doi:10.1007/978-3-642-04076-4_16

Kramer, A. F., Hahn, S., Irwin, D. E., & Theeuwes, J. (2000). Age differences in the control of looking behavior: Do you know where your eyes have been. *Psychological Science, 11*, 210–217. doi:10.1111/1467-9280.00243

Krulik, S., & Rudnick, J. A. (1993). *Reasoning and problem solving: A handbook for elementary school teachers.* Boston, MA: Allyn and Bacon.

Krutetskii, V. A. (1976). *The psychology of mathematical abilities in schoolchildren.* Chicago, IL: Chicago University Press.

Kuratko, D. F. (2005). The emergence of entrepreneurship education: Development, trends and challenges. *Entrepreneurship Theory & Practice, 29*(5), 577–598. doi:10.1111/j.1540-6520.2005.00099.x

Kurrek, M., & Fish, K. (1996). Anaesthesia crisis management training: An intimidating concept, a rewarding experience. *Canadian Journal of Anaesthesia, 43*, 430–434. doi:10.1007/BF03018101

Laabs, J. J. (1991). The golden arches provide golden opportunities. *The Personnel Journal, 70*(7), 52–57.

Lacasa, P., & Gipi. (2006). *Aprendiendo periodismo digital: Historias de pequeñas escritoras.* Madrid, Spain: Machado Libros.

Lacasa, P., & Gipi. (2009). *Video games at the institute: Digital leisure as a learning tool.* Research Report. Madrid, Spain: Academic Press.

Lacasa, P. (2011). *Los videojuegos: Aprender en mundos reales y virtuales.* Madrid, Spain: Morata.

Lakatos, I. (1976). *Proofs and refutations*. Cambridge, UK: Cambridge University Press. doi:10.1017/CBO9781139171472

Lane, J., Slavin, S., & Ziv, A. (2001). Simulation in medical education: A review. *Simulation & Gaming, 32*(3), 297–314. doi:10.1177/104687810103200302

Latour, B. (1987). *Science in action*. Cambridge, MA: Harvard University Press.

Lean, E. (1983). Learning disabled trainees: Finding and helping the "hidden handicapped". *Training and Development Journal, 37*(9), 56–62.

Leinhart & Byrness. (1996). *Schemata serve several functions in learning, categorizing, remembering, comprehending and problem solving*. Academic Press.

Lemay, P. (2007). Developing a pattern language for flow experiences in video games. In *Proceedings of DiGRA 2007 Conference*. DiGRA.

Lenhart, A., Kahne, J., Middaugh, E., Macgill, A. R., Evans, C., & Vitak, J. (2008). *Teens, video games and civics*. Retrieved September 15, 2012, from http://www.pewinternet.org/Reports/2008/Teens-VideoGames-and-Civics.aspx

Leonard, K., Van Scotter, J., & Pakdil, F. (2009). Culture and communication: Cultural variations and media effectiveness. *Administration & Society, 41*(7), 850–877. doi:10.1177/0095399709344054

Lepper, M. R. (2000). Turning "play" into "work" and "work" into "play": 25 years of research on intrinsic versus extrinsic motivation. In Sansone, C., & Harackiewicz, J. M. (Eds.), *Intrinsic and Extrinsic Motivation The Search for Optimal Motivation and Performance* (pp. 257–307). San Diego, CA: Academic Press. doi:10.1016/B978-012619070-0/50032-5

Levinsen, K. (2006). Collaborative on-line teaching: The inevitable path to deep learning and knowledge sharing. *Electronic Journal of E-Learning, 4*(1), 41–48.

Lewis, G., Robertson, I., Watson, P., & Datta, A. (1998). Circadian rhythm of sleepiness and vigilance studied in man. *The Journal of Physiology, 27*(1), 506.

Lewis, M. W. (2007). Analysis of the roles of serious games in helping teach health-related knowledge, skills, and in changing behavior. *Journal of Diabetes Science and Technology, 1*(6).

Lieberman, D. A. (2006). What can we learn from playing interactive games? In Vorderer, P., & Bryant, J. (Eds.), *Playing Video Games: Motives, Responses, and Consequences* (pp. 379–397). Mahwah, NJ: Erlbaum.

Lieberman, D., Chamberlin, B., Medina, E., Franklin, B., Sanner, B., & Vafiadis, D. (2011). The power of play: Innovations in getting active summit 2011: A science panel proceedings report from the American heart association. *Circulation, 123*, 2507–2516. doi:10.1161/CIR.0b013e318219661d

Lind, E., & Welch, A., Ekkekakis, & Panteleimon. (2009). Do 'mind over muscle' strategies work? Examining the effects of attentional association and dissociation on exertional, affective and physiological responses to exercise. *Sports Medicine (Auckland, N.Z.), 39*(9), 743–764. doi:10.2165/11315120-000000000-00000

Linehan, C., Lawson, S., Doughty, M., & Kirman, B. (2009). There's no "I" in "emergency management team": Designing and evaluating a serious game for training emergency managers in group decision making skills. In *Proceedings of the 39th Conference of the Society for the Advancement of Games & Simulations in Education and Training*, (pp. 20-27). IEEE.

Linehan, C., Lawson, S., Doughty, M., Kirman, B., Haferkamp, L., & Krämer, N. C. … Nigrelli, M. L. (2012). Teaching group decision making skills to emergency managers via digital games. In A. Lugmayr, H. Franssila, P. Näränen, O. Sotamaa, J. Vanhala, & Z. Yu (Eds.), *Media in the Ubiquitous Era: Ambient, Social and Gaming Media*. Hershey, PA: IGI Global.

Lin, Y.-L., & Tu, Y.-Z. (2012). The values of college students in business simulation game: A means-end chain approach. *Computers & Education, 58*(4), 1160–1170. doi:10.1016/j.compedu.2011.12.005

Lopes, A. V., Bernardes, A., Loureiro, C., Varandas, J. M., Oliveira, M. J. C., & Delgado, M. J. (1990). *Actividades matemáticas na sala de aula*. Lisboa, Portugal: Texto Editores.

Lopez-Moreto, G., & Lopez, G. (2007). Computer support for learning mathematics: A learning environment based on recreational learning objects. *Computers & Education, 48*, 618–641. doi:10.1016/j.compedu.2005.04.014

Lund, J., & Tannehill, D. (2009). *Standards-based physical education curriculum development.* Sudbury, MA: Bartlett Publishers.

Mackenzie, A. (2011). *Games for deaf kids.* Retrieved on March 20, 2012 from www.ehow.com/list_6399398_games-deaf-kids.html

Magnussen, R. (2011). Game-like technology innovation education. *International Journal of Virtual and Personal Learning Environments, 2*(2), 30–39. doi:10.4018/jvple.2011040103

Mallon, B., & Webb, B. (2005). Stand up and take your place: Identifying narrative elements in narrative adventure and role-play games. *Computers in Entertainment, 3*(1).

Manning, P. (2005). Continuing medical education 1906-1975: How the past influences the present. *Almanac, Alliance for CME, 27*(12).

Manouselis, N., Drachsler, H., Vuorikari, R., Hummel, H., & Koper, R. (2011). Recommender systems in technology enhanced learning. In Ricci, F., Rokach, L., Shapira, B., & Kantor, P. B. (Eds.), *Recommender Systems Handbook* (pp. 387–415). Berlin, Germany: Springer. doi:10.1007/978-0-387-85820-3_12

Manovich, L. (2001). *The language of new media.* Cambridge, MA: MIT Press.

Mapp, K. M. (2012). *The gamification of learning and instruction: Game-based methods and strategies for training and education.* New York, NY: Pfeiffer.

Markowska, M. (2011). *Entrepreneurial competence development: Triggers, processes & competences.* (Dissertation). Jönköping International Business School. Jönköping, Sweden.

Marlow, C. M. (2009). *Games and learning in landscape architecture.* Paper presented at the Conference of Digital Landscape Architecture. New York, NY.

Martin, A. (2000). The design and evolution of a simulation/game for teaching information systems development. *Simulation & Gaming, 31*(4), 445–463. doi:10.1177/104687810003100401

Mayer, R. E. (2001). *Multimedia learning.* Cambridge, UK: Cambridge University Press. doi:10.1017/CBO9781139164603

Mayer, R. E., & Moreno, R. (2003). Nine ways to reduce cognitive load in multimedia learning. *Educational Psychologist, 38*, 43–52. doi:10.1207/S15326985EP3801_6

McDaniel, R., & Telep, P. (2009). Best practices for integrating game-based learning into online teaching. *Journal of Online Learning and Teaching, 5*(2), 424–438.

McFarlane, A., Sparrowhawk, A., & Heald, Y. (2002). *Report on the educational use of games.* Cambridge, UK: TEEM.

McGaghie, W., Issenberg, B., Petrusa, E., & Scalese, R. (2010). A critical review of simulation-based medical education research: 2003–2009. *Medical Education, 44*(1), 50–63. doi:10.1111/j.1365-2923.2009.03547.x

McGee, M. R. (2002). *Investigating a multimodal solution for improving force feedback generated textures.* (PhD Thesis). University of Glasgow. Glasgow, UK.

McGivern, R. F., Hilliard, V. R., Anderson, J., Reilly, J. S., Rodriguez, A., Fielding, B., & Shapiro, L. (2007). Improving preliteracy and premath skills of head start children with classroom computer games. *Early Childhood Services: An Interdisciplinary Journal of Effectiveness, 1*, 71–81.

McGonigal, J. (2012). *Reality is broken: Why games make us better and how they can change.* New York, NY: Random House.

McLester, S. (2005). Game plan. *Tech & Learning, 26*, 18.

McMillan, J. H. (2008). *Assessment essentials for standards-based education.* London, UK: Corwin.

Mercer, N. (2000). *Words and mind: How we use language to think together.* New York, NY: Routledge. doi:10.4324/9780203464984

Merenluoto, K., & Lehtinen, E. (2004). Number concept and conceptual change: Towards a systematic model of the processes of change. *Learning and Instruction, 14*, 519–534. doi:10.1016/j.learninstruc.2004.06.016

Michael, D., & Chen, S. (2006). *Serious games: Games that educate, train, and inform.* Boston, MA: Thomson.

MicroSim. (2012). *Website*. Retrieved May 1, 2012, from http://www.laerdal.com/docid/5899175/MicroSim

Miller, C. S., Lehman, J. F., & Koedinger, K. R. (1999). Goals and learning in microworlds. *Cognitive Science, 23*(3), 305–336. doi:10.1207/s15516709cog2303_2

Miller, D. J., & Roberstson, D. P. (2010). Article. *British Journal of Educational Technology, 41*(2), 242–255. doi:10.1111/j.1467-8535.2008.00918.x

Miller, G. (1956). The magical number seven, plus or minus two: Some limits on our capacity for processing information. *Psychological Review, 63*, 81–97. doi:10.1037/h0043158

Miller, G. (1992). Making training accessible to people with disabilities. *Training (New York, N.Y.), 92*(8), 94.

Mills, A. K. (2010). A review of the "digital turn" in the new literacies studies. *Review of Educational Research, 80*(2), 246–271. doi:10.3102/0034654310364401

Mishra, P., & Koehler, M. J. (2006). Technological pedagogical content knowledge: A framework for teacher knowledge. *Teachers College Record, 108*(6), 1017–1054. doi:10.1111/j.1467-9620.2006.00684.x

Mitchell, A., & Savill-Smith, C. (2004). *The use of computer and videogames for learning: A review of the literature*. Retrieved from http://www.lsda.org.uk/files/PDF/1529.pdf

Mitchell, A., & Savill-Smith, C. (2004). *The use of computer and video games for learning: A review of the literature*. London, UK: Learning and Skills Development Agency.

Mominó, J., Sigalés, C., & Meneses, J. (2008). *La escuela en la sociedad en red: Internet en la educación primaria y secundaria*. Barcelona, Spain: Ariel.

Monroy-Hernández, A., Hill, B. M., González-Rivero, J., & boyd, d. (2011). Computers can't give credit: How automatic attribution falls short in an online remixing community. In *Proceedings of the 29th International Conference on Human Factors in Computing Systems (CHI 2011)*. IEEE.

Monteiro, M., Corredoura, A., Candeias, M., Morais, P., & Diniz, J. (2011). Central hospital - Master of resuscitation: An immersive learning approach. In *Proceedings of the IEEE 1st International Conference on Serious Games and Applications for Health*, (pp. 74-77). IEEE Press.

Moreira, D., & Oliveira, I. (2004). *O jogo e a matemática*. Lisboa, Portugal: Universidade Aberta.

Moreno-Ger, P., Burgos, D., Martínez-Ortiz, I., Sierra, J., & Fernández-Manjón, B. (2008). Educational game design for online education. *Computers in Human Behavior, 24*, 2530–2540. doi:10.1016/j.chb.2008.03.012

Moreno-Ger, P., Burgos, D., & Torrente, J. (2009). Digital games in e-learning environments: Current uses and emerging trends. *Simulation & Gaming, 40*(5), 669–687. doi:10.1177/1046878109340294

Morgan, S., & Forster, J. (1999). Creativity in the classroom. *Gifted Education International, 14*(1), 29–43. doi:10.1177/026142949901400105

Mor, Y., Winters, N., Cerulli, M., & Björk, S. (2006). *Literature review on the use of games in mathematical learning, part I: Design. Report of the Learning Patterns for the Design and Deployment of Mathematical Games project*. Academic Press.

Mote, D. (2011). Management. In *Encyclopedia of Business* (2nd ed). Retrieved on March 15, 2012 from http://www.referenceforbusiness.com/encyclopedia/Kor-kids-with-learn

Mott, B. W. (1999). Towards narrative-centered learning environments. In Proceedings of the Narrative Intelligence Symposium, AAAI 1999 Fall Symposium Series. AAAI.

Mueller, F., & Bianchi-Berthouze, N. (2012). Evaluating exertion games experiences from investigating movement-based games. In R. Bernhaupt (Ed.), *Evaluating User Experiences in Games*. Berlin, Germany: Springer. Retrieved from http://www.uclic.ucl.ac.uk/people/n.berthouze/MullerBerthouze2010

Mueller, F., Agamanolis, S., & Picard, R. (2003). Exertion interfaces: Sports over a distance for social bonding and fun. In *Proceedings of the SIGCHI Conference on Human Factors in Computing Systems*. Ft. Lauderdale, FL: ACM.

Mueller, F., Agamanolis, S., Vetere, F., & Gibbs, M. R. (2009). A framework for exertion interactions over a distance. In *Proceedings of ACM SIGGRAPH 2009*. ACM.

Mueller, F., Edge, D., Vetere, F., Gibbs, M. R., Agamanolis, S., Bongers, B., & Sheridan, J. G. (2011). Designing sports: A framework for exertion games. In *Proceedings of the SIGCHI Conference on Human Factors in Computing Systems*. Vancouver, Canada: ACM Press.

Mumtaz, S. (2006). Factors affecting teachers' use of information and communications technology: A review of the literature. *Journal of Information Technology, 9*(3), 312–342.

Murray, H. J. R. (1952). *A history of board-games other than chess*. Oxford, UK: Clarendon Press.

Murray, J. H. (1997). *Hamlet on the holodeck, the future of narrative in cyberspace*. New York, NY: The Free Press.

Musafiri, E. (2011). *Maters program-responsible management and sustainable economic development*. Kigala, Rwanda: Natural University.

NAMI. (2011). *Website*. Retrieved on April 5, 2012 from www.nami.org//template.clm?section=about_mental_illness

Narayanasamy, V. (2006). Distinguishing games and simulation games from simulators. *Computers in Entertainment, 4*(2), 9. doi:10.1145/1129006.1129021

National Council of Teachers of Mathematics. (2000). *Principles and standards for school mathematics*. Reston, VA: National Council of Teachers of Mathematics.

Nauta, H., & Spil, T. (2011). Change your lifestyle or your game is over: The design of a serious game for diabetes. In *Proceedings of the IEEE 1st International Conference on Serious Games and Applications for Health*, (pp. 62-68). IEEE Press.

NCTM. (1991). *Normas para o currículo e a avaliação em matemática escolar*. Lisboa, Portugal: A.P.M e I.I.E.

NCTM. (2007). *Princípios e normas para a matemática escolar*. Lisboa, Portugal: A.P.M e I.I.E.

Neto, J. P. (2012). *Snort*. Retrieved April 2, 2012 from http://homepages.di.fc.ul.pt/~jpn/gv/catdogs.htm

Neto, J. P., & Silva, J. N. (2004). *Jogos matemáticos, jogos abstractos*. Lisboa, Portugal: Gradiva.

Neumann, J. (1972). *Theory of games and economic behaviour*. Princeton, NJ: Princeton University Press.

New Media Consortium & EDUCAUSE. (2011). *The horizon report*. Austin, TX: The New Media Consortium.

North, D. C. (1990). *Institutions, institutional change and economic performance*. Cambridge, MA: Cambridge University Press. doi:10.1017/CBO9780511808678

O'Neil, H. F., Wainess, R., & Baker, E. L. (2005). Classification of learning outcomes: Evidence from the computer games literature. *Curriculum Journal, 16*(4), 455–474. doi:10.1080/09585170500384529

Oblinger, D. (2004). The next generation of educational engagement. *Journal of Interactive Media in Education, 8*. Retrieved September 15, 2012, from http://jime.open.ac.uk/article/2004-8-oblinger/198

OECD. (2006). *Evolution of student interest in science and technology studies – Policy report*. Paper presented at the Global Science Forum. Paris, France.

Ogbor, J. O. (2000). Mythicizing and reification in entrepreneurial discourse: Ideology critique of entrepreneurial studies. *Journal of Management Studies, 37*(5), 605–635. doi:10.1111/1467-6486.00196

Okan, Z. (2003). Edutainment: Is learning at risk? *British Journal of Educational Technology, 34*(3), 255–264. doi:10.1111/1467-8535.00325

Okuda, Y., Bryson, E., DeMaria, S. Jr, Jacobson, L., Quinones, J., Shen, B., & Levine, A. (2009). The utility of simulation in medical education: What is the evidence? *The Mount Sinai Journal of Medicine, New York, 76*(4), 330–343. doi:10.1002/msj.20127

Oliveira, F., Andersen, B., Pereira, J., Seager, W., & Ribeiro, C. (2011). The use of integrative framework to support the development of competences. In *Proceedings of the Second International Conference on Serious Games Development and Applications*, (pp. 117-128). Berlin, Germany: Springer-Verlag.

Olsen, A. (2010). *Educational games for the visual impaired*. Retrieved on March 20, 2012 from www.brighthub.com/education/special/articles/65405.aspx

Ortoll, E. (Ed.). (2007). *La alfabetización digital en los procesos de inclusión social*. Barcelona, Spain: UOC.

Osborne, J. F., & Collins, S. (2001). Pupils' views of the role and value of the science curriculum: A focus-group study. *International Journal of Science Education, 23*, 441–468. doi:10.1080/09500690010006518

Ott, M., & Pozzi, F. (2011). Digital games as creativity enablers for children. In *Behaviour and Information Technology*. New York, NY: Taylor & Francis.

Ozcetin, N., & Eren, A. (2010). The effects of perceived instrumentality and future time perspective on students' graded performance and attitudes regarding English class. *International Journal on New Trends in Education and Their Implications, 1*(4), 5.

Paas, F. G. W. C., Renkl, A., & Sweller, J. (2003). Cognitive load theory: Instructional implications of the interaction between information structure and cognitive architecture. *Instructional Science, 32*(1), 1–8. doi:10.1023/B:TRUC.0000021806.17516.d0

Pacheco, J. (2000). *A flexibilização das políticas curriculares: Actas do seminário O papel dos diversos actores educativos na construção de uma escola democrática*. Guimarães, Portugal: Centro de Formação Francisco de Holanda.

Palhares, P. (2004). O jogo e o ensino/aprendizagem da matemática. *Revista da ESEVC, 5*, 129–146.

Panoutsopoulos, H., & Sampson, D. G. (2012). A study on exploiting commercial digital games into school context. *Journal of Educational Technology & Society, 15*(1), 15–27.

Papastergiou, M. (2009). Digital game-based learning in high school computer science education: Impact on educational effectiveness and student motivation. *Computers & Education, 52*(1), 1–12. doi:10.1016/j.compedu.2008.06.004

Papastergiou, M. (2009). Exploring the potential of computer and video games health and physical education: A literature review. *Computers & Education, 53*, 603–622. doi:10.1016/j.compedu.2009.04.001

Papert, S. (1980). *Mindstorms*. New York, NY: Basic Books.

Paras, B., & Bizzocchi, J. (2005). *Game, motivation and effective learning: And integrated model for educational game design*. Paper presented at the Changing Views--Worlds in Play. Vancouver, Canada.

Pasch, M., Bianchi-Berthouze, N., van Dijk, B., & Nijholt, A. (2009). Movement-based sports video games: Investigating motivation and gaming experience. *Entertainment Computing, 1*, 49–61. doi:10.1016/j.entcom.2009.09.004

Pastore, R. S., & Falvo, D. A. (2010). Video games in the classroom: Pre- and in-service teachers' perceptions of games in the K-12 classroom. *International Journal of Instructional Technology and Distance Learning, 7*(12), 49–57.

Patrick, J. J. (1991). *Teaching the responsibilities of citizens*. Bloomington, IN: ERIC Clearinghouse for Social Studies/Social Sciences Education.

Pearson, H. H. (2009). *Idealism and education*. Retrieved on February 29, 2012 from pearsonhighered.com/.../0132540746.p

Peavler, R. (2012). *What is capitalism?* Retrieved from http://www.about.com

Peetsma, A., & Thea, T. D. (1999). Future-time perspective: Analysis of a facet-designed questionnaire. *European Journal of Psychological Assessment, 15*(2), 99–105. doi:10.1027//1015-5759.15.2.99

Pellegrino, J., & Quellmalz, E. S. (2010). Perspectives on the integration of technology and assessment. *Journal of Teacher Education, 43*(2), 119–134.

Pelletier, C. (2009). Games and learning: What's the connection? *International Journal of Learning and Media, 1*(1), 83–101. doi:10.1162/ijlm.2009.0006

Perkins, G., Green, C., & Farquharson, W. (2006). Microsim: A new tool for advanced life support training. *Resuscitation, 69*, 54.

Philip, J. (1986). Gas man: An example of goal oriented computer-assisted teaching which results in learning. *Journal of Clinical Monitoring and Computing, 69*, 387–394.

Pivec, M., Dziabenko, O., & Schinnerl, I. (2003). Aspects of game-based learning. In *Proceedings of I-KNOW 2003*. Graz, Austria: UCS.

Pivec, P., & Pivec, M. (2009). Collaborative online roleplay for adult learners. In Ratan & Ritterfeld (Eds.), *SG: Mechanisms and Effects*. Hershey, PA: IGI Global.

Pivec, M. (2007). Play and learn: Potentials of game-based learning. *British Journal of Educational Technology, 38,* 387393. doi:10.1111/j.1467-8535.2007.00722.x

Pivec, M., Koubek, A., & Dondi, C. (Eds.). (2004). *Guidelines on game-based learning.* Berlin, Germany: Pabst Vrlg.

Pivec, M., & Pivec, P. (2009). What do we know from research about the use of games in education? In Wastiau, P., Kearney, C., & van den Berghe, W. (Eds.), *How are Digital Games used in School* (pp. 123–156). Brussels, Belgium: European Schoolnet.

Portela, F., Fonseca, J., Correia, R., & Andrade, J. (2011). Wii therapy on seniors: Effects on physical and mental domains. In *Proceedings of the IEEE 1st International Conference on Serious Games and Applications for Health,* (pp. 84-88). IEEE Press.

Posamentier, A. S., & Krulik, S. (1998). *Problem-solving strategies for efficient and elegant solutions: A resource for the mathematics teacher.* Thousand Oaks, CA: Corwin Press, Inc.

Pratt, D., Winters, N., Cerulli, M., & Leemkuil, H. (2009). A patterns approach to connecting the design and deployment of mathematical games and simulations. In Balacheff, N., Ludvigsen, S., de Jong, T., Lazonder, A., & Barnes, S. (Eds.), *Technology-Enhanced Learning: Principles and Products* (pp. 215–232). Dordrecht, The Netherlands: Springer. doi:10.1007/978-1-4020-9827-7_13

Prensky, M. (2001). Digital natives, digital immigrants on the horizon. *MCB University Press, 9*(5).

Prensky, M. (2005). In digital games for education, complexity matters. *Educational Technology, 45*(4), 22–28.

Prensky, M. (2006). *Don't bother me mom: I'm learning!* St. Paul, MN: Paragon House.

Prensky, M. (2007). *Digital game based learning.* New York, NY: Paragon House.

Prensky, M. (2008). Students as designers and creators of educational computer games: Who else? *British Journal of Educational Technology, 39*(6), 1004–1019. doi:10.1111/j.1467-8535.2008.00823_2.x

Prince, A. (2011). *Games for emotionally disturbed children.* Retrieved on March 20, 2012 from http://www.ehow.com/info_81.007533_games-emotionally-disturbed

Propp, V. (1987). *Morfología del cuento.* Madrid, Spain: Fundamentos.

Prospects.Net. (2011). *The impact of higher education on employment prospects and earnings.* Retrieved on February 15, 2012 from http://ww2-prospects.ac.uk/cms/ShowPage

Quinn. (2005). Engaging learning: Designing e-learning simulation games. San Francisco, CA: Pfeiffer.

Ranalli, J. (2008). Learning English with the Sims: Exploiting authentic computer simulation games for L2 learning. *Computer Assisted Language Learning, 21*(5), 441–455. doi:10.1080/09588220802447859

Randel, J. M. (1992). The effectiveness of games for educational purposes: A review of recent research. *Simulation & Gaming, 23*(3), 261–276. doi:10.1177/1046878192233001

Ratey, J., & Hagerman, E. (2008). *Spark: The revolutionary new science of exercise and the brain.* New York, NY: Little, Brown, and Company.

Redecker, C., Ala-Mutka, K., Bacigalupo, M., Ferrari, A., & Punie, Y. (2009). *Learning 2.0: The impact of web 2.0 innovations on education and training in Europe.* JRC Scientific and Technical Reports. Retrieved September 15, 2012, from http://ipts.jrc.ec.europa.eu/publications/pub.cfm?id=2899

Reid, M., et al. (2002). *Evaluation report of the becta digital video pilot project.* Coventry, UK: Becta. Retrieved from http://www.becta.org.uk/research/reports/digitalvideo/

Rendas, A. (2006). Towars meaningful learning in undergraduate medical education using concept maps in a PBL pathophysiology course. *Advances in Physiology Education, 30*(1), 23–29. doi:10.1152/advan.00036.2005

Resnick, M., Bruckman, A., & Martin, F. (1996). Pianos not stereos: Creating computational construction kits. *Interaction, 3*(6).

Resnick, M., Maloney, J., Monroy-Hernandez, A., Rusk, N., Eastmond, E., & Brennan, K. (2009, November). Scratch: Programming for all. *Communications of the ACM.* doi:10.1145/1592761.1592779

Reynolds, M. (1999). Critical reflection and management education: Rehabilitating less hierarchical approaches. *Journal of Management Education, 23*, 537–553. doi:10.1177/105256299902300506

Ribeiro, C., Fernandes, J., & Pereira, J. (2011). Didactical competence modeller: Dynamic story creation for serious games. In *Proceedings of KMEL 2011: The 1st International Symposium on Knowledge and E-Learning*. Springer.

Rice, J. W. (2007). New media resistance: Barriers to implementation of computer video games in the classroom. *Journal of Educational Multimedia and Hypermedia, 16*(3), 249–261.

Ridley, R., Wilks, D., & Freeman, J. (1997). Anaesthetists' attitudes towards an anesthesia simulator: A comparative survey: USA and Australia. *Anaesthesia and Intensive Care, 25*, 514–519.

Rieber, L. P. (1996). Seriously considering play- Designing interactive learning environments: Based on the blending of microworld, simulations and games. *Educational Technology Research and Development, 44*(2). doi:10.1007/BF02300540

Riedl, M. O. (2006). Believable agents and intelligent story adaptation for interactive storytelling. In Proceedings of the 3rd International Conference on Technologies for Interactive Digital Storytelling and Entertainment (TIDSE06), (pp. 1-12). TIDSE.

Robertson, J., & Howells, C. (2008). Computer game design: Opportunities for successful learning. *Computers & Education, 50*, 559–578. doi:10.1016/j.compedu.2007.09.020

Romero, M., & Usart, M. (2012). Game based learning time-on-task and learning performance according to students' temporal perspective. In *Proceedings of ECGBL*, (pp. 424-431). Cork, Ireland: ECGBL.

Romero, M., Usart, M., Ott, M., Earp, J., de Freitas, S., & Arnab, S. (2012). Learning through playing for or against each other? Promoting collaborative learning in digital game based learning. In *Proceedings of the 20th European Conference on Information Systems*. Barcelona, Spain: ESADE.

Romero, M. (2010). *Gestion du temps dans les activités projet médiatisées à distance*. Editions Européenes Universitaires.

Romero, M. (2011). Distance learners' work life balance. *Journal of Instructional Technology and Distance Learning, 8*(5), 43–47.

Romero, M., & Barberà, E. (2011). Quality of e-learners' time and learning performance beyond quantitative time-on-task. *International Review of Research in Open and Distance Learning, 12*(5), 122–135.

Romero, M., Hyvönen, P., & Barbera, E. (2012). Creativity in collaborative learning across the life span. *Creative Education, 3*(4), 422–429. doi:10.4236/ce.2012.34066

Romero, M., & Lambropoulos, N. (2011). Internal and external regulation to support knowledge construction and convergence in CSCL. *Electronic Journal of Research in Educational Psychology, 9*(1), 309–330.

Romero, M., Usart, M., & Almirall, E. (2011). Serious games in a finance course promoting the knowledge group awareness. *Proceedings of EDULEARN, 2011*, 3490–3492.

Rosen, K. (2008). The history of medical simulation. *Journal of Critical Care, 23*, 157–166. doi:10.1016/j.jcrc.2007.12.004

Roslina, I., & Azizah, J. (2008). *Web based computer games as an educational tools: Mapping the Malaysian surrounding issues*. Retrieved October 13, 2011 from http://eprints.utm.my/24577/2/RoslinaIbrahim2009.pdf

Roslina, I., & Azizah, J. (2009). *Educational games (EG) design framework: Combination of game design, pedagogy and content modeling*. Paper presented at the International Conference on Electrical Engineering and Informatics. Selangor, Malaysia.

Rowe, J., Shores, L., Mott, B., & Lester, J. (2010). Integrating learning and engagement in narrative-centered learning environments. In *Proceedings of the 10th International Conference on Intelligent Tutoring Systems*, (pp. 166-177). IEEE.

Rutkowski, A. F., Saunders, C., Vogel, D., & van Genuchten, M. (2007). Is it already 4am in your time zone: Focus immersion and temporal dissociation in virtual teams. *Small Group Research, 38*(1), 98–129. doi:10.1177/1046496406297042

Salen, K., & Zimmerman, E. (2003). *Rules of play: Game design fundamentals.* Cambridge, MA: The MIT Press.

Sandford, R., Ulicsak, M., Facer, K., & Rudd, T. (2006). Teaching with games. *Futurelab report.* Retrieved from http://archive.futurelab.org.uk/projects/teaching-with-games

Sandford, R., & Williamson, B. (2005). *Games and learning.* Bristol, UK: Futurelab.

Sarama, J., & Clements, D. H. (2009). Building blocks and cognitive building blocks: Playing to know the world mathematically. *American Journal of Play, 1,* 313–337.

Sarasvathy, S. D. (2001). Causation and effectuation: Toward a theoretical shift from economic inevitability to entrepreneurial contingency. *Academy of Management Review, 26*(2), 243–263.

Sardone, N. B., & Devlin-Scherer, R. (2010). Teacher candidate responses to digital games: 21st-century skills development. *Journal of Research on Technology in Education, 42*(4), 409–425.

Sauvé, L., Renaud, L., & Kaufman, D. (2010). Games, simulations, and simulations games for learning: Definitions and distinctions. In Kaufman, D., & Sauvé, L. (Eds.), *Educational Gameplay and Simulation Environments: Case Studies and Lessons Learned* (pp. 1–26). Hershey, PA: IGI Global. doi:10.4018/978-1-61520-731-2.ch001

Schaffer, S. Halverson, & Gee. (2004). *Video games and the future of learning.* Retrieved from http://www.wisconsin.gov/state/core/education.html

Schiesel, S. (2007, April 30). P.E. classes turn to video game that works legs, not thumbs. *The New York Times.* Retrieved March 5, 2009, from http://www.nytimes.com/2007/04/30/health/30exer.html

Schmidt, J. T., & Werner, C. H. (2007). Designing online instruction for success: Future oriented motivation and self-regulation. *The Electronic Journal of e-learning, 5*(1), 69-78.

Schön, D. (1983). *The reflective practitioner: How professionals think in action.* New York, NY: Basic Books.

Schuman, H., Walsh, E., Olson, C., & Etheridge, B. (1985). Effort and reward: The assumption that college grades are affected by quantity of study. *Social Forces, 63*(4), 945–966.

Scott, L. M., Scott, D., Bedic, S. P., & Dowd, J. (1999). The effect of associative and dissociative strategies on rowing ergometer performance. *The Sport Psychologist, 13,* 57–68.

Scribner, S. (1997). Situating the experiment in cross-cultural research. In Tobach, E., Falmage, R. J., Parlee, M. B., Martin, L. M., & Scribner, A. (Eds.), *Selected Writings of Silvia Scribner* (pp. 94–105). Cambridge, UK: Cambridge University Press.

Scribner, S., & Cole, M. (1978). Literacy without schooling: Testing for intellectual effects. *Harvard Educational Review, 48*(4).

Sefton-Green, J. (2006). Youth, technology and media cultures. *Review of Research in Education, 30,* 279–306. doi:10.3102/0091732X030001279

Seidel, T., & Prenzel, M. (2006). Stability of teaching patterns in physics instruction: Findings from a video study. *Learning and Instruction, 16,* 228–240. doi:10.1016/j.learninstruc.2006.03.002

Sengupta, S. (2011). *Causes of unemployment.* Retrieved on February 18, 2012 from www.buzzle.com/articles/causes-of-unemployment.html

Serrano, A., Marchiori, E. J., del Blanco, A., Torrente, J., & Fernandez-Manjon, B. (2012). A framework to improve evaluation in educational games. In *Proceedings of the Global Engineering Education Conference (EDUCON).* IEEE.

Shaffer, D. W. (2006). *How computer games help children learn.* New York, NY: Palmgrave Macmillan. doi:10.1057/9780230601994

Shaffer, D. W., Squire, K. R., Halverson, R., & Gee, J. P. (2005). Video games and the future of learning. *Phi Delta Kappan, 87*(2), 104–111.

Sharma, A. (2011). What is the relationship between education and education and psychology? *Preserve Articles*. Retrieved on February 23, 2012 from www.preservearticles.com/about_preservedarticles.com.html

Shawer, S. F. (2010). Classroom-level curriculum development: EFL teachers as curriculum-developers, curriculum-makers and curriculum-transmitters. *Teaching and Teacher Education*, *26*(2), 173–184. doi:10.1016/j.tate.2009.03.015

Sheked, A. (2005). *Multiple case narrative: A qualitative approach to studying multiple populations*. Amsterdam, The Netherlands: John Benjamins Publishing Company.

Shelton, B. E., & Scoresby, J. (2011). Aligning game activity with educational goals: Following constrained design approach to instructional computer games. *Educational Technology Research and Development*, *59*, 113–138. doi:10.1007/s11423-010-9175-0

Shi, W., Lee, G., Hinchley, J., Corriveau, J.-P., Kapralos, B., & Hogue, A. (2010). Using a virtual learning environment with highly interactive elements in second life to engage millennial students. In *Proceedings of the International Conference on e-Education, e-Business, e-Management, and e-Learning, 2010*, (pp. 255-259). IC4E.

Shulman, L. S. (1986). Those who understand: Knowledge growth in teaching. *Educational Researcher*, *15*(2), 4–14.

Siemens, G., & Long, P. (2011). Penetrating the fog: Analytics in learning and education. *EDUCAUSE Review*, *46*(5).

Silseth, K. (2012). The multivoicedness of game play: Exploring the unfolding of a student's learning trajectory in a gaming context at school. *International Journal of Computer-Supported Collaborative Learning*, *7*(1), 63–84. doi:10.1007/s11412-011-9132-x

Silva, J. N., & Santos, C. P. (2011). Jogos e matemática. In Palhares, P., Gomes, A., & Amaral, E. (Eds.), *Complementos de Matemática para Professores do Ensino Básico* (pp. 303–334). Lisboa, Portugal: Lidel.

Silverman, D. (2005). *Doing qualitative research: A practical handbook* (2nd ed.). London, UK: Sage Publications.

Simon, H. A. (1992). The game of chess. In Aumann, R. J., & Hart, S. (Eds.), *Handbook of Game Theory with Economic Applications* (Vol. 1, pp. 1–17). Amsterdam, The Netherlands: Elsevier Science Publishers B.V. doi:10.1016/S1574-0005(05)80004-9

Simons, J., Vansteenkiste, M., Lens, W., & Lacante, M. (2004). Placing motivation and future time perspective theory in a temporal perspective. *Educational Psychology Review*, *16*(2), 121–139. doi:10.1023/B:EDPR.0000026609.94841.2f

Simpson, E., & Stansberry, S. (2008). Video games and teacher development: Bridging the gap in the classroom. In Miller, C. T. (Ed.), *Games: Purpose and Potential in Education* (pp. 163–184). New York, NY: Springer.

Simpson, G., Hoyles, C., & Noss, R. (2006). Exploring the mathematics of motion through construction and collaboration. *Journal of Computer Journal of Computer Assisted Learning*, *22*, 114–136. doi:10.1111/j.1365-2729.2006.00164.x

Sinclair, J., Hingston, P., & Masek, M. (2007). Considerations for the design of exergames. [Perth, Australia: GRAPHITE.]. *Proceedings of GRAPHITE, 2007*, 289–295. doi:10.1145/1321261.1321313

Sitzmann, T., Ely, K., Brown, K. G., & Bauer, K. N. (2010). Self-assessment of knowledge: A cognitive learning or affective measure? *Academy of Management Learning & Education*, *9*(2), 169–191. doi:10.5465/AMLE.2010.51428542

Sitzman, T. (2011). Analytic examination of the instructional effectiveness of computer-based simulation games. *Personnel Psychology*, *64*(2), 489–528. doi:10.1111/j.1744-6570.2011.01190.x

Sjøberg, S., & Schreiner, C. (2006). How do learners in different cultures relate to science and technology? Results and perspectives from the project ROSE. *APFSLT: Asia-Pacific Forum on Science Learning and Teaching*, *7*(1).

Slater, M., Usoh, M., & Steed, A. (1995). Taking steps: The influence of a walking metaphor on presence in virtual reality. *ACM Transactions on Computer-Human Interaction*, *2*, 201–219. doi:10.1145/210079.210084

Smith, A. (1776). *The wealth of nations*. Retrieved on February 18, 2012 from www.bibliomania.com/2/1/65/112/frameset.html

Smith, J. (2012). *How to develop teaching materials.* Retrieved on March 10, 2012 from www.ehom.com/how_6592423_develop_teaching-materials.html

Smith, R. (2009). *Military simulation & serious games: Where we came from and where we are going.* Modelbenders Press.

Smith, R. (2010). The long history of gaming in military training. *Simulation & Gaming, 41*(1), 6–19. doi:10.1177/1046878109334330

Snyder, R. M. (2007). *Winning chess tournaments: Methods and materials training guide.* Lincoln, NE: iUniverse.

Sothern, M. (2004). Obesity prevention in children: Physical activity and nutrition. *Nutrition (Burbank, Los Angeles County, Calif.), 20*(7-8), 704–708. doi:10.1016/j.nut.2004.04.007

Spindler, G., & Hammond, L. (2006). *Innovations in educational ethnography: Theory, methods and results.* New York, NY: LEA.

Spires, H. (2008). *The 21st century skills and serious games – Preparing the N generation in serious educational games.* Rotterdam, The Netherlands: Sense Publishing.

Squire, K. (2002). Cultural framing of computer/video-games. *Game Studies, 2*(1).

Squire, K. (2005). Changing the game: What happens when video games enter the classroom?. *Innovate Journal of Online Education, 1*(6).

Squire, K. (2005). Game-based learning: An X-learn perspective paper. *MASIE Center: e-Learning Consortium Report.* Retrieved from http://www.masieweb.com/research-and-articles/research/game-based-learning.html

Squire, K. (2005b). *Game-based learning: Present and future state of the field.* Retrieved from http://www.newmediaforlearning.com/research/Game-Based_Learning.pdf

Squire, K. (2003). Video games in education. *International Journal of Intelligent Simulations and Gaming, 2*(1).

Squire, K. (2004). *Replaying history: Learning world history through playing civilization III.* Bloomington, IN: Indiana University.

Squire, K. (2006). From content to context: Videogames as designed experience. *Educational Researcher, 35*(8), 19–29. doi:10.3102/0013189X035008019

Squire, K. (2008). Open-ended video games: A model for developing learning for the interactive age. In Salen, K. (Ed.), *The Ecology of Games: Connecting Youth, Games and Learning* (pp. 167–198). Cambridge, MA: MIT Press.

Squire, K. (2011). *Video games and learning: Teaching and participatory culture in the digital age.* Cambridge, MA: Teachers College Press.

Squire, K. A. (2005). From users to designers building a self-organizing game-based learning. *TechTrends, 49*(5), 32–42. doi:10.1007/BF02763688

Squire, K. D. (2006). From content to context: Videogames as designed experiences. *Educational Researcher, 35*(8). doi:10.3102/0013189X035008019

Squire, K., & Jenkins, H. (2004). Harnessing the power of games in education. *Insight (American Society of Ophthalmic Registered Nurses), 3*(1), 5–33.

Srinivasan, V., Butler-Purry, K., & Pedersen, S. (2008). Using video games to enhance learning in digital systems. In *Proceedings of the 2008 Conference on Future Play Research Play Share Future Play.* (pp. 196-199). London, UK: ACM.

St. Amant, K., & Kelsey, S. (2011). *Computer mediated communication: Issues and approaches in education.* Hershey, PA: IGI Global.

Stacey, R. D. (1996). *Complexity and creativity in organizations.* San Francisco, CA: Berret-Koehler.

Stacy, C. Marsella, W. L. (2003). Interactive pedagogical drama for health interventions. In *Proceedings of the Eleventh International Conference on Artificial Intelligence in Education,* (pp. 341-348). IEEE.

Staiano, A., & Calvert, S. (1998). Exergames for physical education courses: Physical, social, and cognitive benefits. *Child Development Perspectives, 5*(2), 93–98. doi:10.1111/j.1750-8606.2011.00162.x

Steen, L. A. (1990). *On the shoulders of giants: New approaches to numeracy.* Washington, DC: National Academy Press.

Steinkuehler, C. (2010). Video games and digital literacies. *Journal of Adolescent & Adult Literacy, 54*(1), 61–63. doi:10.1598/JAAL.54.1.7

Stern, E., & Aprea, C., & Ebner. (2003). Improving cross-content transfer in text processing by means of active graphical representation. *Learning and Instruction, 13*(2), 191–203. doi:10.1016/S0959-4752(02)00020-8

Steyaert, C. (2004). The prosaics of entrepreneurship. In Hjorth, D., & Steyaert, C. (Eds.), *Narrative and Discursive Approaches in Entrepreneurship* (pp. 8–21). Cheltenham, UK: Edward Elgar.

Stigler, M., & Hiebert, J. (1999). *The teaching gap.* New York, NY: Free Press.

Suh, S., Kim, S. W., & Kim, N. J. (2010). Effectiveness of MMORPG-based instruction in elementary English education in Korea. *Journal of Computer Assisted Learning, 26,* 370–378. doi:10.1111/j.1365-2729.2010.00353.x

Susi, T., Johannesson, M., & Backlund, P. (2007). *Serious games - An overview.* Skövde, Sweden: University of Skövde.

Sweller, J., Van Merriënboer, J., & Paas, F. (1998). Cognitive architecture and instructional design. *Educational Psychology Review, 10*(3), 251–296. doi:10.1023/A:1022193728205

Szczesna, A., Grudzinski, J., Grudzinski, T., Mikuszewski, R., & Debowski, A. (2011). The psychology serious game prototype for preschool children. In *Proceedings of the IEEE 1st International Conference on Serious Games and Applications for Health*, (pp. 58-61). IEEE Press.

Szezurek, M. (1982). *Meta-analysis of simulation games effectiveness for cognitive learning.* Bloomington, IN: Indiana University.

Taffinder, N., Russell, R., & Manus, I. (1998). An objective assessment of laparoscope psychomotor skills: The effect of a training course on performance. *Surgical Endoscopy, 12,* 493.

Tang, S., Hanneghan, M., & El Rhalibi, A. (2009). Introduction to games-based learning. In Connolly, T. M., Stansfield, M. H., & Boyle, E. (Eds.), *Games-Based Learning Advancement for Multisensory Human Computer Interfaces: Techniques and Effective Practices.* Hershey, PA: IGI Global. doi:10.4018/978-1-60566-360-9.ch001

Tan, W. H., Neill, S., & Johsnston-Wilder, S. (2012). How do professionals' attitude differ between what game-based learning could ideally achieve and what is usually achieved. *International Journal of Game-Based Learning, 2*(1), 1–15. doi:10.4018/ijgbl.2012010101

Tate, W. F. (2005). *Access and opportunities to learn are not accidents: Engineering mathematical progress in your school.* Paper presented at the Southeast Eisenhower Regional Consortium for Mathematics Science at SERVE. Orlando, FL.

Tate, W. F., & Rousseau, C. (2002). Access and opportunity: The political and social context of mathematics education. In English, L. D. (Ed.), *Handbook of International Research in Mathematics Education* (pp. 271–299). London, UK: Erlbaum.

Tenenbaumb, G., & Connollya, T. C. (2008). Attention allocation under varied workload and effort perception in rowers. *Psychology of Sport and Exercise, 9*(5), 704–717. doi:10.1016/j.psychsport.2007.09.002

Tenenbaum, G. (2001). A social-cognitive perspective of perceived exertion and exertion tolerance. In Singer, R. N., Hausenblas, H., & Janelle, C. (Eds.), *Handbook of Sport Psychology* (pp. 810–820). New York, NY: Wiley.

Teteris, E., Fraser, K., Wright, B., & McLaughlin, K. (2012). Does training learners on simulators benefit real patients? *Advances in Heath Sciences Education, 17*(1), 137–144. doi:10.1007/s10459-011-9304-5

Thatcher, D. (1990). *Promoting learning through games and simulations.* Thousand Oaks, CA: Sage Publications.

Thomas, S. (2006). Pervasive learning games: Explorations of hybrid educational gamescapes. *Simulation & Gaming, 37*(1), 41–55. doi:10.1177/1046878105282274

Thue, D., Bulitko, V., & Spetch, M. (2008). Making stories player-specific: Delayed authoring in interactive storytelling. In *Proceedings of the 1st Joint International Conference on Interactive Digital Storytelling: Interactive Storytelling*, (pp. 230-241). IEEE.

Tiberghien, A., & Buty, C. (2007). Studying science teaching practices in relation to learning: Times scales of teaching phenomena. In Pintó, R., & Couso, D. (Eds.), *ESERA Selected Contributions Book* (pp. 59–75). Berlin, Germany: Springer. doi:10.1007/978-1-4020-5032-9_5

Trahtemberg, L. (2000). El impacto previsible en las nuevas tecnologías en la enseñanza y la organización escolar. *Revista Iberoamericana de Educación, 24*. Retrieved from http://www.campus-oei.org/revista/rie24a02.htm

Trautwein, U. (2007). The homework-achievement relation reconsidered: Differentiating homework time, homework frequency, and homework effort. *Learning and Instruction, 17*(3), 372–388. doi:10.1016/j.learninstruc.2007.02.009

Tubella, I., Tabernero, C., & Dwyer, V. (2008). *Internet i televisió: La guerra de les pantalles*. Barcelona, Spain: Editorial Ariel.

Turkle, S. (1984). *Video games and computer holding power*. The New Media Reader.

Turkle, S. (1995). *Life on the screen: Identity in the age of the internet*. New York, NY: Touchstone.

U.S. Department of Education, National Center for Education Statistics. (2000). *Entry and persistence of women and minorities in college science and engineering education*. Washington, DC: NCES.

UEMS. (1993). *Charter on training of medical specialists in the European community*. European Union of Medical Specialists.

Ulicsak, M., & Wright, M. (2010). *Games in education: Serious games*. Bristol, UK: Futurelab. Retrieved from http://www.futurelab.org

UNESCO. (2006). *Report on education for all: Literacy for life*. Retrieved on February 26, 2012 from www.uis.unesco.org/Library/Documents/gmr06.en.pdf

United Nations. (1976). *General assembly resolution 31/123 – The international year of disabled persons, 1981*. Geneva, Switzerland: United Nations.

United Nations. (1993). *General assembly, standard rules on the equalization of opportunities for persons with disabilities*. Retrieved on March 5, 2012 from www.un.org/documents/ga/res/48/ar096.htm

University of Nottingham. (2012). *Corporate social responsibility*. Retrieved on February 29, 2012 from http://pgstudy.nottingham.ac.uk/postgraduate-courses

Usart, M., & Romero, M. (2012). Students' time perspective and its effects on game based learning. In *Proceedings of the 8th International Scientific Conference eLearning and Software for Education*. Bucharest, Romania: IEEE.

Usart, M., Romero, M., & Almirall, E. (2011). Impact of the feeling of knowledge explicitness in the learners' participation and performance in a collaborative game based learning activity. *Lecture Notes in Computer Science, 6944*, 23–35. doi:10.1007/978-3-642-23834-5_3

Uthalsangchai, P. (2011). *Qualities of a successful international manager*. Retrieved on March 15, 2012 from www.bangkokbank.com

Valente, J., Kozlova, V., & Lima, C. (2011). Virtual tutor in MRI learning. In *Proceedings of the IEEE 1st International Conference on Serious Games and Applications for Health*, (pp. 37-41). IEEE Press.

Van Eck, R. (2006). Digital game-based learning: It's not just the digital natives who are restless. *EDUCAUSE Review, 41*(2).

Van Eck, R. (2006). Digital game-based learning: It's not just the digital natives who are restless.... *EDUCAUSE Review, 41*(2).

Van Eck, R. (2009). A guide to integrating COTS games into your classroom. In Ferdig, R. (Ed.), *Handbook of Research on Effective Electronic Gaming in Education* (pp. 179–199). New York, NY: Information Science Reference.

Van Langen, A. M. L. (2005). *Unequal participation in mathematics and science education*. Antwerpen, Belgium: Garant-Uitgevers.

Vanderwater, E. A., Shim, M. S., & Caplovitz, A. G. (2004). Linking obesity and activity level with children's television and video game use. *Adolescence, 27*(1), 71–85. doi:10.1016/j.adolescence.2003.10.003

VanSickle, R. L. (1986). A quantitative review of research on instructional simulation gaming: A twenty-year perspective. *Theory and Research in Social Education, 14*(3), 245–264. doi:10.1080/00933104.1986.10505525

Virvou, M., Katsionis, G., & Manos, K. (2005). Combining software games with education: Evaluation of its educational effectiveness. *Journal of Educational Technology & Society, 8*, 54–65.

Vogel, J. J., Vogel, D. S., Cannon-Bowers, J., Bowers, C. A., Muse, K., & Wright, M. (2006). Computer gaming and interactive simulations for learning: A meta-analysis. *Journal of Educational Computing Research, 34*(3), 229–243. doi:10.2190/FLHV-K4WA-WPVQ-H0YM

Völgyi, E., Lyytikäinen, A., Tylavsky, F., Nicholson, P., Suominen, H., Alén, M., & Cheng, S. (2010). Long-term leisure-time physical activity has a positive effect on bone mass gain in girls. *Journal of Bone and Mineral Research, 25*(5), 1034–1041.

Voogt, J., & Pareja Roblin, N. (2010). *21st century skills – Discussion paper*. Enschede, The Netherlands: University of Twente. Retrieved 25 November 2012 from http://onderzoek.kennisnet.nl/onderzoeken-totaal/21stecentury

Voogt, A. J. (1999). Distribution of mancala board games: A methodological inquiry. *Board Games Studies, 2*, 104–114.

Vos, N., Meijden, H. V. D., & Denessen, E. (2011). Effects of constructing versus playing an educational game on student motivation and deep learning strategy use. *Computers & Education, 56*, 127–137. doi:10.1016/j.compedu.2010.08.013

Vosniadou, S. (2007). Conceptual change approach and its re-framing. In Vosniadou, S., Baltas, A., & Vamvakoussi, X. (Eds.), *Re-Framing the Conceptual Change Approach in Learning and Instruction* (pp. 1–15). Oxford, UK: Elsevier Press.

Vygotskiĭ, L. A. (1978). *Processes, mind in society: The development of higher psychological*. Boston, MA: Harvard University Press.

Vygotsky, L. S. (1978). *Mind in society: The development of higher psychological processes*. Cambridge, MA: Harvard University Press.

Wagner, P., Schober, B., & Spiel, C. (2008). Time students spend working at home for school. *Learning and Instruction, 18*, 309–320. doi:10.1016/j.learninstruc.2007.03.002

Wagner, T. (2008). *The global achievement gap*. New York, NY: Basic Books.

Wagstaff, R., & Mahmoudi, H. (1976). Relation of study behaviors and employment to academic performance. *Psychological Reports, 38*, 380–382. doi:10.2466/pr0.1976.38.2.380

Walker, J. (2010). Being a responsible citizen. *Responsible Citizen Co*. Retrieved on February 28, 2012 from www.resposblecitizen.co.uk/being-a-responsible-citizen.html

Wallace, B. (1986). Creativity: Some definitions: The creative personality; the creative process; the creative classroom. *Gifted Education International, 4*(2), 68–73. doi:10.1177/026142948600400202

Wassarman, H. S. (2002). The role of expectancies and time perspectives in gambling behaviour. *The Sciences and Engineering, 62*(8B), 3818.

Watson, W. R., Mong, C. J., & Harris, C. A. (2011). A case study of the in-class use of a video game for teaching high school history. *Computers & Education, 56*, 466–474. doi:10.1016/j.compedu.2010.09.007

Wellman, G. S., & Marcinkiewicz, H. (2004). Online learning and time-on-task: Impact of proctored vs. unproctored testing. *Journal of Asynchronous Learning Networks, 8*(4), 93–104.

Whitton, N. (2012). The place of game-based learning in an age of austerity. *Electronic Journal of e-Learning, 10*(2), 249 – 256.

Wiles, J., & Bondl, J. (1979). *Curriculum development- A guide to practice*. Columbus, OH: Chales E. Merril Publishing Company.

Williamson, B. (2009). *Computer games, schools, and young people: A report for educators on using games for learning*. Bristol, UK: NESTA FutureLab.

Wilson, L. O. (2005). *Curriculum index*. Retrieved on March 5, 2012 from www4.uwsp.edu/education/Wilson.index

Winnicott, D. W. (1971). *Playing and reality*. Harmondsworth, UK: Penguin Books.

Wittgenstein, L. (1958). *Philosophical investigations* (Anscombe, G. E. M., Trans.). Oxford, UK: Basil Blackwell.

Workbench, E. (2005). *Electronics workbench - A national instruments company*. Retrieved May 1, 2012, from http://www.electronicsworks.com/

Worspace. (2005). *Workspace 5 PC based robotic simulation software*. Retrieved May 1, 2012, from http://www.workspace5.com/

Wouters, P., van der Spek, E. D., & van Oostendorp, H. (2009). *Current practices in serious game research: A review from a learning outcomes perspective*. Retrieved from http://www.cs.uu.nl/docs/vakken/b3elg/literatuur_files/Wouters.pdf

Yatim, M. H. M., & Masuch, M. (2007). GATELOCK: A game authoring tool for children. In *Proceedings of the 6th International Conference on Interaction Design and Children*, (pp. 173–174). IEEE.

Young-Loveridge, J. (2005). Students' views about mathematics learning: A case study of one school involved in the great expectations project. In Higgins, J., Irwin, K. C., Thomas, G., Trinick, T., & Young Loveridge, J. (Eds.), *Findings from the New Zealand Numeracy Development Project 2004* (pp. 107–114). Wellington, New Zealand: Ministry of Education.

Younis, B. L. (2010). Integrating serious games in higher education programs. In *Proceedings of the Academic Colloquium 2010: Building Partnerships in Teaching Excellence*. Ramallah, Palestine: Virtual Environment Lab (V-LAB).

Zagal, J. P., & Mateas, M. (2010). Time in videogames: A survey and analysis. *Simulation & Gaming, 41*(6), 844–868. doi:10.1177/1046878110375594

Zakay, D. (1989). Subjective time and attentional resource allocation: An integrated model of time estimation. In Levin, I., & Zakay, D. (Eds.), *Time and Human Cognition: A Life-Span Perspective* (pp. 365–397). Amsterdam, The Netherlands: North-Holland. doi:10.1016/S0166-4115(08)61047-X

Zemliansky, P. (Ed.). (2010). *Design and implementation of educational games: Theoretical and practical*. Hershey, PA: IGI Global. doi:10.4018/978-1-61520-781-7

Zhang, Y., Goonetilleke, R. S., Plocher, T., & Liang, S.-F. M. (2005). Time-related behaviour in multitasking situations. *International Journal of Human-Computer Studies, 62*, 425–455. doi:10.1016/j.ijhcs.2005.01.002

Zimbardo, P. G., & Boyd, J. N. (1999). Putting time in perspective: A valid, reliable individual-differences metric. *Journal of Personality and Social Psychology, 77*, 1271–1288. doi:10.1037/0022-3514.77.6.1271

Zimbardo, P. G., Keough, K. A., & Boyd, J. N. (1997). Present time perspective as a predictor of risky driving. *Personality and Individual Differences, 23*, 1007–1023. doi:10.1016/S0191-8869(97)00113-X

Zyda, M. (2005). From visual simulation to virtual reality to games. *IEEE Computer, 38*(9), 25–32. doi:10.1109/MC.2005.297

About the Contributors

Sara de Freitas is Director of Research and Professor of Virtual Environments at Coventry University with responsibility for applied research, teaching and learning and business development. Sara was responsible for setting up the Serious Games Institute, a hybrid model of research, business and study, the first institute of its kind. Sara currently holds Scientific Coordination of a European-Union funded Network of Excellence in serious games. She also holds 23 research and development projects: including three from the Joint Information Systems Committee (JISC), two from the UK Engineering and Physical Sciences Research Council and 12 from FP7 European Union funds. Sara publishes widely in the areas of: pedagogy and e-learning; change management and strategy development for implementing e-learning systems and serious games and virtual worlds for supporting training and learning. Her most recent book, the e-Learning Reader (edited with J. Jameson) has just been published by Continuum Press. Other recent books include Rethinking Learning for a Digital Age (edited with R. Sharpe and H. Beetham) which was published in 2010 by Routledge and Digital Games and Learning (edited with P. Maharg) which was published in 2011 by Continuum Press. Interdisciplinary Advancements in Gaming, Simulations and Virtual Environments: Emerging Trends (edited with R. Ferdig) was published by IGI Global. Her book series with Routledge: Digital Games and Learning (edited with P. Maharg) will include ten books published from 2012.

Michela Ott is a Senior Researcher at the Institute for Educational Technology within the Italian National Research Council (ITD-CNR). She has participated in, led, and coordinated many national and international research projects in the field of Educational Technology. She is a member of the editorial board of important journals, and is the author of more than 100 scientific publications published in national and international journals, books, and conference proceedings. She is the author of several educational software packages and has contributed to the design and implementation of hypermedia systems. She leads national research projects dealing with the use of digital Mind Games to support and enhance students' reasoning skills. She is involved in both STELLAR (Sustaining Technology Enhanced Learning at a LARge scale – www.stellarnet.eu) and GaLA (Game and Learning Alliance – www.galanoe.eu) Networks of Excellence: the former focuses on Technology Enhanced Learning and the second on Serious Games.

Maria Magdalena Popescu is Associate Professor at the Carol I National Defence University, in Bucharest, Romania. She has been working closely with the ADL Department within the Carol I NDU and participated in many research projects and initiatives on e-learning and technology-enhanced education. Her research focuses on educational software tools, open educational resources, use and policy, online education, e-pedagogy and eLearning, instructional design, towards a wider implementation of all these within the educational system at large. At present, she is involved with the GaLA European Network (Game and Learning Alliance) as task leader in Serious Games metrics and taxonomy.

Ioana Andreea Stănescu is a Senior Researcher at Advanced Distributed Learning Romania. Her research focuses on knowledge management, e-learning and m-learning, game-based learning, collaborative technology, and human computer interaction. She has been involved in the development and management of R&D projects that support knowledge acquisition, interoperability, and reuse, and that target the improvement of the learning milieu through systems integration and intelligent solutions. The results of her research have been published in international conference proceedings and scientific journals and have been integrated in educational products. Currently, she is active in the European Game and Learning Alliance (GaLA) Network of Excellence.

* * *

Leona Achtenhagen is Professor of Entrepreneurship and Business Development as well as Associate Dean of Accreditation at Jönköping International Business School in Sweden. Her current research interests comprise, for example, entrepreneurial and strategic issues of small firm growth, the representation of entrepreneurship in different media, as well as entrepreneurship education. Her research results have been published in journals such as *Entrepreneurship Theory & Practice*, *Long Range Planning*, and *Entrepreneurship & Regional Development*.

Sylvester Arnab is a Senior Researcher at the Serious Games Institute. He is currently project managing the coordination of the R&D activities under the EU-funded Games and Leaning Alliance (GALA) as well as the various game development projects. The recent one is a game for Relationship and Sex Education in conjunction with a team in Singapore, which is currently being deployed in the schools in Coventry and Warwickshire. He has various publications within the area of virtual worlds and simulation, and he has published an edited book: *Serious Games for Healthcare: Applications and Implications*, IGI Global.

Nurul Aini Bakar is currently a PhD student at the National University of Malaysia. Her research interest is to study the effect of game-based learning on students' learning, particularly on 21st century skills, as well as motivation towards science subject.

Fernanda Sande Candeias graduated in History at the University of Évora in 1989. She has a Master's degree in Contemporary History by the University of Lisbon. She had also special training in auditing. From 2004 to 2008, she audited the quality of Safety and Health at Work courses at Portuguese Universities for the Portuguese Institute for Safety and Health at Work, where she was the head of the Training Division. Fernanda is an experienced trainer and teacher and has taught young students and adults for more than twenty years. She has explored the potential of new technologies applied to teaching.

She designed curricula for distance learning, namely e- and b-Learning, and monitored several courses in that field. In 2011, she co-founded Stand Clear Lda., a startup engaged in developing innovative tools for medical education.

Héctor del Castillo is Assistant Professor and Senior Researcher in the Department of Educational Science at the University of Alcala (Spain). He holds a degree in Sociology and a PhD in Psychological Development, Learning, and Education; he has developed an interest for the analysis of multimedia and digital literacy contexts, focusing his work as a teacher and researcher on the fields of Education and Sports. Academically, he has concentrated on exploring new virtual educational environments participating in various innovation projects.

Ana Sofia Corredoura graduated in Medicine at the Universidade Nova de Lisboa in 1993. She is specialist in Internal Medicine since 2002 and works as a Medical Chief in a major teaching hospital in Lisbon. She has experience in training medical students and residents and is also an instructor in advanced life support by the European Resuscitation Council. In 2010, she obtained a Certificate of Teaching Ability by the Portuguese Public Employment and Vocational Training Institute. Videogames for medical education is a major area of interest and research. In 2011, she co-founded Stand Clear Lda., a startup engaged in developing innovative tools for medical education.

Ian Dunwell is a Senior Researcher at the Serious Games Institute, currently leading the area of educational games. Having obtained his PhD in Computer Science in 2007, he also holds a degree in Physics from Imperial College London, and is an Associate of the Royal College of Science. His research interests lie primarily in the application of an understanding of cognitive processes as a means for providing optimised, evaluated, and effective learning experiences. He led the final stage delivery of the evaluation of Code of Everand, commissioned in 2009 by the Department for Transport and the largest public-funded serious game developed in the UK to date. He also led the SGI contribution to ALICE, a €2.2m EU-funded FP7 project developing next-generation adaptive learning environments, which was awarded the highest possible evaluation rating on its conclusion by the European Commission. Other European-funded project involvement has included defining the overarching pedagogic design for four serious games within the European Union funded e-Vita (European Life Experiences) project, and preliminary design work towards the repurposing of medical learning objects within the mEducator consortium. He is currently leading the SGI contribution to MASELTOV, a €3m FP7 STREP targeting at providing mobile assistive services to migrants entering the EC. In addition to completing an Erasmus placement at Fraunhofer IPA, developing an architecture linking real-world service robotics to virtual worlds; recent exploratory work has included the use and evaluation of a wide range of novel HCI interface technologies, including the NeuroSky and Emotiv headsets, eyetracking, and Near Infrared-Spectroscopy (NIRS) in collaboration with the Department of Computing, Imperial College London, and Graz University. In the domain of serious games, he has consulted with a number of leading serious game companies including Blitz Games, PlayGen, and Zynga to design and develop evaluation strategies for serious games such as Patient Rescue, Ward Off Infection, i-Seed, and Parent Know-How, and worked extensively with games aimed at reaching difficult demographics and changing the affect and motivation of learners. He has also worked in an advisory role with Warwick University Digital Lab in the development of a game tackling childhood obesity, and with Coventry University Faculty of Health and Life Sciences developing and evaluating games enabling parents to communicate difficult topics to their children effectively.

Ronald Dyer has held technology positions in the USA at such organization as Salomon Smith Barney, Goldman Sachs with responsibility for ICT integration as well as in the Caribbean as a consultant with the Inter-American Development Bank, where his project portfolio focused on Institutional Strengthening with ICT. He possesses over 20 years of experience in the area of Technology Strategy, Transformation, and Change Management for capacity building and performance improvement within public and private sector institutions, specifically education and service industries. Currently Mr. Dyer is a 3rd year Doctorate in Business Administration (DBA) candidate at Grenoble Ecole de Management, France, where his research focus is on Serious Games for Technology, Innovation, and Change. He is a graduate of Wilfrid Laurier University, Waterloo, Ontario, Canada, and holds an MBA in Project Management from Henley Graduate School of Business, University of Reading, United Kingdom.

Dores Ferreira is a Primary Teacher with a Master's in Teaching and Learning Mathematics. Is a PhD student in Child Studies: Elementary Mathematics at the Institute of Education of the University of Minho, Braga, Portugal, and collaborator of the CIEC at this institute. She is also Vice-President of the Association for Elementary Mathematics Education (AEME).

Ana Belén Garcia-Varela is Assistant Professor and Senior Researcher in the Department of Educational Science at the University of Alcala (Spain). She holds a PhD in Developmental Psychology and Education, a diploma on Teaching Studies: Early Childhood, and a degree in Psychopedagogy, Learning, and Education. Her research interest is related to new literacies and the analysis of different contexts of development. She also has participated in projects related to innovation and improvement in the quality of teaching, focusing on the analysis of virtual teaching environments.

Despoina Goutou holds a BSc in Economics from the University of Toulouse (France), spent a year abroad at the University of Nottingham (UK) doing Economics. She is an MSc candidate at the University of Exeter in International Management for the academic year 2012-2013. Currently, she is an Assistant Researcher at the educational organization e-DEKA in Greece. Her areas of research are social and educational development. She is author of scientific papers published in international journals. She has presented two papers related to (a) the Geoengineering Method and (b) What is the Hartwick rule? What does it have to do with sustainability? She is member of the services involved in students learning mobility through the EU ERASMUS project. She is, also, member of the LinkedIn e-Learning Think Tank Team Group.

Thorkild Hanghøj is an Associate Professor at the Department for Communication and Psychology at Aalborg University, Copenhagen, where he is affiliated with ILD – The Research Lab on ICT and Designs for Learning. He has a MA in cultural studies and media studies, and has a PhD on the design and use of ICT-supported debate games within educational settings. His current work is mainly focused on game pedagogy and the role of the teacher in facilitating computer games based upon the research project "Serious Games on a Global Market Place" (2007-2011) and on-going research on how games may be used for teacher development.

David Herrero is a research fellow and PhD candidate at the Faculty of Education of Universidad de Alcalá (Spain). He has a degree in in Physical Education, a BA in Educational Psychology, and a MA in Communication and Learning (UAH). His research interests are directed to the links between video games and learning processes, focusing his PhD dissertation in the possibilities to transfer that learning to other contexts.

Bengt Johannisson is Senior Professor of Entrepreneurship at Linnaeus University in Sweden. Previously, he held chairs at Lund University and at Jönköping International Business School in Sweden and at Roskilde University in Denmark. He has also been a Visiting Scholar at universities in England, Canada, Austria, and Italy. 1998-2007, he was the Editor-in-Chief of Entrepreneurship and Regional Development, and he himself has published widely on entrepreneurship, personal networking, family business, as well as on local and regional development. His current research interest is social entrepreneurship. A special concern is entrepreneurship education, and in this field, he has been an expert to the Swedish government. In Sweden, Bengt Johannisson has initiated inter-university networks on research and post-graduate studies in entrepreneurship, and for fifteen years, he was a Director of the European Doctoral Programme in Entrepreneurship and Small Business Management. Bengt Johannisson is the 2008 Winner of the FSF-Nutek Global Award in Entrepreneurship Research.

Harri Ketamo, Ph.D., is a CEO and Founder at eedu ltd. and Adjunct Professor at Tampere University of Technology. He has a strong academic background in Educational Technology, Complex Adaptive Systems, Cognitive Psychology of Learning, Neural Computing, and Game Design. Before founding eedu, Harri was a Director of Education at Satakunta University of Applied Sciences, CEO and founder at GameMiner ltd., and Academy of Finland granted Post-Doc Researcher.

Kristian Kiili, Ph.D., Ed.M., works as a Senior Research Fellow and an Adjunct Professor at the Tampere University of Technology (TUT) in Pori, Finland, in which he heads the multidisciplinary Advanced Multimedia Center research laboratory. His current research focuses on game-based learning, learning by designing games approach, user-centered game design issues, and educational exergames. He is a member on the committee of the European Conference on Games-Based Learning and has act as reviewer in several scientific journals. Results received from his studies have been published in several scientific publications as well as applied in commercial products. Kiili is a co-founder and director of Flow Factory company.

Maria Meletiou-Mavrotheris is an Associate Professor at the European University, Cyprus, and Director of the Research Laboratory in ICT-Enhanced Education. She has a Ph.D. in Mathematics Education (University of Texas at Austin), an M.Sc. in Statistics (University of Texas at Austin), an M.Sc. in Engineering (University of Texas at Austin), an M.A. in Open and Distance Learning (UK Open University), a B.A. in Mathematics (University of Texas at Austin), and Teacher's Diploma in Elementary Education (Pedagogical Academy of Cyprus). Her research interests focus on the educational applications of advanced eLearning technologies in mathematics and science education. She has coordinated numerous EU and locally funded projects and has a respectable publication record in scholarly national and international journals.

Natalia Monjelat is a research assistant and PhD candidate at the Faculty of Education of Universidad de Alcalá (Spain). She has a BA in Psychology and Education (Universidad de San Martín, Argentina) and a MA in Communication and Learning (UAH). She is interested in the relationship between technologies and learning, focusing her PhD dissertation in the new media and technologies that may be used as resources to tackle learning difficulties and create innovative scenarios in the school.

Micaela Seemann Monteiro is a Physician and Specialist in Internal Medicine. She was conferred the Competence in Emergency Medicine by the Portuguese Medical Board. She is also an Instructor in Advanced Life Support by the European Resuscitation Council. She graduated at the Heinrich-Heine-Universität in Düsseldorf, Germany, in 1994, and trained in Germany, Great Britain, and Portugal. As the Director of an Emergency Department of a major Lisbon teaching hospital, she has a vast experience in training medical students and residents. Videogames for medical education is a major area of interest and research. In 2011, she co-founded Stand Clear Lda., a startup engaged in developing innovative tools for medical education.

George S. Mouzakitis: Manager of the LinkedIn Group entitled "e-Learning Think Tank Team." Currently engaged in educational research referring to (a) "Education/Training for Market Needs," (b) Inclusion of disabled persons in education/workforce, (c) The use of games in education of disabled and not disabled individuals, (d) English for ESP. Author of twelve books, total pages 5,460, under the general title *The English we Use for....* He has a B.A. in English/Greek Language (Athens), M.A. in Special Education (Western Michigan, USA), Ph.D. in Communication (Columbia State). Teaching experience totals 43,245 hours in tertiary education participation in 43 international conferences. Publications: Chapters in two books on educational trends and disabled persons issues in USA and one in Croatia on learning disabilities. Member of the editorial team of the *Global Journal of Management and Research*, India. Member of Scientific committees of international conferences.

Kamisah Osman, Assoc. Prof. Dr., is currently the Deputy Director, Centre of Academic Advancement, the National University of Malaysia. After completing her undergraduate education at the National University of Malaysia in 1993, she then taught Chemistry and Physics at one of the secondary schools in Malaysia. Her passion towards effective pedagogy in science towards meaningful acquisition of scientific knowledge and dispositions has inspired her to pursue her studies in Science Education. She is an Executive Editor of *Asian Journal of Learning and Teaching in Higher Education*, an Editorial Board Member of the *Eurasian Journal of Science and Mathematics Education*, *Science Education Review*, *Malaysian Journal of Education*, and *Malaysian Action Research Journal*. Her passion towards inspiring innovative teaching, particularly at the university level, has made her one of the key players of Action Research Committee at the National University of Malaysia.

Pedro Palhares is an Associate Professor at the Institute of Education of the University of Minho in Portugal. He teaches Mathematics and Mathematics Pedagogy to preschool and elementary teachers. His research interests include ethnomathematics, patterns in the teaching and learning of mathematics, mathematical games, and problem solving. He is currently director of the PhD program on Child Studies.

João Pereira is Associate Professor at the Computer Science Department of the Technical University of Lisbon (Instituto Superior Técnico – IST/UTL), where he teaches Computer Graphics. João Pereira holds a PhD in Electrical and Computers Engineering (Computer Graphics) from IST/UTL, Technical University, December 1996. He received also a MSc and a BsEE degrees in Electrical and Computers Engineering from IST/UTL, respectively, in 1989 and 1984. He coordinates the Visualization and Simulation action line of the VIMMI group at INESC-ID (Computer Systems Engineering Institute). His main research fields are real-time rendering, 3D game programming, serious games, networked virtual environments, augmented reality, and parallel computer graphics. He has been involved with several European (RESOLV, IMPROVE, RTP11.13, MAXIMUS, SATIN, INTUTION, TARGET, GALA) and National projects. He was also proposal evaluator of the FET during 2009. Professor Pereira is member of the Eurographics Association and EuroVR Association.

Arttu Perttula is a Researcher at the Tampere University of Technology in Pori, Finland. He got his Master of Science (M.Sc.) from the Tampere University of Technology in 2007. His research is related to mobile human computer interaction. Perttula has been working in different research projects concentrating mainly on mobile social media, mobile learning, and mobile games. In the year 2008, Perttula spent six months with Fuji Xerox Palo Alto Laboratory, Inc. as an intern. In the year 2010, Perttula spent three months as a Visiting Researcher at Stanford University, H-STAR Institute.

Claudia Ribeiro is finalist PhD student at the Computer and Information Systems Department at the Technical University of Lisbon (Instituto Superior Técnico – IST/UTL), Portugal, where she has been teaching classes in the areas of Artificial Intelligence, Databases, 3D Programming for Simulation and Games, 3D Visualization and Animation. In 2003, she received her M.Sc. degree in Computer Science and Bs.E.E. (2001) both from IST/UTL. She is a Researcher at INESC since 2009, where she works in several European and national funded projects. Her research interests are agent-based modeling and simulation, simulation, artificial intelligence, serious games, game design, and digital game-based learning. She is a member of the ACM Special Interest Group (SIG) on Simulation and Modeling (SIM).

Margarida Romero is a European Ph.D. in Psychology by UMR CNRS (France) and Universitat Autonoma de Barcelona (Extraordinary Ph.D. Award in Psychology). Associate Director of E-learning in ESADE Law & Business School, and Associate Professor of Psychology in UAB and e-Learning in UOC. Her research is focused in collaborative learning, game-based learning, and the time factor in e-learning.

Mirian Checa Romero is Assistant Professor and Senior Researcher in the Department of Educational Science at the University of Alcala (Spain). She holds a PhD in Developmental Psychology and Education, a diploma on Teaching Studies: Early Childhood, and a degree in Psychopedagogy, Learning, and Education. She is interested in the analysis of media such as film or video games, understood as tools that promote digital literacy in different contexts of development and learning.

Jorge Nuno Silva is a Professor at the Department of History and Philosophy of Science of the University of Lisbon, Portugal. He got his PhD in UC Berkeley in Pure Mathematics. His research interests include teaching of mathematics, mathematical games, history of mathematics, and history of board games.

Mireia Usart is M.Sc. in e-Learning by Universitat Oberta de Catalunya (UOC). PhD candidate in the eLearning Center (UOC). PhD paper awarded with 1st prize in eLSE 2012 conference. Fellowship in the Direction of Educational Innovation and Academic Quality in ESADE Law & Business School. Her research aims to advance the understanding of the time factor in game-based learning in the contexts of blended learning.

Index